File Techniques for Data Base Organization in COBOL

File Techniques for Data Base Organization in COBOL

LeRoy F. Johnson and Rodney H. Cooper

University of New Brunswick
Fredericton, New Brunswick, Canada

Prentice-Hall, Inc.

Englewood Cliffs, New Jersey 07632

Library of Congress Cataloging in Publication Data

Johnson, LeRoy Frank (date)
File techniques for data base organization in COBOL.

Includes index.
1. COBOL (Computer program language)
2. File organization (Computer science)
3. Data base management. I. Cooper, Rodney H., joint author. II. Title.
QA76.73.C25J64 001.64'25 80-23372
ISBN 0-13-314039-3

Editorial/production supervision
and interior design by Kathryn Gollin Marshak
Cover design by Miriam Recio
Manufacturing buyer: Joyce Levatino

Printed in the United States of America

10 9 8 7 6 5

Prentice-Hall International, Inc., *London*
Prentice-Hall of Australia Pty. Limited, *Sydney*
Prentice-Hall of Canada, Ltd., *Toronto*
Prentice-Hall of India Private Limited, *New Delhi*
Prentice-Hall of Japan, Inc., *Tokyo*
Prentice-Hall of Southeast Asia Pte. Ltd., *Singapore*
Whitehall Books Limited, *Wellington, New Zealand*

To our parents
who implemented us from genetic specifications
and debugged us as best they could.

Contents

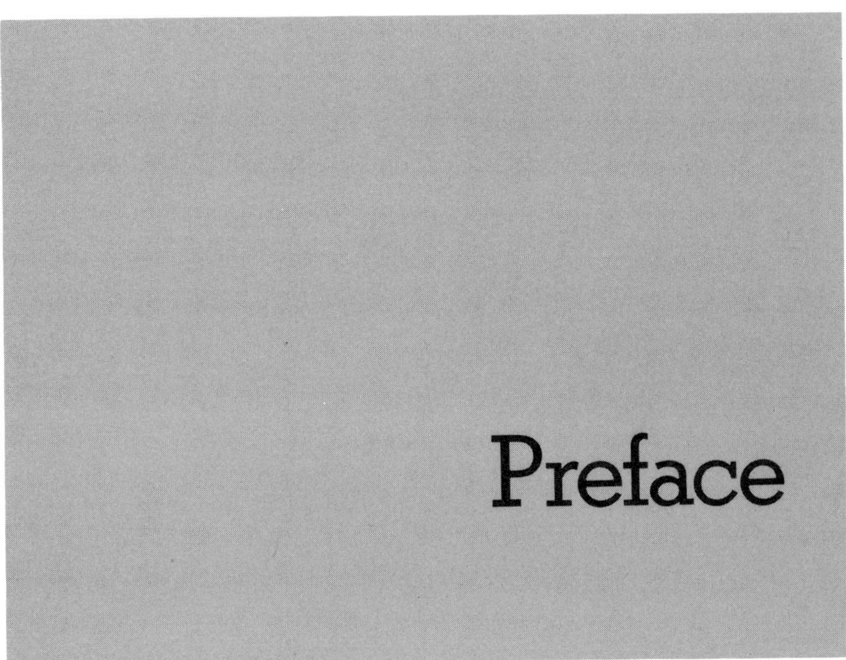

Preface

The material in this book was mainly developed because our experience with students and professionals indicated a real need for such an approach. As teachers, we found that students, as prospective programmers, had trouble relating the general theory of data structures to the effective implementation of files. In our consulting, we found to our surprise that professional programmers and analysts often had a faulty understanding of the various file systems and were not fully aware of their design parameters. The result was often a specialization in the use of one system to the exclusion of all other solutions. This is understandable, for many professionals cut their teeth on sequential tape systems, so the change to direct access methods can be traumatic when done on the job, with the pressures caused by elusive deadlines and the even more elusive "one remaining bug."

Accordingly, the book is aimed at these two groups, and the efforts made to satisfy their differing demands have provided interesting constraints, which have greatly improved our original class notes.

This text is intended to be used for a second course in COBOL programming and file processing at the university level and for independent study by professionals. It is intended to provide an introduction to advanced COBOL language features for file handling and data base management. The discussion of COBOL is based on the ANSI standard manual and relevant CODASYL documents.

The basic material has been class tested at the University of New Brunswick in various courses taken by upperclassmen and by graduate students, many of whom enter the professional areas of computing. Their input has strongly influenced the book's scope and intent.

This book is directed to the student of computing who works, or will work, with files in some capacity. We consider ourselves students of computing also, and as such, identifying with our audience, we have tried to write a book we would have liked to read when we began to learn about files. By no means have we exhaustively covered file techniques, but we have included what we feel is basic and should prove useful in the future.

At times we will refer to various functions performed by people involved with files, using the following terminology. A *user* is a consumer of a system product. A *programmer* is a language specialist. An *analyst* is a system specialist. *Designer* is a general term for a person making intelligent decisions that affect the design of the system at any level.

We regret that with the exception of words such as "one" there are no pronouns that address both men and women. We adopt the convention of using "he" and "his" and do so sparingly as the demands of the language require.

Although we have tried to deal with the subject in a broad and acceptable manner, we would be naive to expect complete accord with our selection and presentation of material. We believe that instructors who have alternate views of the subject will only enhance the learning experience of their students. Our views are contained herein; instructors have the classroom in which to present theirs. We hope the debate will be lively and rewarding.

ACKNOWLEDGMENTS

It is a pleasure to acknowledge the help we have received in preparing this book. First, we would each like to thank the other author.

In addition we had help from Pat Emin, Rufus McKillop, Professors Albert M. Stevens and Fred Cogswell, and a host of students, in particular Ron Ho, Joe Marriot, Jim Carmont, Luc Frenette, Jamie Campbell, Mike Good, and Ronnie Losier.

The book was carefully reviewed by Ray Strong and by Prentice-Hall's reviewers. Thank you for being cruel. Karl Karlstrom of Prentice-Hall deserves a round of applause, because he made the book possible and was great to work with.

A warm thanks to Dr. William Knight, our resident statistician, for his oblique and random encouragements at all hours of the day and night. Our sincere thanks to Mrs. Anna Anderson, who typed endless versions and who now knows that a final draft is final in name only.

All of these people contributed to improving the book you are reading, and we are most grateful to them.

Introduction

As the computing field has matured, those in the field have changed their attitude to data, realizing that data exists independently of the programs that access it and that files can be more valuable than the individual programs that access them. The development of data management techniques has tended to isolate applications programmers from the physical storage structures of the data their programs access and even from the programs' logical structure in a data base. Nevertheless, in his own programs the applications programmer must deal with files that are ultimately mapped to a physical storage structure resident on some physical storage medium. Thus the logical and physical limitations of the data base are ultimately present in every program, and their effects may seriously degrade it.

Although a data base may alleviate the programmer's need to construct physical files, he must still construct logical files. Since data bases cannot at present manipulate data in a completely arbitrary way, a knowledge of physical file structure will be to the programmer's advantage. Similarly, a deep understanding of file techniques will always be important because applications are neither completely general nor physically independent. On the other hand, someone must ultimately construct the physical files that store the data base. Therefore, the current trend toward large data base systems only accentuates the need for file techniques, for it is upon techniques discussed in this book that data base systems ultimately depend for implementation.

Although the vast data base argument is persuasive, considerable argument exists for distributed data bases and some enterprises are returning to distributed computing. Basic file techniques will remain fundamentally important since the data base management system philosophy is, in general, of large scale. No matter what the future brings, there will be large systems with data base management and small systems without.

It is not possible to do language-independent computing; at best, in the search for generality, a deep understanding of the particular is required. One approach is to use a pseudocode. We do not believe, however, that a pseudocode that cannot be run on a computer and is used by few people is superior, for teaching of file techniques, to a commonly used programming language—both can be improved upon. The techniques of this book are illustrated using COBOL, for while we do not always love COBOL, the fact that it is *the* business language makes all counterargument spurious. Since design is really just the search for optimal choice subject to the constraints of the real world, we trust that the reader will accept COBOL as one example of a real system of constraints that he is likely to encounter frequently in the business world. Practical file techniques have been difficult to acquire not because of any intrinsic difficulty but because the requisite information is scattered among many sources. The purpose of this book is to gather in one source a description of basic methods for the logical and physical description of files along with the appropriate COBOL statements for definition and access. We discuss the effective use of file techniques while relating our discussion to data base organization.

We stress the how and why of good design and demonstrate style by example rather than precepts. Our approach is to provide a good background in the fundamentals along with sufficient detail to allow immediate use in a COBOL work environment. By no means will the reader become an instant expert, but he should acquire the ability to approach and solve file problems in a reasonable time. On the one hand, the book can be considered as an intermediate COBOL text; on the other hand, the book is basically about file techniques using COBOL simply as an extended example of how one language handles fundamental file techniques.

We would be remiss if we did not apply our principles of design and style to the organization of the book. The essence of the approach is to move from a specific example to a generalization of the concept suggested by the example, then to a COBOL instance of their use. We move from a creation and discussion of logical structure to the realization and storage of the logical structure as a physical structure. This mapping is the fundamental problem of file design. Only after we have provided a firm grasp of the various major techniques do we attempt to discuss their interrelationship and their role in the file design process.

In our view, it can be quite traumatic for a student to move from a general concept to his first realization of that concept in a programming language. However, once this first dichotomy has been bridged, the student rapidly gains facility with the concept. In substance, we move from the particular to the general and back to the particular because this is how man creates.

Some authors believe in the multiple-language approach. We do not. In our experience, given a thorough understanding of a single language, language skills are transferable. We believe in a thorough and workable conceptual structure for files expressed in one language which may be worked with directly and which may be used indirectly as a stable frame of reference for future needs.

COBOL

This book uses COBOL as defined in ANSI X3.23-1974. Other books which refer to ANSI COBOL may refer to earlier versions of the standard. In addition, manufacturers' compilers that claim to be ANSI COBOL may in fact differ by including features not in the standard. Where possible, programs should conform to the standard; although the standard is not an instructional text, the programmer is advised to refer to it.

It must also be noted that various levels of implementation exist. Thus a compiler may not have all the features necessary to implement a given subset of COBOL. To this purpose COBOL refers to eleven processing modules. Those of main concern for this book are Sequential I-O, Relative I-O, Indexed I-O, and Sort-merge. Each module has two or three levels of implementation. Lower levels are subsets of higher levels in that module. The null level has *no* features.

The COBOL standard not only gives the language description but also provides information to the implementer and leaves certain decisions to him. In actual use the implementer provides a translator that transforms the COBOL program to a language or to another translator (usually a compiler) that the machine understands. Since programming in COBOL cannot be divorced from the computer, we will refer to the IBM OS/VS COBOL compiler and JCL for the IBM 370 system control language in our examples. There are two reasons for this choice: first, this is the COBOL implementation at our installation; and second, it is in wide use. We will differentiate between the standard and the IBM implementation where necessary. Those readers who use other implementations should experience no difficulties; rather they should find this approach a useful exercise in the variations in interpretation of the standard.

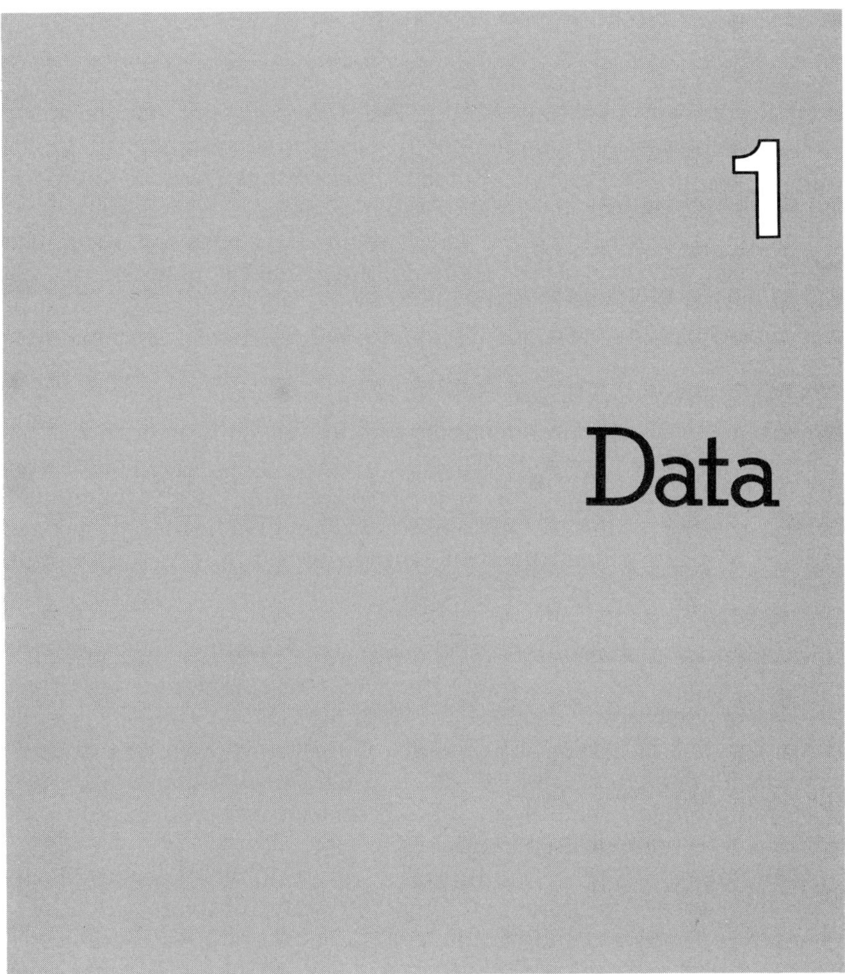

1 Data

What is data? How is it related to computing? Why are we concerned with it? Although these are elementary questions, the answers are neither simple nor static. For our purposes, *data* is that information manipulated by programs and stored external to those programs. Because of the high cost of main memory compared to secondary or external memory, data resides in main memory only temporarily. It is most often stored on external, secondary memory such as disks or magnetic tapes.

The view that stored data belongs to a particular program has gradually shifted to the view that stored data exists independently of the programs that manipulate it. This shift has occurred as a result of the change in several factors. As programming systems became more complex, it was realized that the same data was present in various files of different programs (or even the same program) and that the cost of collecting, storing, and accessing data was becoming an increasingly major component of the overall system cost. In addition, the inevitability of organizational change leads to the need to lessen its impact on programming systems. The separation of data from the programs that manipulate it is intended to reduce the impact of change by reducing the software maintenance effort required to accommodate such change. Thus a new importance was placed on the relation of data to the algorithms that manipulate it.

The shift in the ways we view data has been made possible by advances in computer technology and this shift in turn has influenced the development of stored data technology. Increases in the cost of data in relation to the total computing cost combined with the need to protect data from future organizational changes require a more general view of stored data; however, only recent significant advances in computer technology have made a more general view possible.

A growing realization of the true cost of data has forced a reconsideration of its role in effective, cost-conscious computing. The rapid increase in demand for data and the consequent growth in storage is well known. The result of this growth is a serious compounding of the problems of efficient data management. Although the data problem is intrinsic to information processing, solutions have been technological in nature.

Because of the constant change in technology, solutions to problems once considered effective are now obsolete. In effect, computer programs, like automobiles, deteriorate with time and use, and just as it may ultimately cost less to buy a new car than to keep an old car running, some computer solutions are best improved by throwing the old programs away. Unfortunately, like certain automobiles, the effective life of software and hardware can be very short indeed. The cost of data can leave us with, in effect, an automobile we cannot afford to keep and yet cannot afford to throw away. The data base concept, which considers data independently of the programs that use it, is an attempt to solve such a dilemma by keeping the data while changing its apparent structure so that it can be used by a new set of programs. Informally, a *data base* is a collection of data files that are in some way related and serve many application programs. A *data base management system* (DBMS) consists of a data base and the necessary software to manipulate and relate the data files. This description is an oversimplification, but it is sufficient for now.

A rapidly decreasing cost per bit has led to increased on-line and interactive use of data. Because of this the cost of acquiring, changing, and providing rapid access to vast amounts of data has a tremendous impact on the total cost of computing. That is, managing data for such systems is a significant part of the total cost. It is the major costs of a system that determine our degree of concern, and so today data has a high profile as a problem area. Since file handling is fundamental to data, the more design alternatives the systems analyst and programmer have, the better will be the cost-effective use of data. *Data base organization* refers to the formal interactions and relationships of the data files that constitute the data base. The field of data base organization is vast, growing, and the technology rapidly evolving; however, we believe that a firm grasp of basic file techniques and principles will be of continuing use and value.

Accordingly, the thrust of this book is on the techniques and principles of files: their use in COBOL and their relationship to data bases.

In designing files a question must be continually asked. How should data be related to programs? Three basic answers are: it should be possible to use data easily for a variety of programs; data should be independent of programs; and it should be easy to examine the data as required. Not all the techniques we examine will satisfy these requirements, but they will ultimately lead to methods that can do so.

1.1 INFORMATION

The advent of the computer with its ability to provide easy access to large quantities of data has made the use and storage of vast amounts of data not only practical but a common occurrence. However, it is one thing to collect volumes of data but quite another matter to be able to access and interpret this data in a meaningful manner. The many recorded bankruptcies of businesses as a direct consequence of implementing a data processing system is stark evidence of the difficulties that can be encountered. Of course, many data processing failures have not been as severe, but they have been costly nevertheless. As a result, the collecting of large amounts of data must be approached with a considerable degree of respect and attention to the needs of the organization as well as its ability to support the costs that will arise.

The purpose of computing is *not* to collect data but to enable the making of decisions. A *decision* is the choice of a particular course of action among alternatives. If a decision is not to be haphazard or illogical, then it must be based on information that indicates one alternative as preferable. In some instances decisions can be made by the computer with the provision of a suitable algorithm. For example, if an account is outstanding 60 days, the computer can automatically send a form letter requesting payment or threatening legal action. More complex decisions may require human interaction. The importance of information determines the effort we are willing to expend to obtain it. Various file techniques have been developed in an attempt to match the cost of this to the ultimate importance of the information.

The Cost/Benefit Tradeoff

What then is the value of information? Why is it important? Certainly, the costs of obtaining information can be extremely high. Consider a data form that requires 15 minutes to fill out under ideal conditions. Suppose that the 10 supervisors of a company complete the form once a month. Since they are not readily familiar with the form, they take 30 minutes, and because they dislike filling out the form, another 30 minutes is required for them to cool off and return to normal. If each supervisor earns $20,000 a year, a rough cost to the company of filling out the form each month is twice his hourly rate or approximately $20. The costs have hardly begun. Imagine an error that requires return of the form, once, twice,. . . .

In the decision to acquire a data processing system, the possible benefits to be derived must be weighed against the costs of obtaining these benefits. This is called a *cost/benefit tradeoff.* In order to determine this, the system is broken into its component parts. The more a component contributes to total cost, the more important are the benefits obtained from that component. Simply stated, do the benefits derived justify the cost? Insofar as the cost/benefit tradeoffs are largely determined by the computing system, this relationship is a fundamental question in the design of files and data bases. In the subsequent study of file techniques, the cost/benefit tradeoffs will be of particular concern.

Although this discussion of cost may appear to digress from the technical aspects of file design and data bases, we cannot overstress its important influence in the ultimate choice of technical alternatives for an implementation. Cost is an important constraint of any system implementation, and it is not always apparent in dollars. The determination of cost is complex and uncertain; the cost of what is not done must be considered in addition to the cost of what is done.

1.1.1 The Information Asset

In examining the assets of a company, accountants consider only those things to which a meaningful dollar value can be assigned, while managers are just as likely to consider their staff as a critical asset. Of course, a good stock market analyst will consider both in his evaluation of the assets of a company. But the most important asset that many companies have does not appear on the balance sheet nor on the organizational chart; it is the knowledge of its business that resides in the organization independently of the individuals that constitute that organization.

Operating a business requires capital, people, and information. The fundamental importance of each is illustrated by the fact that any single element can generate the other two. For example, capital or information can be used to attract good people because people want to be well paid and wish to acquire knowledge. Indeed, good technical people will often accept a lower salary in order to be able to work with the latest concepts in an area.

For the knowledge within an organization to be effective, it must be possible to put this knowledge to use as information readily available to the individuals of the organization. How to accomplish this is a difficult problem, and although file techniques have contributed immensely to solutions, the problem is far from solved. The all-knowing computer that responds to verbal requests exists as yet only in science fiction.

In the past, information was regarded primarily as a byproduct. Financial information resided in the accounting department, marketing information in the sales department, engineering information in the design and production departments, and so on. The technology of manual filing systems effectively limited other choices. Since, from the management view, money is the essential raw material, early computing functions began in the accounting departments, which provided the basic information for management decisions, and data processing reported through that function. This ignored the essential importance of the common requirements for information. Recognizing this as a deficiency, many companies have revised the reporting structure of computing to make it independent of any particular departmental bias. Although the user must influence the design of files and, ultimately, the system should be biased in the direction of profits, the undue pressures of more powerful users may warp the system to such an extent that this degrades the overall return to the organization.

That the critical information inherent in an organization be independent of individuals is extremely important to the ongoing success of the organization. Compare an organization to biological organisms consisting of cells; they live, are made up of individuals, yet they are independent of individual cells that die and are replaced or change function. This illustrates one of the reasons for the survival of large organizations and the high fatality rate of small organizations. The larger the organization the less significant any one person is to the whole. For this reason, the threat of resignation based on indispensability is a dangerous tactic. The organization hires a replacement and, thus repaired, lives on.

Such repairs nevertheless are not without cost. People leaving the organization constitute an information leakage and the loss of organizational energy. Such leakage along with the inability to access and apply information effectively can be the prime causes of the decline of a once successful organization. Data must be stored in files to prevent this, but what data?

1.1.2 Information Systems

The determination of the value of information is a major difficulty in deciding what data to collect and how to store it. The failure to determine the proper value of information has been the basis of many programming system failures. It is impossible to collect all available data and, indeed, unnecessary. Our concern with data, then, arises from the use we can make of it, or the information we can derive from the raw data so to speak.

As facts increase in volume, they soon become incomprehensible and are thus of little use by themselves. It is the meaningful interpretation of facts that give rise to their utility. *Information* can be thought of as an interpretation or use of data that is meaningful to a person. Thus in the broad or generic sense, an *information system* is one that provides for the collection and storage of suitable raw facts or data and provides for the means to manipulate this data to produce output suitable for direct human use.

Figure 1.1 shows the outline of several possible features of an information system. Four main divisions of any information system are: input, system processors, external data storage, and output.

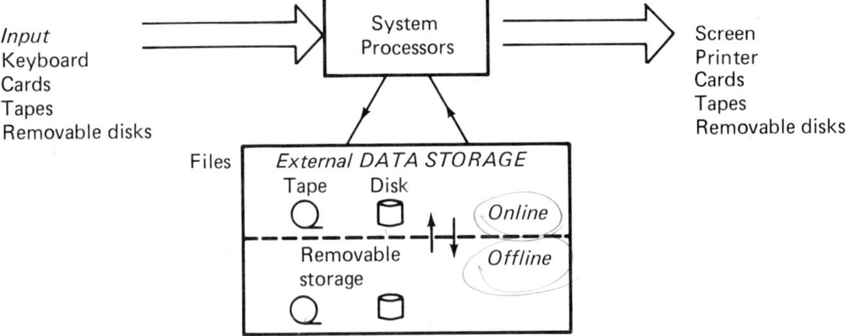

Figure 1.1 Information systems.

The following list gives an idea of some of the diverse applications of information systems:

- accounting
- airline reservations
- charge cards
- customer records
- income tax records
- insurance records
- inventory control
- land registration records
- patients' medical records
- welfare records.

It is not difficult to imagine the diversity of such applications and that the performance requirements may themselves be just as diverse. For instance, Table 1.1 indicates three broad levels of the requirements for information: operational, managerial, and executive. Of course all three levels may be present in a single system.

System Performance

For any job, certain performance criteria or measurements must be defined in order to determine the best system design. For instance, an airline reservation system has a critical response time for booking and checking reservations. Essentially, information is required in a demand time measured in seconds. Solutions that are inexpensive but slow are unacceptable. Updating of the

Table 1.1 Activity Levels in Information Systems

Level	*Activity*
Executive decision	Intellectual Unpredictable Browsing
Management control	Interpretation Summary Statistical
Operational control	Automatic Factual

data must also be essentially instantaneous since several seat requests on a particular flight may arrive simultaneously. The cost to obtain a reservation system that meets the performance requirements is tremendous but so too are the cost of a plane and the cost of moving empty seats through the air. Of course, once an airline upgrades service with an efficient reservation system, others are forced to follow to remain competitive.

Performance criteria must be determined before a system is defined and will form part of the system definition. For instance, that the data should be error free, timely, and current and that the system should satisfy the user and meet cost objectives are obvious criteria, which, however, are seldom met.

When the criteria can be quantified, then we have a performance measure. If we specify that the data error rate is to be less than one per thousand requests, we have a measure. Similarly, the criterion of timeliness could be stated as: 80% of requests will be answered in 30 sec and 95% in 60 sec with no request exceeding 2 minutes.

Ultimately, performance of a system is measured in terms of user satisfaction with the quality of the service provided by the system. Of course user satisfaction is achieved by more specific systems performance such as mean search time of a file, mean response time for random access to a record, and minimum throughput of transactions per day.

The *purpose* of data processing is twofold.

1. To organize vast amounts of data for efficient machine consumption.
2. To organize interpretations of the data for efficient human consumption.

With earlier information systems, or classical data processing, these two purposes were intertwined. It is now generally realized that to a large degree they can be separated and that in fact it is advantageous to do so.

In response to the first purpose, machine stored data is now usually referred to informally as a data base. In response to the second purpose, programs that provide the algorithms to obtain information are called applications programs. The efficiency referred to can only acquire meaning within the criteria set for the system, not as a result of criticism from those ignorant of the basis for design. A study of the first purpose is in large part the subject of the rest of this book.

1.2 FILES

The need to organize the storage of data for efficient access was recognized long before computers arrived. The scroll, devised by the ancients, is an example of a sequential file. Unfortunately, a scroll has severe disadvantages. One must carefully unroll it to access information. If it is very long, the part unrolled gets rolled into a second roll making it inconvenient to glance back at what was read. Changes can only be accomplished by recopying to a new scroll. Its advantage, however, is simplicity: all that is needed is a continuous sheet of paper. The disadvantages outweighed the advantages and the scroll gave rise to the bound book, allowing random access to chapters and pages. The innovations of the bound book required not only a change in the physical organization of the recording media but also in the technology to provide for printing and binding of the pages. On a more modern note, we have filing cabinets, card index systems, and other mechanical aids to storage retrieval.

There are a number of reasons for using a computer file system as a source of information:

- expected reduced costs of operation
- increased use of data
- government reporting requirements
- increased throughput over manual systems
- increased flexibility over manual systems.

Depending on the user, the source and importance of the reasons used to justify a file system will vary. However, we can express the basic reason and measure of value as that of profit to the organization, although the profit expected may be impossible to measure in dollars. The reasons put forward may be technically sound, result from the pressures of hardware and software salesmen, or simply be based on prestige requirements. Basically our concern is with technical reasons, but one must be aware of the political reasons that usually come disguised in pseudotechnical terms.

1.2.1 Subgroupings

Data is a collection of facts. These facts are obtained through observation or measurement. For purposes of storage and processing, well-defined subgroupings of data are necessary. In computing, a number of subgroupings have acquired common usage and a relatively common terminology. They are summarized in Table 1.2.

For computing, a precise and common terminology has not been developed yet, particularly in the data processing area where a proliferation of manufacturer-spawned names has added to the usual confusion generated by the academic privilege of defining your own terms in a new field. In Table 1.2 and throughout the book, we give only a single name for a concept because we believe that once understood it will be recognized by other names. In the beginning, a profusion of alternate names can be confusing.

Table 1.2 File Terminology

Term	*Definition*
Data	Collection of facts in an accessible form
Data base	Organized collection of related files
File	Organized collection of related data grouped in individual elements called records
Record	Collection of related data identified as the element of a file
Item	Smallest accessible unit of named data in a file
Aggregate	Named set of items in a record referred to as a whole
Group	Named set of *contiguous* items in a record referred to as a whole
Bit	Smallest unit of information storage (binary digit)
Byte	Smallest addressable group of bits (usually a unit consisting of eight bits)

The subgrouping of data in Table 1.2 that is of prime concern and used as the unit for processing reference is the *record*. A collection of similar records, that is, records having a similar structure, is called a computer *file*, which resides on external storage media. A collection of related files is now usually referred to as a *data base*, but more about that later. The smallest accessible unit of data that we refer to by a name is an *item*. We may now redefine a record as the collection of data items that is identified as a file element. It is possible for the computer to refine the data in an item. For instance, a byte can be extracted from an item, but this goes beyond a discussion of files.

It is often useful or necessary to have subgroupings of the items of a record. *Aggregate* refers to such a subgrouping. If, in addition, we require the items to be contiguous, then we call such an aggregate a *group*. The distinction between a record and a group is that a record is an element of a file while a group is an element of a record. This hierarchy of the definitions is usually quite clear in actual application.

As an illustration, suppose that an enterprise requires *data* on the people employed. For each person *a record* is kept in a personnel *file*. *Items* of a record would be name, personnel number, salary, and so on. An *aggregate* could be all data items of a personal nature. A *group* could be all positions held in the company by one employee. There could be many other files such as one for job description records. The collection of all files in the personnel office form a *data base*.

A more important distinction is in the number of occurrences of each subgrouping. The size of a record is fixed, or if it is variable, then it has an upper limit. Thus the number of groups in a record is limited. The number of records, however, is unbounded; that is, given more hardware, more records can be added to the file. It is characteristic of files that the number of records increases, and provision for this should always be incorporated in the design.

Within a record certain items called *keys* are used to identify the record or some property of the record. In some cases the key is unique to a record, in which case it is then called a *primary key*. For example, in a personnel file the social security number provides a primary key for the individual record. The item "sex," on the other hand, can be used as a key to identify all records of male employees. Obviously, this would not be a primary key.

Basically it is the size of files that warrants the techniques discussed in this book. Currently, large files require secondary storage. The cost per bit of secondary storage is much less than that of main memory, and it would appear that this differential will be maintained since the speed of main memory must match or approach that of the central processor unit (CPU) in order to make effective use of the CPU's processing capability. Attaining such speed is expensive, thus limiting the size of main memory used in a computer system. Of course, another reason for using secondary storage is the need to remove the storage media from the system for back up, security, transportation, and so on.

1.2.2 File Organization

Files can be characterized by the methods used to organize their records. Well-known file organization methods are sequential, indexed sequential, direct, and indexed. Each of these has different system performance characteristics when used for storage and processing. Associated with these organizations are access methods for adding, updating, and deleting records. The decisions as to which organization and access methods to be used are based on the two fundamental measures of computing: *space* and *time.* Space refers to the amount and cost of hardware; in the case of files, this means the amount of storage media which is related to the size of the file and the method of organization used. Time is the processing speed; in the case of files, this refers to the time required to fetch an arbitrary record, add a record, update a record, and delete a record. The file design problem arises from the time/space tradeoff, which says, essentially, that you can have more of one at the expense of the other but not both for the same cost. The basic constraint on a file system is the cost limit. As the cost of hardware decreases, the main source of cost is time, and this is increasingly a function of people costs.

There are other performance measures as observed by the user; the data should be error free, timely, current, and the system should provide satisfaction in its use. The system performance measures we have indicated provide for the attainment of these more general performance characteristics but do not guarantee them. The user ultimately does not really care about the wonderful technical performance; he wants the data when he wants it and he wants it to be usable. However, such performance can only be attained if particular care is taken to see that the subsystems have the appropriate performance characteristics. Perhaps most crucial are the file subsystems because the performance of secondary devices is the weakest link in the computing chain.

1.2.3 Integrity and Security

To obtain satisfactory performance from the system files there are a number of considerations beyond the organization of data and access to it that must be considered. The *integrity* of a file concerns the extent that the data is accurate at all times. This is a complex question for there are limits to maintaining integrity. For instance, it is not always possible to verify the correctness of an individual entry but bound checks may be employed such as numeric type, upper bound on a number, sign, and so on. When the same item appears in various files, its value may differ among files due to difficulties in updating all occurrences. Hopefully, this is only temporary, but it can still have serious consequences. Thus integrity, like freedom from errors, is not an absolute but a performance objective at which to aim.

The loss of integrity arises from three main areas: hardware failure, human error, and programming errors that allow invalid modification of data. By data *security* we mean the protection of data against unauthorized access. Such access may involve disclosure, alteration, or even destruction of data. No system is totally secure; all that can be hoped for is that the cost of penetration exceeds the value of penetration. Since this is expensive to achieve, the cost of security is related to the value of the data files to be protected. Unfortunately, the best technical security will not protect against careless human procedures that allow security mechanisms to be opened or whole files to be copied.

Integrity and security can be treated together in many aspects. It is important to be able to detect and recover from alterations and destruction of data by whatever cause. Procedures to do so must be designed into a file system and may well be its most important feature.

1.3 LOGICAL ORGANIZATION

Given a set of named objects, we may wish to consider how the names are organized and recorded. In lieu of any information concerning the objects, it is highly likely that the names would be ordered alphabetically. This recognizes that, if nothing else, at least the symbols that represent the objects (i.e., alphabetic names) have a logical relationship of alphabetic order.

Another possibility could be the order derived from listing the names sequentially. For example, we might ask for the sixth name and, because of the integer ordering conventions we all learn from an early age, chances are we would know where to find that name. The relationship in this case is one of physical position.

Although the names are physically organized, by the act of constructing the written list, they may have no logical organization. However, names may appear to be disorganized merely because the ordering function is not recognized. For instance, the names of acquaintances may be arranged in the order they were first met.

Thus there are two major ways to organize data: *logically*, whereby the data items are arranged according to some abstract relationship; and *physically*, whereby the data items are arranged by their physical adjacencies.

The purpose of files is to provide a representation of data and the relationships among the data items. The organization or structure of data that we store in files is logical, but because the structure of the file in storage is physical, the file ultimately has a physical organization. It is advantageous to preserve the logical nature of the ways in which the organizing of future data can be perceived as distinct from its present physical organization. The pure logical view is as a *data structure* which is a model for data, and we will briefly consider some examples that provide a contrast to the file structures of COBOL.

1.3.1 Linear Ordering Structures

When we speak of structure, we mean that some relationship of order is present. The alphabetic and integer orders are linear orders. They have the form of a straight line: every element is related by the order to every other element. The importance of these two orders is signified by the fact that they are the first two formal orders taught to children. There are many linear orders, and we spend a great deal of time learning them and being asked to recognize them.

Linear orders all have the important property of sequentiality. That is, an element in the order is located by position with respect to its logically adjacent elements: each element is in forward order from the preceding element and in reverse order from the following element. Thus, although the linear orders may differ, they can all be recognized as having a serial structure, and any linear order can be stored quite naturally in a sequential file.

Data can, however, often have more than one linear relationship present, and it is unlikely that they can all be simultaneously expressed in one serial list. Sorting is one answer to this problem.

The purpose of linear sorting is to rearrange a sequential list of objects so as to obtain in explicit form a linear order we know to be implicitly present among the list elements. This is the basis of sequential file processing.

This multiple ordering of data allows us to view different relationships of the data. For instance, while a personnel file may be ordered on a personnel number, it makes more sense for it to be ordered on names. If we wish to examine the effect of age on salary, we may wish to order the file on age and on salary for a given age. Reports are always more useful when appropriately ordered.

To express order, a model or representation of the order is required. Data structures are representations and thus *models* of the structure of data. Many representations have been discerned and formally defined. A brief overview will indicate the pattern, and a more detailed consideration is given in Chapter 10. Common representations for linear orders are the stack, queue, and the linear linked list. The distinctions among these representations are in the access methods: how we locate, add, and delete elements, as illustrated in Fig. 1.2.

Stack

A *stack* is a serial list of records where access is restricted to one end of the list. This end is usually called the *top.* Thus we may think of a stack conceptually as having a variable upper boundary and a fixed lower boundary.

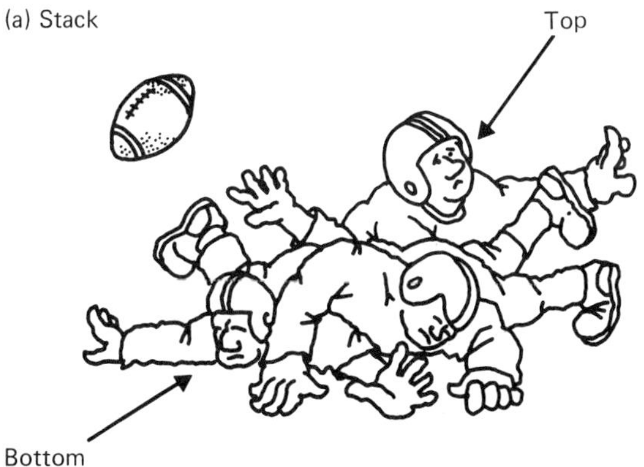

Figure 1.2 Access to data structures: (a) stack

(b) Queue

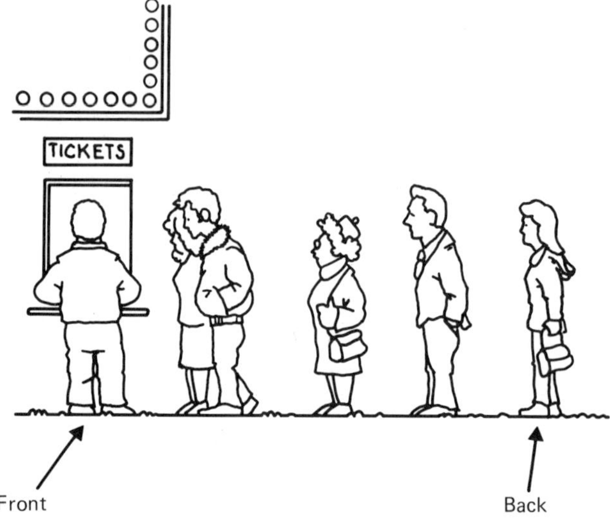

Movie line-up

(c) Linear linked list

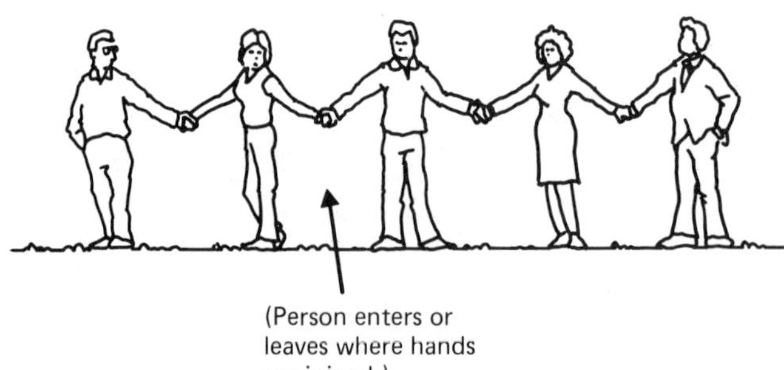

Group of people joining hands

Figure 1.2 Access to data structures (*cont.*): (b) queue; (c) linear linked list.

Queue

A *queue* is a serial list of records with restricted access where deletions occur at one end called the *front* and additions at the other end called the *back*. Theoretically the lineup for a movie is a queue. Line crashers illustrate that the real world does not always obey the nice distinctions of theory. In computer storage, unlike a movie lineup, the records do not move each time there is a record deleted, rather the front of the queue recedes.

Linear Linked List

A linear linked list is a general form of a list with unrestricted access. Additons, deletions, and record access can occur anywhere in the list. For instance, in the line of people in Fig. 1.2(c), access can occur at any point where hands are joined. The physical order does not have to bear any relation to the logical order of the list. This is achieved by pointer variables in each record that point to the next record in the list, as shown in Fig. 1.3. Nonlinear lists have multiple pointers and shall be discussed later. The linear linked list can be used as a stack or a queue if desired, and thus the latter are special cases of the general linked list. Linked lists are very important in file organization both logically and physically.

1.3.2 Nonlinear Ordering Structures

Some orderings cannot be simply expressed as a linear sequence. A number of nonlinear relational structures have been devised to describe such orderings. Perhaps the simplest and best known is the tree.

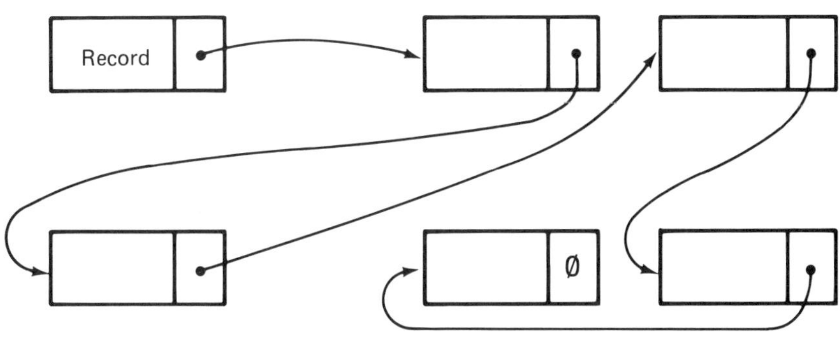

Figure 1.3 Linked list.

Tree Structure

Consider the set of male descendants of Adam to the third generation. If we wish to illustrate the descendants of Adam and at the same time show both the ancestors and descendants of each of Adam's male descendants, we require a structure more complex than a linear list. The structure of Fig. 1.4 gives the required ordering and this structure is called a *tree*. Any descendant is reached in a downward direction. Given a descendant only his ancestors can be reached in an upward direction.

The point or *vertex* labeled "Adam" is a distinguished vertex called the *root* of the tree. The lines or *edges* joining the names have an implied downward direction. Such a tree is called a *rooted tree*, and it is a very common relationship in computing. An important property of a tree is that there are *no* circular relationships. A rooted tree is a hierarchical structure.

Trees are a special class of a more general structure called a *graph*. Although the tree structure may appear to be very simple, its properties are mathematically complex, and its use in computing fundamental. Many files are naturally structured as trees.

Plex Structure

Many structures contain circular relationships. Because these are nonhierarchical, they cannot be expressed as trees. For example, in a retail store the owner may find that rather complex relationships exist among inventory items, their classification, and the suppliers. In Fig. 1.5, items are classified by supplier and by type, such as glassware. The complex structure obtained is called a *plex*. A plex is a labeled graph or network and is the most general type of data structure. The term "plex" is reserved for those structures that cannot be represented by trees or other simple data structures.

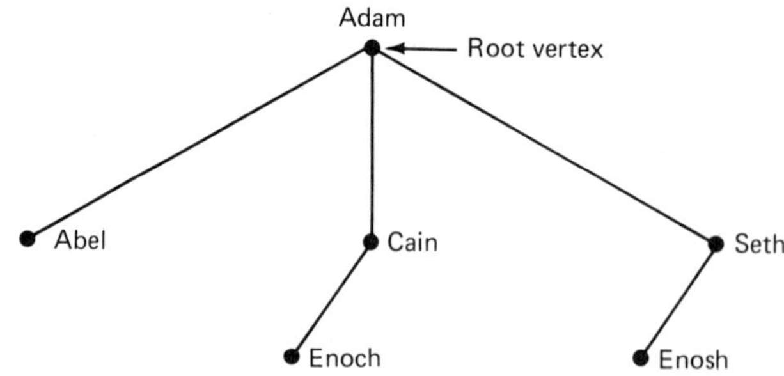

Figure 1.4 Tree structure of some male descendants of Adam.

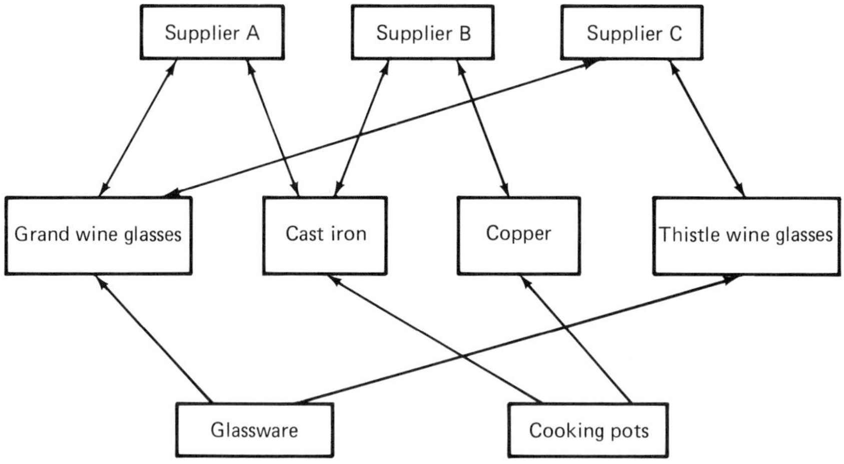

Figure 1.5 Plex structure of inventory records.

Few computer languages have storage structures for defining plexes, and so the programmer must resort to their definition within the program.

Partial Orderings

What kind of order is represented by trees and plexes? *Partial ordering* is a concept that is applicable. In a partial ordering some elements may not be ordered with respect to one another; they are in effect incomparable. Some subsets of the set of elements are linearly ordered. However, if X is ordered with respect to Z and Y is also ordered with respect to Z, then X and Y may be incomparable. The subset relation on a set is a partial ordering. In effect a partial ordering may be thought of as a collection of linear orderings that are in some sense connected. There are more restrictive forms of partial orders, and a linear order is one such. A tree is a partial order on the vertices where every element is ordered with respect to at least one element, namely, the root.

The nature of data structures is far more complex than the file structures that have so far been provided in computer languages.

The intent of these comments is merely to indicate the place of data structures in the organization of data and their relation to files. A more detailed consideration is provided in Chapter 10. The reader should realize that the best organization of the data may not be directly expressible in a file organization.

1.3.3 Data Structure Synopsis

In summary, a *data structure* is an organized representation of data that is explicitly intended to display certain interrelationships among the data items. The central problem of the theory of data structures is how to provide representations that express most simply those interrelationships of the data, or structures, that we perceive as important and to analyze the consequences of such structures. Thus data structures provide models for data bases.

Unfortunately, the logical organizations a programmer devises cannot always be directly defined in the programming language we may wish to use. Nor do the physical organizations possible on a computer system's available external storage devices always correspond to the data structure we choose. The basic problem of file design is to determine how *best* to move from the perceived logical organization of the data to its ultimate physical organization on a storage device, where "best" is determined by some performance measure chosen for the design. We shall examine this problem and performance measures in some detail within a COBOL context in subsequent chapters.

1.3.4 Language Data Structures

The purpose of data structures, as we have discussed, is to provide as simply as possible a suitable representation of the logical relationships of the data that concern us. In other words, data structures provide abstract models of the structure of the data. The various data structures are devised without any great concern for how or where individual records and items are to be physically inserted or deleted, for how the computer system works, and for how these structures might be created within a programming language context. Indeed, this lack of concern is necessary for the theory of data structures to develop, since it is not at all clear what kind of computing systems will be available in future. In fact, the theory of data structures will strongly influence the development of future systems. Because a language may only have certain data structures incorporated, we will refer to such data structures as *language data structures.*

Since the computer system cannot be ignored in the representation of data, certain mechanisms for storing data on external storage have been devised for most programming languages. These mechanisms, taking into account the physical properties of external storage, provide means of access, insertion, deletion, and modification of records. In addition, they determine the physical organization of the data on the external storage media. Thus these mechanisms determine the physical representation of a data structure and provide for the creation and manipulation of the resulting physical storage organization. Such a mechanism is termed a *storage structure* to differentiate it from a data structure; in the case of external devices, it is usually referred to as a *file structure.*

How the logical relations of a language data structure correspond to the actual physical storage is determined by the software. It is quite possible for a language data structure to have a different physical organization in different systems. In a given system, the language data structures may be considered synonymous with the physical structure or organization; this assumption is a convenience that can be misleading.

In the beginning, a language data structure corresponded to the physical organization of the data in a very direct way. Sequential files on magnetic tape are a good example. The program considers records as being sequentially ordered, and they are physically placed on the tape in that order except that it is possible to group the records into blocks, with physical access of the tape involving a block (or group of records) rather than a single record. The reason for this, as we shall see, is the physical characteristic of a tape drive that involves the start and stop time. A language data structure is simply the implementation of a data structure within the context of a programming language and the realities imposed by the need for efficient use of physical storage devices. Insofar as it is consistent in this context, a good language data structure attempts to provide a simple conceptual mechanism and it may, as in COBOL indexed files, hide a great deal of the actual physical organization from the programmer. In COBOL there are presently three major file structures referred to as modules: Sequential, Relative I-O, and Indexed I-O. We shall examine these file structures of COBOL in detail and use them in our programs to illustrate file techniques.

1.4 PHYSICAL ORGANIZATION

The actual way data is stored on a physical device may bear little resemblance to how the programmer has organized it or how the language data structure appears to organize it. This is primarily because the two objectives of physical organization are to conserve space and to optimize the speed at which storage locations can be accessed. In general, these requirements conflict and the difficulty of the design problem is to determine an acceptable trade off. In other words, you can have more of one only at the expense of the other.

A good file structure does not require that the programmer know how the data is physically organized nor even on what kind of device it may reside. However, more efficient use of a file structure can usually be made if the programmer is aware of the physical organization, the reasons for it, and the device to be used. As the amount of storage used increases, this knowledge assumes increasing importance because any attempt to conserve space degrades the access time which is generally more important.

Let us consider how the physical characteristics of a device may affect the access time of records and a simple solution called *blocking*. A tape drive has a time delay before it reaches full speed. To examine this, play a tape recorder for a few minutes. Since reading or writing is done at full speed, the portion of the tape that moves past the read/write heads during the delay period is *unusable*, and it is called the *interblock gap*. To reduce the amount of unused tape, several records are written at one time. This group of records that is written at one time is called a *block* or physical record. The programmer must have a knowledge of the computer system to determine the optimal block size. It is also possible for the storage structure to determine the block size, however, this may not be ideal for the particular application. Figure 1.6 illustrates

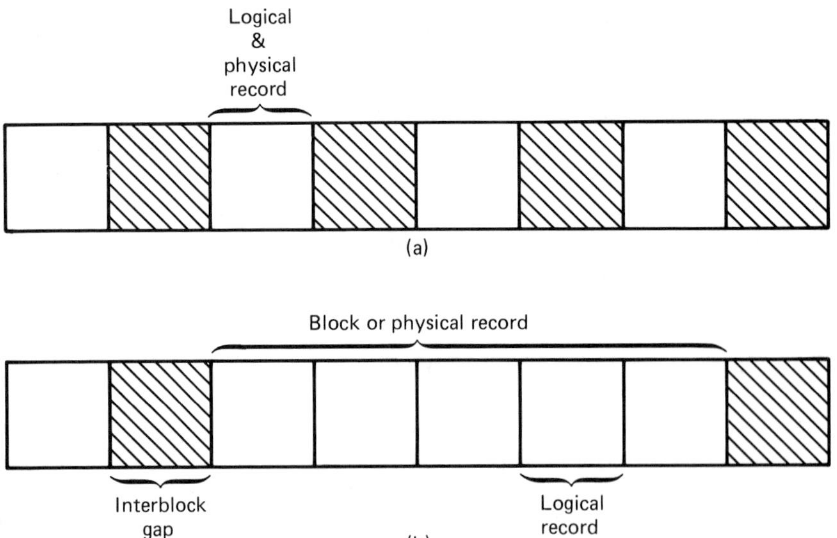

Figure 1.6 Physical organization of fixed-length logical records on a magnetic tape: (a) unblocked; (b) blocked.

the physical organization of a sequential file on a tape with unblocked (a) and blocked (b) designs.

A disk permits direct access to a record; therefore, a file need not be sequential. Nevertheless, the time required to physically locate the record may exceed the read or write time of the record and blocking may be advantageous here also. Figure 1.7 illustrates consecutive blocks on a disk. The unused portions of a disk may not be contiguous and, in order to use several such portions, a linked pointer system may be used. Figure 1.8 illustrates this con-

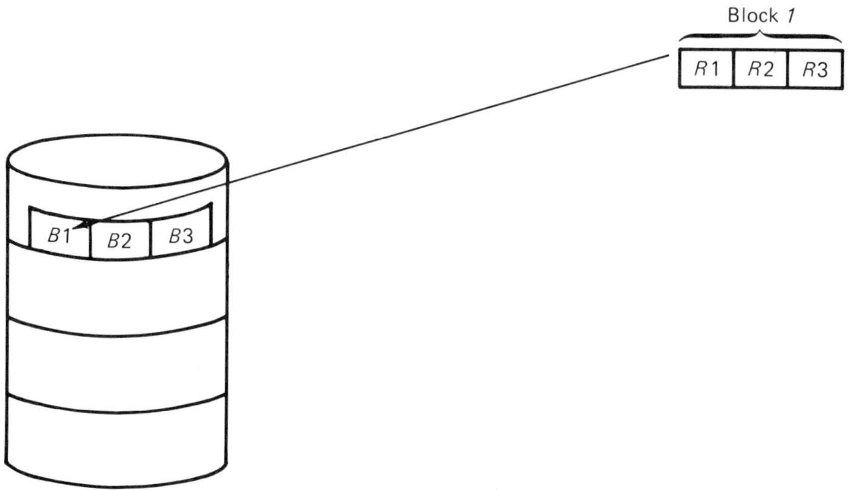

Figure 1.7 Consecutive blocks on a disk.

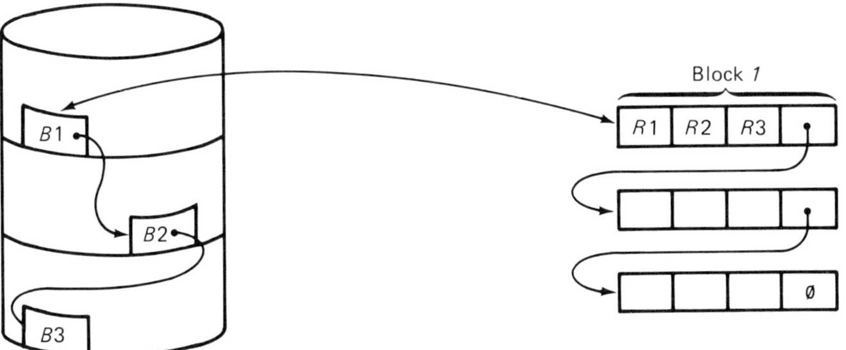

Figure 1.8 Linked blocks on a disk.

cept. There are other reasons for the linked technique which shall be examined later.

1.5 WORKING WITH DATA

As we have seen, there are essentially two kinds of perceived relationships among data items. These are the logical relationships, or how the programmer wishes to view the structure of the data, and the physical adjacencies, or how the data items are physically stored with respect to each other.

Logical organization can be further subclassified into data structures and language data structures. The concept of a data base, as we shall see, suggests further subdivisions.

What is the correspondence among these various ways of viewing data? For simplicity, let us assume that the data structure and the language structure coincide. We consider then the relation between logical organization and physical organization. Ideally these two types of relationships should also coincide. This can occur in, for instance, sequential files. However, the fact that this is not always possible nor desirable poses a major difficulty in file design.

There exists then the set of physical organizations that are available in a computing system and the set of logical relationships that we can conceive. The object of data structures, as we have mentioned, is to provide explicit expression of the logical relationships we consider important; however, they are far more varied and extensive than the physical relationships presently available on storage devices. Thus it is a major problem to derive a correspondence between how we wish to perceive the data and how we are forced to store it.

1.5.1 Mapping

To consider the way one view is transformed into another, we require a concept called a *mapping*. As an illustration let us consider the representation of a matrix in the main memory. Computer memory is generally a linear store, that is, it has the characteristics of a vector where the words are the locations of the items and the addresses of the words act as the index into the words. Storage of a matrix is achieved by mapping it into a vector.

In FORTRAN, for instance, a matrix is stored column by column, as illustrated by Fig. 1.9. The location map of A to memory

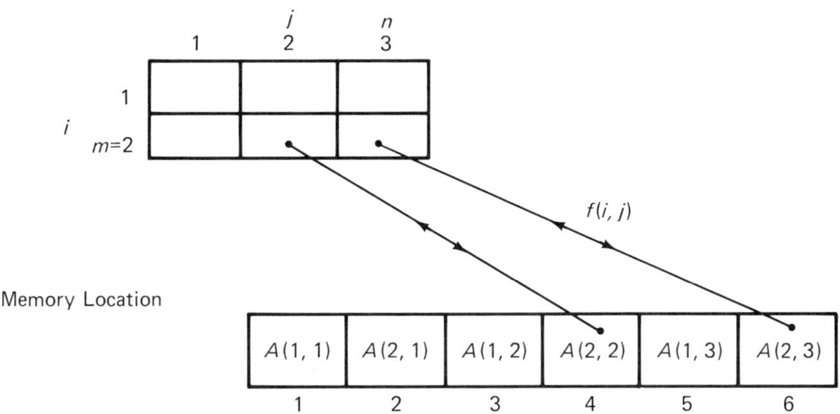

Figure 1.9 Matrix storage in FORTRAN.

is defined by the following function which, for simplicity, maps to the locations 1 to 6 of memory:

$$f(i, j) = i + [m \cdot (j - 1)]$$

For practice with mapping, try Problem 11 at the end of the chapter. Conceptually a mapping is a correspondence of the elements of a set X to the elements of a set Y. There are several kinds of mappings according to the properties of the correspondence. Functions are mappings, and when the function has a unique inverse it is called a one-to-one function. In computing, the mappings are always between *finite* sets. The reader can refer to a text on discrete structures for a more formal discussion of mappings.

The mapping of a language data structure to a physical storage organization is provided by the program language software. It may be possible for the programmer to influence the form of the mapping, for example, by specifying the blocking factor. In later chapters we examine how the mapping is done because the selection of a particular language data structure is determined to some extent by the physical organizations that result.

When the logical structure chosen by the programmer is not available as a language data structure provided by COBOL, the programmer must determine an appropriate mapping from the data structure to an available storage structure. This is done by controlling the program access to the language data structure records using suitable algorithms to perform the required mappings. Not all COBOL structures are available for all COBOL compilers.

Interestingly, all data structures can be mapped into a sequential file; it may not be very efficient, but it can be done.

1.5.2 Processing

How the data is to be processed influences how it should be organized. Basically there are two types of processes used to apply transactions to files.

Batch Processing

Batch processing applies a set of transactions against the master file that they affect. Each transaction concerns a record of the master file and the transactions are first sorted in the order of the master records so sequential processing of the transaction file against the master file is possible. If magnetic tape is the only external storage available, batch processing is necessary. When more than one master file is affected by the transactions, resorting of the transaction file may be required. In batch processing, a considerable amount of the total processing time is usually consumed by sorting. Knuth (1975) states that computer manufacturers claim over 25% of computer time is used for sorting. Since many programs do no sorting, some must do a great deal.

Another disadvantage of batch processing is that the processing is scheduled so that the transaction file is sufficiently large to make a run worthwhile. This is because the complete master file must be examined in sequential processing.

Transaction Processing

Transaction processing, sometimes called *inline* processing, applies a transaction against all master files before dealing with the next transaction. When no sorting of the transactions is involved, direct access is required, so files cannot be on tape while being processed. The major advantage then is that a transaction can be processed immediately online as received. However, transaction processing may be used in a batch system.

Computer processing has a jargon with which you should become familiar. *On demand* means the request for processing need not await a scheduled operation which could be as infrequent as monthly. Processing is then single transaction oriented. *Real time* means that the response is linked to a physical process as it occurs.

Interactive processing means that the user can modify the processing in some manner in real time.

The file designer must know the type of processing to be used and anticipate future processing requirements.

1.6 DATA BASE

1.6.1 Overview

The concept of data as external to the program gives rise to the idea of a data base. There is some confusion about the meaning of the term "data base" because the scope of the idea is large and allows many specific instances. In brief, a *data base* is a collection of data consisting of multiple files arranged so that it may be readily accessed by different programs usually devised by different programmers.

In actual use this definition can and must be expanded. Other considerations are the level of redundancy allowed in the data, the degree of independence from application programs, the control of access to data, and the provision for optimal use of a set of application programs with conflicting requirements.

Martin (1976), among others, states that a data base must include the considerations mentioned to differentiate it from a collection of files. Because the boundary between a data base and a collection of files is vague, we relax this definition somewhat and use *data base management system* (DBMS) to refer to a data base with the software required to implement to a significant degree the considerations previously mentioned.

Primarily, the data base system concept is a result of the realization that, ideally, data and the files that contain data items exist independently of the program that accesses the data and should be treated accordingly. However, the complexity that arises from this view is immense and poses limits to a complete realization of the view, for carried to its ultimate the result would be one world data base. Thus the idea must be tempered by reality. Nevertheless, the limits of such a view are still to be explored. It should also be realized that the requirements of the large organization and the small organization do not necessarily coincide. We note that some corporations have compounded their data problems by premature implementations of data base systems.

The concept of a data base system does not lessen the need to consider physical files; rather, it says that the definition of physical files should not be located in the application program but in the data base system. The purpose of this transfer of location, as shown in Fig. 1.10, is to move from a static storage defined by the application program mapping to a dynamic storage mapping independent of the application program. This dynamic mapping is to be controlled by the data base software. Unfortunately in practice, such an idea has not been fully realized.

In a data base system the data item is the main element of data rather than the file, and it is in the various ways that the data base system can organize the relational structure of these elementary elements of information that differentiate it from a simple collection of files. Of course, in the data base, as seen by the application program, it is the record structure that is of primary interest. Flexibility of organization and use is the key concept of data base systems, and data base management is the means by which it occurs. However, before such flexibility can be examined, it is necessary to understand static structures both logically and physically. We

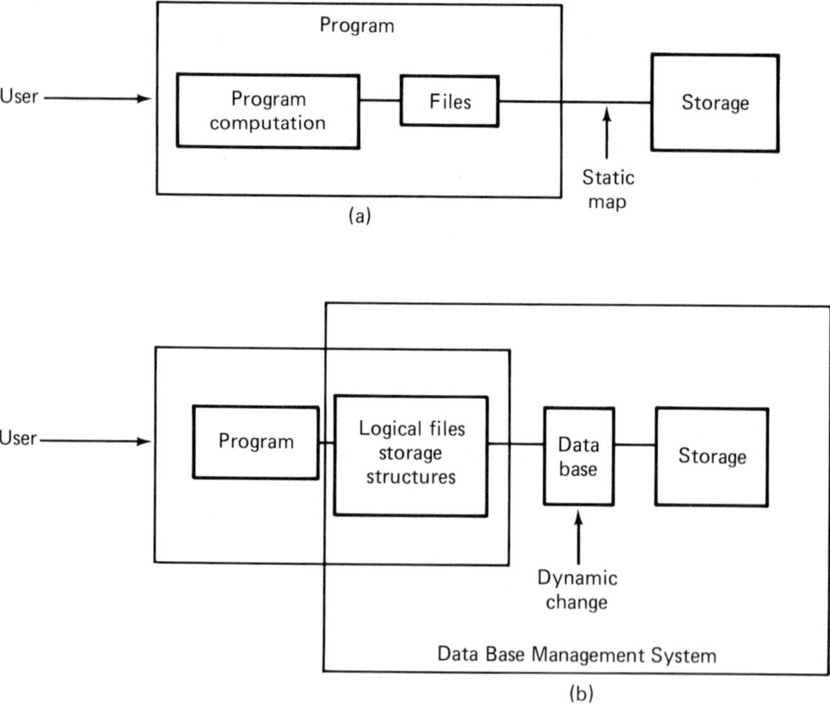

Figure 1.10 Mappings: (a) static; (b) dynamic.

shall do this in subsequent chapters before returning to a consideration of the data base philosophy.

Virtual files and transparent files are two concepts toward which computing has been moving. A virtual file is one that appears to exist to the programmer but that is not normally present in the computer system. A simple instance is the logical file defined within a program that has a physical storage structure other than the one of which we are aware. A transparent file does not appear to the programmer to exist, but it does. The actual physical file in the above example is, ideally, transparent.

Because a data base system is simply a high-level file management technique, the development of data base systems has a good analogy in the development of high-level languages. The same pros and cons will be advanced and the same emotional debates will ensue. Of course, you still need an assembler language but no one uses it unless it is absolutely necessary, the point being that the simplest and most direct solutions are chosen unless *good* reasons are given to the contrary. Complex detail and so-called clever solutions should never be tolerated for their own sake.

1.6.2 History of Data Files

Basically, the history of data files can be viewed in three main stages of progression. They illustrate the move to isolate the physical storage of data from the applications program. This has been achieved by delaying the point at which the logical record is tied or bound to a physical address. This is called the *binding time.*

Stage 1: *Static physical organization*
The physical storage of data is performed by the applications programmer. Example: sequential files. Physical address used by programmer for direct access. Device sensitive.

Stage 2: *Dynamic physical organization and static storage structures*
The physical storage of data is performed by a software processor accessed indirectly by the applications program. Physical data restructured independently of the application program. Examples: relative files, indexed files. Device independent but a fixed logical view.

Stage 3: *Dynamic logical organization*
The logical structure of program files may change while the physical organization remains fixed. The logical files of the data base may change without affecting the application program's logical files. In other words, multiple logical files can be obtained from the same physical data. This is achieved by the data base system software.

1.7 THE FUTURE

From the discussion so far, it is not difficult to see the future trend in storage techniques. The cost of acquiring and maintaining data will increase with respect to the costs of processing it. Thus greater and greater effort will be made to isolate the applications programmer from the impact of change in physical storage. At the same time the problem of storage utilization, time utilization, response time, complexity, and provision for anticipated use will be of major concern, continually requiring the need for complex tradeoffs that will be dynamic because of improvement in storage technology and the dynamic nature of the data base. To quote James Martin (1976):

> One of the most difficult tricks that we have to learn is how to introduce automation without introducing rigidity. The computer industry is only now beginning to glimpse how that can be done. Data base techniques are an important part of the answer.*

We might add that the telephone industry has dealt with this problem for many years. Its immense plant investment has forced new solutions to integrate with old solutions. The trend shown in Fig. 1.11 is developing rapidly.

The question remains. What will the applications programmer see as a file in the future? We believe that it will be the same file he now sees in his COBOL program but it may only be a logical figment of this program's imagination. Thus the file structures of COBOL will live on as long as COBOL does. Love it or hate it; COBOL does not appear about to die.

*James Martin, *Principles of Data-Base Management* (Englewood Cliffs, N.J.: Prentice-Hall, Inc., 1976), p. 39.

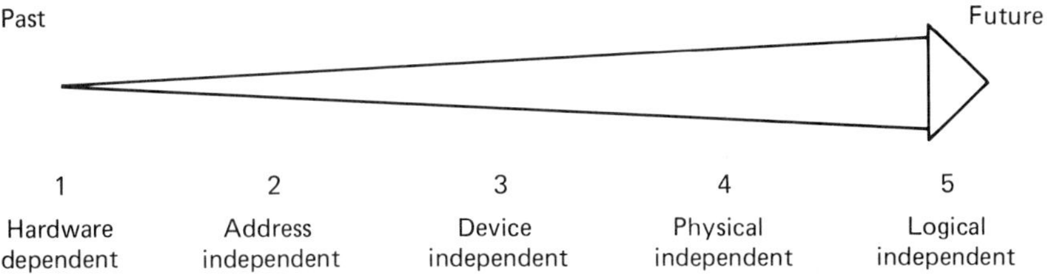

Figure 1.11 Trends in applications programming.

PROBLEMS

1. Explain the difference between data and information.

2. Determine measures of the value of information.

3. Determine ten functions that could be performed by an information system.

4. Discuss the information requirements of a small retail store.

5. Discuss the information requirements of a retail chain with central buyers and management.

6. Discuss the information requirements of a university. Is a single data base suitable? Is it necessary?

7. Suppose each home could afford a data terminal that could request computing service in the same way we now have telephone services.

(a) As the computer company, how would you charge for services?

(b) As the subscriber, how would you make use of this service?

8. Suppose you are engaged as a consultant to a small company that wishes to computerize their operations. What general advice would you give? Devise a feasibility study. Remember you do not know their business, but they do.

9. Comment on the human aspects of introducing a data processing system to an organization.

10. Does your installation have a data base? Write a brief report on its success.

11. (a) Change the function of Fig. 1.9 to begin at location k of memory.

(b) Map a three-dimensional array to memory and determine a function to describe your map.

2

Data Management

The physical storage problem of data is complex, primarily because of the storage hierarchy, the need to move data, and the desirability of making the hardware as transparent to the user as possible in the process. *Data management* refers to the methods used to store and retrieve data, including input/output as well as external storage devices. Our concern with data management is limited mainly to the use of external storage for files, but since data is physically stored, data management necessarily involves consideration of hardware also. We restrict our discussion of hardware to the essential details of tape and disk drives that influence how data is managed on these devices.

The main purpose of this chapter is to provide the essential device and system background for understanding the COBOL file structures and their relation to hardware requirements. To do this, a knowledge of how and why data is managed in a computer system is necessary in order to appreciate the form storage structures take and the reasons files are processed in certain ways.

2.1 STORAGE DEVICES

An intense competition by hardware technology manufacturers has provided a large variety of storage devices. Apart from their physical construction, storage devices are characterized by cost per byte, storage capacity, and access speed. Indeed, the use of data base technology is largely due to the decreased cost per byte and the availability of large storage capacity. In addition, reduction in access time has made many on-line systems possible.

Storage devices consist of a storage media and an access mechanism. Two storage media were already in use before 1900: the Hollerith card and paper tape. Since these media are permanently altered when data is stored, they can only be recorded on once. For both media, it is possible to read faster than it is to record. The use of magnetic media, on the other hand, allows the rewriting of a particular storage location. Furthermore, reading and writing have identical characteristics. Tape, disk, and drum are common examples of magnetic media.

The operation of a device requires an access mechanism that locates the beginning of a physical record on the media and provides the flow of data: either a READ or copy of the record and a WRITE or placement of a new record. A sequential access storage device can only locate a record by moving from the location of an adjacent record. Examples of sequential devices are card readers and tape drives. While tape drives normally move forward, some have a backspace capability. Ideally, a direct access storage device locates a record independently of the position of other records. Examples of direct access are disks and drums. In practice, record access is not usually completely random as in memory. Disks locate the storage area, called the track, directly but sequentially scan the track for a record.

Magnetic media are relatively cheap and have large capacity. The access mechanisms are generally mechanical, much slower than electronic access, but less expensive.

2.1.1 Tape Devices

The first major large-capacity, external storage device was the magnetic tape drive, and today magnetic tape is still the primary off-line storage media. The traditional data processing operation has been predominantly tape oriented, and the limitations of tape have resulted in processing procedures that are less than ideal when using more general storage devices. From the mid 1960s there has been a general move away from tape-oriented processing. The weight or inertia of traditions has often caused tape processing procedures to be applied unnecessarily by programmers to more general devices. Of course, the cost of conversion may also prevent existing procedures being upgraded to new device capabilities.

A tape drive and magnetic tape are similar in essence to the audio tape recorder. However, the recording mode is digital. Tape media may be reel-to-reel or cartridge, with cartridge being faster for mounting and demounting on the drive. It should be noted that the labor costs of mounts and demounts is increasingly significant.

Tapes store an immense amount of data. A standard 2400-feet tape with a recording density of 1600 bytes/in. potentially stores $1600 \times 12 \times 2400 = 46{,}080{,}000$ bytes. Longer tapes are available. The effect of interblock gaps (IBG), as we shall see, can significantly decrease the amount of data actually stored. Magnetic tape is error prone and elaborate re-entry procedures are performed by better operating systems. Error detection is incorporated into the reading and writing of records.

Like the audio recorder, a tape drive can have different speeds. A typical speed is 125 in./sec. The speed of the tape and the density of the recording give the *transfer rate*. For instance, a speed of 100 in./sec at a density of 1600 bytes/in. gives a transfer rate of 160,000 bytes/sec. Choosing the highest recording density for a fixed speed maximizes the transfer rate but increases cost. Drives are now available with 6250 bytes/in.

Normally, sequentially accessed files are stored on magnetic tape because of its portability and because of the relatively low cost of this storage medium in comparison to more sophisticated devices such as disks and drums. Although storage media allow sequential access to records stored on them, the advantage of devices such as disks and drums as opposed to magnetic tape is that access to a given record is much faster. Unfortunately, the cost is much greater, and these devices provide far less portability. Of course, any file can be stored on a tape and portability is obtained in this manner as well as backup copies. For these reasons alone, tape will continue to be used.

Tape Organization

The standard nine-track tape contains nine parallel tracks running the length of the tape, with any point on a track recording a binary zero or one. Looking at right angles to the tracks, we have nine binary bits, eight used to record a character and the ninth, called a *parity bit*, used to detect errors in the character.

The basic data unit of a tape is the physical record or block. This is that portion of the tape on which data is recorded between a start and the following stop. The tape only moves at full speed while writing or reading.

In addition to data, tape control information must also be present on a tape. The logical beginning of a tape is a reflective strip of aluminum attached to the tape several feet from its physical beginning.

The first block of a tape is often a label used to describe the tape. It should contain such information as file identification, creation date, security date, retention date, and reel number if the file requires more than one tape. To determine that there are no more records an end-of-file marker is written on a tape after the last record is written. In the event that we try to write beyond the end of the tape, there must be an indicator to prevent tape from running off the reel. A reflective strip of aluminum is again used to indicate the logical end of the tape.

2.1.2 Disk Devices

The one-dimensional and mechanical nature of a tape drive limits it to sequential access. Early computers used magnetic drums with a two-dimensional access; this permitted direct high-speed access but limited capacity. The use of drums has decreased as disks developed. The development of magnetic disks provided high-speed direct access of large capacity. The cost of disks has drastically dropped and many installations now use disks solely as the processing external memory, limiting tapes to I/O and library storage. This is because disks have relatively low access times, in the order of milliseconds, and fast data transfer, in the order of megabytes per second.

In Fig. 2.1, the general construction of a magnetic disk and its

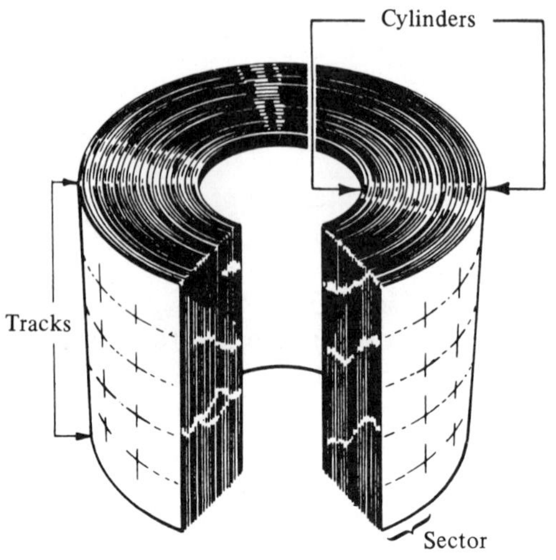

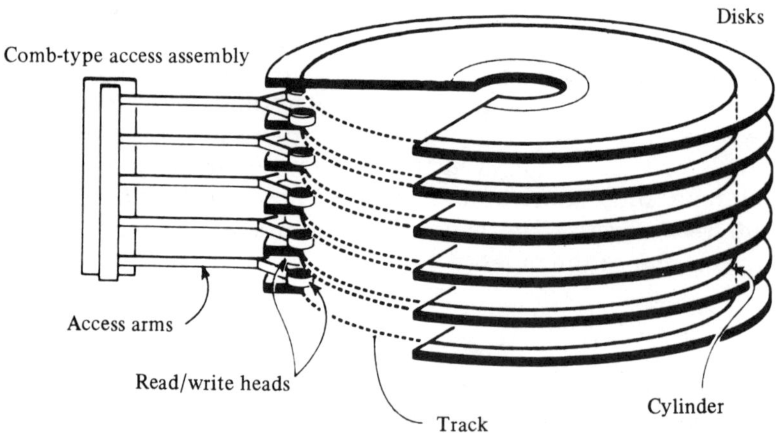

Figure 2.1 Typical disk unit structure: (top) logical storage structure; (bottom) physical access structure. (Courtesy IBM).

access mechanism is sketched; the mechanical drive and control other than the access assembly containing the READ/WRITE heads is absent as it does not concern us. The phonograph with which the reader is familiar provides a convenient descriptive analogy to a disk. The basic physical unit of recording media on a disk is a platter that resembles a record and likewise rotates. As the platter rotates, it passes a READ/WRITE head. When the head is held fixed, it scans a portion of the disk called a *track*. Unlike the spiral tracks of a record, these tracks are concentric circles because the READ heads are located at fixed discrete points along the diameter of the platter when reading or writing information, whereas a phonograph arm has continuous motion toward the center while playing. On some devices each track is subdivided into sectors which are the addressable storage units. One might expect the inner tracks to store less information since they have a smaller radius but all tracks have the same capacity. This is achieved by increasing the recording density of the inner tracks and consequently decreasing the size of the sectors toward the center of the platter. Access mechanisms are of two types—fixed and movable. When fixed, there must be a READ/WRITE head for every track.

A disk is usually composed of several platters which are fixed to a central shaft or spindle and which rotate together. A movable arm resembles a comb where the teeth pass between the platters moving in and out to seek the track desired and each tooth of the comb contains two READ/WRITE heads, one for the platter above and one for that below. Thus the platters are recorded on each side. This arrangement gives a large surface area in a small volume which is why a disk has greater capacity than a drum.

Disk Characteristics

The advantage of the direct access device over the sequential access device is speed of access. For a movable arm, disk drive access time has two components: the time required to move the READ/WRITE head to the proper track, called the *seek time*, and the rotational delay time required to locate the beginning of the record on the track, called the *latency time*. Seek time varies nonlinearly according to the initial position of the recording head. The manufacturer usually only provides an average value. The average seek time can be reduced by programming but multiple users of the disk in a multiprogramming environment will perturb the expected results. Of course, with fixed heads the seek time is essentially zero.

The speed with which data can be read or written is known as the *transfer rate* and is usually measured in bytes per second. On disks the read and write rates are identical. The effective rate of data transfer is less than the transfer rate since the track contains control information in addition to data and this control information is not useful to the program.

Disks differ with respect to mechanical construction, the number of recording surfaces, the number of cylinders, and the track data capacity. In short, there are wide variations in speed, capacity, and, as a consequence, cost. Any variation can make it difficult to do a comparative analysis of disk drives. The costs of on-line and off-line storage can be difficult to determine but estimates provide a useful relative comparison.

Disk Organization

The basic data unit is the recording track which is that area of a platter that rotates under a READ/WRITE head when fixed in position. The track is organized into a beginning, designated by an *index point* (this also serves as the end of the track), and blocks separated by physical gaps. Each track contains some control information about the track itself. In addition, a poor fit of the blocks will cause lost space at the end of the track. For these reasons not all the track can be used for recording data.

The set of tracks on the top and bottom of each platter that can be accessed with one position of the READ/WRITE heads is known as a *cylinder*. That is, a cylinder consists of all the tracks in the same position on every platter. If there are ten recording surfaces, then there are ten tracks in a cylinder.

Data is recorded in a *data block*. Each data block also contains control information about the block. A block address is obtained from the cylinder number, the track number, and the block number.

2.2 BLOCKING

We have referred to a block as the physical equivalent of a logical record. The correspondence or mapping between the records of a file and the blocks of the file on the storage media is known as *blocking*. There are several forms of blocking. When one logical record corresponds to one block, it is called an *unblocked* record. If two or more records make up a block, we have blocked records and a blocked file. In the event a record is so large that it requires more than one block (the logical record exceeds the physical record size), we say that the record *spans* the blocks and it is called a *spanned* record. There are two reasons for blocking.

1. Less external storage is consumed.
2. The input/output time is reduced.

Note that spanned records may not be supported; in this case, the record size is limited to the maximum block size, which is one track, and the organization of a file must be designed to fit this maximum block size. In many disk systems, the physical record size is fixed.

The reason less external storage is used in blocking is that each interblock gap is quite large compared to a byte. Thus, the more bytes we write together, the larger the physical record compared to the interblock gap. Large blocking can significantly reduce the ratio of wasted space. Since access time is slow relative to data transmission, increasing the block size decreases the average time to transmit a byte when access time is included. Indeed, the blocking factor for sequential files is the most significant efficiency parameter that is easily controlled. When blocking a disk, the blocking factor should integer divide the track size. Typically two or three blocks per track are used. In some cases only a track can be accessed and this determines the block size.

2.3 BUFFERS

Since a block of records is retrieved from or written to the file, how is a logical record accessed by the program? The difference in the program record access and the device access is resolved by a concept called a *buffer*, which is an area of memory that is equal in size to the maximum block size and used to store blocks for program reference. Data management software provides and uses buffers for the blocking and deblocking of records. Good management of the buffers maximizes the performance of a device while minimizing the demand for CPU cycles and memory by that device.

When a READ statement which is used to obtain a record is executed and the file buffer is empty, a block of records is moved from external storage to the file buffer. However, if the buffer contains unused records, the execution of a READ statement causes the next record to be moved to the data area.

Similarly, the execution of a WRITE statement moves program data to the buffer. As soon as the buffer contains a complete block it is immediately written to the file storage device.

The foregoing procedure is called *single buffering*. Commonly two buffers would be used, as a buffer is not otherwise available when a transfer between that buffer and a device is taking place. To maintain a maximum transfer rate, two buffers are required.

Optimal block size is determined by the size of logical records, the memory available for buffers, and the device in use. Choice of block size is complicated by the fact that in modern systems one may not necessarily determine the device to be used nor even be able to. Nevertheless because blocking is such an important component of program efficiency it cannot be ignored. Perhaps more ideally the software should determine the blocking factor.

2.4 FILES

Since files reside external to main memory, file access necessarily involves the location of the file and the establishment of data flow between memory and the file device. Communication with a file requires that it exist and be identifiable. A file is created by having the operating system allocate secondary storage for the number of records expected and reserving this space for this file only as long as it exists. How the operating system does this is not our concern; how the creation of the file is defined is the concern of the file user. Within COBOL a file is created by the file definition; however, the file must also be created within the system. In the IBM 370, for example, system file creation is specified by JCL, or Job Control Language, and we will provide several illustrations.

In System 370 a tape reel or other unit of storage media is called a *volume*. Volumes usually have labels, and each file stored on a volume should have a file label. These labels allow the physical file to be identified.

In communicating with a file, two types of information are involved: file control and file data. Our concern here is file control. Files are identified by file names, and with COBOL there are two file names: the program or COBOL file name and the system file name. The COBOL file name is determined in the file definition or FD declaration and the system file name in the JCL declaration. The correspondence between the two is obtained via the ENVIRONMENT DIVISION with the ASSIGN clause.

Before a file can be used, it must be located and, in the case of a sequential file, positioned to the starting point. If necessary, a message is sent to the operator to mount the storage media. Storage for the file buffers must be assigned and any other requirements for processing completed. The file must be *connected* to the program before use. This is called *opening a file*, and in COBOL the OPEN verb is used to prepare a file for program use. *Closing a file* releases the file buffer area and any associated tables for other use. Tape drives are rewound and the storage device released to the system. In COBOL, the CLOSE verb is used to initiate file closing.

Other information concerning the type of file organization and access mode must also be provided. This is more appropriately discussed in the relevant chapters.

2.5 IBM RECORD FORMATS

There are three types of record formats: fixed length, variable length, and undefined length. As their actual characteristics vary with the particular computer system, we restrict the discussion to the IBM 370 system. *Fixed length records*, as the name implies, all have the same length. For *variable length records*, four bytes prefix the logical record to specify the record length. Four bytes are used to specify the block size. *Undefined length records* differ from variable length records in that the record length is *not* contained in the record; rather, the records are separated physically by an interblock gap. Undefined length records cannot be blocked.

In some cases a record is very long and exceeds the block size requiring the logical record to be contained in two or more blocks (a form of inverse blocking if you like). Spanned records (in System 370) are actually a special form of fixed or variable length records.

2.6 CONCLUSIONS

Our discussion of devices has been brief because it is necessarily of a general nature. The point we would like to make is that the physical characteristics of storage devices can determine the kind of logical or abstract solutions we choose. Since storage devices are continually being improved, we should be careful to avoid ignoring the fundamental reasons for past solutions when those reasons no longer exist.

Devices come and go but concepts of access speed, capacity, transfer rates, and the physical organization of data will continue to apply. It may well be that the reader will gain a deeper appreciation by a more detailed study of a particular device. We cannot choose the device for him. In our view such detailed study should only be on need-to-know and when-required basis. Life is too unpredictable and short for any other approach.

PROBLEMS

1. Suppose physical records 800 bytes in length are written on a tape of density 800 bytes/in. If the interblock gap is ½ in., how much of the tape available is used for physical records?

2. Suppose records 50 bytes in length are blocked in groups of 100 and written on a tape of density 1600 bytes/in. If the interblock gap is ¾ in., how much of the tape is consumed by interblock gaps (IBGs)?

3. Suppose records are 92 bytes long and an I/O buffer is available with 1000 bytes. You have a choice of tape recording densities of 800 and 1600. What blocking factor and density would you use to get the highest recording density of records on the tape? To get the lowest recording density of records on the tape?

4. Obtain the characteristics of the most common tape drive in your computer center. List in decreasing order of importance those characteristics important to programmers, if any.

5. If there is more than one tape drive in the center, determine the best one to use.

6. Determine the essential programming characteristics of the disk drives in your computer center. Which drive is best? Comment on this question.

7. (a) What is the importance of the surface area of the recording media?
   (b) What is the importance of the transfer rate?
   (c) For which kind of access is the seek time important?
   (d) How can seek time be eliminated?

8. If a disk has 10 platters with 20 tracks and the very top and bottom platter surfaces are not used, what is the cylinder size? If a track stores 4000 bytes, what is the disk capacity?

9. Investigate two storage devices that we have not considered; discuss their operation and list the advantages and disadvantages of these devices.

3 COBOL Sequential Files

3.1 INTRODUCTION

Recall that a *sequential file* is simply a serial list of records where, except for the first and last records, each record has a unique predecessor and a unique successor record. This serial order is established when the file is created, by storing the records one following the other in the order of writing. Thus the records are physically stored in their logical sequential order. Essentially, a sequential file has a static linear physical order, records being accessed in the order that they were originally written.

A file is said to be *sequentially organized* when the records which comprise it are sequenced (possibly according to one or more fields within each record) and are stored and accesssed in consecutive order according to this sequence. A deck of COBOL statements with sequence numbers from 1 to 100 stored in numerically ascending order on these sequence numbers is an example of a sequentially organized file. The file would still be sequentially organized if the cards were numbered 10, 20, 30, to 1000 or even if stored in the same order without the sequence numbers being present at all. On the other hand, a file is said to be *sequentially accessed* when the records are processed in the consecutive order in which they are physically located on a storage media. A sequentially organized file *must*, by definition, be sequentially accessed, but as we shall see, it is possible to sequentially access files that are not sequentially organized.

The card deck mentioned above is sequentially accessed when it is placed in a card reader prior to compiling. If the deck is shuffled, destroying its sequence, the program will not execute properly. Note that a deck of playing cards is usually shuffled before being used. This is done in order to achieve a random distribution but playing cards are dealt sequentially, one card at a time, hopefully, off the top of the deck. Thus a deck of playing cards is randomly organized but sequentially accessed.

There are many examples of *sequentially organized* files, such as:

(a) a list of all employees of a company in ascending order by social security number

(b) a list of all students in a high school in decreasing order by student ID number

(c) a list of the hit parade songs played by a radio station during one hour, arranged in the order in which they were played

Sequential files may be placed on external storage devices such as tape drives, disks, magnetic drums, cards, etc. Actually, the physical limitations of magnetic tape drive mechanisms in present use only allow for sequential access. Records stored on magnetic tape can only be fetched consecutively. Some sophisticated tape drives allow reading in both directions, as noted in Chapter 2, but the records are still processed sequentially. Changing directions severely limits the speed of a tape device and is not normally done.

In terms of data base organization, there are two major reasons for using sequential access to records. First, the occurrence of records is sequentially organized for purposes of the application;

hence, sequential access to the records is a necessary requirement. Second, the cost or availability of equipment requires the use of magnetic tape drives or other devices that permit only sequential access to the records.

Sequentially organized files are found most often in batch-oriented data processing. Transactions relevant to some application are collected into a batch and kept until enough have accumulated to warrant their processing as a group. An example of this is the recording of purchases made with credit cards. Each purchase is not immediately debited to a credit card account by a clerk. Rather, it is forwarded by mail to a central clearing house where it is batched together with many other credit slips before being processed. These transactions are arranged in some sequence (usually in increasing order by corresponding credit card number) and then processed by a program to each individual account where the accounts are stored in the same sequence.

Batch-oriented data processing is also performed when data is to be processed for monthly billings, semi-annual inventories, quarterly tax reports, and other applications. A major factor is that processing is scheduled by the cyclic nature of the application. Thus the need for data is not a sudden demand; rather it is known in advance and can be planned for. Batch can be very efficient in such cases. Sudden demand reports tend to require organization of the data base in a manner other than sequential.

Reading a sequential file normally begins with the first record. However, some systems allow an offset, and reading may begin with the *n*th record. In COBOL a START instruction is used to obtain the offset. Records can be added to the end of the file, but some installations forbid such operations, requiring a new file copy to be made. This is really a matter of the file back-up procedures in use, since an error in the program could inadvertently wipe out a portion of the file. A sequential file record can only be rewritten on a direct access device. Records *cannot* be rewritten in place on *magnetic* tape as there is *no* guarantee that they can be returned to the same physical location and, consequently, adjacent records may be overwritten, destroying them.

Whether sequential access to the records is required because the data is sequentially organized or whether the storage devices permit only sequential access, the operating systems of most machines provide routines that store and retrieve records from storage devices sequentially. Such routines, called *access methods* by manufacturers, are responsible for providing all the machine commands that transfer data between the memory of the machine and a storage device. These routines are usually complicated, machine dependent, and very sophisticated. Fortunately, the details required to use them normally need not be known directly by the programmer as most of the higher-level languages and, in particular, COBOL contain language statements that direct their execution. When the programmer is unaware of the access method, we say it is *transparent.*

In COBOL, the language elements necessary for handling sequential files are termed the *Sequential I–O module.* This is the ANSI term; it may or may not be used by a particular manufacturer's implementation. The Sequential I–O module has two levels of implementation called *Level 1* and *Level 2.* Level 1 contains the basic facilities for the definition and access of sequential files as well as specification of check points. Level 2 provides the full facilities for use of the sequential module. Although we cannot examine every feature, we have not restricted our discussion to Level 1. Since Level 1 does not provide for the full capabilities of COBOL sequential files, the programmer must determine the level of the compiler he is to use. The file language statements provided by the Sequential I–O module are translated by a COBOL compiler into commands that direct the sequential access method of a computer's operating system to physically store and fetch records on a storage device.

In summary, *sequential organization* means that the file records are stored consecutively on the file media and can only be retrieved serially in the order that they are stored. Records are thus addressed implicitly. Sequential access transmits records between the program and the file media in the physical order of storage; that is, transmission of a record requires that all previous records have been transmitted. Sequential processing refers to the use of sequentially accessed files.

3.2 CASE STUDY: MUSIC LOG

The disc jockeys of radio station XJBC maintain a written report that lists the music selections they play during their radio programs. This report is known as the *music log* and is very useful to management for determining advertising costs and daily programming content. This log is also studied to advise the government's radio and television authority of the amount of air time allocated to music of national and international origin and to help the station's listeners obtain the names of selections and performers of music they have enjoyed.

The increased use of the log, particularly the statistics required by government, has excessively increased administrative costs. Protests to the government officials concerned have been to no avail. And in view of last year's submissions being lost in the mail, management has decided that it is essential to improve present procedures by placing the music log on a computer.

3.2.1 Logical Analysis: Music Log

The music log is a sequentially organized file in which the records are sequenced in the order in which the musical selections were played. Each record contains the name of the music selection, the name of the performer, the time the music was played, the name of the recording label, and the duration of the selection. The music log grows with the passing of time, but entries in the log are not changed as they record historical events, unless an error was made.

The music log is easily adapted to a computer file and is to be stored on magnetic tape. In addition, the countries of origin of the record and of artist are to be added to the file. Further, since the statistical calculations are to be automatic, management has decided to classify the music into country, classical, popular, jazz, teenage, and folk. This is encoded into a single field of the record.

Program 3.1 Narrative. Program 3.1 creates the sequential music log file for station XJBC. The COBOL procedure is accomplished with four paragraphs driven by the first paragraph in a top down structured manner. The reader should examine this program skimming over points he does not understand as the next section introduces the Sequential I-O module of COBOL and refers back to Program 3.1 for specific examples.

Exercise (Program 3.1)

There is a problem with Program 3.1. Suppose a record is entered incorrectly. How do we correct it? First, we must find it which means it must be uniquely identified. Determine what changes should be made to the music log record in order to solve the problem.

In discussing COBOL programs we shall not concern ourselves unduly with those segments of the programs not pertinent to the discussion at hand. Although, for purposes of simplicity, we shall write these programs to read their data from a standard card deck, it should be realized that with a sophisticated I/O environment

Program 3.1

```
IDENTIFICATION DIVISION.
PROGRAM-ID. PROG3PT1.
AUTHOR. R H COOPER.
DATE-COMPILED. MAR 14,1980.
ENVIRONMENT DIVISION.
CONFIGURATION SECTION.
SOURCE-COMPUTER. IBM-370.
OBJECT-COMPUTER. IBM-370.


INPUT-OUTPUT SECTION.
FILE-CONTROL.
    SELECT CARD-READER
           ASSIGN TO UT-CARD-S-SYSIN
           ORGANIZATION IS SEQUENTIAL
           ACCESS MODE IS SEQUENTIAL.
    SELECT MUSIC-LOG
           ASSIGN TO UT-DISK-S-MUSIC
           ORGANIZATION IS SEQUENTIAL
           ACCESS MODE IS SEQUENTIAL.
    SELECT PRINTER
           ASSIGN TO UT-PRNT-S-SYSOUT
           ORGANIZATION IS SEQUENTIAL
           ACCESS MODE IS SEQUENTIAL.


DATA DIVISION.
FILE SECTION.

FD  CARD-READER
    BLOCK CONTAINS 1 RECORDS
    RECORD CONTAINS 80 CHARACTERS
    LABEL RECORDS ARE OMITTED
    DATA RECORD IS CARD-IMAGE.
01  CARD-IMAGE.
    02  FILLER                    PIC X(80).

FD  MUSIC-LOG
    BLOCK CONTAINS 100 RECORDS
    RECORD CONTAINS 149 CHARACTERS
    LABEL RECORDS ARE STANDARD
    DATA RECORD IS MUSIC-LOG-RECORD.
01  MUSIC-LOG-RECORD.
    02  FILLER                    PIC X(149).

FD  PRINTER
    BLOCK CONTAINS 1 RECORDS
    RECORD CONTAINS 133 CHARACTERS
    LABEL RECORDS ARE OMITTED
    DATA RECORD IS PRINT-LINE.
01  PRINT-LINE.
    02  FILLER                    PIC X(133).


WORKING-STORAGE SECTION.
77  EOF-CARD-FLAG                 PIC X(3).
    88  EOF-CARD VALUE IS 'ON'.
```

Program 3.1 (cont.)

```
           01  WS-MUSIC-LOG-RECORD.
               02  FIRST-CARD.
                   03  NAME-OF-SELECTION  PIC X(30).
                   03  NAME-OF-ARTIST     PIC X(30).
                   03  NAME-OF-RECORDING-LABEL
                                          PIC X(20).
               02  SECOND-CARD.
                   03  TIME-PLAYED        PIC 9(4).
                   03  DURATION           PIC 9(4).
                   03  ORIGIN-OF-RECORD   PIC X(30).
                   03  ORIGIN-OF-ARTIST   PIC X(30).
                   03  MUSIC-CLASSIFICATION
                                          PIC X.


           PROCEDURE DIVISION.
               PERFORM INITIALIZATION.
               PERFORM PROCESS-CARDS UNTIL EOF-CARD.
               PERFORM TERMINATION.
               STOP RUN.


           INITIALIZATION.
               OPEN INPUT CARD-READER
                    OUTPUT PRINTER
                           MUSIC-LOG.
               MOVE 'OFF' TO EOF-CARD-FLAG.
               READ CARD-READER INTO FIRST-CARD
                    OF WS-MUSIC-LOG-RECORD
                    AT END MOVE 'ON' TO EOF-CARD-FLAG.
               IF NOT EOF-CARD THEN
                  READ CARD-READER INTO SECOND-CARD
                       OF WS-MUSIC-LOG-RECORD.


           PROCESS-CARDS.
               WRITE MUSIC-LOG-RECORD FROM WS-MUSIC-LOG-RECORD.
               WRITE PRINT-LINE FROM FIRST-CARD OF
                     WS-MUSIC-LOG-RECORD.
               WRITE PRINT-LINE FROM SECOND-CARD OF
                     WS-MUSIC-LOG-RECORD.
               READ CARD-READER INTO FIRST-CARD
                    OF WS-MUSIC-LOG-RECORD
                 AT END MOVE 'ON' TO EOF-CARD-FLAG.
               IF NOT EOF-CARD THEN
                  READ CARD-READER INTO SECOND-CARD
                       OF WS-MUSIC-LOG-RECORD.


           TERMINATION.
               CLOSE CARD-READER
                     PRINTER
                     MUSIC-LOG.
```

modifications of these programs to accept their data from other files or terminals can be done. No attempt will be made to use files as detailed as those encountered in the real world, but the reader should constantly realize that he may well need to operate with records containing many more fields and files containing many more records.

3.3 SEQUENTIAL I-O MODULE OF COBOL

In order to organize and access a sequential file, statements selected from the Sequential I-O module of COBOL are used. These statements of the COBOL language can be divided into three classes, specifically:

(a) statements that *name* the file, *define* its mode of organization and access, and *link* the file to a physical storage device

(b) statements that *describe* the records that comprise the file

(c) statements that *prepare* the file for use, *write* records to the file, *read* records from it once created, and, lastly, *disconnect* the file from the program once work with it is completed.

The actual allocation of physical storage space for a sequential file—that is, the labeling and selection of a magnetic tape, the reservation of space on a disk, or the setting aside of some of the capacity of any storage device—is not a function that can be done within the COBOL language. This is a function of specialized operating system routines or the job control language at a given installation. For help in this matter it is best to consult a systems analyst or the consulting service department at the installation where you work.

Today many installations forbid users from reserving physical storage space themselves and strictly police the availability of storage devices. This is done in an effort to provide increased reliablility, integrity, and security for all the users of data at an installation, and it is another step forward in the realization that data exists independently of the programs that process it. Once the problem of reserving storage space has been settled, the user is in a position to write COBOL programs that will create and use the sequential file.

The COBOL program to create the music log file on tape (Program 3.1) is fairly complex for what it does, but this is typical for creating a COBOL sequential file. Unfortunately, the flexibility allowed by COBOL in defining files and the desire for system independence requires considerable explanation. The following description of COBOL corresponds to the order in which a program is written and concentrates on the statements concerned with the definition and processing of a sequential file. The reader should refer to Program 3.1 for examples in the following discussion.

The management of external storage is provided by the operating system. Thus the program must communicate to the operating system the necessary information for it to handle the input/output operations required. COBOL statements are provided to describe the file name, record size, block size, record format, and type of file organization. The INPUT-OUTPUT section describes the file environment; this may only be the system file name or it may also specify the type of storage device. A file on external storage must also include control information for system use; IBM refers to a file and its control information as a *data set.* The program file description is provided in a COBOL FD entry.

3.3.1 INPUT-OUTPUT SECTION: Defining the File

The FILE-CONTROL paragraph of the INPUT-OUTPUT SECTION defines the name of a file, its organizational type, and the type of access permitted. In addition, it provides a link between the internal COBOL name of a file and the physical storage address of the file itself. A standard ANSI COBOL entry form is[1]

```
FILE-CONTROL.
    SELECT file-name
        ASSIGN TO implementor-name
        ORGANIZATION IS SEQUENTIAL
        ACCESS MODE IS SEQUENTIAL.
```

File-name is the name by which the file will be known within the COBOL program and is a user-defined word. Such words are at

[1] Since COBOL is very flexible and quite complex, the standard and manufacturers' manuals provide very general entry skeletons. To do so here would provide unwarranted detail. We give the basic structure that is normally used and refer the reader to the appropriate manuals for special options.

most 30 characters in length. *Implementor-name* is a system-name COBOL word that is used to communicate with the operating system environment and whose definition may differ among installations.

As an example, a typical IBM COBOL entry for the INPUT–OUTPUT SECTION defines the MUSIC-LOG file of Program 3.1. The ASSIGN clause entry UT-DISK-S-MUSIC specifies that this file is to be stored on a disk device, that it is a sequential file ('S'), and that the *ddname* on the job control language card associated with this file is MUSIC.

Finally, in the preceding COBOL entry form, ORGANIZATION IS SEQUENTIAL specifies that the file is to be sequentially organized, and ACCESS MODE IS SEQUENTIAL specifies that the file is to be sequentially accessed.

3.3.2 FD Entry: Describing the Records

The FD entry furnishes information concerning the identification, record names, and physical structure of a file. A standard ANSI COBOL entry is

```
FD file-name
        BLOCK CONTAINS integer RECORDS
        RECORD CONTAINS integer CHARACTERS
        LABEL RECORDS ARE STANDARD
        DATA RECORD IS data-name.
```

These clauses may appear in any order but, for consistency, it is advisable to follow the order used in the standard.

The BLOCK CONTAINS clause designates how many logical records constitute one physical record. As a physical record is the unit of information transferred to or from main memory during a physical READ/WRITE, it is useful to combine as many logical records of a sequential file as possible into one physical record to increase the efficiency of transfer. However, this can only be achieved at the cost of main memory. This grouping is transparent to the user and is entirely handled by the compiler and the operating system. If more than one logical record is to make up a physical record, a buffer will be provided in the memory of the machine to store the records prior to their transfer to the physical storage device.

The BLOCK CONTAINS clause is used with the record size to determine the buffer size. A record will be stored in this buffer area each time a WRITE statement is executed. When the buffer is full, an entire physical record is transferred to the storage device.

Exactly the opposite action occurs on reading a blocked file. The first READ statement executed brings an entire physical record into memory and makes the first logical record available to the programmer. Successive READ statements will result in more logical records being made available until the physical record in the buffer is depleted at which time a READ will initiate the transfer of another physical record.

The BLOCK CONTAINS clause is not required in the event that a physical record and a logical record are of the same size or where the hardware device assigned to the file, such as a printer, has a fixed physical record size.

The RECORD CONTAINS clause specifies the number of characters in a data record. This clause is optional as the size of each data record can be obtained by an examination of the PICTURE clauses of the level 01 entry that follow its FD entry. However, most COBOL implementations compare the length of a record as stated with the sum of the record's elementary item PICTURE clauses and warn of a discrepancy.

The LABEL RECORDS clause indicates whether or not the physical file has a label. It is a *required* clause. STANDARD indicates that the file has a label and that it conforms to the specifications for labels at the installation. In the event that labels are not present, as, for example, card and print files,

```
LABEL RECORDS ARE OMITTED
```

must be coded. (See Program 3.1.)

The DATA RECORD clause is optional and serves only as documentation. It associates the level 01 entry record description whose record name is *data-name* with the file with which it is associated.

3.3.3 PROCEDURE DIVISION: Accessing the File

The OPEN Statement for a Sequential I-O File

The following form of the OPEN statement should be used when records are to be written to a sequential file.

OPEN OUTPUT *file-name*

If the records are to be read from a sequential file, the following form is used.

```
OPEN INPUT file-name
```

The OPEN statement indicates that the file is to be prepared for processing. No statements may be executed that reference a file until an OPEN has been performed on that file (except in the sort module). After an OPEN has been issued, the program is positioned at the beginning of the sequential file.

The WRITE Statement

The general form of the WRITE statement is

```
WRITE record-name [FROM identifier]
```

The *record-name* is the name of a logical record in the FILE SECTION FD entry of the file in question and may be a qualified name. If the optional FROM is used, the record is first moved from the WORKING-STORAGE SECTION area, denoted *identifier*, to *record-name* before writing.

The READ Statement

The general format of the READ statement is

```
READ file-name [INTO identifier]
AT END imperative statement
```

The execution of this statement causes one logical record to be read from the file and made available to the user. As mentioned previously, the record may already be in the buffer if the file is blocked; that is, the actual transfer of the data from the I/O device to memory may already have taken place. In the event that the optional INTO clause is added, the record will be transferred from the buffer to the area in the WORKING-STORAGE SECTION named *identifier* by a group MOVE.

The *imperative statement* following the key words AT END is required and is executed in the event that an attempt is made to read beyond the end of the file. Once this imperative statement, indicating what action is to be taken, is executed, control is returned to the statement following the READ.

The CLOSE Statement

A CLOSE statement should be issued whenever all WRITE statements to the file are completed or once end-of-file has been reached on reading. Once a file has been closed, it can be repositioned for more processing at the beginning by issuing another OPEN statement. The CLOSE statement disconnects the file from the program, thus making it available to other users. A CLOSE also ensures that any logical records left in a buffer for writing to the file (even if they do not exactly complete a physical record) are transferred to the file. In addition, an end-of-file marker is placed on the file if the file has been opened for OUTPUT. The general form of the CLOSE statement is

CLOSE *file-name*

If a file is opened for OUTPUT, the previous contents of the file are lost when the file is closed.

3.4 SEQUENTIAL FILE PROCESSING

File processing can be classified into four basic functions: edit, sort, update, and report. *Edit* involves the creation of a valid set of transactions to be applied to update a file or files. *Sorting* is required to make the update process more efficient or to rearrange the order of a report. *Update* involves any change to a file. The *report* function is the ultimate purpose for which the files exist and for which the other functions are required.

How these functions are performed varies greatly; however, there are some fairly common types of procedures for sequential files known as *batch processing.* These procedures have been developed to deal efficiently with the limitations of sequential organization. Basically, processing is arranged to occur in large blocks of records. For instance, input transactions are collected into large batches (whence the name) before being entered into the computer. There are two kinds of files in a batch system: transaction and master.

A *transaction* is the recording of an enterprise event that produces data. Before transactions are applied to a master file to update it, they are collected in a transaction file. Such a file could well be simply a deck of cards. A transaction file is temporary, unless it must be saved for historical purposes.

The stored data of an enterprise resides in *master* files; these files are permanent except as the records they contain are modified by transactions. A master file is sequenced on a primary key.

The classical method of applying transactions to a sequential master file is to order the transactions on the same key as the master and then to search the master file for the record that matches the transaction record. Since transactions can be insertions or deletions as well as changes, the master file is rewritten to a new master. Incidently, the old master automatically becomes a backup copy of the master. When a record update is made, the master record is changed and rewritten to the new master and the next transaction obtained before proceeding. Records are deleted by failing to rewrite them. Records are inserted by writing to the new master before the following record of the master is written. We formalize this procedure in the next section.

A general batch processing cycle on a single master file is indicated in Figs. 3.1–3.4. The first step of the cycle consists of creating a transaction file. Input transactions are examined by the edit program shown in Fig. 3.1. Valid transactions are written to the transaction file and invalid transactions are printed on an error file, usually with flags on the errors. The error transactions are corrected by the user and resubmitted to the edit process.

When the transaction file is ready for processing, it is sorted to match the key sequence of the master to which it will be applied. This step is indicated by Fig. 3.2 (sorting is discussed in the next chapter). The update process of Fig. 3.3 merges the transaction file into the old master to create a new master. The error report is necessary to indicate invalid update attempts. For instance, we cannot correct a master record that does not exist. This could indicate loss of a master record or an invalid key in a transaction record. The programmer must take care to allow for recovery from processing errors.

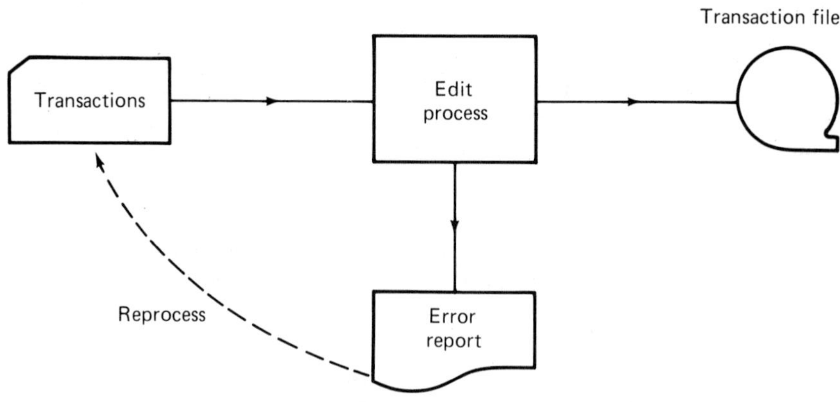

Figure 3.1 Creation of a transaction file.

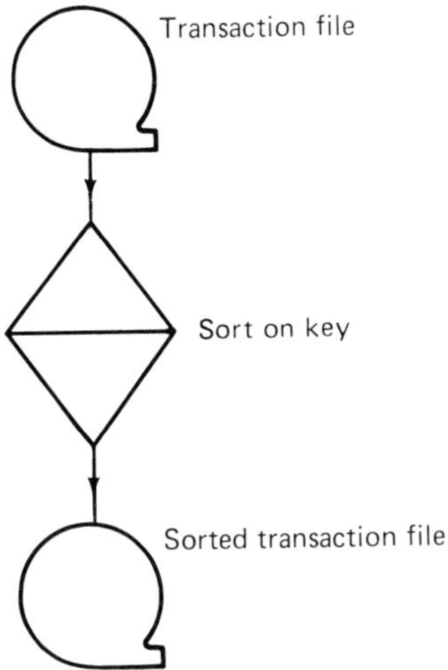

Figure 3.2 Sort process.

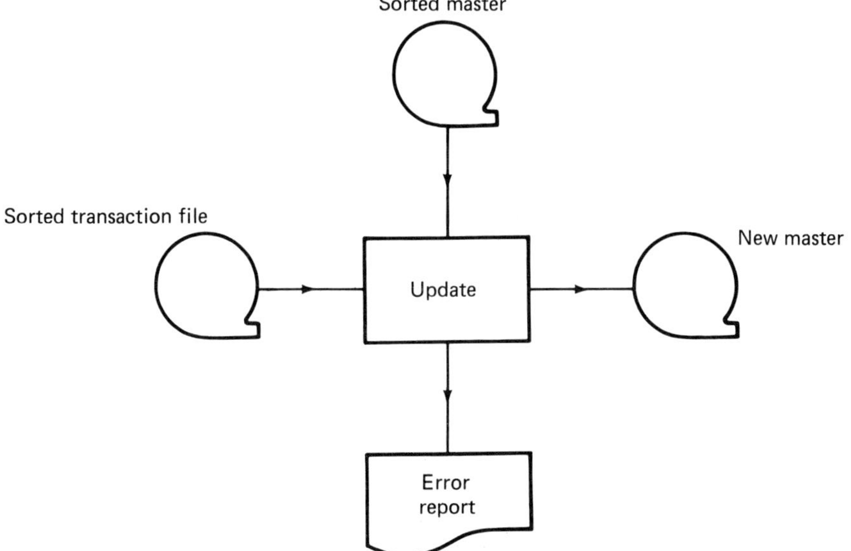

Figure 3.3 Update process.

When the master file is updated, which may take more than one run because of errors, we are ready to produce a report. A simple report process is shown in Fig. 3.4. It is parameter driven by input cards. Often the report phase also updates the master (father) producing, for instance, year to date totals and then we have a new master (son). If we only need to modify existing record values and the file is on disk, we could rewrite in place and not need to copy over the file. This may not provide the saving it appears to, as the need for a copy of the old master may require a copy to be made at this time anyway. Of course, most systems will require more than one file and more than one report. Often the same report is available sorted on different keys at various levels of detail.

While the data of an enterprise changes continuously, batch processing delays the effect of such change on master files into lengthy discrete steps. Change is recognized usually on a regular cycle or after some determined interval. The time chosen between processing transactions is important. The smaller the interval, the more costly the process of updating because of the overhead associated with a run and because few transactions will cause less efficient processing of the master file, since all records of a sequential file

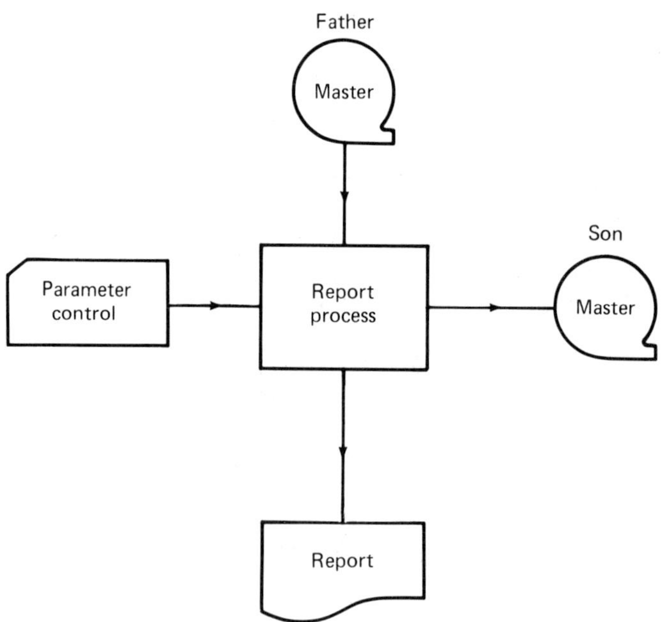

Figure 3.4 Report process.

must be examined. On the other hand, a greater time between runs decreases the value of the information obtained by the enterprise. Because the volume of transactions is increased, the run will be more complex, which could also increase the cost of the run.

3.5 UPDATING A SEQUENTIAL FILE: THE BALANCE LINE ALGORITHM

In Program 3.1 we have seen the creation of a sequential file. This program is not too useful as a production program because it assumes that the records entered are correct. The correct assumption with files is to assume that, no matter what, bad records will somehow get onto the file.

The balance line algorithm is a standardized approach to updating sequentially ordered master files by one or more transaction files in the same sequence. It should more properly be called a process as it gives rise to many specific algorithms. It is a structured generalization of the update process discussed in the previous section. Many examples are given in the work by Cooper *et al.* (1973).

The balance line algorithm requires at least three files: a transaction file, an original master, called the *father*, and a new master, called the *son.* Transaction files and fathers *must* be sorted in ascending order on the same key, and this key is unique or a primary key of the master files. Transactions to be applied consist of three types: additions of new records, orders to delete records, and changes to existing records of the master files. A transaction can affect only one record of a master file, while several transactions may be applied to one record. The key of the transaction file is called the *transaction key* and that of the master file the *master key.* A transaction record may only update a master record if the current transaction key matches the current master key. We note that the transaction record layout need not resemble the master record layout. Before proceeding to the algorithm proper it is useful to consider what can happen to both types of records.

A master record is read into the WORKING-STORAGE SECTION and it is either

(a) copied as is to the new master file or

(b) copied with changes to the new master file or

(c) not copied at all to the new master file.

Each master record is thus left alone, changed, or deleted.

A transaction record is read into the WORKING-STORAGE SECTION and it is either

(a) added as is to the new master file or
(b) used to change the contents of a master record or
(c) used to delete a master record, by *inhibiting* its copy to the new master file.

The fundamental idea of the balance line algorithm is to synchronize the interaction of master and transaction records in a standard manner so that the appropriate actions can be taken. The process is in two parts: an initialization phase and a process phase.

3.5.1 Initialization

The following steps are taken in the initialization phase:

1. Read a master file record. If end-of-file is reached, set the master key to HIGH-VALUES.
2. Read a transaction record from each transaction file and set the transaction key to HIGH-VALUES for each file that is positioned at end-of-file.
3. Extract the smallest key from among the master and transaction keys and place this value in a separate key called the *active key*.

3.5.2 Process Phase

In the process phase the following steps are repeated until the value of the active key is HIGH-VALUES.

4. If the master key matches the active key, move the master record to the output area and read another master record. Set the master key to HIGH-VALUES if end-of-file is reached.
5. For each transaction record (there may be one or more per file) whose key matches the active key, process the transaction; that is, change the master record awaiting output, or inhibit output of the master record, or, in the event a transaction record is a new master record, move it to the output area. Then read a new transaction record

for each transaction file processed. Repeat this step if transaction key equals active key. Set the new transaction key of any file that reaches end-of-file to HIGH-VALUES.

6. Write the record in the output area if the WRITE is not inhibited.
7. Redetermine a new active key setting as in step 3.

The active key acts like a policeman directing traffic at a busy intersection. Only those records whose keys equal the active key are allowed to participate in the update process. Of course, eventually all the keys on all the files will equal HIGH-VALUES and the algorithm will terminate. Rush hour through the intersection is then over.

3.6 CASE STUDY: PROFIT INC.

O.R. Capital, the president of Profit Inc., a small company, has realized that continued growth of his company will soon be limited by lack of current detailed information on its operations. Realizing that computer systems will eventually be required, he wishes to move slowly in that direction before the need becomes pressing. He has contacted an old school buddy, R. Matrix, who owns a small consulting company. Matrix also has a problem; he has specialized in scientific programming but wishes to move into the data processing area. They have met together, discussed their mutual problems, and come to the conclusion that a process of incremental design, where usable subsystems supported by manual assistance are produced, will give them both the required experience and ultimately develop the systems needed by Profit Inc. with close cost controls on development stages along with early results for immediate payback on the company's investment. As a result of these meetings, the correspondence shown in Figs. 3.5–3.7 takes place.

3.6.1 Logical Analysis: Profit Inc.

We need only understand those aspects of Profit Inc.'s accounting process that will be manipulated by the computer. While the more the analyst understands about accounting the more he can contribute to the design of an effective accounting system, it must be realized that he will often be called upon to develop systems for areas in which he is *not* an expert. Thus he must work with the user

Profit Incorporated

14 WEST OHIO STREET
NEW YORK, NY 10011

May 10, 1980

Mr. R. Matrix, President
Matrix & Associates
65001 Pennsylvania Ave.
Washington, DC 20028

Dear Mr. Matrix,

Further to our meeting on May 5 concerning computer systems for my firm, please find attached a summary of my thoughts on the matter.

My present concern is that while our revenue is currently too low to support extensive computer work, our projected revenues should be sufficient to cover this investment. In order to achieve this projected revenue, very close management control is needed to optimize our resources. I am hopeful that your work will be directed to benefiting us in this area.

In terms of project funds, I feel that 1% of revenue is the most that we can spend outside the firm. However, I can devote considerable time to this project provided that it is productive.

Sincerely yours,

O.R. Capital

O.R. Capital
President

ORC:aa
Attachment

Figure 3.5

MEMO TO: Mr. R. Matrix, President
Matrix & Associates

FROM: O.R. Capital, President, Profit Inc.

DATE: May 10, 1980

SUBJECT: Problem Area Definition for Computer Systems

Profit Incorporated is a small retail firm which is growing past the current limitations imposed by its manual bookkeeping and accounting system. I have decided that further growth cannot be maintained unless accounting, inventory, and personnel computer systems are introduced. Because our firm must currently be viewed, however, as a relatively small enterprise, the basic restriction to this advanced strategy must be considerations of capital outlay. It should be specifically understood at the outset that I am not prepared to hire additional staff with a computer science background. Any systems designed must keep this fact in mind. Profit has grown in large measure because of the dedication of a very few hardworking and loyal individuals, and I am not prepared to consider their replacement to support the introduction of computer systems. I am vitally concerned at this time with growth maximization, tight monetary control and increased profits.

The objective of the systems you are to design is to provide support for ensuring tight monetary control through the monitoring of cash flow. Information output by these systems will be used to gauge the firm's performance. At the outset I would envisage the following limited systems being converted to computer:

(a) general journal

(b) income statement

(c) balance sheet

(d) company accounts.

The idea behind putting these items on computer is to make it possible to calculate trial balances quickly. Further modifications can be considered as our relationship matures.

Figure 3.6

MATRIX & ASSOCIATES
65001 PENNSYLVANIA AVENUE
WASHINGTON, DC 20028

May 15, 1980

Mr. O.R. Capital, President
Profit Incorporated
14 W. Ohio Street
New York, NY 10011

Dear Mr. Capital,

Initially, we propose to provide as main output a trial balance from which your accountant can then determine the adjusted trial balance and income statement. Hopefully you should be able to produce these reports monthly instead of semi-annually as is the case at present. When this is working well, we will discuss further improvements.

Changes will be as per our standard rates which I have enclosed.

Because of our lack of experience in this area I will not myself directly take charge of this phase.

I would appreciate a letter of intent to proceed before I send an analyst to your firm. Delivery of Phase One will be six months from your letter.

Sincerely,

R. Matrix

R. Matrix
President

RM:lj
Enclosure

Figure 3.7

or another professional expert in the area and use his skills to determine by careful questioning what is important to the computer solution.

Any accounting system must record the flow of money in an enterprise. For example, *expenses* are those goods and services consumed by Profit Inc., *cash* are those monies paid out or a debt incurred; *sales* result in income, which is cash received or money owed Profit Inc. These events result in accounting transactions that must be recorded as they happen. Then they are classified by accountants to provide meaningful information and summarized in reports to control cash flow and determine profits. Debts are *liabilities.* The resources owned by the enterprise are *assets.* The money invested in the enterprise is its *capital.* The fundamental accounting equation relating these terms is

$$\text{Assets} = \text{Liabilities} + \text{Capital}$$

Every accounting transaction in a double entry bookkeeping transaction is expressed in terms of how it effects this accounting equation. Obviously, if we add to assets, we must have an identical increase in either liabilities or capital. Thus we talk of *balance.* Assets and liabilities are grouped into accounts of like transactions. Each account has two entries for increase and decrease. The first entry is called a *debit* and the second a *credit.* It is important to realize that debit does not necessarily decrease an account; in fact if it is an asset account, a debit increases it. Simply think of a debit as the right entry and credit as the left entry of an account.

Any accounting transaction affects two accounts, one on each side of the accounting equation in order to keep the equation balanced. Thus an accounting transaction debits an account and credits a balancing account. We need not worry how this is done; Profit Inc. will provide the proper accounting transactions. We need only concern ourselves with their *form.* For instance, if the rent is paid, the amount is debited to the account RENT and since the money came from somewhere, the account CASH is credited if the rent is paid by check. Remember, for our purpose we need not know how to create a proper accounting transaction but only how to manipulate it in a computer system.

Profit Inc. records all transactions chronologically in a General Journal as shown in Table 3.1. In order to better relate like entries, a separate ledger is kept for each account and this contains the record of entries for that account obtained from the General Journal. The transfer from journal to ledger account is called *posting.* Ac-

Table 3.1 Sample of General Journal Entries

Date	*Comments*	*Check No.*	*Debit*	*Credit*
'date'	'debit account name' 'credit account name' Comments		'amount'	 'amount'
80/01/5	RENT CASH RENT FOR JAN 1980 Note 10% increase	 2001	1000.00	 1000.00

counts are posted once a month. Each account has the form shown in Table 3.2.

The first summary of accounting transactions is the trial balance; from this the two most important summaries are made: the income statement that determines profit or loss and the balance sheet that indicates the financial health of the enterprise. The main problem that Profit Inc. has is in quickly determining the trial balance, as this is the most time-consuming part of determining the two latter summaries.

To this end a Phase One solution by Matrix & Associates is to create the General Journal as a sequential file and from this file to find the total or balance of each account and provide a trial balance. The accounts are created as a sequential file and they carry only the account total. This is not a satisfactory long-term solution (see the Problems at the end of this chapter) because account detail is not provided except as scattered in the General Journal: however, a

Table 3.2 Sample of Account Ledger Posting

	RENT Account Ledger				
Date	*Comments*	*Debit*	*Credit*	*Code*	*Balance*
80/01/5	Jan	1000		D	1000.00

trial balance is obtained in a simple manner with minimal programming and consequent cost. The system is to be expanded in Phase Two where a sequential file of accounts with transaction detail will be maintained.

The trial balance of accounts, as shown in Table 3.3, consists of a list of all accounts, ordered according to accounting principles, along with their balances and an indication of whether these balances are debit or credit entries. The sum of the debits *must* equal the sum of credits of the accounts in the trial balance. This indicates that all entries have been properly made and that totals are correct. In effect, a double entry bookkeeping system is an *error*-detecting system.

3.6.2 Profit Inc.'s Accounting System

The system for Phase One consists of four programs as illustrated in Figs. 3.8–3.11, and the accounting cycle is on a monthly basis.

Accounting transactions are assigned a transaction number as a unique identifier and are entered on the General Journal file as in Fig. 3.8 until transactions are complete for the period just ended. The General Journal file will be used to update a master

Table 3.3 Trial Balance

		Debit	*Credit*
Assets			
	Cash	10,000	
	Equipment	5,000	
	Inventory	6,000	
Liabilities			
	Loans		3,000
	Capital		20,000
Income			8,000
Expenses			
	Rent	3,000	
	Supplies	1,000	
	Wages	6,000	
		31,000	31,000

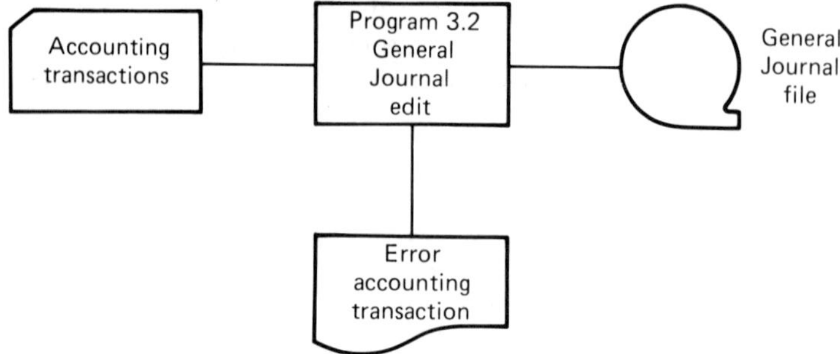

Figure 3.8 Creation of a General Journal transaction file for Profit Inc.

file of account information. This account directory file is initialized in Fig. 3.9.

When the General Journal is complete for the period just ended, the accounts are totaled and entered in the master account directory file. This is indicated in Fig. 3.10. A trial balance report can be obtained as in Fig. 3.11. This trial balance covers the period or periods represented by the totals in the master account file.

Note:

The following program examples use a simple-minded approach that works only for the very first accounting period. To run subsequent periods, Program 3.4 must make provision to carry through previous account balances. As well, new account transactions must be added onto the previous General Journal file. At this point it is convenient to generate an expense report for the expense account totals as they are found. The dashed lines indicate that this is not present in the program examples.

Program 3.2 Narrative. The purpose of Program 3.2 is to read a deck of data cards containing accounting transactions to be entered in the General Journal of Profit Inc. Debit and credit en-

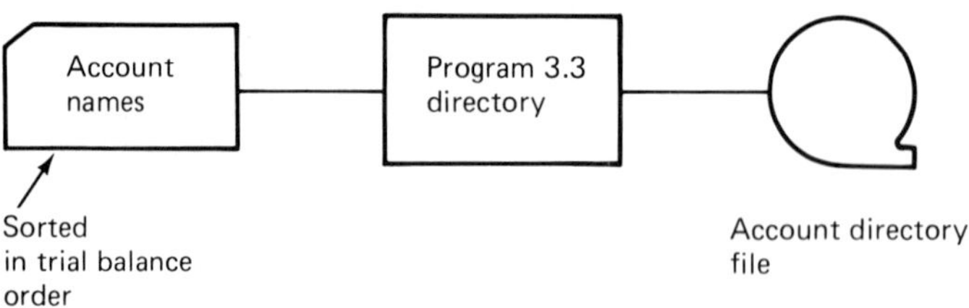

Figure 3.9 Creation of an account directory file.

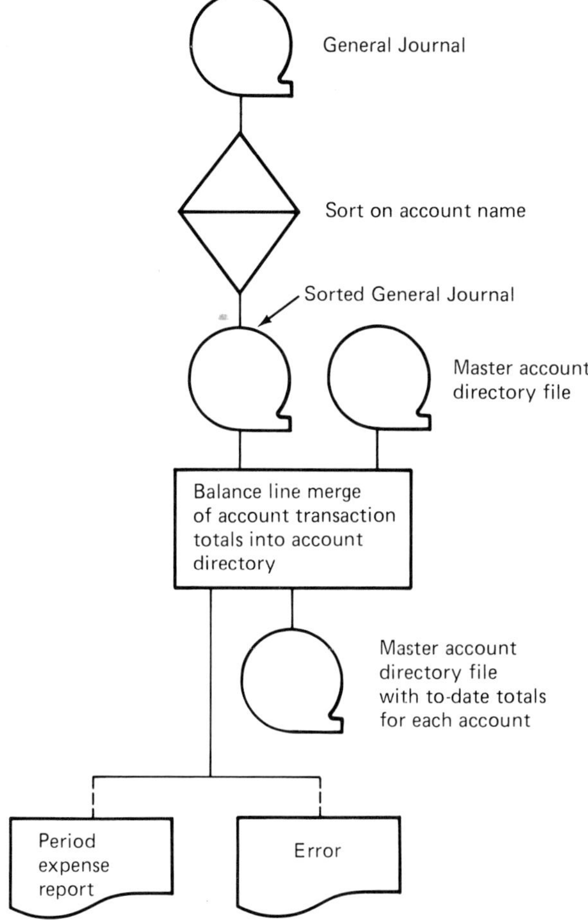

Figure 3.10 Update of account totals of master account file.

tries are punched on separate cards and each debit–credit pair is followed by any number (including zero) of comments. The general format of a debit or credit entry data card is as follows:

(a) an 8-digit transaction number
(b) a 'D' or 'C' for debit or credit, respectively
(c) the date of the entry in the form

Month	3 alphabetic characters
Day	2 digits from 01 to 31
Year	2 digits from 00 to 99

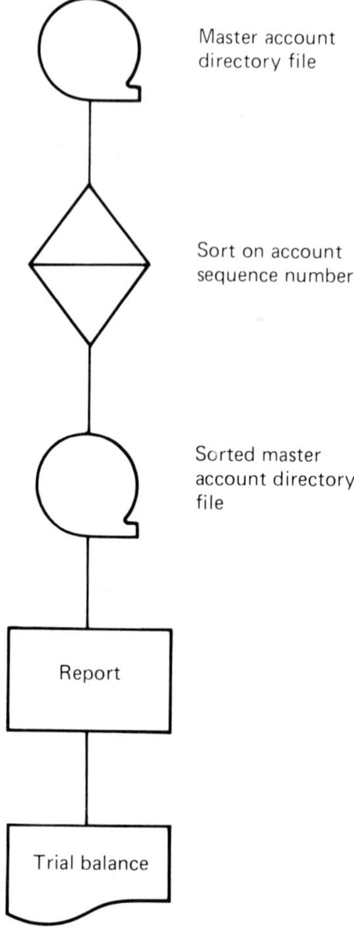

Figure 3.11 Trial balance generation.

(d) the name of the account to which the entry is posted using at most 30 characters
(e) the transaction amount
(f) a 3-digit batch number.

An input card will be posted to the General Journal provided that it is a valid member of a debit–credit pair or a valid comment. A debit–credit pair is a set of two data cards, the first of which is a debit entry and the second the corresponding credit entry. A credit

Program 3.2

```
IDENTIFICATION DIVISION.
PROGRAM-ID. PROG3PT2.
ENVIRONMENT DIVISION.
CONFIGURATION SECTION.
SOURCE-COMPUTER.  IBM-370.
OBJECT-COMPUTER.  IBM-370.
INPUT-OUTPUT SECTION.
FILE-CONTROL.
    SELECT CARD-READER
      ASSIGN TO CARD-S-SYSIN
      ORGANIZATION IS SEQUENTIAL
      ACCESS MODE IS SEQUENTIAL.
    SELECT GENERAL-JOURNAL-FILE
      ASSIGN TO DISK-S-DD1
      ORGANIZATION IS SEQUENTIAL
      ACCESS MODE IS SEQUENTIAL.
DATA DIVISION.
FILE SECTION.
FD  CARD-READER
      BLOCK CONTAINS 1 RECORDS
      LABEL RECORDS ARE OMITTED
      RECORD CONTAINS 80 CHARACTERS
      DATA RECORDS IS CARD-READER-RECORD.
01  CARD-READER-RECORD.
    02 FILLER                         PIC X(80).
FD  GENERAL-JOURNAL-FILE
      BLOCK CONTAINS 1 RECORDS
      LABEL RECORDS ARE STANDARD
      RECORD CONTAINS 80 CHARACTERS
      DATA RECORD IS GENERAL-JOURNAL-FILE-RECORD.
01  GENERAL-JOURNAL-FILE-RECORD.
    02 FILLER                         PIC X(80).
WORKING-STORAGE SECTION.
77  ERROR-IN-INPUT-FLAG               PIC X(3).
    88 ERROR-IN-INPUT VALUE IS 'ON'.
77  NO-MORE-COMMENTS-FLAG             PIC X(3).
    88 NO-MORE-COMMENTS          VALUE IS 'ON'.
77  NO-MORE-ENTRIES-FLAG              PIC X(3).
    88  NO-MORE-ENTRIES          VALUE IS 'ON'.
    88  MORE-ENTRIES             VALUE IS 'OFF'.
77  NUMBER-OF-ERROR-RECORDS           PIC 9(5)
                 USAGE IS             COMP SYNC.
77  NUMBER-OF-RECORDS-TO-WRITE        PIC 9(5)
                 USAGE IS             COMP SYNC.
77  PROCEED-FLAG                      PIC X(3).
77  VALID-DEBIT-ENTRY-FLAG            PIC X(3).
    88  VALID-DEBIT-ENTRY        VALUE IS 'ON'.
    88  INVALID-DEBIT-ENTRY      VALUE IS 'OFF'.
77  READ-BUFFER-EMPTY-FLAG            PIC X(3).
    88  READ-BUFFER-EMPTY        VALUE IS 'OFF'.
77  VALID-CREDIT-ENTRY-FLAG           PIC X(3).
    88  VALID-CREDIT-ENTRY       VALUE IS 'ON'.
```

Program 3.2 (cont.)

```
          88  INVALID-CREDIT-ENTRY    VALUE IS 'OFF'.

      01  WS-COMMENT-RECORD.
          02 TRANSACTION-NUMBER              PIC X(8).
          02 COMMENT-ASTERISK                PIC X.
             88 COMMENT                VALUE IS '*'.
          02 COMMENT-ENTRY                   PIC X(71).


      01  WS-CREDIT-ENTRY.
          02 TRANSACTION-NUMBER              PIC X(8).
          02 DEBIT-OR-CREDIT                 PIC X.
             88 CREDIT-RECORD          VALUE IS 'C'.
          02 ENTRY-DATE.
             03 MONTH                        PIC X(3).
             03 ENTRY-DAY                    PIC 9(2).
             03 YEAR                         PIC 9(2).
          02 NAME-OF-ACCOUNT                 PIC X(30).
          02 CREDIT-AMOUNT                   PIC 9(5)V9(2).
          02 FILLER                          PIC X(24).
          02 BATCH-NO                        PIC 9(3).

    . 01  WS-DEBIT-ENTRY.
          02 TRANSACTION-NUMBER              PIC X(8).
          02 DEBIT-OR-CREDIT                 PIC X.
             88 DEBIT-RECORD           VALUE IS 'D'.
          02 ENTRY-DATE.
             03 MONTH                        PIC X(3).
             03 ENTRY-DAY                    PIC 9(2).
             03 YEAR                         PIC 9(2).
          02 NAME-OF-ACCOUNT                 PIC X(30).
          02 DEBIT-AMOUNT                    PIC 9(5)V9(2).
          02 FILLER                          PIC X(24).
          02 BATCH-NO                        PIC 9(3).


      PROCEDURE DIVISION.
          PERFORM INITIALIZATION.
          PERFORM ADD-ENTRIES-TO-GENERAL-JOURNAL
                  UNTIL NO-MORE-ENTRIES.
          PERFORM TERMINATION.
          STOP RUN.


      INITIALIZATION.
          OPEN INPUT  CARD-READER
               OUTPUT GENERAL-JOURNAL-FILE.
          MOVE SPACES TO WS-DEBIT-ENTRY.
          MOVE SPACES TO WS-CREDIT-ENTRY.
          MOVE SPACES TO WS-COMMENT-RECORD.
          PERFORM ZERO-COUNTERS-SET-FLAGS.
          MOVE 'OFF' TO READ-BUFFER-EMPTY-FLAG.
          PERFORM OBTAIN-JOURNAL-ENTRIES.


      ADD-ENTRIES-TO-GENERAL-JOURNAL.
          PERFORM ERROR-PRESENT-ROUTINE.
          IF NOT ERROR-IN-INPUT
             THEN PERFORM WRITE-GENERAL-JOURNAL-RECORD
             ELSE PERFORM ERROR-RTN.
```

Program 3.2 (cont.)

```
            IF MORE-ENTRIES
               PERFORM ZERO-COUNTERS-SET-FLAGS
               PERFORM OBTAIN-JOURNAL-ENTRIES.


        TERMINATION.
            IF NUMBER-OF-RECORDS-TO-WRITE
                IS GREATER THAN ZERO THEN
                PERFORM WRITE-GENERAL-JOURNAL-RECORD.
            IF NUMBER-OF-ERROR-RECORDS
                IS GREATER THAN ZERO THEN
                PERFORM ERROR-RTN.
            CLOSE CARD-READER
                  GENERAL-JOURNAL-FILE.


        ERROR-PRESENT-ROUTINE.
            IF INVALID-DEBIT-ENTRY
               OR INVALID-CREDIT-ENTRY
               THEN
                    MOVE 'ON' TO ERROR-IN-INPUT-FLAG
               ELSE
                    MOVE 'OFF' TO ERROR-IN-INPUT-FLAG.


        WRITE-GENERAL-JOURNAL-RECORD.
            PERFORM WRITE-DEBIT-ENTRY.
            PERFORM WRITE-CREDIT-ENTRY.
            PERFORM WRITE-COMMENT-RTN
                    UNTIL NO-MORE-COMMENTS OR NO-MORE-ENTRIES.
            MOVE SPACES TO WS-CREDIT-ENTRY.


        ERROR-RTN.
            EXIT.
        ZERO-COUNTERS-SET-FLAGS.
            MOVE ZERO TO NUMBER-OF-RECORDS-TO-WRITE.
            MOVE ZERO TO NUMBER-OF-ERROR-RECORDS.
            MOVE 'OFF' TO ERROR-IN-INPUT-FLAG.
            MOVE 'ON' TO PROCEED-FLAG.
            MOVE 'OFF' TO VALID-DEBIT-ENTRY-FLAG.
            MOVE 'OFF' TO VALID-CREDIT-ENTRY-FLAG.
            MOVE 'OFF' TO NO-MORE-ENTRIES-FLAG.
            MOVE 'OFF' TO NO-MORE-COMMENTS-FLAG.


        OBTAIN-JOURNAL-ENTRIES.
            PERFORM GET-DEBIT-ENTRY.
            PERFORM VERIFICATION-OF-DEBIT-ENTRY.
            IF VALID-DEBIT-ENTRY
               PERFORM PREPARE-DEBIT-RECORD
               ELSE
                    PERFORM INVALID-DEBIT-ENTRY-ROUTINE.
            IF PROCEED-FLAG EQUAL 'ON'
               THEN
                    PERFORM GET-CREDIT-ENTRY
                    IF MORE-ENTRIES THEN
                    PERFORM VERIFICATION-OF-CREDIT-ENTRY
                    IF VALID-CREDIT-ENTRY
                       PERFORM PREPARE-CREDIT-RECORD.
```

Program 3.2 (cont.)

```
       GET-DEBIT-ENTRY.
           IF READ-BUFFER-EMPTY
              THEN
                   PERFORM READ-DEBIT-ROUTINE
              ELSE
                   PERFORM COPY-DEBIT-ROUTINE.


       VERIFICATION-OF-DEBIT-ENTRY.
           IF DEBIT-RECORD
              MOVE 'ON' TO VALID-DEBIT-ENTRY-FLAG.


       PREPARE-DEBIT-RECORD.
           ADD 1 TO NUMBER-OF-RECORDS-TO-WRITE.
           MOVE 'OFF' TO READ-BUFFER-EMPTY-FLAG.


       INVALID-DEBIT-ENTRY-ROUTINE.
           MOVE 'OFF' TO READ-BUFFER-EMPTY-FLAG.
           MOVE 'OFF' TO PROCEED-FLAG.


       GET-CREDIT-ENTRY.
           IF READ-BUFFER-EMPTY
              THEN
                   PERFORM READ-CREDIT-ROUTINE
              ELSE
                   PERFORM ERROR-RTN.


       VERIFICATION-OF-CREDIT-ENTRY.
           IF CREDIT-RECORD AND CREDIT-AMOUNT
              IS EQUAL TO DEBIT-AMOUNT
              AND TRANSACTION-NUMBER OF WS-DEBIT-ENTRY
              IS EQUAL TO TRANSACTION-NUMBER
              OF WS-CREDIT-ENTRY
              THEN
                   MOVE 'ON' TO VALID-CREDIT-ENTRY-FLAG.


       PREPARE-CREDIT-RECORD.
           ADD 1 TO NUMBER-OF-RECORDS-TO-WRITE.
           MOVE 'OFF' TO READ-BUFFER-EMPTY-FLAG.


       READ-DEBIT-ROUTINE.
           READ CARD-READER
                AT END MOVE 'ON' TO NO-MORE-ENTRIES-FLAG.
           MOVE 'ON' TO READ-BUFFER-EMPTY-FLAG.
           IF MORE-ENTRIES
              MOVE CARD-READER-RECORD
                   TO WS-DEBIT-ENTRY.


       COPY-DEBIT-ROUTINE.
```

Program 3.2 (cont.)

```
                MOVE CARD-READER-RECORD
                      TO WS-DEBIT-ENTRY.


            READ-CREDIT-ROUTINE.
                READ CARD-READER
                     AT END MOVE 'ON' TO NO-MORE-ENTRIES-FLAG.
                MOVE 'ON' TO READ-BUFFER-EMPTY-FLAG.
                IF MORE-ENTRIES
                   MOVE CARD-READER-RECORD
                        TO WS-CREDIT-ENTRY
                ELSE
                   SUBTRACT 1 FROM NUMBER-OF-RECORDS-TO-WRITE
                   MOVE 'OFF' TO VALID-DEBIT-ENTRY-FLAG.




            WRITE-DEBIT-ENTRY.
                MOVE WS-DEBIT-ENTRY
                     TO GENERAL-JOURNAL-FILE-RECORD.
                WRITE GENERAL-JOURNAL-FILE-RECORD.
                MOVE SPACES TO WS-DEBIT-ENTRY.
                MOVE SPACES TO WS-COMMENT-RECORD.




            WRITE-CREDIT-ENTRY.
                MOVE WS-CREDIT-ENTRY
                     TO GENERAL-JOURNAL-FILE-RECORD.
                WRITE GENERAL-JOURNAL-FILE-RECORD.


            WRITE-COMMENT-RTN.
                READ CARD-READER INTO WS-COMMENT-RECORD
                    AT END MOVE 'ON' TO NO-MORE-ENTRIES-FLAG.
                IF COMMENT AND TRANSACTION-NUMBER
                   OF WS-COMMENT-RECORD
                   EQUAL TRANSACTION-NUMBER OF WS-CREDIT-ENTRY
                   THEN
                        WRITE GENERAL-JOURNAL-FILE-RECORD
                              FROM WS-COMMENT-RECORD
                        MOVE SPACES TO WS-COMMENT-RECORD
                   ELSE
                        MOVE 'ON' TO NO-MORE-COMMENTS-FLAG
                        MOVE 'ON' TO READ-BUFFER-EMPTY-FLAG.
```

entry corresponds to a debit entry if it has the same transaction number and the same amount field as the debit. No posting of a debit entry is made unless a corresponding credit directly follows it in the data deck. A debit entry is saved in WS-DEBIT-ENTRY before the corresponding credit is processed. In the event that a corresponding credit entry cannot be found, an error condition is raised and an error handling routine (not actually coded) is entered. This error routine should void all cards with the current transaction number. Processing will resume on the first new transaction number that is found on a debit entry. Following the posting of a debit-credit pair, any number of comments are posted to the journal provided they are valid. A comment is valid if it directly follows a debit-credit pair and has the same transaction number as the pair or if it directly follows a valid comment with the same transaction number. Processing is continued until the data deck is exhausted.

Since a debit-credit pair can be followed by any number of comments, the number of logical records used to record a single business transaction can vary. There is thus a variable amount of space used on the storage device to store the results of a single business transaction. The actual size of the logical records, however, remains fixed at 80 characters. Later we shall study a method whereby even the logical records of the file themselves may vary in length.

Note, also, that there are three types of logical records that have different record formats; namely, the debit record, the credit record, and the comment record. These records are blocked as well, which means that they are grouped together to form physical records before being written to the storage device. Accordingly, this is a very interesting file. The business transaction contains any number of logical records made up of one debit logical record, one credit logical record, and any number of comment logical records. The logical records, though of the same length, have different fields. The physical records, while they have the same length and contain the same number of logical records, do not necessarily contain the same mix of logical records.

Before entering a transaction, it must be tested for correctness; if an error is found, the transaction is rejected. An error report will list such transactions, and they must be found and corrected and reentered. The most obvious test is that the debit amount equal the credit amount. Data verification is treated in Chapter 12.

Program 3.3 Narrative. The purpose of Program 3.3 is to create the account directory file, a listing of all the accounts named in the General Journal with added fields for debit and credit totals for the

Program 3.3

```
       IDENTIFICATION DIVISION.
       PROGRAM-ID. PROG3PT3.
       ENVIRONMENT DIVISION.
       CONFIGURATION SECTION.
       SOURCE-COMPUTER. IBM-370.
       OBJECT-COMPUTER. IBM-370.
       INPUT-OUTPUT SECTION.
       FILE-CONTROL.
           SELECT ACCOUNT-DIRECTORY
                  ASSIGN TO DISK-S-DD1
                  ORGANIZATION IS SEQUENTIAL
                  ACCESS MODE IS SEQUENTIAL.
          SELECT ACCOUNT-DIRECTORY-SORT-FILE
                  ASSIGN TO DISK-S-SORTWK01
                  ORGANIZATION IS SEQUENTIAL
                  ACCESS MODE IS SEQUENTIAL.
           SELECT CARD-READER
                  ASSIGN TO CARD-S-SYSIN
                  ORGANIZATION IS SEQUENTIAL
                  ACCESS MODE IS SEQUENTIAL.


       DATA DIVISION.
       FILE SECTION.

       FD  ACCOUNT-DIRECTORY
           LABEL RECORDS ARE STANDARD
           RECORD CONTAINS 63 CHARACTERS
           DATA RECORD IS ACCOUNT-DIRECTORY-RECORD.
       01  ACCOUNT-DIRECTORY-RECORD.
           02  FILLER                      PIC X(63).

      SD  ACCOUNT-DIRECTORY-SORT-FILE
          RECORD CONTAINS 63 CHARACTERS
          DATA RECORD IS ACCOUNT-DIRECTORY-SORT-RECORD.
      01  ACCOUNT-DIRECTORY-SORT-RECORD.

          02 SEQUENCE-NUMBER               PIC X(3).
          02 NAME-OF-ACCOUNT               PIC X(30).
          02 FILLER                        PIC X(30).

       FD  CARD-READER
           LABEL RECORDS ARE OMITTED
           RECORD CONTAINS 80 CHARACTERS
           DATA RECORD IS CARD-IMAGE.
       01  CARD-IMAGE.
           02 NAME-OF-ACCOUNT              PIC X(30).
           02 TYPE-OF-ACCOUNT              PIC X.
           02 EXPENSE-ACCOUNT-FIELD        PIC X.
           02 FILLER                       PIC X(48).
       WORKING-STORAGE SECTION.
       77 COUNTER                          PIC S9(8)
                                               COMPUTATIONAL
                                               SYNCHRONIZED.
       77  EOF-CARD-FLAG                   PIC X(3).
           88  EOF-CARD VALUE IS 'ON'.

       01  WS-ACCOUNT-DIRECTORY.

           02 SEQUENCE-NUMBER              PIC S9(3).
```

Program 3.3 (cont.)

```
            02 NAME-OF-ACCOUNT              PIC X(30).
            02 TYPE-OF-ACCOUNT              PIC X.
            02 EXPENSE-ACCOUNT-FIELD        PIC X.
            02 TRIAL-DEBIT-TOTAL            PIC 9(5)V9(2).
            02 TRIAL-CREDIT-TOTAL           PIC 9(5)V9(2).
            02 ADJUSTED-DEBIT-TOTAL         PIC 9(5)V9(2).
            02 ADJUSTED-CREDIT-TOTAL        PIC 9(5)V9(2).
        PROCEDURE DIVISION.
            PERFORM INITIALIZATION.
            PERFORM BUILD-DIRECTORY UNTIL EOF-CARD.
            CLOSE CARD-READER
                  ACCOUNT-DIRECTORY.
            PERFORM SORT-DIRECTORY.
            STOP RUN.


        INITIALIZATION.
            OPEN INPUT CARD-READER
                 OUTPUT ACCOUNT-DIRECTORY.
            MOVE 'OFF' TO EOF-CARD-FLAG.
            MOVE 0 TO COUNTER.
            READ CARD-READER
                 AT END MOVE 'ON' TO EOF-CARD-FLAG.


        BUILD-DIRECTORY.
            ADD 1 TO COUNTER.
            MOVE CORRESPONDING CARD-IMAGE
                 TO WS-ACCOUNT-DIRECTORY.
            MOVE ZERO TO TRIAL-DEBIT-TOTAL.
            MOVE ZERO TO TRIAL-CREDIT-TOTAL.
            MOVE ZERO TO ADJUSTED-DEBIT-TOTAL.
            MOVE ZERO TO ADJUSTED-CREDIT-TOTAL.
            MOVE COUNTER TO SEQUENCE-NUMBER
                 OF WS-ACCOUNT-DIRECTORY.
            WRITE ACCOUNT-DIRECTORY-RECORD
                FROM WS-ACCOUNT-DIRECTORY.
            READ CARD-READER
                 AT END MOVE 'ON' TO EOF-CARD-FLAG.



        SORT-DIRECTORY.
            SORT ACCOUNT-DIRECTORY-SORT-FILE
                 ASCENDING KEY
                    NAME-OF-ACCOUNT
                    OF ACCOUNT-DIRECTORY-SORT-FILE
                 USING ACCOUNT-DIRECTORY
                 GIVING ACCOUNT-DIRECTORY.
```

trial balance and the adjusted trial balance. A sequence number is carried with each account to specify the order of printing of accounts in the Trial Balance Report (to be written later). The sequence number is taken to be the order in which the account names are read from a data deck supplied as data to the program. This deck must be in the order accounts appear in the trial balance.

Program 3.3 has three phases: initialization, building the directory, and sorting it.

During initialization the ACCOUNT-DIRECTORY and CARD-READER files are opened for OUTPUT and INPUT, respectively.

The BUILD-DIRECTORY paragraph initializes totals to zero, assigns the sequence number to each card read, writes the ACCOUNT-DIRECTORY-RECORD, and reads another card. Processing of this paragraph halts when end-of-file is encountered on the CARD-READER.

The SORT-DIRECTORY paragraph sorts the records of ACCOUNT-DIRECTORY in NAME-OF-ACCOUNT order. Note that the input and output files to the sort routine are identical.

Program 3.4 Narrative. The first step in Program 3.4 is to sort the GENERAL-JOURNAL file on NAME-OF-ACCOUNT. Recall that the ACCOUNT-DIRECTORY is already sorted in this order by Program 3.3.

Next the SORTED-GENERAL-JOURNAL and ACCOUNT-DIRECTORY files are opened for INPUT and the TRIAL-BALANCE file is opened as an output file. An initial record is read from each of the input files and the lowest key of these records determined and placed in ACTIVE-KEY.

The balance line routine is now entered. Records on the ACCOUNT-DIRECTORY are treated as master records. They are copied into WS-TRIAL-BALANCE-RECORD. Records from the GENERAL-JOURNAL are treated as transaction records. When a transaction record is read, a debit entry is added to the TRIAL-DEBIT-TOTAL of WS-TRIAL-BALANCE-RECORD; a credit entry is added to the TRIAL-CREDIT-TOTAL of WS-TRIAL-BALANCE-RECORD. Comment records on the GENERAL-JOURNAL file are ignored. When all transaction records whose NAME-OF-ACCOUNT match the ACTIVE-KEY are processed, the WS-TRIAL-BALANCE-RECORD, which now contains the debit and credit totals for that account, is written to the TRIAL-BALANCE file. Processing is continued until the records of both files are exhausted. The ACTIVE-KEY will be set to HIGH-VALUES at this time. Files are then closed and the program terminates.

Program 3.4

```
IDENTIFICATION DIVISION.
PROGRAM-ID.  PROG3PT4.
ENVIRONMENT DIVISION.
CONFIGURATION SECTION.
  SOURCE-COMPUTER.  IBM-370.
  OBJECT-COMPUTER.  IBM-370.
INPUT-OUTPUT SECTION.
FILE-CONTROL.
    SELECT ACCOUNT-DIRECTORY
      ASSIGN TO DISK-S-DD1
      ORGANIZATION IS SEQUENTIAL
      ACCESS MODE IS SEQUENTIAL.
    SELECT ACCOUNT-DIRECTORY-SORT-FILE
      ASSIGN TO DISK-S-SORTWK01
      ORGANIZATION IS SEQUENTIAL
      ACCESS MODE IS SEQUENTIAL.
    SELECT GENERAL-JOURNAL
      ASSIGN TO DISK-S-DD2
      ORGANIZATION IS SEQUENTIAL
      ACCESS MODE IS SEQUENTIAL.
    SELECT GENERAL-JOURNAL-SORT-FILE
      ASSIGN TO DISK-S-SORTWK01
      ORGANIZATION IS SEQUENTIAL
      ACCESS MODE IS SEQUENTIAL.
    SELECT PRINTER
      ASSIGN TO DISK-S-DD3
      ORGANIZATION IS SEQUENTIAL
      ACCESS MODE IS SEQUENTIAL.
    SELECT SORTED-GENERAL-JOURNAL-FILE
      ASSIGN TO DISK-S-DD4
      ORGANIZATION IS SEQUENTIAL
      ACCESS MODE IS SEQUENTIAL.
    SELECT TRIAL-BALANCE
      ASSIGN TO DISK-S-DD5
      ORGANIZATION IS SEQUENTIAL
      ACCESS MODE IS SEQUENTIAL.
DATA DIVISION.
FILE SECTION.
FD  ACCOUNT-DIRECTORY
      BLOCK CONTAINS 1 RECORDS
      LABEL RECORDS ARE STANDARD
      RECORD CONTAINS 63 CHARACTERS
      DATA RECORD IS ACCOUNT-DIRECTORY-RECORD.
01  ACCOUNT-DIRECTORY-RECORD.
    02 SEQUENCE-NUMBER            PIC X(3).
    02 NAME-OF-ACCOUNT            PIC X(30).
    02 TYPE-OF-ACCOUNT            PIC X.
    02 EXPENSE-FIELD              PIC X.
    02 TRIAL-DEBIT-TOTAL          PIC 9(5)V9(2).
    02 TRIAL-CREDIT-TOTAL         PIC 9(5)V9(2).
    02 ADJUSTED-DEBIT-TOTAL       PIC 9(5)V9(2).
    02 ADJUSTED-CREDIT-TOTAL      PIC 9(5)V9(2).
FD  GENERAL-JOURNAL
      LABEL RECORDS ARE STANDARD
```

Program 3.4 (cont.)

```
                BLOCK CONTAINS 1 RECORDS
                RECORD CONTAINS 80 CHARACTERS
                DATA RECORD IS GENERAL-JOURNAL-RECORD.
       01   GENERAL-JOURNAL-RECORD.
            02 TRANSACTION-NUMBER          PIC X(8).
            02 DEBIT-OR-CREDIT-FLAG        PIC X.
            02 ENTRY-DATE.
               03 MONTH                    PIC X(3).
               03 ENTRY-DAY                PIC 9(2).
               03 YEAR                     PIC 9(2).
            02 NAME-OF-ACCOUNT             PIC X(30).
            02 AMOUNT                      PIC 9(5)V9(2).
            02 CARD-NO                     PIC 9(3).
            02 FILLER                      PIC X(24).

       SD   GENERAL-JOURNAL-SORT-FILE
                RECORD CONTAINS 80 CHARACTERS
                DATA RECORD IS GENERAL-JOURNAL-SORT-RECORD.
       01   GENERAL-JOURNAL-SORT-RECORD.
            02 FILLER                      PIC X(16).
            02 NAME-OF-ACCOUNT             PIC X(30).
            02 FILLER                      PIC X(34).

       SD   ACCOUNT-DIRECTORY-SORT-FILE
                RECORD CONTAINS 63 CHARACTERS
                DATA RECORD IS ACCOUNT-DIRECTORY-SORT-RECORD.
       01   ACCOUNT-DIRECTORY-SORT-RECORD.
            02 SEQUENCE-NUMBER             PIC X(3).
            02 FILLER                      PIC X(60).

       FD   PRINTER
                BLOCK CONTAINS 1 RECORDS
                LABEL RECORDS ARE OMITTED
                RECORD CONTAINS 133 CHARACTERS
                DATA RECORD IS PRINTER-RECORD.
       01   PRINTER-RECORD.
            02 FILLER                      PIC X.
            02 DATA-AREA                   PIC X(132).

       FD   SORTED-GENERAL-JOURNAL-FILE
                BLOCK CONTAINS 1 RECORDS
                LABEL RECORDS ARE STANDARD
                RECORD CONTAINS 80 CHARACTERS
                DATA RECORD IS SORTED-GENERAL-JOURNAL-RECORD.
       01   SORTED-GENERAL-JOURNAL-RECORD.
            02 TRANSACTION-NUMBER          PIC X(8).
            02 DEBIT-OR-CREDIT             PIC X.
            02 ENTRY-DATE.
               03 MONTH                    PIC X(3).
               03 ENTRY-DAY                PIC 9(2).
               03 YEAR                     PIC 9(2).
            02 NAME-OF-ACCOUNT             PIC X(30).
            02 AMOUNT                      PIC 9(5)V9(2).
            02 CARD-NO                     PIC 9(3).
            02 FILLER                      PIC X(23).
            02 COMMENT-ENTRY               PIC X.
               88 COMMENT            VALUE IS '*'.

       FD   TRIAL-BALANCE
                BLOCK CONTAINS 1 RECORDS
```

Program 3.4 (cont.)

```
               LABEL RECORDS ARE STANDARD
               RECORD CONTAINS 63 CHARACTERS
               DATA RECORD IS TRIAL-BALANCE-RECORD.
       01  TRIAL-BALANCE-RECORD.
           02 SEQUENCE-NUMBER              PIC X(3).
           02 NAME-OF-ACCOUNT              PIC X(30).
           02 TYPE-OF-ACCOUNT              PIC X.
           02 EXPENSE-ACCOUNT-FIELD        PIC X.
           02 TRIAL-DEBIT-TOTAL            PIC 9(5)V9(2).
           02 TRIAL-CREDIT-TOTAL           PIC 9(5)V9(2).
           02 ADJUSTED-DEBIT-TOTAL         PIC 9(5)V9(2).
           02 ADJUSTED-CREDIT-TOTAL        PIC 9(5)V9(2).


       WORKING-STORAGE SECTION.
       77  ACCOUNT-DIRECTORY-EOF-FLAG  PIC X(3).
           88 END-OF-FILE-AD       VALUE IS 'ON'.
       77  ACTIVE-KEY                      PIC X(30).
           88 FINISHED             VALUE IS HIGH-VALUES.
       77  SORTED-JOURNAL-EOF-FLAG         PIC X(3).
           88 END-OF-FILE-SGJ      VALUE IS 'ON'.
       77  WRITE-SWITCH                    PIC X(3).

       01  WS-TRIAL-BALANCE-RECORD.
           02 SEQUENCE-NUMBER              PIC X(3).
           02 NAME-OF-ACCOUNT              PIC X(30).
           02 TYPE-OF-ACCOUNT              PIC X.
           02 EXPENSE-ACCOUNT-FIELD        PIC X.
           02 TRIAL-DEBIT-TOTAL            PIC 9(5)V9(2).
           02 TRIAL-CREDIT-TOTAL           PIC 9(5)V9(2).
           02 ADJUSTED-DEBIT-TOTAL         PIC 9(5)V9(2).
           02 ADJUSTED-CREDIT-TOTAL        PIC 9(5)V9(2).


       PROCEDURE DIVISION.
           PERFORM SORT-JOURNAL-ACCOUNT-NAME.
           PERFORM INITIALIZE-BALANCE-LINE.
           PERFORM BALANCE-LINE UNTIL FINISHED.
           PERFORM TERMINATION.
           STOP RUN.

       SORT-JOURNAL-ACCOUNT-NAME.
           SORT GENERAL-JOURNAL-SORT-FILE
                ASCENDING KEY
                   NAME-OF-ACCOUNT OF GENERAL-JOURNAL-SORT-FILE
                USING GENERAL-JOURNAL
                GIVING SORTED-GENERAL-JOURNAL-FILE.

       INITIALIZE-BALANCE-LINE.
           OPEN INPUT SORTED-GENERAL-JOURNAL-FILE
                      ACCOUNT-DIRECTORY
                OUTPUT TRIAL-BALANCE.
           MOVE 'OFF' TO SORTED-JOURNAL-EOF-FLAG
                         ACCOUNT-DIRECTORY-EOF-FLAG.
           MOVE 'OFF' TO WRITE-SWITCH.
           PERFORM READ-SORTED-JOURNAL-RECORD.
           PERFORM READ-ACCOUNT-DIRECTORY-RECORD.
           PERFORM DETERMINE-ACTIVE-KEY.

       BALANCE-LINE.
```

Program 3.4 (cont.)

```
        IF NAME-OF-ACCOUNT OF ACCOUNT-DIRECTORY-RECORD
           EQUAL ACTIVE-KEY
          THEN
           PERFORM PROCESS-MASTER-RECORD.
        PERFORM PROCESS-TRANSACTION-RECORD
            UNTIL NAME-OF-ACCOUNT
                  OF SORTED-GENERAL-JOURNAL-RECORD
                  NOT EQUAL ACTIVE-KEY.
        PERFORM WRITE-TRIAL-BALANCE-RECORD.
        PERFORM DETERMINE-ACTIVE-KEY.

    TERMINATION.
        CLOSE ACCOUNT-DIRECTORY
              SORTED-GENERAL-JOURNAL-FILE
              TRIAL-BALANCE.

    READ-SORTED-JOURNAL-RECORD.
        READ SORTED-GENERAL-JOURNAL-FILE
             AT END MOVE 'ON' TO
                SORTED-JOURNAL-EOF-FLAG.
        IF END-OF-FILE-SGJ
           MOVE HIGH-VALUES TO NAME-OF-ACCOUNT OF
                SORTED-GENERAL-JOURNAL-RECORD.

    READ-ACCOUNT-DIRECTORY-RECORD.
        READ ACCOUNT-DIRECTORY
             AT END MOVE 'ON' TO
                        ACCOUNT-DIRECTORY-EOF-FLAG.
        IF END-OF-FILE-AD
           MOVE HIGH-VALUES TO NAME-OF-ACCOUNT OF
                ACCOUNT-DIRECTORY-RECORD.

    DETERMINE-ACTIVE-KEY.
        IF NAME-OF-ACCOUNT OF
           SORTED-GENERAL-JOURNAL-RECORD
           IS LESS THAN
           NAME-OF-ACCOUNT OF ACCOUNT-DIRECTORY
          THEN
           MOVE NAME-OF-ACCOUNT OF
                SORTED-GENERAL-JOURNAL-RECORD
                TO ACTIVE-KEY
          ELSE
           MOVE NAME-OF-ACCOUNT OF ACCOUNT-DIRECTORY
                TO ACTIVE-KEY.
    PROCESS-MASTER-RECORD.
        MOVE CORRESPONDING ACCOUNT-DIRECTORY-RECORD
             TO WS-TRIAL-BALANCE-RECORD.
        MOVE 'ON' TO WRITE-SWITCH.
        PERFORM READ-ACCOUNT-DIRECTORY-RECORD.

    PROCESS-TRANSACTION-RECORD.
        IF DEBIT-OR-CREDIT OF
            SORTED-GENERAL-JOURNAL-RECORD
          EQUAL 'D' AND NOT COMMENT
          THEN
           ADD AMOUNT OF SORTED-GENERAL-JOURNAL-RECORD
           TO TRIAL-DEBIT-TOTAL OF
           WS-TRIAL-BALANCE-RECORD
          ELSE
           IF DEBIT-OR-CREDIT OF
```

Program 3.4 (cont.)

```
                SORTED-GENERAL-JOURNAL-FILE
             EQUAL 'C' AND NOT COMMENT THEN
             ADD AMOUNT OF SORTED-GENERAL-JOURNAL-RECORD
             TO TRIAL-CREDIT-TOTAL OF
             WS-TRIAL-BALANCE-RECORD.
          PERFORM READ-SORTED-JOURNAL-RECORD.
          PERFORM READ-SORTED-JOURNAL-RECORD
              UNTIL NOT COMMENT OR END-OF-FILE-SGJ.

      WRITE-TRIAL-BALANCE-RECORD.
          IF WRITE-SWITCH EQUAL 'ON' THEN
                  WRITE TRIAL-BALANCE-RECORD
                      FROM WS-TRIAL-BALANCE-RECORD
                  MOVE 'OFF' TO WRITE-SWITCH.
```

3.7 CASE STUDY: MISSILE TARGET SYSTEM

A Titan missile can be armed with a MIRV (a multiple independently targeted reentry vehicle) for a retaliatory nuclear strike against a possible enemy. Basically this means that the rocket contains a package of several atomic weapons, each of which has a different selected target and all of which are released when the Titan reaches a certain distance from the target area. A computer program is to be written to keep track of the targets assigned to each missile at a missile launch center.

3.7.1 Logical Analysis: Missile Target System

The number of warheads assigned to each individual Titan is a variable and depends on the general area targeted by it. For example, a missile launched against a hydroelectric plant in the Ukraine may have no other targets in the general area whereas another launched against an industrial complex near Moscow may have several nearby vital targets. If each Titan Complex is capable of launching 25 such missiles and each missile carries a maximum of 5 warheads, there exists a potential of 25 to 125 possible first targets.

In view of the fact that the nature of the defense against an incoming missile strike is not entirely known beforehand, tactical counterdefense planning allows for each Titan to have a series of one or more secondary strike centers. This requires each of the individual MIRV warheads to carry various secondary targets.

The logical record in this case is the record associated with each individual missile at the launch site. The launch complex at Norman Falls, South Dakota which we shall use for this study, has 25 missiles, each in its own silo. The missiles are labeled USAFN1, USAFN2, USAFN3, . . . , USAFN25. Each missile contains a MIRV with from 1 to 5 different warheads. The following information is kept for each warhead:

(a) name of target
(b) class of target
  (i) primary
  (ii) secondary
(c) expected time to target
(d) warhead payload in megatonnage
(e) expected nature of defense
  (i) ground-to-air missiles
  (ii) air-to-air missiles
  (iii) both of the above
  (iv) none of the above
(f) time required to launch
(g) warhead number (a label from 1 to 5)
(h) abort mission code (a secret number which, if telegraphed to the missile in flight, causes self destruct).

While each of the fields mentioned above, "name of target," "class of target," etc., is fixed in length, the number of targets associated with each Titan rocket is not. One rocket may carry a MIRV with three warheads, each with a secondary target, whereas another missile may have only two warheads, neither of which has a secondary target. The first rocket will thus have six targets (three warheads, two targets each) and the second rocket will have only two targets (two warheads, one target each). Thus the length of each record will not be fixed in length for each individual rocket but will vary with the number of targets. This is unlike the fixed-length records we have dealt with so far.

One solution to this problem is to arrange for each record associated with an individual rocket to contain space for the maximum possible number of targets whether assigned or not. As this wastes a great deal of space and is not very imaginative, we term this a *bureaucratic solution.*

An alternate solution is to make use of variable-length records. This is more space efficient; and considering the large number of missiles and targets, we as taxpayers have implemented the second approach. The fact that such saving is insignificant in comparison to the cost of the missiles does not concern us here (after all they are not constructed according to ANSI standards).

3.8 VARIABLE-LENGTH RECORDS

Variable-length records permit a varying number of character positions. When the records in a file are the same length, they are called *fixed-length records.*

3.8.1 Processing Variable-Length Records in COBOL

If a COBOL file contains variable-length records, the level 01 description of the records in the file FD or in the WORKING-STORAGE SECTION must reflect this variance in size. This can be accomplished in one of two ways. Either a different level 01 record description can be coded for each separate record size in the file FD or the format of the OCCURS clause containing the DEPENDING ON option can be used.

The former of these methods is generally used only when a file contains a few different record sizes or when the records of differing size vary considerably in format. The following ANSI COBOL statements describe a file that contains 12 different length records and a level 01 entry is included for each:

```
FD File-name
   LABEL RECORDS ARE STANDARD
   BLOCK CONTAINS integer RECORDS
   RECORD CONTAINS integer-1 TO integer-2 CHARACTERS
   DATA RECORDS ARE record-name-1
                    record-name-2
                    record-name-3
                         .
                         .
                         .
                    record-name-12.
01 record-name-1.
   02 FILLER  PIC X(n1).

01 record-name-2.
   02 FILLER PIC X (n2).

01 record-name-3.
```

```
    02 FILLER PIC X(n3).
              .
              .
              .
  01 record-name-12.
    02 FILLER PIC X(n12).
```

As with all FD file descriptions the LABEL RECORDS clause is required.

The BLOCK CONTAINS clause specifies the length of each physical record. It will be assumed that the size of each block is *integer* times the size of the largest of the various individual record sizes.

The RECORD CONTAINS clause indicates the size of the smallest of various variable record sizes in characters (*integer-1*) and the size of the largest (*integer-2*) of the record sizes in characters. In the above then

$$\textit{integer-1} = \min \{n1, n2, n3, \ldots, n12\} \quad \text{and}$$
$$\textit{integer-2} = \max \{n1, n2, n3, \ldots, n12\}$$

The DATA RECORDS clause specifies the record names of each of the individual record descriptions. It is assumed that at least two of the integers, *n1*, *n2*, *n3*, . . . , *n12*, are different; otherwise each will be considered as an automatic redefinition of *record-name-1* and strictly speaking we would then not be dealing with variable-length records.

The following IBM COBOL statements describe a variable-length record file containing records of three different types:

```
FD  AIRPLANE-FILE
    LABEL RECORDS ARE STANDARD
    BLOCK CONTAINS 5 RECORDS
    RECORD CONTAINS 30 TO 50 CHARACTERS
    DATA RECORDS ARE  CARGO-PLANE
                      PASSENGER-PLANE
                      MILITARY-PLANE.

01  CARGO-PLANE.
    02 FILLER  PIC X(40).

01  MILITARY-PLANE.
    02 FILLER PIC X(30).

01  PASSENGER-PLANE.
    02 FILLER PIC X(50).
```

This FD describes a variable-length record file called AIRPLANE. There are three different record descriptions for records of 30, 40, and 50 characters. Actual elementary field descriptions have not been included and the reader should assume the records are generated in the WORKING-STORAGE SECTION and later moved to the above level 01 record descriptions of the appropriate length.

In order to understand the action initiated by the BLOCK CONTAINS *integer* RECORDS clause in IBM OS/VS COBOL, it is important to realize that it does not specify what its meaning in English would imply. BLOCK CONTAINS 5 RECORDS does not mean that each physical record actually contains five logical records (as it does with fixed-length records) but rather that the physical record shall take up no more space on the storage device than would be occupied by five records of the largest possible size. Several bytes are added to the physical record size in order to maintain internal bookkeeping. This extra storage space amounts to

(a) four bytes for each logical record in the block *plus*

(b) four additional bytes.

Thus the statement BLOCK CONTAINS 5 RECORDS actually allows a maximun physical record size of 274 bytes in the above example. This is calculated from the fact that the largest variable-length record permitted is 50 bytes long; there are 5 of these for a total of 5 × 5 = 250 bytes; for each of these 5 records there are 4 additional bytes, 5 × 4 = 20 making a total of 250 + 20 = 270 bytes; and, lastly, an additional 4 bytes is added for a grand total of 274 bytes. The maximum physical record that could be stored is thus 274 bytes.

A physical record may not actually contain this number of bytes as the logical records are not all of the same length. A physical record is completed and written to the storage device whenever the sum of the number of bytes in each logical record in the block, plus 4 bytes for each of these records, plus 4 additional bytes is subtracted from the maximum physical record size and the difference does not leave enough space for a variable-length record of the maximum size. An example will make this clear.

The BLOCK CONTAINS clause permitted a maximum physical record size of 274 bytes. Suppose the user wishes to write one 30-byte record followed by five 40-byte records. The sum of space occupied by these logical records is

$$\begin{aligned}
1 \times 30 &= 30 \\
5 \times 40 &= 200 \\
6 \times 4 &= 24 \\
1 \times 4 &= \underline{\ \ 4} \\
\text{Total}\ & 258
\end{aligned}$$

The amount of space remaining is 274 - 258 = 16, which is not enough for a record of 50 bytes, the maximum variable-record length. As a result, a 258-byte physical record is written.

It should be noted that BLOCK CONTAINS 5 RECORDS was chosen for illustrative purposes and that the number 5 may be a very poor choice depending on the storage device used and the amount of space available for storing logical records prior to their being written on a storage device. The correct choice of this number is a topic for a much later discussion on choosing blocking factors.

3.8.2 Variable-Length Records in the Missile Target System

In the missile target system each record contains information about one or more targets associated with an individual Titan rocket. Thus the length of each varies with the number of targets. In this case, however, the fields associated with each target are identical and what actually varies is the group item of targeting information. For each rocket, this group item will occur as many times as there are targets and what is needed is a variable form of the OCCURS clause which permits the length of the group item to vary from record to record.

OCCURS DEPENDING ON

The following code, valid for IBM COBOL, describes the record associated with each missile:

```
01  TITAN-MISSILE.
02  NUMBER-OF-TARGETS   PICTURE 99.
02  TARGET OCCURS 0 TO 5 TIMES
        DEPENDING ON NUMBER-OF-TARGETS.
    03 NAME-OF-TARGET PIC X(20).
    03 CLASS-OF-TARGET PIC X(9).
    03 EXPECTED-FLIGHT-TIME PIC 9(4).
    03 WARHEAD-PAYLOAD PIC 9(3).
```

```
03 EXPECTED-DEFENSE PIC 9.
03 LAUNCH-TIME PIC 9(3).
03 WARHEAD-NUMBER PIC 9.
03 ABORT-CODE PIC 9(5).
```

Each of the level 03 elementary items describes one unit of information concerning the target. The level 02 group item thus contains all the information concerning each target and it is itself a table. For any record this table may have from 0 to 5 entries. The number of entries varies from record to record but is given in the elementary data item named NUMBER-OF-TARGETS. If this data item contains 5, then the group item TARGET is a table of 5 entries. If NUMBER-OF-TARGETS is 3, the group item TARGET is a table of 3 entries. In the example given, the entry TARGET for any record cannot have more than 5 entries.

Program 3.5 Narrative: Missile Target. The input to Program 3.5 consists of keypunched data cards. Each card contains a 7-character missile identification code called MISSILE-IDENTIFICATION and carries the information about one particular target. As any missile can have up to five first strike targets, there are a maximum of five data cards having the same missile identification code. We shall refer to a group of five or less such data cards as the "target group" of one missile. To aid in processing, the data cards are sorted by hand into target groups.

As each card of the target group is read, its targeting information is moved to the array TARGET in MISSILE-FILE-RECORD. The array TARGET is defined with an OCCURS DEPENDING ON clause which has as its object a variable called NUMBER-OF-TARGETS. As the variable controls the size of the array TARGET, it is stored in the fixed part of the record. Before any information from a data card is moved to the array, the variable NUMBER-OF-TARGETS is incremented by 1 to allow the array to expand by one more entry to hold the additional information.

The missile identification code of the first data card within a target group is stored in a variable called ACTIVE-KEY and only cards whose codes match the ACTIVE-KEY are processed to the same MISSILE-FILE-RECORD. The ACTIVE-KEY is updated to another code when the target group is written.

Processing is terminated when end-of-file is encountered on the card reader.

It should be noted that the elementary item NUMBER-OF-TARGETS which expresses the size of the corresponding OCCURS

Program 3.5

```
IDENTIFICATION DIVISION.
PROGRAM-ID.  PROG3PT5.
ENVIRONMENT DIVISION.
CONFIGURATION SECTION.
OBJECT-COMPUTER.  IBM-370.
SOURCE-COMPUTER.  IBM-370.
INPUT-OUTPUT SECTION.
FILE-CONTROL.
    SELECT CARD-READER
    ASSIGN TO CARD-S-SYSIN
    ORGANIZATION IS SEQUENTIAL
    ACCESS MODE IS SEQUENTIAL.
    SELECT PRINTER
    ASSIGN TO PRNT-S-SYSOUT
    ORGANIZATION IS SEQUENTIAL
    ACCESS MODE IS SEQUENTIAL.
    SELECT  MISSILE-FILE
    ASSIGN TO DISK-S-MISSILE
    ORGANIZATION IS SEQUENTIAL
    ACCESS MODE IS SEQUENTIAL.
DATA DIVISION.
FILE SECTION.
FD  CARD-READER
    BLOCK CONTAINS 1 RECORDS
    LABEL RECORDS ARE OMITTED
    RECORD CONTAINS 80 CHARACTERS
    DATA RECORD IS CARD-READER-RECORD.
01  CARD-READER-RECORD.
    02 MISSILE-IDENTIFICATION    PIC X(7).
    02 NAME-OF-TARGET            PIC X(20).
    02 CLASS-OF-TARGET           PIC X(9).
    02 EXPECTED-FLIGHT-TIME      PIC 9(4).
    02 WARHEAD-PAYLOAD           PIC 9(3).
    02 EXPECTED-DEFENCE          PIC 9.
    02 LAUNCH-TIME               PIC 9(3).
    02 WARHEAD-NUMBER            PIC 9.
    02 ABORT-CODE                PIC 9(5).
    02 FILLER                    PIC X(27).
FD  MISSILE-FILE
    BLOCK CONTAINS 5 RECORDS
    LABEL RECORDS ARE STANDARD
    RECORD CONTAINS 55 TO 239 CHARACTERS
    DATA RECORD IS MISSILE-FILE-RECORD.
01  MISSILE-FILE-RECORD.
    02 MISSILE-IDENTIFICATION    PIC X(7).
    02 NUMBER-OF-TARGETS         PIC 99.
    02  TARGET OCCURS 0 TO 5 TIMES
        DEPENDING ON NUMBER-OF-TARGETS
                     OF WS-MISSILE-FILE-RECORD.
```

Program 3.5 (cont.)

```
               03 NAME-OF-TARGET       PIC X(20).
               03 CLASS-OF-TARGET      PIC X(9).
               03 EXPECTED-FLIGHT-TIME PIC 9(4).
               03 WARHEAD-PAYLOAD      PIC 9(3).
               03 EXPECTED-DEFENCE     PIC 9.
               03 LAUNCH-TIME          PIC 9(3).
               03 WARHEAD-NUMBER       PIC 9.
               03 ABORT-CODE           PIC 9(5).
       FD  PRINTER
           BLOCK CONTAINS 1 RECORDS
           LABEL RECORDS ARE OMITTED
           RECORD CONTAINS 132 CHARACTERS
           DATA RECORD IS PRINTER-RECORD.
       01  PRINTER-RECORD.
           02 FILLER                   PIC X(5).
           02 NAME-OF-TARGET           PIC X(20).
           02 FILLER                   PIC X(5).
           02 MISSILE-IDENTIFICATION   PIC X(7).
           02 FILLER                   PIC X(95).
       WORKING-STORAGE SECTION.
       77  ACTIVE-KEY                  PIC X(7).
       77  COUNTER                     PIC S9(8).
       77  EOF-CARD-FLAG               PIC X(3).
           88 EOF-CARD VALUE IS 'ON'.
       01  WS-MISSILE-FILE-RECORD.
           02 MISSILE-IDENTIFICATION   PIC X(7).
           02 NUMBER-OF-TARGETS        PIC 99.
           02  TARGET OCCURS 0 TO 5 TIMES
               DEPENDING ON NUMBER-OF-TARGETS
                            OF WS-MISSILE-FILE-RECORD.
               03 NAME-OF-TARGET       PIC X(20).
               03 CLASS-OF-TARGET      PIC X(9).
               03 EXPECTED-FLIGHT-TIME PIC 99.
               03 WARHEAD-PAYLOAD      PIC 9(3).
               03 EXPECTED-DEFENCE     PIC 9.
               03 LAUNCH-TIME          PIC 9(3).
               03 WARHEAD-NUMBER       PIC 9.
               03 ABORT-CODE           PIC 9(5).
       PROCEDURE DIVISION.
           PERFORM INITIALIZATION.
           PERFORM READ-AND-COPY-TO-FILE-ROUTINE
                   UNTIL EOF-CARD.
           PERFORM TERMINATION.
           STOP RUN.
       INITIALIZATION.
           OPEN INPUT  CARD-READER
                OUTPUT PRINTER
                       MISSILE-FILE.
           MOVE 'OFF' TO EOF-CARD-FLAG.
           MOVE ZERO TO NUMBER-OF-TARGETS
                        OF WS-MISSILE-FILE-RECORD.
           READ CARD-READER
```

Program 3.5 (cont.)

```
         AT END MOVE 'ON' TO EOF-CARD-FLAG.
     IF NOT EOF-CARD THEN
        MOVE MISSILE-IDENTIFICATION
             OF CARD-READER TO ACTIVE-KEY
        MOVE MISSILE-IDENTIFICATION
             OF CARD-READER TO
             MISSILE-IDENTIFICATION
             OF WS-MISSILE-FILE-RECORD.


READ-AND-COPY-TO-FILE-ROUTINE.
    PERFORM COPY-CARD-TO-WORKING-STORAGE
            UNTIL MISSILE-IDENTIFICATION
                  OF CARD-READER
                  NOT EQUAL ACTIVE-KEY
                  OR EOF-CARD.
    MOVE NUMBER-OF-TARGETS
         OF WS-MISSILE-FILE-RECORD
         TO NUMBER-OF-TARGETS
         OF MISSILE-FILE-RECORD.
    DISPLAY NUMBER-OF-TARGETS
             OF WS-MISSILE-FILE-RECORD.
    WRITE MISSILE-FILE-RECORD
          FROM WS-MISSILE-FILE-RECORD.
    IF NOT EOF-CARD  THEN
       MOVE MISSILE-IDENTIFICATION
            OF CARD-READER TO ACTIVE-KEY
       MOVE ZERO TO NUMBER-OF-TARGETS
                         OF WS-MISSILE-FILE-RECORD
       MOVE MISSILE-IDENTIFICATION
            OF CARD-READER
            TO MISSILE-IDENTIFICATION
            OF WS-MISSILE-FILE-RECORD.


COPY-CARD-TO-WORKING-STORAGE.
    ADD 1 TO NUMBER-OF-TARGETS
             OF WS-MISSILE-FILE-RECORD.
    MOVE NUMBER-OF-TARGETS OF WS-MISSILE-FILE-RECORD
            TO COUNTER.
    MOVE NAME-OF-TARGET OF CARD-READER-RECORD
            TO NAME-OF-TARGET
            OF TARGET
            OF WS-MISSILE-FILE-RECORD (COUNTER).
    MOVE CLASS-OF-TARGET OF CARD-READER-RECORD
            TO CLASS-OF-TARGET
            OF TARGET
            OF WS-MISSILE-FILE-RECORD (COUNTER).
    MOVE EXPECTED-FLIGHT-TIME
            OF CARD-READER-RECORD
            TO EXPECTED-FLIGHT-TIME
            OF TARGET
            OF WS-MISSILE-FILE-RECORD (COUNTER).
    MOVE WARHEAD-PAYLOAD OF CARD-READER-RECORD
            TO WARHEAD-PAYLOAD
            OF TARGET
            OF WS-MISSILE-FILE-RECORD (COUNTER).
    MOVE EXPECTED-DEFENCE OF CARD-READER-RECORD
            TO EXPECTED-DEFENCE
            OF TARGET
```

Program 3.5 (cont.)

```
                        OF WS-MISSILE-FILE-RECORD (COUNTER).
                MOVE LAUNCH-TIME OF CARD-READER-RECORD
                        TO LAUNCH-TIME
                        OF TARGET
                        OF WS-MISSILE-FILE-RECORD (COUNTER).
                MOVE WARHEAD-NUMBER
                        OF CARD-READER-RECORD
                        TO WARHEAD-NUMBER
                        OF TARGET
                        OF WS-MISSILE-FILE-RECORD (COUNTER).
                MOVE ABORT-CODE OF CARD-READER
                        TO ABORT-CODE
                        OF TARGET
                        OF WS-MISSILE-FILE-RECORD (COUNTER).
                PERFORM PRINT-VERIFY-ROUTINE.
                READ CARD-READER
                     AT END MOVE 'ON' TO EOF-CARD-FLAG.


            PRINT-VERIFY-ROUTINE.
                MOVE SPACES TO PRINTER-RECORD.
                MOVE MISSILE-IDENTIFICATION OF CARD-READER
                     TO MISSILE-IDENTIFICATION OF PRINTER.
                MOVE NAME-OF-TARGET OF CARD-READER
                     TO NAME-OF-TARGET OF PRINTER.
                WRITE PRINTER-RECORD
                      AFTER ADVANCING 2 LINES.


            TERMINATION.
                CLOSE CARD-READER
                      MISSILE-FILE
                      PRINTER.
```

clause is found in that part of the record that does not itself vary in size. This part of the record is usually referred to as the *fixed part of the record.* The data item referred to by the DEPENDING ON option of the OCCURS clause should always occur within the fixed part of the record. In addition, it should be described as a positive unsigned integer item that is defined with either USAGE IS DISPLAY (the default option) or as a COMPUTATIONAL or COMPUTATIONAL-3 item. It must never be a table entry or exceed in value the maximum size specified in the TIMES portion of the OCCURS clause. Note that the former of these restrictions prohibits the DEPENDING ON option of an OCCURS clause from naming data item within another OCCURS DEPENDING ON clause.

ANSI COBOL does not permit an OCCURS clause of any format to describe an item whose size is variable, that is, an item containing an OCCURS DEPENDING ON clause or having subordinate to it an item containing an OCCURS DEPENDING ON clause. IBM COBOL has relaxed this restriction. Check your manual for details.

The OCCURS DEPENDING ON option can be used either in the WORKING-STORAGE SECTION or in the FD entry for a given file. For either case, the object of the DEPENDING ON option, that is, the number that specifies how large the variable table is in size, should be updated to the correct value in order to reflect this size before any data is moved into the variable table. The table length is changed to reflect the updated value whenever the value of the data item that specifies this size is changed. This is done automatically when data is read into a buffer by a READ statement.

It is particularly important to note this if there is any data item that follows a portion of a group description containing an OCCURS DEPENDING ON option, as the contents of this subsequent item will be destroyed as the variable table grows and overwrites it. For example, in the following code the value of data item C will be lost if a new value is moved to A as this will change the size of variable table B.

```
01   RECORD-DESCRIPTION.
     02   A  PIC 99.
     02   B  OCCURS 0 TO 10
             TIMES  DEPENDING ON A
             PIC  X(4).
     02   C  PIC X(2).
```

The contents of C can be saved in a temporary location and returned once A has been updated. The size of B changes as soon as the value of A is modified.

The user must employ caution when executing group moves to storage areas containing subordinate items described with the OCCURS DEPENDING ON option. This is best explained by describing the result of a MOVE operation to the following group item A:

```
01    A.
      02   B  PIC 9(2).
      02   C  OCCURS 5 TO 10
              TIMES DEPENDING ON
              B  PIC X(5).
01    E.
      02   FILLER PIC X(50).
```

If the statement

```
MOVE E TO A
```

is executed, the size of variable table C is determined by the previous contents of B. After the MOVE is executed, if the data moved to the area defined by B within A is of the correct format (i.e., it can legally be defined as PIC 99) then the length of table C will be updated. In the event that the data transferred to B is not of the correct format, the value within B will be ignored and the length of table C will not change.

As a WRITE statement with the FROM option and a READ with the INTO options involve group moves, the user is cautioned that care must be taken to ensure that any variable-length tables within the receiving field are of the correct size. It may be advisable to avoid using these two options if confusion arises and move data to and from the buffer areas with individual MOVE statements after correctly updating the object data items of any DEPENDING ON options involved.

3.8.3 A Final Note

Variable-length records are not fully defined in the 1974 ANSI COBOL standard, and in the standard neither an OCCURS DEPENDING ON clause nor multiple FD level 01 entries of differing sizes really allow for logical records of variable length to be stored. Recent work of the COBOL CODASYL Committee would seem to indicate that future revisions of the standard will permit an approach very similar to that employed in IBM OS/VS COBOL. If you are using another COBOL compiler, careful reading of the manuals supplied is highly advised.

3.9 POSTSCRIPT: A WORD ON PROGRAM STYLE

We would like to draw attention to the fact that none of the programs in this chapter contain a GO TO statement. Although we do not insist that GO TO's be forbidden, we adhere to the belief that GO TO's should only be used with care, as in most programs an overabundance of GO TO's can and does lead to unnecessary program complexity. Satisfying as it may be to a programmer's ego, program complexity is not a desirable attribute of *good* programming style. Our experience has shown that the decision to avoid GO TO's does not magically transform a bad program into a good program, but such a decision does bring discipline to the programming process. Certainly, there are many techniques that lead to good programming. If having a coffee, sharpening a pencil, or avoiding nested IF's (a good idea) do the same for our reader, so be it. Style arises from good and consistent habits. Choose a method and stick to it. Although good style requires hard work, the benefits that result are so profitable you cannot afford to neglect it. Programming takes effort, brains, and time; sloppy work leads to more effort and time than expected. The history of missed deadlines in the manufacture of software speaks for itself.

PROBLEMS

1. Discuss the limitations of sequential files as you see them.

2. What is the major disadvantage of batch processing?

3. Write a COBOL program to access the MUSIC LOG file and determine the amount of time records have been played, the number of records, and the average duration of a record.

4. The purpose of this exercise is to master the concepts of a case study by doing.
   (a) Write a program to create a sequential FIRE-STATISTICS file on disk.
   (b) Write an update program that rewrites in place. Are there any back-up problems? How would you solve them?

Case Study: Fire Statistics

The city council of Johnsonburg has delegated the responsibility of drafting a new budget for the city's fire department to a small subcommittee. This decision was taken as a result of complaints brought forward by the Ratepayers' Association concerned with the alarming increase in fire losses suffered by the city's citizens and businesses. The Association has charged that the recent introduction of a large cereal factory and an addition to the pulp and paper mill necessitate appropriate expansion of the city's firefighting equipment. A recent newspaper report has further agitated the situation by suggesting that arson is increasing with the current growth in population. As a first step, the subcommittee has requested that the fire chief keep statistics on the nature and extent of the fires his department will be called on to fight in the coming months. He is to provide a quarterly report to the committee.

Logical Analysis: Fire Statistics

The prime directive is to collect data on the city's fires. To this end a report form is prepared, in consultation with the fire department, to collect details on the various areas of concern to the fire chief and the subcommittee. A completed sample of this report is shown in Fig. 3.12 and is to be filled out by the fire chief or designated fireman as soon after the blaze as possible. Manpower does not permit a more detailed report at this time. Later the form may be revised if the subcommittee expresses detailed interest in one or more areas designated or in a new area altogether (such as the type of construction of the burned buildings).

Since these forms will be used to prepare quarterly reports, it is decided to keypunch and store them on a magnetic tape file once a week. No one has requested instant access to any of these reports, therefore, storage on direct access devices is not required. Magnetic tape storage is expected to be less expensive for this aplication.

Several decisions are required concerning what information is to be written to the sequential tape file. The fires are first classified as to cause. Each fire cause is assigned a code, and it is decided that for purposes of reporting neither the type of injury nor the names of the injured need be recorded. The latter decision protects the privacy of the individuals from the city council subcommittee, and the exact extent of injuries can only be determined by a competent examining physician.

In particular, as shown in Table 3.4, it is decided to reserve space in a record for each of the fields that will store the data items.

5. Whenever cash is paid out, it should be done by check. To control checks they are assigned consecutive check numbers. Missing check numbers must be explained—perhaps they have been stolen. Show how to add check numbers to the transaction records of the GENERAL JOURNAL file. How could you detect missing check numbers?

6. Program 3.2 assumes that entries that reach the file are correct. Accounting errors are corrected by entering a *correcting entry*.

   (a) Revise Program 3.2 so that transactions on the General Journal can be corrected.
   (b) If the amount of a transaction was found a month later, how would you correct it?

7. Write a program to print out the GENERAL JOURNAL file.

JOHNSONBURG FIRE DEPARTMENT			FORM - 1980 1A-315-4
LOCATION OF FIRE		OWNER OF ESTABLISHMENT	
DATE	TIME OUT	ARRIVAL TIME SCENE Duration	UNITS DISPATCHED
CASUALTIES		TYPE OF INJURY	
FIRE CAUSE	CODE	PROPERTY DAMAGED	AMOUNT
□ ACCIDENT □ ARSON □ BURNING LEAVES □ CHEMICAL □ CHILDREN □ CIGARETTE □ FALSE ALARM □ FAULTY WIRING □ FIRE SPREAD □ EXPLOSION □ UNKNOWN			
		NO. OF ALARMS	TIME RETURNED
		REPORT PREPARED BY	INSPECTOR
		REPORT ACCEPTED BY	DATE
		FILE NO.	

Figure 3.12 Sample form for Fire Statistics Case Study.

Table 3.4 Information to be Stored in FIRE-STATISTICS FILE

Entry	*No. of Characters*
Fire location	30 – alphabetic
Owner of building	20 – alphabetic
Date of fire	6 – digits
Time of alarm	4 – military (24-hour) time
Time at scene	4 – military time
Duration of fire	4 – digits
Number of trucks dispatched	2 – digits
Dollar damage estimate	7 – digits
Number of casualties	3 – digits
Cause of fire	2 – digit code
Number of fire alarms	1 – digit
Time returned from fire	4 – military time
File number	6 – digits
	93 – total

8. At the end of the fiscal year, Profit Inc.'s expense accounts are zeroed. Explain how you might do this. Is a knowledge of accounting required or can the programmer just see that zeros get entered?

9. Profit Inc.'s accountant, John Figures, is pleased with the speed at which he gets his trial balance and with the fact that he no longer has to do posting and total accounts. However, last month there was an error in the supplies account and it took him quite a while to find it in the General Journal. He wonders if it would be possible to print out the Account entries as well as the totals. He also feels it will be easier for him to audit entries in Accounts rather than the General Journal.

(a) Advise him of solution, cost, and delivery.
(b) Implement solution.
(c) Propose a test of the solution.

10. Investigate which files in your computer installation make use of variable-length records. Why are they used in these cases? What part of the records in these files vary in size?

11. Make a list of your favorite baseball, hockey, or football players and indicate which teams they have played for. Write a program that reads in this data and prints it out. Make use of variable-length records to record the teams. If you dislike sports, try to design a file that would require variable-length records.

12. Describe the contents of the record you think the income tax department keeps concerning you. Draw a diagram of the record indicating the various fields and the lengths that would be needed in characters for the information in each field. This is called making a *record layout*. Can you think of any part of this file that would require variable-length fields? Is it likely or even reasonable that every field you fill out on your income tax form is included? Often indivduals write letters to the tax department trying to clarify what level of tax to pay on certain incomes or questioning a decision of the government that affects the amount they are assessed. How would you keep track of this form of data? Remember you are not the only taxpayer and no two letters are the same.

13. One thing many students often fail to get is enough experience presenting their material in public. Imagine that you are a member of the tax department and are asked to explain and justify the record layout in Problem 12 to management. Ask your fellow students or your teacher to arrange for a small public talk. If you cannot do this, try to lecture to yourself in a mirror or even to an empty classroom. Your future employers will often ask you to explain to them or another group what you are planning to do in your programming, and valuable experience can be had now without penalty.

4 Sorting in COBOL

4.1 INTRODUCTION

Sorting consists of arranging records in the sequence of a key contained in the records. This key is referred to as a *sort key*. For instance, if the keys are numeric, then they can be placed in numeric order either ascending or descending. It must be possible to compare all keys, so there must exist a linear order on the keys. Since the sort key need not be unique, it is possible to sort those records further without destroying the first sort order on yet another sort key, and so on.

Some systems, particularly batch systems, often spend most of their processing time sorting. Thus sorting, while not a major topic of this book, is a very important technique for file processing. Our purpose here is to develop the essential background for the use of sorting in the book. The reader may skip this chapter if he wishes.

When two or more files are already sorted, combining them to form as single sorted file can be done by a process called a *merge*. Merging is more efficient because it assumes that the files to be combined are already in order. It is easily done by keeping a pointer to each file that indicates the next record to be removed from that file. Simply determine which of these records pointed to is next, move it to the sorted file, and update that record pointer; then repeat the selection.

Most computer installations own or rent a library of prepackaged sorting programs. These SORT-MERGE packages, as they are usually called, are designed to provide a wide range of sorting techniques depending on the number of items to be sorted and the amount of computer memory that can be devoted to the program. Each SORT-MERGE package has its own command statements or language, and a program can be written in this language to solve a particular sorting problem. The user must designate which file is to be sorted, on which keys the records are to be sorted, and where the file, once sorted, is to be stored.

The fact that a file to be sorted may not fit into memory poses an additional problem of considerable magnitude. Sorting methods that assume that all records to be sorted are stored in memory are called *internal sorts*. When a method need not have all records in memory at the same time, it is called an *external sort*.

Most data processing files cannot be placed in the available memory, thus external sort methods are required. This is a serious restriction and affects the efficiency of the methods used for sorting. Efficiency of sorting is a function of the structure of the unsorted records and no best method is known. Thus SORT-MERGE packages can be rather complex.

The COBOL language has constructs for describing the necessary sorting information within a program. The COBOL compiler will provide a call to the SORT-MERGE package for you and translate your COBOL sort instructions into the command language of the SORT-MERGE package. When the sort is described in COBOL, there are several immediate advantages realized. First, the user need only know COBOL; he need not learn the language of the SORT-MERGE package. Second, while the sort statements within COBOL are standardized by the ANSI Language Committee, the command language of each SORT-MERGE package is often different. This makes the program written in COBOL portable; that is, it can be run on different machines to attain the same result, and it also isolates the program from system changes. Third, the sorting statements can be embedded in a COBOL program. This enables a programmmer to write COBOL statements that will govern when the sorting routines are to be called and which records in the file are to be sorted. It is also possible to write one's own sort in a COBOL program. This is not likely to be necessary, but a situation could occur, such as a limit on memory, in which it would be advantageous to do so. However, chances are that someone will have a COBOL sort that he will be pleased to give you.

The SORT-MERGE module provides the capability to sort the records of a file according to the sort keys of the records specified by the user. Special procedures provide the flexibility to edit the files and increase the efficiency of the sort phase. COBOL Level 1 limits the sorting of a file to once per program execution, while COBOL Level 2 allows multiple sorting of files.

4.2 INTERNAL SORTING

In order to understand the process of sorting, we examine a simple yet reasonable sort algorithm which we refer to as the *simple selection sort*. Assuming that the records before the current record position are in order, select from the remaining records the one that belongs in the current position. Record selection from the yet unsorted records consists of simply selecting the maximum or minimum key of these records. The process is illustrated in Fig. 4.1. Here the pointer top indicates the first of the as yet unsorted records. Initially no records are sorted, but when the top points to the last record, the set of records must be sorted in ascending order from the first record.

The number of operations used by this algorithm is proportional to n^2, where n is the number of records. More efficient algorithms provide far better bounds for the size of the number of operations, Heapsort, discovered by J.W.J. Williams (1964), is one such sort. One of the best all-around internal sorts is that proposed by Hoare (1962), called Quicksort. Its average processing time is very good; unfortunately, it can run very badly in the worst case. A very clever technique is that of Dobosiewicz (1978).

4.3 EXTERNAL SORTING

When all of the records do not fit into the available memory, we can only sort subsets. We then require a method of combining two

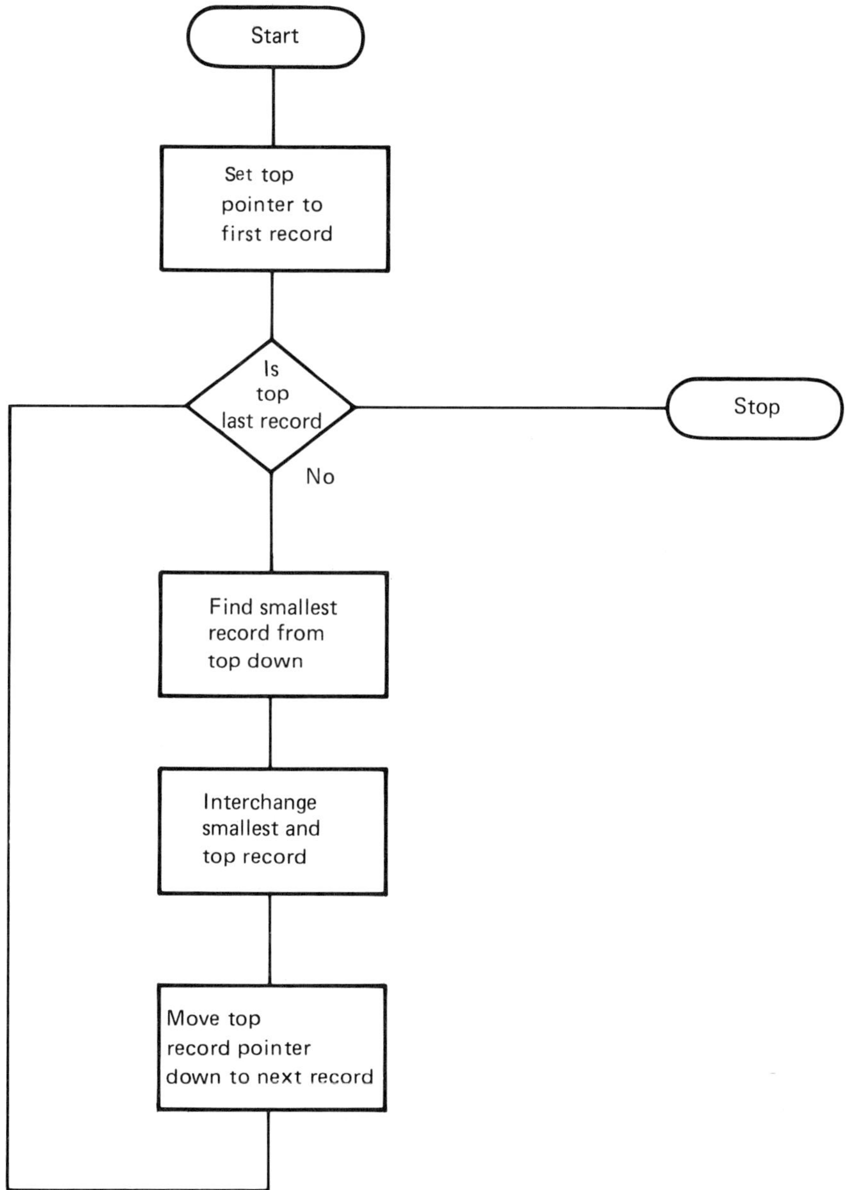

Figure 4.1 Simple selection sort.

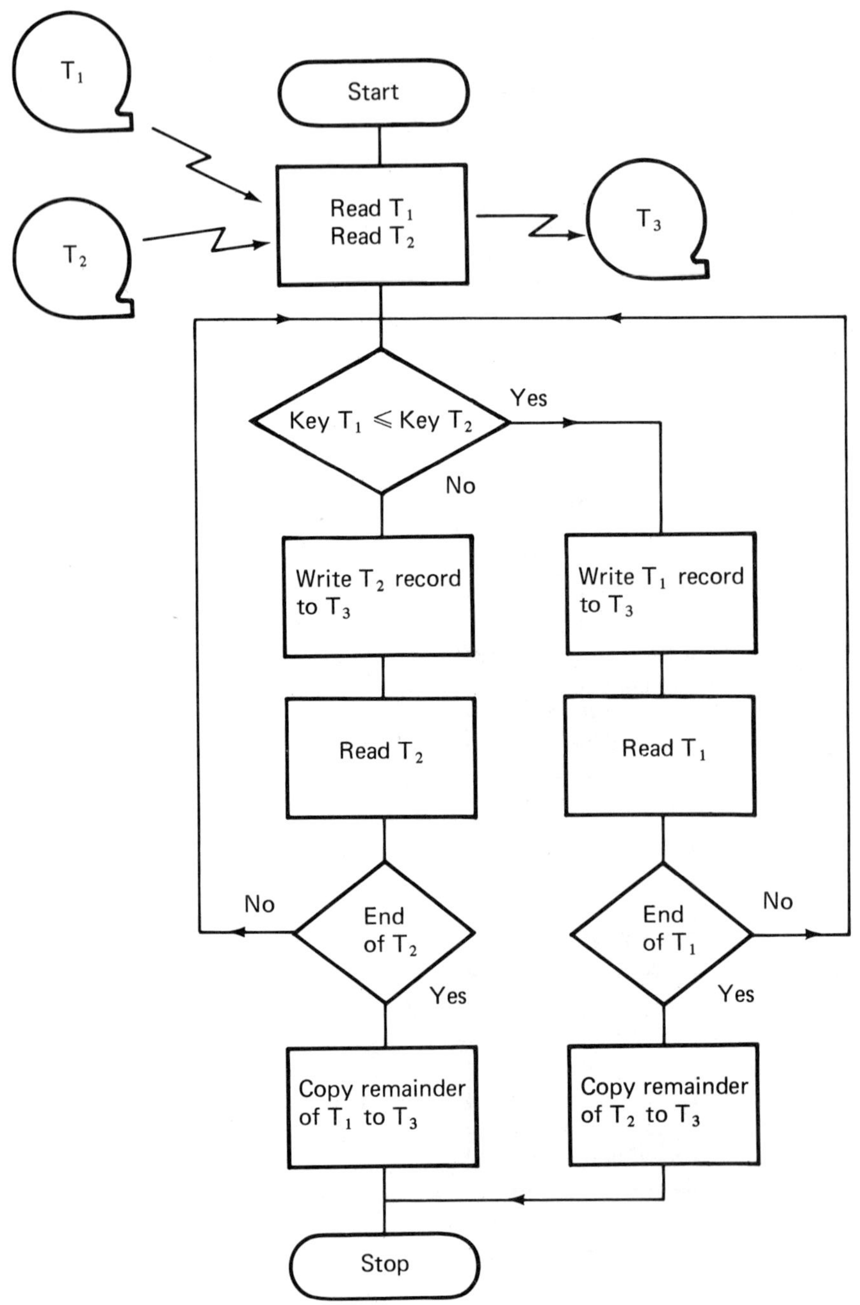

Figure 4.2 Merging sorted tapes into ascending order.

sorted subsets, while maintaining their sorted nature. This process is called *merging*, which we mentioned in the introduction to this chapter. In Fig. 4.2 we give the basic logic flow to merge two sorted tapes into a single sorted tape. Merging as part of a single sort is more complicated as two output tapes may be required to contain the two input tapes.

When using an external sort, the largest blocking possible should be used to reduce I/O operations. Increasing the number of tapes being merged can be advantageous. However, there is usually a limit to the number of files that can be opened, and the results are system dependent, especially in a time-sharing environment.

4.4 BASIC SORTING IN COBOL

Sorting in COBOL requires that certain statements be added to each of the three main divisions of a COBOL program, namely, the ENVIRONMENT, DATA, and PROCEDURE DIVISIONs. These statements indicate which file is to be sorted, what fields within the records of this file are to be sorted, and where the sorted file is to be stored.

The program requirements for sorting can be more easily understood when it is realized that COBOL asks the SORT-MERGE package to sort a special file known in COBOL as a *sort file.* This sort file is not the file you wish to have sorted. It is a special internal file *that the program may not open or close* but into which the records the program requires to be sorted are placed for actual sorting. This internal sort file, once it contains the records that are to be sorted is turned over to the SORT-MERGE package. Upon completion of sorting, the internal file is returned in sort order, and a copy can be made of its contents. Because this internal file is central to the whole idea of COBOL sorting, we shall begin with those COBOL statements used to describe it.

The file you wish to have sorted and the file in which you wish to store the sorted result are defined in the normal way except that in the FILE-CONTROL paragraph they *must* contain the clause ACCESS IS SEQUENTIAL. The internal sort file is described in the FILE-CONTROL paragraph as a sequential file. As an example, if the internal sort file is to be called INTERNAL-SORT-FILE, its SELECT clause might appear as

```
SELECT INTERNAL-SORT-FILE
    ASSIGN TO UT-DISK-S-SORTWK11.
```

The most important change in describing this internal sort file comes in the FILE SECTION of the DATA DIVISION where *it receives the special designator SD instead of the normal FD.* This informs the COBOL compiler that this particular file is to be treated as a special internal sort file. The rest of the SD entry is, in other respects, the same as an ordinary FD entry except that *neither a* BLOCK CONTAINS *clause nor a* LABEL RECORDS *clause can appear.* For example, a typical SD entry might appear as follows:

```
SD  INTERNAL-SORT-FILE
    RECORD CONTAINS 100 CHARACTERS
    DATA RECORD IS INTERNAL-SORT-FILE-RECORD.

01  INTERNAL-SORT-FILE-RECORD
    02  LICENSE-NUMBER  PIC  X(6).
    02  FILLER          PIC  X(17).
    02  COLOR           PIC  X(9).
    02  FILLER          PIC  X(68).
```

This entry acts in most respects just like a buffer for an ordinary file. Each record that is to be sorted will first be moved to INTERNAL-SORT-FILE-RECORD and then written to the INTERNAL-SORT-FILE. Later we shall see exactly how this writing (or *releasing* as it is called) to an internal sort file is accomplished.

Each record is sorted on selected fields within the record. For example, we might wish to sort a stolen vehicle file by license number or color of car or perhaps first by color of car and then within each color by license number. Since the SORT-MERGE package must know exactly where in each record the fields to be used as sort keys are located, these fields must be described in the 01 entry of the SD. Other fields not to be used as sort keys may be designated as FILLER. In the SD example for INTERNAL-SORT-FILE, only the fields LICENSE-NUMBER and COLOR have been shown. Presumably one or both of these fields might be used as sort keys.

In the PROCEDURE DIVISION, sorting is initiated by the verb SORT which must specify, the following three things:

(a) which field(s) within each record are to act as the sort keys for purposes of the sort
(b) which records of which file are to be moved to the internal sort file before sorting takes place
(c) once sorting is completed, to which file the sorted records

on the internal sort file are to be transferred for program access.

The SORT verb, which may be used anywhere within the PROCEDURE DIVISION, has several formats which can best be illustrated by example. The following illustrates the simplest form:

```
SORT INTERNAL-SORT-FILE
ON ASCENDING KEY LICENSE-NUMBER
USING POLICE-FILE
GIVING SORTED-POLICE-FILE.
```

This instruction asks that *all* the records on POLICE-FILE be transferred to the INTERNAL-SORT-FILE where they are to be sorted into ascending sequence by the field LICENSE-NUMBER. Upon completion, *all* the records are to be transferred over to the file SORTED-POLICE-FILE.

The program to accomplish this is Program 4.1. Note that in the case of Program 4.1, the SORTED-POLICE-FILE has been assigned to the printer. It is for this reason that the file has in fact appeared as printed output to the program.

Sometimes we may wish to sort a file on more than one key. Suppose, for instance, that we have a directory of employees working in various departments of various factories. We might wish to sort all employees within the factory, then within the factory by department, and within the department by name. A typical SORT statement to do this might be:

```
SORT  INTERNAL-SORT-FILE
ON ASCENDING KEY
      FACTORY, DEPARTMENT, NAME
USING DIRECTORY-FILE
GIVING DIRECTORY-FILE-SORTED.
```

This instruction asks that *all* the records on the file DIRECTORY-FILE be transferred to the INTERNAL-SORT-FILE where they are to be sorted by factory, then within factory by department, and finally within department by name. On conclusion of the sorting routines, all the records are to be placed in a file named DIRECTORY-FILE-SORTED.

As a last example of this form of the SORT verb, we want to sort the directory of the preceding example, first by factory and then by department. Instead of sorting within department by name,

Program 4.1

```
IDENTIFICATION DIVISION.
PROGRAM-ID. PROG4PT1.
AUTHOR. R H COOPER.
INSTALLATION. UNIVERSITY OF NEW BRUNSWICK.
DATE-WRITTEN. FEB 13,1977.
DATE-COMPILED. MAR 19,1980.
SECURITY. THIS PROGRAM IS CLASSIFIED
          AND CAN ONLY BE VIEWED BY
          SPECIAL PERMISSION OF THE PRESIDENT.
REMARKS. THIS PROGRAM SORTS THE POLICE-FILE.


ENVIRONMENT DIVISION.

CONFIGURATION SECTION.

SOURCE-COMPUTER. IBM-370.
OBJECT-COMPUTER. IBM-370.

INPUT-OUTPUT SECTION.

FILE-CONTROL.

    SELECT INTERNAL-SORT-FILE
        ASSIGN TO DISK-S-SORTWK01
        ORGANIZATION IS SEQUENTIAL
        ACCESS MODE IS SEQUENTIAL.
    SELECT OUTPUT-FILE
        ASSIGN TO PRNT-S-SYSOUT
        ORGANIZATION IS SEQUENTIAL
        ACCESS MODE IS SEQUENTIAL.
    SELECT POLICE-FILE
        ASSIGN TO DISK-S-POLICE
        ORGANIZATION IS SEQUENTIAL
        ACCESS MODE IS SEQUENTIAL.


DATA DIVISION.

FILE SECTION.

SD  INTERNAL-SORT-FILE
    RECORD CONTAINS 100 CHARACTERS
    DATA RECORD IS INTERNAL-SORT-FILE-RECORD.
01  INTERNAL-SORT-FILE-RECORD.
    02  LICENSE-NUMBER            PICTURE X(6).
    02  FILLER                    PICTURE X(94).

FD  OUTPUT-FILE
    LABEL RECORDS ARE OMITTED
    RECORD CONTAINS 133 CHARACTERS
    DATA RECORD IS PRINT-LINE.
01  PRINT-LINE.
    02  FILLER                    PICTURE X(133).

FD  POLICE-FILE
    LABEL RECORDS ARE STANDARD
    RECORD CONTAINS 100 CHARACTERS
    DATA RECORD IS POLICE-FILE-RECORD.
```

Program 4.1 (cont.)

```
        01  POLICE-FILE-RECORD.
            02  FILLER                       PICTURE X(100).

        WORKING-STORAGE SECTION.


        PROCEDURE DIVISION.
            SORT INTERNAL-SORT-FILE
                ASCENDING KEY LICENSE-NUMBER
                    OF INTERNAL-SORT-FILE-RECORD
                USING POLICE-FILE
                GIVING OUTPUT-FILE.
            STOP RUN.
```

we decide to sort by descending salary within department. The output might appear as in Fig. 4.3. To accomplish this sort, we code as follows:

```
SORT  INTERNAL-SORT-FILE
ON ASCENDING KEY
     FACTORY, DEPARTMENT
ON DESCENDING KEY
```

FACTORY	DEPARTMENT	NAME	SALARY
.	.	.	.
.	.	.	.
.	.	.	.
1	2	Johnson	$125,000
1	2	Anderson	50,000
1	2	Penton	2,000
1	2	Hardy	1,000
1	2	Cooper	0
1	3	Smith	20,000
1	3	Jones	17,000
.	.	.	.
.	.	.	.
.	.	.	.
2	1	Carmen	25,000
2	1	Frenette	17,000
2	1	Smith	10,000
2	2	White	16,000
2	2	Lee	15,999
.	.	.	.
.	.	.	.
.	.	.	.

Figure 4.3 Output for DIRECTORY-FILE-SORTED.

```
SALARY
USING DIRECTORY-FILE
GIVING DIRECTORY-FILE-SORTED.
```

We should emphasize here the meaning of the words USING and GIVING. These two words indicate that *all* the records stored on DIRECTORY-FILE are to be transferred to the INTERNAL-SORT-FILE, and once sorting is finished *all* the records are to be transferred to the file DIRECTORY-FILE-SORTED. The word to note here is *all*. In the next section, we shall discuss a method that will allow us control over which records on the file are moved to the internal sort file and which records on completion of sorting are copied from the internal sort file.

4.5 INPUT AND OUTPUT PROCEDURES

In the previous section, we discussed the simplest form of the SORT verb: the form containing the key words USING and GIVING. The word USING named a file each record of which was to be transferred to an internal sort file for processing. Similarly, the key word GIVING specified a file to which all sorted records were to be transferred once the SORT-MERGE package had completed its sort of the internal sort file. COBOL provides for more complex sort procedures, some of which we discuss here.

4.5.1 Input

Sometimes it is desirable to exclude certain records from the sorting process. A detective might request a list of those automobiles stolen since the first of January; but the stolen vehicle file may contain automobiles dating back several years. Machine time is wasted if these old records are sorted. We do not want to use the word GIVING as all records will move to the internal sort file, so we need a filter of some kind to sift out the unwanted older records.

Surprisingly enough there may even be occasions when the file has been sorted but we do not want to have a copy of it at all. Suppose, as an example, that we wish to ensure that our file contains no duplicated license numbers (which is a possibility in view of the fact that cars from different states are represented). One simple way of locating duplicates is to sort the file by license number. Any two that are the same will occur together. The internal sort file can then be read record by record and each license number matched with the one preceding it. The duplicates, if they exist, can be printed out; the sorted file itself is of no interest. In other words, what we need is access to the records as soon as the sort is accomplished.

COBOL provides for these requirements by letting the user write the records to the internal sort file himself (before sorting commences) and by permitting him to copy selected records from the internal sort file once the sorting has finished. To do this a new form of the SORT verb is required. We begin by illustrating a SORT verb with the additional features and discuss what happens.

Suppose, as an example, that we wish to sort the stolen vehicle file by color of vehicle, deleting red ones from the sorting phase. Then, once sorting is accomplished, we shall print out the entire internal sort file and exclude all yellow vehicles. As a result neither red nor yellow cars should appear. Reds are not sorted; yellows are not printed. The SORT verb would look like this:

```
SORT  INTERNAL-SORT-FILE
ASCENDING KEY COLOR
INPUT PROCEDURE REMOVE-RED-RECORDS
OUTPUT PROCEDURE SELECT-NON-YELLOW-RECORDS.
```

The key words INPUT PROCEDURE name a group of one or more paragraphs headed by the words REMOVE-RED-RECORDS SECTION within the PROCEDURE DIVISION. (Recall that one or more paragraphs are made into a SECTION by giving them a name followed by the word SECTION.)

Within the REMOVE-RED-RECORDS SECTION the following actions will take place:

1. The POLICE-FILE will be OPENed for INPUT. (Remember that the internal sort file must *never* be OPENed by the programmer.)
2. Records will be read from the POLICE-FILE and, providing the COLOR field does not indicate a RED vehicle, these records will be MOVEd one by one to the SD area of the internal sort file.
3. Once each record is moved to the SD area of the internal sort file, it will be written out on the internal sort file.
4. After all records have been moved to the internal sort file, control will be transferred to the last paragraph within the REMOVE-RED-RECORDS SECTION thereby terminating

the INPUT PROCEDURE. Note that the programmer does not CLOSE the internal sort file although he may CLOSE the POLICE-FILE if he so wishes.

Two of the above steps require futher clarification.

Once a record has been MOVEd to the internal sort file, it should be written out to the internal file with the word RELEASE used in place of the word WRITE. In other words, we would make the change from WRITE INTERNAL-SORT-FILE to RELEASE INTERNAL-SORT-FILE. The key word RELEASE can be thought of as a command to give the record to the SORT-MERGE package rather than writing out to a file as is normally the case.

As with the usual form of the WRITE statement, we may employ the word FROM and have the MOVE to the SD area done automatically. We might, for instance, write

```
RELEASE INTERNAL-SORT-FILE-RECORD
        FROM POLICE-RECORD
```

As with WRITE statements, this will cause a group move of the record from the 01 entry POLICE-RECORD to the 01 entry INTERNAL-SORT-FILE-RECORD.

A word of explanation should be given regarding the need to terminate the INPUT PROCEDURE by transferring control to the last paragraph in the SECTION. The reader should think of a SECTION as a "super-paragraph" that is being PERFORMED by the SORT verb. A PERFORM is not terminated until the last statement of a paragraph or SECTION is reached. It is often convenient to have a paragraph labeled END-PARAGRAPH or some equivalent at the end of the SECTION. Once control is passed to this paragraph, the input procedure is terminated. This paragraph could contain a CLOSE of the POLICE-FILE or simply the null statement EXIT (which does nothing).

The reader should now carefully examine Program 4.2 which contains a REMOVE-RED-RECORDS SECTION. In particular, attention should be paid to the flow of control within this SECTION and to the manner in which records are transferred to the INTERNAL-SORT-FILE.

4.5.2 Output

Let us now consider the output procedure. As with the INPUT PROCEDURE the OUTPUT PROCEDURE is again a SECTION

Program 4.2

```
IDENTIFICATION DIVISION.
PROGRAM-ID. PROG4PT2.
AUTHOR. R H COOPER.
INSTALLATION. UNIVERSITY OF NEW BRUNSWICK.
DATE-WRITTEN. FEB 11,1977.
DATE-COMPILED. MAR 19,1980.
SECURITY. THIS PROGRAM IS CLASSIFIED
          UNDER THE PROVISIONS OF THE NATIONAL
          AGENCY AND IS AVAILABLE TO
          THOSE WITH A 001-007 SECURITY CLEARANCE.
REMARKS. THIS PROGRAM SORTS POLICE FILE
         USING AN INPUT PROCEDURE.


ENVIRONMENT DIVISION.

CONFIGURATION SECTION.

SOURCE-COMPUTER. IBM-370.
OBJECT-COMPUTER. IBM-370.

INPUT-OUTPUT SECTION.

FILE-CONTROL.

    SELECT POLICE-FILE
        ASSIGN TO DISK-S-POLICE
        ACCESS IS SEQUENTIAL.
    SELECT INTERNAL-SORT-FILE
        ASSIGN TO DISK-S-SORTWK01.

    SELECT PRINTER
        ASSIGN TO PRNT-S-SYSOUT.


DATA DIVISION.

FILE SECTION.

SD  INTERNAL-SORT-FILE
    RECORD CONTAINS 100 CHARACTERS
    DATA RECORD IS INTERNAL-SORT-FILE-RECORD.
01  INTERNAL-SORT-FILE-RECORD.
    02  LICENSE-NUMBER           PICTURE X(6).
    02  MAKE-OF-VEHICLE          PICTURE X(15).
    02  FILLER                   PICTURE X(2).
    02  COLOUR                   PICTURE X(9).
    02  FILLER                   PICTURE X(68).

FD  POLICE-FILE
    LABEL RECORDS ARE STANDARD
    DATA RECORD IS POLICE-FILE-RECORD
    RECORD CONTAINS 100 CHARACTERS.
01  POLICE-FILE-RECORD.
    02  LICENSE-NUMBER           PICTURE 9(6).
    02  MAKE-OF-VEHICLE          PICTURE X(15).
    02  YEAR-OF-MODEL            PICTURE 9(2).
    02  COLOUR                   PICTURE X(9).
    02  TYPE-OF-CAR              PICTURE X(6).
    02  DATE-REPORTED-STOLEN     PICTURE 9(6).
```

Program 4.2 (cont.)

```
         02  OWNER-ADDRESS             PICTURE X(18).
         02  CITY                      PICTURE X(10).
         02  STATE-OR-PROVINCE         PICTURE X(7).
         02  OWNER                     PICTURE X(16).
         02  FILLER                    PICTURE X(5).

     FD  PRINTER
         LABEL RECORDS ARE OMITTED
         DATA RECORD IS PRINT-LINE
         RECORD CONTAINS 133 CHARACTERS.
     01  PRINT-LINE.
         02  FILLER                    PICTURE X(133).

     WORKING-STORAGE SECTION.
     77  INTERNAL-SORT-FILE-EOF        PICTURE X(3).
         88  SORT-FILE-EMPTY VALUE IS 'ON'.
             88  SORT-FILE-NOT-EMPTY VALUE IS 'OFF'.
     77  POLICE-FILE-EOF               PICTURE X(3).
         88  POLICE-FILE-EMPTY VALUE IS 'ON'.
         88  POLICE-FILE-NOT-EMPTY VALUE IS 'OFF'.

     01  WS-POLICE-FILE-RECORD.
         02  LICENSE-NUMBER            PICTURE 9(6).
             02  DUMMY-RECORD-FIELD REDEFINES LICENSE-NUMBER.
                 03  FIRST-CHARACTER PICTURE X.
                     88  DUMMY-RECORD VALUE IS HIGH-VALUES.
                 03  FILLER            PICTURE X(5).
         02  MAKE-OF-VEHICLE           PICTURE X(15).
         02  YEAR-OF-MODEL             PICTURE 9(2).
         02  COLOUR                    PICTURE X(9).
         02  TYPE-OF-CAR               PICTURE X(6).
         02  DATE-REPORTED-STOLEN      PICTURE 9(6).
         02  OWNER-ADDRESS             PICTURE X(18).
         02  CITY                      PICTURE X(10).
         02  STATE-OR-PROVINCE         PICTURE X(7).
         02  OWNER                     PICTURE X(16).
         02  FILLER                    PICTURE X(5).

     01  WS-PRINT-LINE.
         02  FILLER                    PICTURE X.
         02  FILLER                    PICTURE X(5).
         02  LICENSE-NUMBER            PICTURE X(6).
         02  FILLER                    PICTURE X(5).
         02  MAKE-OF-VEHICLE           PICTURE X(15).
         02  FILLER                    PICTURE X(5).
         02  COLOUR                    PICTURE X(9).
         02  FILLER                    PICTURE X(88).


     PROCEDURE DIVISION.
     MAIN-LINE SECTION.
         PERFORM INITIALIZATION.
         PERFORM SORT-THE-RECORDS.
         STOP RUN.

     INITIALIZATION.
         MOVE 'OFF' TO INTERNAL-SORT-FILE-EOF.
         MOVE 'OFF' TO POLICE-FILE-EOF.
         OPEN INPUT POLICE-FILE.
         READ POLICE-FILE INTO WS-POLICE-FILE-RECORD
```

Program 4.2 (cont.)

```
            AT END MOVE 'ON' TO POLICE-FILE-EOF.

SORT-THE-RECORDS.
    SORT INTERNAL-SORT-FILE
        ASCENDING KEY COLOUR
            OF INTERNAL-SORT-FILE-RECORD
        DESCENDING KEY LICENSE-NUMBER
            OF  INTERNAL-SORT-FILE-RECORD
        INPUT PROCEDURE REMOVE-RED-RECORDS
        OUTPUT PROCEDURE SELECT-NON-YELLOW-RECORDS.

REMOVE-RED-RECORDS SECTION.
    PERFORM SELECT-RED-ONES
        UNTIL POLICE-FILE-EMPTY.
    GO TO END-PARAGRAPH.

SELECT-RED-ONES.
    IF COLOUR OF WS-POLICE-FILE-RECORD EQUAL 'RED'
       OR
        DUMMY-RECORD
        THEN
        NEXT SENTENCE
        ELSE
        PERFORM GIVE-SORT-THE-RECORD.
    READ POLICE-FILE INTO WS-POLICE-FILE-RECORD
        AT END MOVE 'ON' TO POLICE-FILE-EOF.

GIVE-SORT-THE-RECORD.
    MOVE WS-POLICE-FILE-RECORD
        TO INTERNAL-SORT-FILE-RECORD.
    RELEASE INTERNAL-SORT-FILE-RECORD.

END-PARAGRAPH.
    EXIT.


SELECT-NON-YELLOW-RECORDS SECTION.
    PERFORM INITIALIZATION.
    PERFORM READ-AND-PRINT-RECORDS
        UNTIL SORT-FILE-EMPTY.
    CLOSE PRINTER.
    GO TO END-PARAGRAPH.

INITIALIZATION.
    OPEN OUTPUT PRINTER.
    RETURN INTERNAL-SORT-FILE
        AT END MOVE 'ON' TO INTERNAL-SORT-FILE-EOF.

READ-AND-PRINT-RECORDS.
    IF COLOUR OF INTERNAL-SORT-FILE-RECORD
        NOT EQUAL 'YELLOW'
    THEN
        PERFORM PRINT-RECORD
    ELSE
        NEXT SENTENCE.
    RETURN INTERNAL-SORT-FILE
        AT END MOVE 'ON' TO INTERNAL-SORT-FILE-EOF.

PRINT-RECORD.
    MOVE SPACES TO WS-PRINT-LINE.
```

Program 4.2 (cont.)

```
           MOVE CORRESPONDING INTERNAL-SORT-FILE-RECORD
               TO WS-PRINT-LINE.
           WRITE PRINT-LINE FROM WS-PRINT-LINE
               AFTER POSITIONING 2 LINES.

       END-PARAGRAPH.
           EXIT.
```

within the COBOL program. In the SELECT-NON-YELLOW-RECORDS SECTION we shall perform the following procedures:

1. OPEN the PRINTER file for OUTPUT.
2. READ each record from the internal sort file.
3. Provided the COLOR field of each record does not designate a YELLOW record, move the record to the FD for the PRINTER and write it out.
4. CLOSE the printer after all records have been examined.
5. Terminate the OUTPUT PROCEDURE by transferring to the last paragraph within the SECTION containing the statement EXIT.

The reader should examine this SECTION within Program 4.2. The only new statement within the SECTION the reader will not have encountered before is the command RETURN. An internal sort file because of its special nature cannot be read. The verb READ must be replaced by the verb RETURN. Other than this, there are no other differences. The programmer may, if he wishes, use the word INTO which has the same effect as always of transferring the record from the 01 record of the input file to another level 01 item.

Previously we noted our inclination to avoid the GO TO instruction. The INPUT PROCEDURE and OUTPUT PROCEDURE have forced us to break this rule. Here, however, because we must get to the end of these sections before the SORT verb can complete its functions, we have no choice. This is perfectly fine with us; our rules do not say *never* use GO TO's; rather they say *avoid* GO TO's when possible. Here the GO TO is used as a forward jump and cannot cause any confusion.

4.6 MERGE

The verb MERGE can, in a similar manner, be used in place of the verb SORT to merge several input files with identical records in the same sort order to be placed into a single output file in this order. The following example would be used when file 1 and file 2 are already sorted:

```
MERGE file 1
ON ASCENDING
KEY key 1
USING file 2
GIVING file 3
```

4.7 CONCLUSIONS

The COBOL SORT verb is to be preferred when following the rules of simplicity and portability. However, there can be advantages to a sort routine external to the COBOL program. Since the external sort is invoked as a separate job step, less memory may be required; also the COBOL program might not need to be recompiled when the sort is changed. In the event that the sort is a single module, use of an external sort saves writing a COBOL program.

The costs of sorting increase nonlinearly with the number of records sorted. When sorts account for a significant portion of the system run time (it is worth while to time them and provide a run time statistic), program efficiency may best be improved by a careful consideration of the sorts. Are they necessary? Are they properly blocked? Are the proper sorting features implemented? When only a small portion of the file records are to be processed, it may be better to first extract these records and then sort the smaller file so obtained. The input-output procedures of COBOL do just this. It is also important to note that for the paying user, cost efficiency is usually determined by the charging algorithm of an installation and not by the run time. Again as a charging algorithm will be changed from time to time, it is worthwhile to have sort cost indicators built into the program run report. Because of the importance of timing sorts for efficient use of machine resources, we would suggest that in general sorting should be considered as a separate job step. This will make it easier to make changes and to localize the source of the inevitable errors made in doing so.

PROBLEMS

1. (a) Investigate the SORT-MERGE package provided at your installation.
   (b) Use it to sort a file.

2. Sort the file in problem 1 using the COBOL verb. Which method do you prefer? What differences are there?

3. If you have never written a sort program, investigate Quicksort and write a COBOL program for it. For references see Hoare (1962) and Knuth, Vol. III (1975). How large a file can you sort?

4. Discuss the differences between internal and external sorting.

5. Devise a flowchart to merge three sorted tapes giving two sorted tapes as output.

5 COBOL Relative I-O Files

5.1 INTRODUCTION

The need to access all the preceding records of a sequential file makes it not only complicated but slow to process a single record. The traditional batch processing methods, based on applying a transaction file against a master file, are an attempt to make the best of these disadvantages, and for many applications they provide a satisfactory solution. Although it is possible to design any on-line system to use sequential files, the result would generally be so slow as to disqualify it as on-line in most people's minds. Thus other solutions are necessary.

Direct access devices overcome the disadvantages of sequential access by permitting records to be stored and fetched independently of each other. Thus processing of records need not rely on any sequential ordering of the records; indeed, there may be no sequential ordering explicitly present. Direct access is often referred to as *random access*, although the selection of a record is not random. Direct access permits an increased flexibility in achieving system performance requirements.

The cost of direct access storage devices (DASDs) has fallen dramatically since the first appearance of drums and disks. In fact, costs have fallen far enough that for many applications the increased performance provided now outweighs price as a design factor, and for many systems on-line is now chosen where once batch would most certainly have been the solution. There are, of course, other factors besides the cost of a DASD: one in particular is the availability of low-cost data entry terminals.

The increased flexibility of random access, however, is obtained at the cost of explicit addressing of records as compared to the implicit addressing of sequential records. In a sequential file, one need only locate the address of the first record of the file, which is done implicitly by an OPEN statement. In a random file, the means to address each and every record must be present outside the file or contained in another record. Determining absolute physical addresses is complicated. Deciding how much information is needed and where extra information must be stored is a problem that can assume nightmare proportions.

With random access, there are two generic address techniques: *explicit*, where the record is specified by address, and *implicit*, where the record is specified by the unique value of a key contained in the record. Of course, ultimately all records are located explicitly by physical address but here we are only concerned with the logical address as seen by a program.

In this book, three random access techniques are treated in COBOL: *direct*, *relative*, and *indexed sequential*. We begin in this chapter with a discussion of the COBOL description of Relative I–O files.

Due to construction, the physical addressing of the storage locations of a device is complex and often the addresses may not be contiguous, which further confuses matters. Addressing within a device is tied to physical record locations, and it is quite complex to move physical records. Ideally, one would prefer to think of addresses as contiguous with simple names such as a set of integers. This is precisely the address scheme of a Relative I–O file. The initial record is assigned address 1, the next record is assigned address 2, and so on. Thus the address of a record is an integer value that reflects its position *relative* to the first record.

Historically, direct access (to be discussed in Chapter 7) came first. However, we choose to examine relative files first for two reasons: one, it is conceptually simpler to think of the addresses as integers (that is why it was devised); and two, direct access is not provided for in ANSI COBOL although it is available in some implementations.

Relative position is a logical concept and this position may not be preserved physically. By definition a *relative position* is a logical address or place name used by the system to locate the physical address. This is a problem of implementation. We should note, however, that because of the difficulties involved, Relative I-O incurs a software processing overhead cost.

The determination of the correspondence between the relative address integer and the physical address is provided by file access methods of the operating system, and the actual transferring of data to and from a storage device is handled entirely by them. Communication with these access methods is handled by the COBOL compiler in use. Thus the programmer is relieved of the need to know the intricate details of the access methods. Consequently, it is only necessary for him to describe the file and its storage structure to COBOL and to initiate access via the PROCEDURE DIVISION. The main disadvantage of Relative files is that the programmer must provide the relative address integer of a record for access but this integer is not always logically related to the content of the record.

Usually, each record must contain one or more keys that uniquely identify that record within the file, so we can associate the record with a unique relative address. Sometimes the record contains a key that can be used directly as the relative address. For instance, the records of a set of consecutive experiments numbered from 1 to *n*. In this chapter we assume that we are dealing with this simple case. In the more usual and difficult cases, the primary key must be mapped to its relative address. In some cases the record key we want to reference may not be unique, as, for example, an individual's name, and to guarantee uniqueness more qualifying information must be supplied.

In the next chapter we study techniques used to establish the mapping between the referenced record key and the relative address of that record. In Chapter 7 we examine the direct access method where we must provide the actual physical address rather than a relative key. In Chapters 8 and 9 we examine Indexed I-O files where this mapping is automatically provided. This last method is the simplest from the programmer's view; however, systems using it do not always give satisfactory performance characteristics and the other methods must be resorted to.

Relative addressing is a solution intermediate between direct physical addressing and primary key addressing. It has nearly the performance advantages of direct addressing with the advantage of simple integer addresses and independence of the need to know the physical addresses. For now, we assume simplistic relationships between the record key and the record address, ignoring efficient use of space. The main concern of this chapter is the definition and access of COBOL Relative I-O files rather than the use of Relative files in programming to construct more complex data files.

5.2 CASE STUDY: LICENSING OF VEHICLES

A state wishes to maintain a computer record of every vehicle issued a license plate within its boundaries. Each record will contain pertinent information about each vehicle licensed and will be updated whenever necessary. This updating is required whenever a vehicle is sold or scrapped, whenever a new car is introduced into the marketplace, or whenever information about the owner (such as his place of residence) is changed.

The file of all these records is to be used to provide information to individual car owners, to verify vehicle ownership, to provide statistics to government, to locate vehicle owners, and to aid police agencies.

5.2.1 Logical Analysis: Licensing of Vehicles

There are three questions that should be asked whenever a computer file is to be designed.

1. What will be the various demands on the file?
2. How is the file to be changed and how often?
3. What constitutes a record and how is it identified?

The first of these questions, "What are the various demands on the file?" helps determine whether to employ random accessing procedures or sequential accessing procedures and ultimately forces the systems analyst to choose among possible storage devices. This question in itself does not provide the final judgment, but it does provide an initial clue to the best form of solution.

In the case of licensing vehicles, we are told that the information from the file is to be used to provide information on selected individuals and on the file as a whole (statistics). These tasks can be accomplished using sequential access procedures alone, provided we are willing to search through large portions of the file to locate a single record. Two essential criteria must be used to determine the ultimate choice. How fast must the response be? How many records will eventually constitute the file?

We assume the file is large (say, at least one million records) and the government desires speedy responses to its queries. Sequential procedures should only be used when queries can be batched together and applied to the file as a whole, preferably at a time convenient to the data processing department. There is a clearly defined requirement in this case: to select records quickly. This indicates that random accessing should be employed.

The second of the first three questions, "How is the file to be changed and how often?" provides information about the maintenance program that will have to be written to update the records and provides information for throughput analysis. In the present procedure, updating of records will be initiated when a vehicle owner fills out data request forms. A built-in delay is provided by issuing a temporary vehicle permit in the case of new ownership or whenever the information carried by a driver must be up-to-date as provided by law. Updating could thus be carried out using a procedure that batches changes and then applies them when convenient.

The third question, "What constitutes a record and how is it identified?" is answered by deciding that each record on the file will contain the following fields:

(a) the make of the vehicle
(b) the vehicle's license number as assigned by the state
(c) the color of the vehicle
(d) the engine serial number
(e) the owner of the vehicle
(f) the current address of the owner
(g) the owner's driver license number (when available)
(h) the previous year's vehicle license number.

Then each record is identified by assigning each vehicle a unique license number.

5.3 RELATIVE FILE PROCESSING: VEHICLE LICENSE FILE

An implementation of the vehicle license file can be accomplished in COBOL using relative addressing. A file that can be relatively accessed is called in COBOL a *Relative I–O file.*

As with all random access files (and a relative access file is only one type of a random access file), the operating system must be able to determine or have determined for it the physical address of any given record. Recall that with Relative I–O files this is done by assigning each record in the file a unique integer called *a relative record number* that designates the logical ordinal position of each record comprising the file relative to the first record of the file. The first record is arbitrarily assigned the integer 1; the second, the integer 2; the third, the integer 3; and so on. Each record is thus ordered numerically within the file. In order to store or retrieve any given record, COBOL passes its relative record number to an appropriate access method. A calculation involving this record number and the actual starting physical address of the file is performed by system software and is used to determine the physical address of the record.

In ANSI COBOL, the records in a Relative I–O file can be of any length, and this length can vary from record to record. However, this may not always be true in the compiler being used. In IBM OS/VS COBOL, the space reserved for each record is the maximum record size specified.

It is important to stress that the relative record numbers constitute a sequential ordering of the records in the file. An individual record's relative record number is determined by the number of records preceding it in the file. In IBM OS/VS COBOL, the size of a file is determined by the amount of space made available. The number of logical records that can be stored is the amount of space available for records divided by the maximum record size.

Sometimes a programmer does not know in advance how large his file will eventually grow to be. In the event that the file becomes larger than the file space available, the file size must be redefined, and this is done by *recreating the file.* In order to overcome the difficulty inherent in recreating the file every time a new record is to be added, the programmer should make an estimate of how many records his file will have at some time in the future and create the file large enough to contain that many records. If, at a later time, it should become apparent that the number of records added at file creation was not sufficient, the programmer is forced to recreate the file to be of a more appropriate size. This is accomplished by creating a new Relative I–O file with records from the original.

5.3.1 The Relative I-O Module of COBOL

Program 5.1 creates a Relative I–O file called the VEHICLE-LICENSE-FILE. The reader should familiarize himself with this program throughout the reading of this section.

Program 5.1

```
IDENTIFICATION DIVISION.
PROGRAM-ID. PROG5PT1.


ENVIRONMENT DIVISION.

CONFIGURATION SECTION.

SOURCE-COMPUTER. IBM-370-158.
OBJECT-COMPUTER. IBM-370-158.

INPUT-OUTPUT SECTION.

FILE-CONTROL.

    SELECT CARD-READER
        ASSIGN TO CARD-SYSIN
        ORGANIZATION IS SEQUENTIAL
        ACCESS MODE IS SEQUENTIAL.

    SELECT VEHICLE-LICENSE-FILE
        ASSIGN TO DISK-LICENSE
        ORGANIZATION IS RELATIVE
    ACCESS MODE IS SEQUENTIAL
        RELATIVE KEY IS VEHICLE-LICENSE-KEY.


DATA DIVISION.

FILE SECTION.

FD  CARD-READER
    BLOCK CONTAINS 1 RECORDS
    RECORD CONTAINS 80 CHARACTERS
    LABEL RECORDS ARE OMITTED
    DATA RECORD IS CARD-READER-RECORD.
01  CARD-READER-RECORD.
    02  FILLER                      PIC X(80).

FD  VEHICLE-LICENSE-FILE
    BLOCK CONTAINS 1 RECORDS
    RECORD CONTAINS 114 CHARACTERS
    LABEL RECORDS ARE STANDARD
    DATA RECORD IS VEHICLE-LICENSE-FILE-RECORD.
01  VEHICLE-LICENSE-FILE-RECORD.
    02  OWNER-DATA.
        03  NAME                    PIC X(20).
        03  PRESENT-ADDRESS.
            04  STREET              PIC X(20).
            04  CITY                PIC X(20).
        03  DRIVER-LICENSE-NUMBER
                                    PIC ^(8).
```

Program 5.1 (cont.)

```
           02  VEHICLE-DATA.
               03  MAKE-OF-VEHICLE       PIC X(20).
               03  VEHICLE-LICENSE-NUMBER
                                         PIC X(6).
               03  COLOUR-OF-VEHICLE     PIC X(6).
               03  ENGINE-SERIAL-NUMBER
                                         PIC X(8).
               03  LAST-YEAR-LICENSE-NUMBER
                                         PIC X(6).

       WORKING-STORAGE SECTION.

       77  CARD-EOF-FLAG                 PIC X(3).
           88  CARD-EOF                  VALUE IS 'ON'.
       77  VEHICLE-LICENSE-KEY           PIC S9(8) COMP SYNC.
       77  WARNING-FLAG                  PIC X(3).

       01  WS-DATA-CARDS.
           02  CARD-1.
               03  PART-1                PIC X(68).
               03  FILLER                PIC X(12).
           02  CARD-2.
               03  PART-2                PIC X(46).
               03  FILLER                PIC X(34).


       PROCEDURE DIVISION.
           PERFORM INITIALIZATION.
           PERFORM READ-AND-COPY-TO-FILE-ROUTINE
               UNTIL CARD-EOF.
           PERFORM TERMINATION.
           STOP RUN.

       INITIALIZATION.
           OPEN  INPUT  CARD-READER
                 OUTPUT VEHICLE-LICENSE-FILE.
           MOVE 'OFF' TO CARD-EOF-FLAG WARNING-FLAG.
           PERFORM READ-DATA-CARDS.

       READ-DATA-CARDS.
           PERFORM READ-CARD-ONE.
           IF  NOT CARD-EOF PERFORM READ-CARD-TWO.

       READ-CARD-ONE.
           READ CARD-READER INTO CARD-1
               AT END MOVE 'ON'  TO CARD-EOF-FLAG.

       READ-CARD-TWO.
           READ CARD-READER INTO CARD-2
               AT END MOVE 'ON'  TO CARD-EOF-FLAG.

       READ-AND-COPY-TO-FILE-ROUTINE.
           MOVE PART-1 TO OWNER-DATA.
           MOVE PART-2 TO VEHICLE-DATA.
           WRITE VEHICLE-LICENSE-FILE-RECORD
               INVALID KEY MOVE 'ON'  TO WARNING-FLAG.
           DISPLAY VEHICLE-LICENSE-KEY.
           PERFORM READ-DATA-CARDS.

       TERMINATION.
           CLOSE CARD-READER VEHICLE-LICENSE-FILE.
```

Program 5.1 Narrative. The purpose of Program 5.1 is to create a Relative I–O file called VEHICLE-LICENSE-FILE, as diagrammed in Fig. 5.1. The input to the program is a deck of data cards containing the information to be stored in the file. Two data cards are required to provide the information for one record of VEHICLE-LICENSE-FILE. The first card of a pair is read into CARD-1; the second into CARD-2. The first card contains information about the owner of the vehicle and is moved from CARD-1 to OWNER-DATA of the VEHICLE-LICENSE-FILE-RECORD. The second card contains information about the vehicle itself and is moved from CARD-2 to VEHICLE-DATA of the VEHICLE-LICENSE-FILE-RECORD. Normally an edit check would be performed on CARD-1 and CARD-2 prior to these move operations to ensure that only correct data is transferred to the output buffer.

The output of the program is the VEHICLE-LICENSE-FILE. There is no printed output. A record is transferred to the VEHICLE-LICENSE-FILE by means of the following COBOL statement:

```
WRITE VEHICLE-LICENSE-FILE-RECORD
    INVALID KEY MOVE 'ON'
    TO WARNING-FLAG.
```

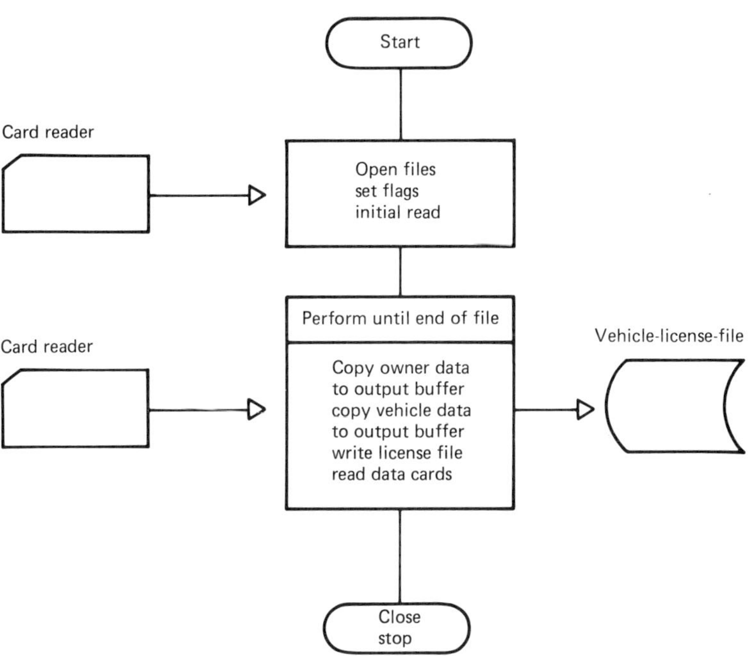

Figure 5.1 VEHICLE-LICENSE-FILE.

found in the paragraph READ-AND-COPY-TO-FILE-ROUTINE. As each record is written, its relative key value is placed in the variable VEHICLE-LICENSE-KEY (this is the file's RELATIVE KEY; compare with the SELECT clause for the file).

The INVALID KEY clause will be invoked whenever an attempt is made to write a record beyond the physical boundary of the file. In the program 'ON' will be moved to WARNING-FLAG should this event occur. No check is made in the program to detect this occurrence, but a program used for production purposes should contain an appropriate error routine.

Finally, it is important to note that the file is being created in SEQUENTIAL mode.

RELATIVE KEY

In COBOL the relative record number variable is known as the RELATIVE KEY. This is an unsigned, positive, integer data item. Recall that, generically, this is a primary key.

ENVIRONMENT DIVISION: Defining a Relative I-O File

A Relative I-O file is defined by a SELECT clause within the INPUT-OUTPUT SECTION of the ENVIRONMENT DIVISION. The following is a standard ANSI COBOL entry:

```
INPUT-OUTPUT SECTION.
        FILE-CONTROL.
        SELECT file-name
        ASSIGN TO implementor-name
        ORGANIZATION IS RELATIVE
        ACCESS MODE IS SEQUENTIAL
        RELATIVE KEY IS data-name.
```

This SELECT clause indicates that the file named is a Relative I-O file that is to be accessed in a sequential mode and names the data item associated with the file that is to be considered as the relative key. If the ACCESS MODE clause is not specified, ACCESS MODE IS SEQUENTIAL is assumed. When the access mode is sequential, the records in the file are stored in the sequence dictated by the file organization. This sequence is the order of ascending relative record numbers.

DATA DIVISION: The FD Entry for a Relative I-O File

A typical FD entry for a Relative I-O file would appear as

follows in ANSI COBOL:

```
FD file name
        BLOCK CONTAINS integer RECORDS
        RECORD CONTAINS integer CHARACTERS
        LABEL RECORDS ARE STANDARD
        DATA RECORD IS record-name.
```

The clauses following the level indicator FD are optional and may appear in any order.

The BLOCK CONTAINS clause specifies the size of a physical record on the storage device. The physical records may be variable in size and the compiler manual should be consulted. The RECORD clause indicates the size of each record (this may also be variable and the compiler manual should be consulted). The LABEL RECORDS clause indicates in this example that the data set or file labels on the storage device have been created according to STANDARD conventions but ANSI COBOL also permits them to be OMITTED (not advised). The DATA RECORD clause names the level 01 record name(s) associated with this file.

Creating a Relative I-O File

In IBM OS/VS COBOL, a file is referred to as an *unloaded* file if it has never at any time contained records. Once a record has been written (even if later it should be deleted), it becomes a *loaded* file. Normally a Relative file is created in the sequential access mode although this is not necessarily the case. In the sequential access mode, the file is opened for OUTPUT and the very first new records written to the file. The records are automatically assigned relative key 1, relative key 2, and so on. The file then becomes a loaded file. This file need not be filled, but any space left over cannot be accessed for reading purposes until records are placed there. *A file may only be opened once for* OUTPUT *in the sequential access mode.* Later, as we shall see, the file may be first opened in the I-O mode. A loaded file must never be opened for OUTPUT in the sequential access mode.

PROCEDURE DIVISION: The OPEN Statement for a Relative I-O File

The following form of the OPEN statement can be used to write records to an unloaded Relative I-O file in the sequential mode:

```
OPEN OUTPUT file-name
```

The WRITE Statement

The general form of the WRITE statement is:

```
WRITE record-name [FROM identifier]
    INVALID KEY imperative statement
```

The *record-name* is the name of the logical record in the FILE SECTION and may be qualified. If the optional FROM is used, the record is first moved from the WORKING-STORAGE SECTION before writing.

The INVALID KEY clause is invoked if an attempt is made to write a record beyond the physical boundary of the file on the storage device, and an *imperative statement* is used to define the action taken if this occurs.

After each WRITE statement, the relative record number of the record just written is placed in the data item named as the RELATIVE KEY.

The CLOSE Statement

A CLOSE statement may only be issued for a file that is already in the OPEN state. It has the form:

```
CLOSE file-name
```

The CLOSE statement should always be issued when all records have been copied to the required file. Its execution assures that the file buffers are emptied, that all required label processing is completed, and an end-of-file marker is written on the file.

5.4 PROCESSING A RELATIVE FILE SEQUENTIALLY

In the logical analysis of our hypothetical vehicle license file problem, it was decided that updates to the file could be collected and batched together for processing at one convenient time. Such updating programs are common and require sequential processing of the file.

The transactions to be applied to a file consist of three kinds: additions to the file of completely new records; orders to delete records from the master file; and changes to fields of existing records within the master file. A transaction against the master file affects only one record although there may be more than one transaction for any given record. For example, a transaction file of a phone company may have three records affecting one telephone number. The first may advise that a customer has paid his account; the second that he is to be removed from the file because he is moving; and the third that a new customer is to be added to the file with the same telephone number as the previous customer. It is a standard rule of thumb in data processing, however, that no transaction should apply to more than one master record.

A transaction and a master file record are associated if they have the same primary key. In the case of the phone company, each customer is uniquely identified by his phone number and each transaction contains the telephone number to which it applies. The primary key that labels each record on the master file is referred to as the *master key* and the primary key that identifies the master record to which a given transaction is to be applied is called a *transaction key*. A file of transactions is called a *transaction file*. As previously mentioned, the transaction file may contain many transactions with the same key; these are transactions that are to be applied to the same record on the master file. The master file consists of only one record for each primary key. This corresponds to the fact that a single customer is responsible for each telephone.

In order to carry out a sequential updating process, it is first necessary that both the master file and the one or more transaction files to be applied to it are sorted in either descending or ascending order by the primary keys distinguishing among the master records. The phone company would sort the master file and transaction file in ascending order by telephone number.

The update process uses the balance line algorithm introduced in Chapter 3. Updating clearly involves the idea of balancing master and transaction records so that records are processed only if they have the same unique keys. Rather than comparing the key from a transaction file record against the key of a master record to determine whether or not updating should take place from one record to another, all keys are compared against an independent key, called, for want of a better name, the *active key*. The active key is the smallest record key of those pointed to by the current record pointer of each file. Each file is handled by a separate routine which is entered whenever the file's current record key matches the active key. If end-of-file is reached on any file, its record key is made equal to HIGH-VALUES. The code shown in Fig. 5.2 will make this clear. Note that processing will halt when *both* files reach end-of-

```
                    .
                    .
                    .
PERFORM DETERMINE-ACTIVE-KEY.
        PERFORM BALANCE-LINE
                UNTIL ACTIVE-KEY EQUAL
                        HIGH-VALUES.
                    .
                    .
                    .
BALANCE-LINE
        IF MASTER-KEY EQUAL
        ACTIVE-KEY PERFORM MASTER-RTN.

        IF TRANSACTION-KEY EQUAL
                ACTIVE-KEY
        PERFORM TRANSACTION-RTN
                UNTIL TRANSACTION-KEY
                        NOT EQUAL ACTIVE-KEY

        PERFORM DETERMINE-ACTIVE KEY.
                    .
                    .
                    .
DETERMINE-ACTIVE-KEY
        IF MASTER-KEY LESS THAN
        TRANSACTION-KEY
        MOVE MASTER-KEY TO ACTIVE-KEY
        ELSE
        MOVE TRANSACTION-KEY TO ACTIVE-KEY.
                    .
                    .
                    .
MASTER-RTN
                    .
                    .
                    .
        READ MASTER-FILE
                AT END
                MOVE HIGH-VALUES TO MASTER-KEY.
TRANSACTION-RTN.
                    .
                    .
                    .
        READ TRANSACTION-FILE
                AT END
                MOVE HIGH-VALUES TO
                TRANSACTION-KEY.
```

Figure 5.2 Code for use of active key.

file since ACTIVE-KEY will then become HIGH-VALUES in the DETERMINE-ACTIVE-KEY routine.

Note that this coding does not show initial reads for the two files. If more transaction files are desired, they can easily be added. Convince yourself of this before proceeding.

5.4.1 COBOL Used in Sequential Processing of a Relative I-O File

A Relative I–O file can be processed sequentially. In this section we shall examine the various language statements in COBOL that make this possible. Program 5.2 reads a data deck containing additions and deletions and creates a new updated file called the NEW-VEHICLE-FILE. The statements needed to create a new Relative I–O file were discussed in the previous section. In Program 5.2, it has been assumed that the files have already been sorted by vehicle license number.

Program 5.2 Narrative. The purpose of Program 5.2, as diagrammed in Fig. 5.3, is to make additions and deletions to the VEHICLE-LICENSE-FILE created in Program 5.1. The balance line algorithm is used. VEHICLE-LICENSE-FILE is the master file; NEW-VEHICLE-FILE is the updated file. It is assumed that the VEHICLE-LICENSE-FILE is sorted by license number before Program 5.2 is executed. This could be done with a sort utility program or by writing another COBOL program. A Relative I–O file can be sorted in a COBOL program by using it in the sequential access mode with the USING format of the COBOL SORT verb or by using an INPUT PROCEDURE. (Sorting is described in detail in Chapter 4.)

The TRANSACTION-FILE contains records of two types: records to be added to the file and records to be deleted. Records to be added come in pairs as in Program 5.1 (two 80-byte records) and have the character string 'ADD' in column 7 of the first record of the pair. A DELETE record consists of only one record and contains the character string 'DELETE' in column 7. The delete transaction record contains a vehicle license number. Any record in the VEHICLE-LICENSE-FILE having this license number is to be deleted. This file is also sorted by license number.

The balance line algorithm is initialized in the usual manner. First the master and transaction files are read. Then the lowest key (license number) becomes the ACTIVE-KEY.

The MASTER-ROUTINE is executed whenever the license number of the VEHICLE-LICENSE-FILE-RECORD matches the

Program 5.2

```
IDENTIFICATION DIVISION.
PROGRAM-ID. PROG5PT2.

ENVIRONMENT DIVISION.

CONFIGURATION SECTION.

SOURCE-COMPUTER. IBM-370-158.
OBJECT-COMPUTER. IBM-370-158.

INPUT-OUTPUT SECTION.

FILE-CONTROL.

    SELECT ERROR-FILE
        ASSIGN TO DISK-ERROR
        ORGANIZATION IS SEQUENTIAL
        ACCESS MODE IS SEQUENTIAL.

    SELECT NEW-VEHICLE-FILE
        ASSIGN TO DISK-NEW
        ORGANIZATION IS RELATIVE
        ACCESS MODE IS SEQUENTIAL.

    SELECT TRANSACTION-FILE
        ASSIGN TO CARD-TRANS
        ORGANIZATION IS SEQUENTIAL
        ACCESS MODE IS SEQUENTIAL.

    SELECT VEHICLE-FILE
        ASSIGN TO DISK-LICENSE
        ORGANIZATION IS RELATIVE
        ACCESS MODE IS SEQUENTIAL.

DATA DIVISION.

FILE SECTION.

FD  ERROR-FILE
    BLOCK CONTAINS 1 RECORDS
    RECORD CONTAINS 80 CHARACTERS
    LABEL RECORDS ARE STANDARD
    DATA RECORD IS ERROR-FILE-RECORD.
01  ERROR-FILE-RECORD.
    02  FILLER                      PIC X(80).

FD  NEW-VEHICLE-FILE
    BLOCK CONTAINS 1 RECORDS
    RECORD CONTAINS 114 CHARACTERS
    LABEL RECORDS ARE STANDARD
    DATA RECORD IS NEW-VEHICLE-FILE-RECORD.
01  NEW-VEHICLE-FILE-RECORD.
    02  FILLER                      PIC X(114).

FD  TRANSACTION-FILE
    BLOCK CONTAINS 1 RECORDS
    RECORD CONTAINS 80 CHARACTERS
```

Program 5.2 (cont.)

```
           LABEL RECORDS ARE OMITTED
           DATA RECORDS ARE TRANSACTION-FILE-RECORD-1
                            TRANSACTION-FILE-RECORD-2.
       01  TRANSACTION-FILE-RECORD-1.
           02  TRANSACTION-KEY          PIC X(6).
           02  TRANSACTION-CODE         PIC X(6).
           02  TRANSACTION-DATA-1       PIC X(68).
       01  TRANSACTION-FILE-RECORD-2.
           02  FILLER                   PIC X(12).
           02  TRANSACTION-DATA-2       PIC X(46).
           02  FILLER                   PIC X(22).

       FD  VEHICLE-FILE
           BLOCK CONTAINS 1 RECORDS
           RECORD CONTAINS 114 CHARACTERS
           LABEL RECORDS ARE STANDARD
           DATA RECORD IS VEHICLE-FILE-RECORD.
       01  VEHICLE-FILE-RECORD.
           02  FILLER                   PIC X(88).
           02  MASTER-KEY               PIC X(6).
           02  FILLER                   PIC X(20).


       WORKING-STORAGE SECTION.
       77  ACTIVE-KEY                   PIC X(6).
       77  MASTER-SWITCH                PIC X(3).

       01  WS-VEHICLE-FILE-RECORD.
           02  DATA-1                   PIC X(68).
           02  DATA-2                   PIC X(46).


       PROCEDURE DIVISION.

           PERFORM INITIALIZATION.
           PERFORM BALANCE-LINE-ROUTINE
               UNTIL ACTIVE-KEY = HIGH-VALUES.
           PERFORM TERMINATION.
           STOP RUN.

       INITIALIZATION.
           OPEN INPUT  VEHICLE-FILE TRANSACTION-FILE
                OUTPUT NEW-VEHICLE-FILE ERROR-FILE.
           MOVE 'OFF' TO MASTER-SWITCH.
           PERFORM READ-MASTER-FILE.
           PERFORM READ-TRANSACTION-FILE.
           PERFORM DETERMINE-ACTIVE-KEY.

       READ-MASTER-FILE.
           READ VEHICLE-FILE
               AT END MOVE HIGH-VALUES TO MASTER-KEY.

       READ-TRANSACTION-FILE.
           READ TRANSACTION-FILE
               AT END MOVE HIGH-VALUES TO TRANSACTION-KEY.

       DETERMINE-ACTIVE-KEY.
           IF  MASTER-KEY < TRANSACTION-KEY
               MOVE MASTER-KEY TO ACTIVE-KEY
               ELSE MOVE TRANSACTION-KEY TO ACTIVE-KEY.
```

Program 5.2 (cont.)

```
BALANCE-LINE-ROUTINE.
    PERFORM MASTER-ROUTINE.
    PERFORM TRANSACTION-ROUTINE
        UNTIL TRANSACTION-KEY NOT = ACTIVE-KEY.
    PERFORM WRITE-RECORD-TO-NEW-FILE.
    PERFORM DETERMINE-ACTIVE-KEY.

MASTER-ROUTINE.
    IF  MASTER-KEY = ACTIVE-KEY
        MOVE VEHICLE-FILE-RECORD
            TO WS-VEHICLE-FILE-RECORD
        MOVE 'ON' TO MASTER-SWITCH
        PERFORM READ-MASTER-FILE.

TRANSACTION-ROUTINE.
    IF  TRANSACTION-CODE = 'ADD'
        IF  MASTER-SWITCH = 'OFF'
            MOVE TRANSACTION-DATA-1 TO DATA-1
            PERFORM READ-TRANSACTION-FILE
            MOVE TRANSACTION-DATA-2 TO DATA-2
            MOVE 'ON' TO MASTER-SWITCH
            ELSE PERFORM ERROR-ROUTINE-1
        ELSE
        IF  TRANSACTION-CODE = 'DELETE'
            IF  MASTER-SWITCH = 'ON'
                MOVE 'OFF' TO MASTER-SWITCH
                ELSE PERFORM ERROR-ROUTINE-2
            ELSE PERFORM ERROR-ROUTINE-2.
    PERFORM READ-TRANSACTION-FILE.

ERROR-ROUTINE-1.
    PERFORM ERROR-ROUTINE-2.
    PERFORM READ-TRANSACTION-FILE.
    PERFORM ERROR-ROUTINE-2.

ERROR-ROUTINE-2.
    DISPLAY TRANSACTION-FILE-RECORD-1.
    WRITE ERROR-FILE-RECORD
        FROM TRANSACTION-FILE-RECORD-1.

WRITE-RECORD-TO-NEW-FILE.
    IF  MASTER-SWITCH = 'ON'
        WRITE NEW-VEHICLE-FILE-RECORD
            FROM WS-VEHICLE-FILE-RECORD
        MOVE 'OFF' TO MASTER-SWITCH.

TERMINATION.
    CLOSE VEHICLE-FILE TRANSACTION-FILE
          NEW-VEHICLE-FILE ERROR-FILE.
```

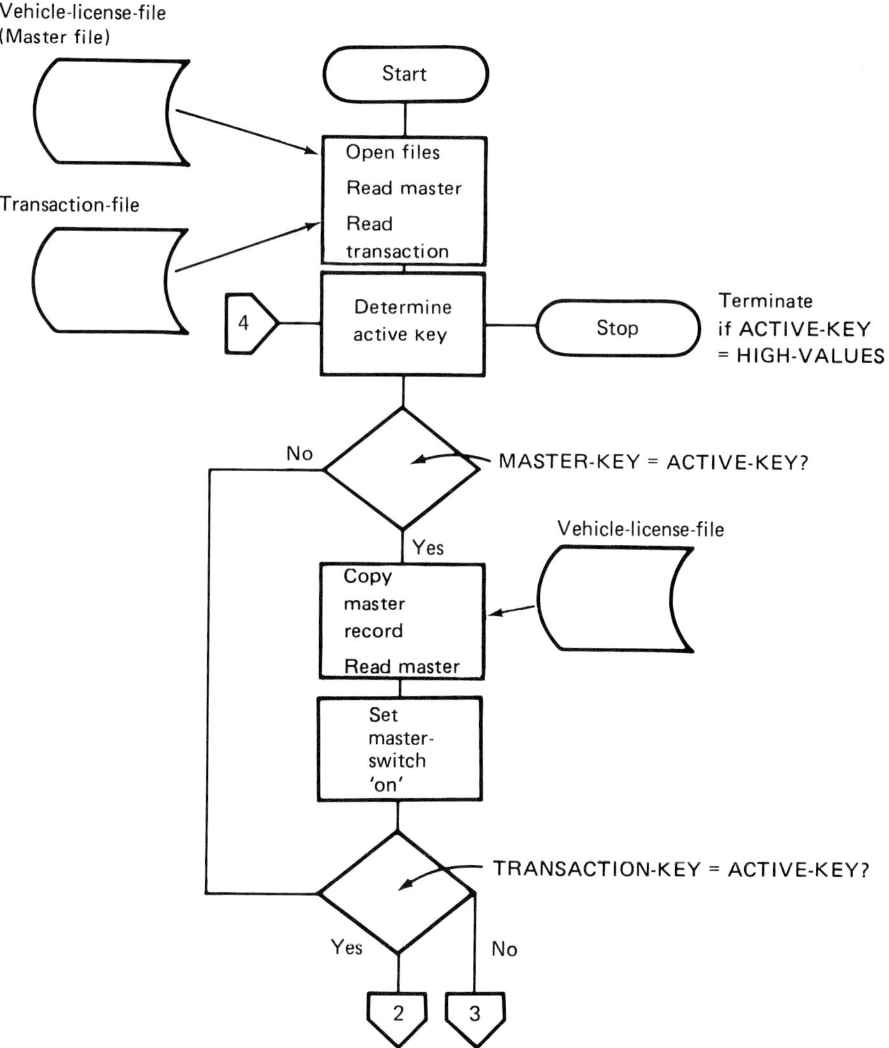

Figure 5.3 Flowchart for Program 5.2.

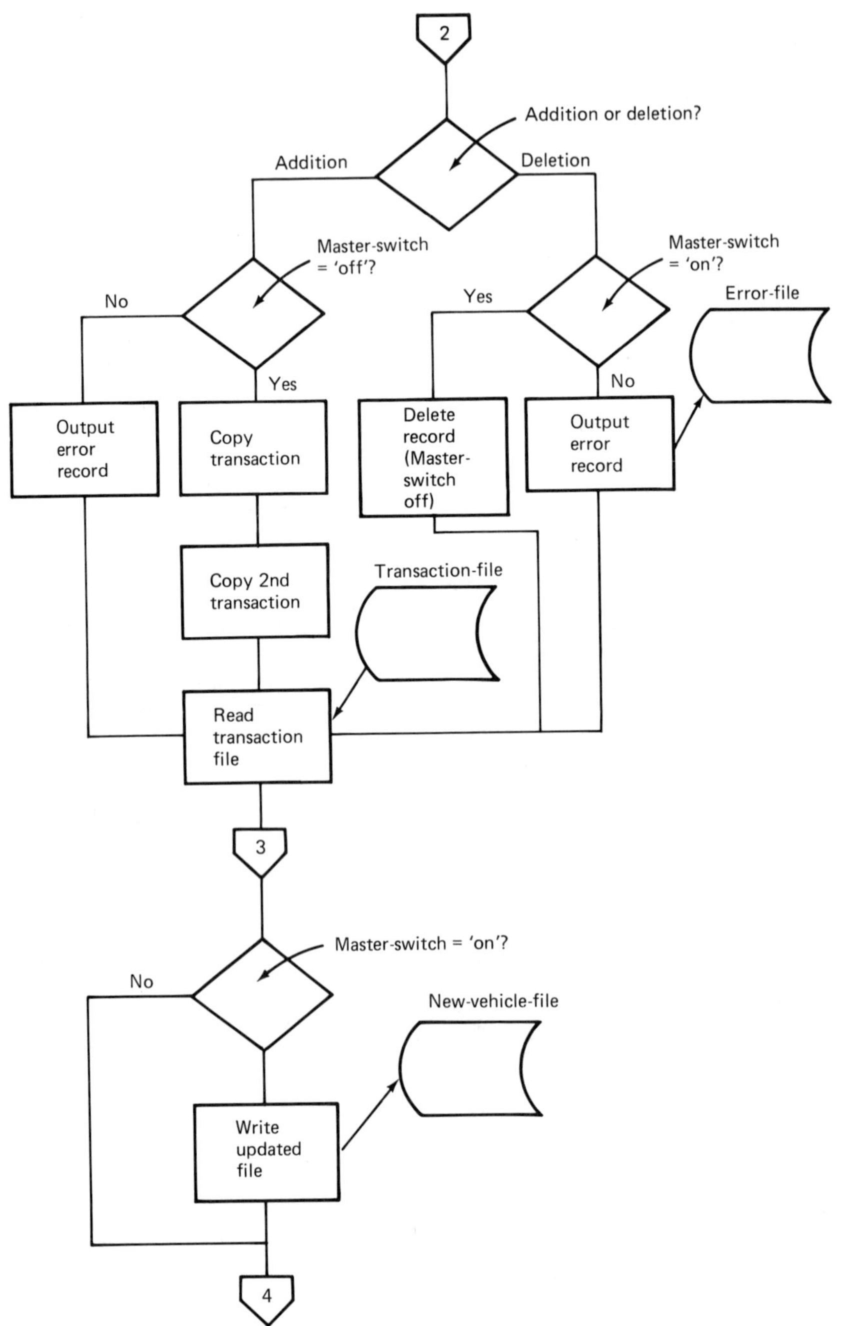

Figure 5.3 (cont.)

active key. The routine moves the VEHICLE-LICENSE-FILE-RECORD to a temporary area called WS-VEHICLE-FILE-RECORD in the WORKING-STORAGE SECTION. It then moves 'ON' to MASTER-SWITCH and reads another record.

Following the conditional execution of the MASTER-ROUTINE, a check is made to see whether or not the TRANSACTION-ROUTINE should be executed. This routine will be executed repeatedly as long as the TRANSACTION-KEY matches the ACTIVE-KEY. On entry to the TRANSACTION-ROUTINE the kind of transaction to be processed is determined. Additions are performed before deletions. In the event that the TRANSACTION-CODE is 'ADD', a check is made to see whether or not the MASTER-SWITCH is 'OFF' . This switch will only register 'ON' if a record having the same license number already exists, i.e., if a definite error has occurred. If the switch is off, the transaction record is moved to working storage and the second record of the add pair is read in. This too is moved to working storage. The MASTER-SWITCH is then turned 'ON' to indicate that a record is ready for copying to the NEW-VEHICLE-FILE. In the event that the transaction is a 'DELETE' , the procedure is almost the opposite to that for an addition. This time the MASTER-SWITCH should be 'ON' , indicating a record is available for copying to the NEW-VEHICLE-FILE (otherwise there is no record to delete). All that need be done in this case is to turn the MASTER-SWITCH off, thereby inhibiting its copy.

Following the TRANSACTION-ROUTINE, the record is written to the NEW-VEHICLE-FILE if the MASTER-SWITCH is 'ON' . Finally, a new determination of ACTIVE-KEY is made. Processing will terminate when both the TRANSACTION-FILE and the VEHICLE-LICENSE-FILE have reached an end-of-file.

Note that we have used the Relative I–O file, VEHICLE-LICENSE-FILE, in the sequential access mode. In the next program we shall use it in the random mode.

The OPEN Statement

To open a file for sequential input that has been declared as a Relative I–O file, code the following:

OPEN INPUT *file-name*

Note that prior to the successful execution of this statement no statement that references this file may be executed.

Reading Records Sequentially

Two statements that are important to reading records sequentially are the START statement and the READ statement.

The START statement is used to provide a logical positioning in the file, or in other words it specifies where in the file sequential reading of the records is to commence. It has the general format:

START *file-name* KEY *relation*
  data-name INVALID KEY *imperative statement*

where *file-name* is the name of the file that is to be positioned and *relation* is one of the following:

IS EQUAL TO
IS =
IS GREATER THAN
IS >
IS NOT LESS THAN
IS NOT <

and *data-name* is the name of the data item specified in the RELATIVE KEY clause of the SELECT statement in the INPUT–OUTPUT SECTION.

An example will clarify the function of the START statement.

```
START VEHICLE-LICENSE-FILE
      KEY IS > VEHICLE-KEY
INVALID KEY MOVE 'ON' TO
WARNING-FLAG.
```

This statement asks that the file named VEHICLE-LICENSE-FILE be positioned at the first record whose relative record number is greater than the integer currently stored in the data item called VEHICLE-KEY which is, in fact, the RELATIVE KEY for this file. The INVALID KEY phrase is invoked when the comparison is not satisfied by any record in the file. Following execution of the INVALID KEY clause, execution returns to the statement following the START statement. If processing is to begin at the first record in the file, the START statement is not required.

Only one format of the READ statement is permitted with Relative I–O files when they are accessed sequentially and this is:

READ *file-name* [INTO *identifier*]
  AT END *imperative statement*

This is the same format of the READ statement encountered with sequential files used in chapter 3 and performs the same function. Specifically, one record is read from the file. If the optional INTO clause is specified, the record once read into the buffer associated with the file is placed in the area of the WORKING-STORAGE SECTION specified as the *identifier.*

The *imperative statement* following the key words AT END is executed when there are no more logical records left to read in the file. Once this *imperative statement* has been executed, control is returned to the statement following the READ statement.

5.5 RANDOM ACCESSING OF RELATIVE I-O FILES

Once a Relative I-O file has been created in the sequential mode, we are free to access its records in the random mode. In the random mode, a record is fetched by specifying its relative record number. Similarly, a record is stored by specifying its relative record number.

In order to read or write a specific record, its relative record number must first be stored in the RELATIVE KEY specified for that file. To illustrate this process, we reconsider the VEHICLE-LICENSE-FILE created in Program 5.1. Suppose now that we wish to write a COBOL program that, given a relative record number on a data card, will fetch the record with this number from the file and rewrite it after changing the owner's address, which is also given on the input data card. The program created for this purpose is Program 5.3. In this section we shall discuss the necessary COBOL language features employed in this program.

Program 5.3 Narrative. In Program 5.2 additions and deletions were made to the VEHICLE-LICENSE-FILE by using it in the sequential access mode and programming the balance line algorithm. VEHICLE-LICENSE-FILE is, however, a Relative I-O file which means that it could have been used in the random access mode (not, of course, with the balance line algorithm which requires a sorted sequential file). The random mode allows direct addition and deletion of records. The DELETE instruction can be used for deletions and the WRITE or REWRITE used for additions. A word of caution, however. A Relative I-O file cannot grow in physical size as was previously mentioned in the text. Additions are thus a tricky business. Additions must replace already existing records. If dummy records are available, this is straightforward. Failing this, a decision must be

Program 5.3

```
IDENTIFICATION DIVISION.
PROGRAM-ID.  PROG5PT3.
ENVIRONMENT DIVISION.
CONFIGURATION SECTION.
SOURCE-COMPUTER. IBM-3032.
OBJECT-COMPUTER. IBM-3032.
INPUT-OUTPUT SECTION.
FILE-CONTROL.
    SELECT INPUT-FILE
        ASSIGN TO CARD-INPUT
        ORGANIZATION IS SEQUENTIAL
        ACCESS MODE IS SEQUENTIAL.
    SELECT VEHICLE-FILE
        ASSIGN TO DISK-VEHICLE
        ORGANIZATION IS RELATIVE
        ACCESS MODE IS RANDOM
        RELATIVE KEY IS FILE-KEY.
DATA DIVISION.
FILE SECTION.
FD  INPUT-FILE
    BLOCK CONTAINS 1 RECORDS
    LABEL RECORDS ARE OMITTED
    RECORD CONTAINS 80 CHARACTERS
    DATA RECORD IS INPUT-FILE-RECORD.
01  INPUT-FILE-RECORD.
    02  RECORD-NUMBER              PIC 999.
    02  NEW-ADDRESS                PIC X(40).
    02  FILLER                     PIC X(37).
FD  VEHICLE-FILE
    BLOCK CONTAINS 1 RECORDS
    RECORD CONTAINS 114 CHARACTERS
    LABEL RECORDS ARE STANDARD
    DATA RECORD IS VEHICLE-FILE-RECORD.
01  VEHICLE-FILE-RECORD.
    02  FILLER          PIC X(20).
    02  PRESENT-ADDRESS            PIC X(40).
    02  FILLER                     PIC X(54).
WORKING-STORAGE SECTION.
77  FILE-KEY                       PIC S9(8)
        USAGE IS COMP SYNC.
77  INPUT-EOF-FLAG                 PIC X(3).
    88  INPUT-EOF       VALUE IS 'ON'.
77  WARNING-FLAG                   PIC X(3).
PROCEDURE DIVISION.
    PERFORM INITIALIZATION.
    PERFORM CHANGE-ADDRESS-ROUTINE
        UNTIL INPUT-EOF.
    PERFORM TERMINATION.
    STOP RUN.
INITIALIZATION.
    OPEN I-O   VEHICLE-FILE
```

Program 5.3 (cont.)

```
                 INPUT INPUT-FILE.
             MOVE 'OFF' TO INPUT-EOF-FLAG.
             MOVE 'OFF' TO WARNING-FLAG.
             PERFORM READ-INPUT-FILE.

         READ-INPUT-FILE.
             READ INPUT-FILE
                 AT END MOVE 'ON' TO INPUT-EOF-FLAG.

         CHANGE-ADDRESS-ROUTINE.
             MOVE RECORD-NUMBER TO FILE-KEY.
             PERFORM READ-VEHICLE-FILE.
             DISPLAY VEHICLE-FILE-RECORD.
             IF WARNING-FLAG = 'OFF'
                 MOVE NEW-ADDRESS TO PRESENT-ADDRESS
                 REWRITE VEHICLE-FILE-RECORD.
             PERFORM READ-VEHICLE-FILE.
             DISPLAY VEHICLE-FILE-RECORD.
             PERFORM READ-INPUT-FILE.

         READ-VEHICLE-FILE.
             READ VEHICLE-FILE
                 INVALID KEY MOVE 'ON' TO WARNING-FLAG.

         TERMINATION.
             CLOSE INPUT-FILE
                   VEHICLE-FILE.
```

made to delete records to make room for new ones. Program 5.3 makes changes to the VEHICLE-LICENSE-FILE in the random mode. Changes to existing records do not entail the same complications as additions. Records to be changed must obviously exist. Making room for them is not a problem.

In order to make a change to a record, its relative key must be known beforehand. We assume in Program 5.3 that the relative keys of records to be changed are available and form part of the input data to the program. In the next chapter, we shall study procedures that enable us to determine the relative keys to records given a more appropriate key, such as the vehicle license number.

The input to Program 5.3 consists of a file labeled INPUT-FILE, a sequential file of records that consists of relative keys and changes to the address field of records in the VEHICLE-LICENSE-FILE. These records are read one by one. The relative key of each record is moved from RECORD-NUMBER in the incoming record to FILE-KEY, the RELATIVE KEY of the VEHICLE-LICENSE-FILE. Next, a READ is executed, bringing in the record to be changed.

The field NEW-ADDRESS of INPUT-FILE-RECORD replaces the PRESENT-ADDRESS in the VEHICLE-LICENSE-FILE-RECORD and a REWRITE is executed. The REWRITE causes the VEHICLE-LICENSE-FILE-RECORD to be written back to the location on the mass storage device from which it came. This is only possible because the record has not changed in size during updating. Unlike Program 5.2, processing halts when there are no further records in the INPUT-FILE of record changes. Only those records that are to be changed are actually read and rewritten. Clearly this form of updating is applicable to on-line terminal systems where instantaneous responses are required. Changes can, as we have seen, be made with a balance line algorithm and sequential files, but many records that are not to be affected by updates must be read as well and the entire file must be recopied. More onus is placed, however, on the programmer when using random access. Changes destroy the current content of the file and adequate backup must be available in the event of error. Random access provides high speeds, but as with cars, the driver must be more careful.

Declaring a File

In order to process a Relative I–O file in the random mode, the clause

```
ACCESS MODE IS RANDOM
```

must be added to the SELECT clause associated with this file. The SELECT clause for a Relative I–O file in the random access mode has the following format:

```
SELECT file-name
        ASSIGN TO implementor-name
        ORGANIZATION IS RELATIVE
        ACCESS MODE IS RANDOM
        RELATIVE KEY IS data-name.
```

This select clause indicates that the file named is a Relative I–O file that is to be processed in the random mode and designates the variable that is to be used as the relative key for the file. As previously mentioned, when the access mode is random, the value of the RELATIVE KEY data item indicates the record to be accessed.

Defining a File

The FD entry for the file is the same as for file creation. Specifically a typical entry is:

```
FD file-name
        LABEL RECORDS ARE STANDARD
        BLOCK CONTAINS integer RECORDS
        RECORD CONTAINS integer CHARACTERS
        DATA RECORD IS record-name.
```

In some implementations it may not be possible to block records with Relative I-O files.

The OPEN Statement

If records are only to be read and not written, the programmer should code:

```
OPEN INPUT file-name
```

and if he desires to do both reading and writing he should code

```
OPEN I-O file-name
```

The READ Statement

The format of the READ statement to be employed with Relative I-O files in the random access mode is as follows:

```
READ file-name [INTO identifier]
        INVALID KEY imperative statement
```

This statement causes one record to be read from the file named and transferred to the WORKING-STORAGE SECTION record named as the *identifier* of the optional INTO clause it specifies.

It is assumed that *prior* to the READ statement being executed, the object record's relative record number has been stored in the RELATIVE KEY data item. If the RELATIVE KEY points to a record that is not an element of the file, then the imperative statement following the key words INVALID KEY is invoked. Upon completion of this imperative statement, control returns to the statement following the READ statement.

The WRITE Statement

The format of the WRITE statement to be used with Relative I-O files in the random access mode is as follows:

```
WRITE record-name [FROM identifier]
        INVALID KEY imperative statement
```

This statement causes one record stored at *record-name* or at *identifier* (if the optional FROM option is used) to be transferred to the associated Relative I-O file. The optional FROM causes a move of the record at *identifier* in the WORKING STORAGE SECTION to the *record-name* which must be the name of the level 01 record named in the FD associated with the file. It is assumed that the relative record number of the record to be written has been stored in the RELATIVE KEY prior to the execution of the WRITE statement. This statement should only be used to add *new* records to the file or to replace records that have been deleted with the DELETE statement.

The REWRITE Clause

COBOL provides for a second output statement for a Relative I-O file and this is the REWRITE statement. The REWRITE statement is specifically intended to be used when the user wishes to logically replace a record in the file. Since a record should not be rewritten to a file unless it has been changed, this statement should be used whenever a record has been updated in a Relative I-O file. The general format for a REWRITE statement is

```
REWRITE record-name [FROM identifier]
    INVALID KEY imperative statement
```

Specifically, the REWRITE statement causes the record named as *record-name* to be rewritten to the file, where *record-name* is the data item named as the level 01 entry for the FD entry of the associated file within the FILE SECTION of the DATA DIVISION. If the optional FROM is included, then the record is first moved to the output buffer from its storage area within the WORKING-STORAGE SECTION called *identifier*.

It is assumed that, prior to rewriting, the relative record number of the record to be rewritten to the file has been stored in the data item named as the RELATIVE KEY of the associated file. In the event that an attempt is made to rewrite a record that does not exist in the file, the *imperative statement* following the key words INVALID KEY is invoked. The REWRITE clause may only be used if the file is opened for I-O.

The DELETE Statement

The DELETE statement can be used to delete a record from a Relative I-O file provided the file has been opened in the I-O mode.

The general format of the DELETE statement is:

```
DELETE file-name RECORD
    INVALID KEY imperative statement
```

where *file-name* is the name of the associated file.

The relative record number of the record to be removed from the file is assumed to be stored in the RELATIVE KEY data item prior to the execution of the DELETE statement. Once the DELETE statement has been executed, the identified record has been logically removed from the file and can no longer be accessed. The contents of the RELATIVE KEY are not affected by execution of the DELETE statement.

If the file does not contain the record that is to be deleted, the *imperative statement* following the key words INVALID KEY is executed and then control returns to the statement following the DELETE statement.

Sequential Accessing of Records Using Random Access

It is worth noting that even though a file is opened in the random access mode, it can still be treated as though it were a file in the sequential access mode by careful programming. Specifically, the user can set the RELATIVE KEY to 1; read the first record; add 1 to the RELATIVE KEY; read record 2; add 1 to the RELATIVE KEY; read record 3; and so on. It is *not*, however, possible to issue a START statement, because a START statement cannot be issued when the file is opened with ACCESS IS RANDOM. ANSI COBOL allows for intermixing of sequential and random access in the dynamic mode; in this case, ACCESS IS DYNAMIC would be used.

5.6 BLOCKING RELATIVE I-O FILES

IBM OS/VS COBOL does not allow the blocking of Relative I-O records. This is not too surprising, as blocking is generally done to provide for the fetching of a group of sequential records with one READ. In essence, the records are batched together, fetched, and stored as one long physical record. This makes most sense with sequential files, as records are then needed one after the other. With Relative I-O files, when access is random, records do not necessarily follow one another. However, there are instances where space saving justifies blocking. The principle of locality of reference says that retrieval of records tends to occur in the same general area. Earlier in this chapter we said that the whole purpose of Relative I-O was to allow flexibility in fetching records. They could be fetched in any order.

There are times, however, when the request for records from a file may well be in sequential order. In an airline reservation system, the requests for information can often be handled sequentially. A traveler often wants to know whether there are seats on any of the flights from New York, say, to Dallas on this coming Saturday. Here it might be useful to read a whole series of records at once, rather than fetch each plane's record individually. If an effort to store similar flights in sequential order on the disk were made, blocking would prove useful. Note, however, that the original request is still random. What flight information is requested? The next user may well be interested in next summer's flights to Mexico. Rather than block these records, perhaps a more appropriate procedure to consider is the storing of the information regarding all flights from city A to city B on a Saturday as one large record. Whenever a user wishes the information, the large record can be brought into core and there broken up into its various flights. The large record is still a Relative I-O record. This technique is sometimes called *internal blocking*. It is really a matter of carefully deciding in the original design stages what should constitute the contents of a record on the file.

5.7 CONCLUSIONS

In summary, the records of a Relative file are addressed as integers relative to their position with respect to the first record of the file. The flexibility of direct access to a record is tempered by the disadvantage that the programmer must establish a relationship between the record key and the integer record address. Although a simple relationship may exist that can be exploited; more often complex programming may be required to establish the relationship and to manage space. Such considerations are explored in the next chapter.

The COBOL Relative I-O module provides either random or sequential access of a relative file. It is an example of an indexed file organization. As it provides few features, it is fast and has little overhead. Basically, it isolates the programmer from the physical address but requires him to manage space and record assignment. These files must exist on DASDs or what is termed *mass storage* in COBOL.

The relative address acts much like an index of a table. One might view a relative file as a table in external memory and the same uses apply. Of course, they are much slower than tables. Obviously, relative files are best associated with records that have ascending consecutive numbers as the file grows.

In the sequential access mode, records are processed in ascending order of the relative record numbers. In the random access mode, the programmer must first determine the relative address number. Module level 2 allows mixing of random and sequential access using the dynamic access mode. There are a number of features we have not discussed; they are best learned from the appropriate software manual.

Backup requirements exist as for sequential files rewritten in place. The two major disadvantages are the need to relate the primary key to the relative address, which may be difficult to do efficiently, and the fact that a file must be completely written when created, which may be before we wish to use the records. Also, when blocking cannot be used, Relative I–O files may be inefficient. They are less efficient than sequential files for sequential access and thus should not be used unless random access is required.

PROBLEMS

1. What is the main difficulty in addressing a Relative I–O file? Give an example where this difficulty is not a problem. Does your example use all of the file records?

2. Change the ACCOUNT-DIRECTORY file of Program 3.3 to a Relative I–O file.

3. In Problem 2, what difficulties will arise with your solution if new accounts are added? How would you solve these problems? Will you be able to obtain the trial balance order of accounts?

4. In Problem 2, suppose you want to maintain account detail rather than just summary totals. Devise a file layout. (You may make assumptions to obtain a solution.) Discuss the problems with your solution, if any, and comment on your assumptions as they affect the future of Profit Inc.'s accounting system.

5. Discuss the limitations of Relative I–O as you see them.

6. Discuss the advantages of Relative I–O as you see them.

7. Write a program to print the names and addresses of car owners.

8. It is necessary to mail letters to the owners of 1976 Fords with rust problems. Write a program to produce a list of such owners in alphabetic order.

6

Record Addressing Techniques

In Chapter 5 the concept of a Relative I-O file was introduced as one technique for organizing records on a mass storage device. With this technique, each record could be retrieved independently of the others in the file by determining its relative record number, storing this integer in the RELATIVE KEY of the file, and then issuing a READ statement. The method required that the relative position of a record in the file be known before it could be accessed. This is because the logical address used to fetch each record is its position *relative* to the first record of the file. Ignored in Chapter 5 was the burden on the file user of remembering each record's relative address. A user is seldom aware of the relative address of the record he wishes to access. Thus, the basic problem of file addressing is: Given a primary key, how does the program locate the record belonging to this primary key?

6.1 INTRODUCTION

Consider the following scenario: A police officer walking his beat, notices a Ford sedan parked in a No Parking Zone, across the street from the Farmer's Loan and Trust. The officer vaguely recalls a car of this description posted on the bulletin board detailing stolen vehicles. Realizing that he needs confirmation and should summon assistance, he quickly walks to the police call box on the corner and phones the station. To his dispatcher he reports the license number and a brief description of the vehicle.

The duty of the dispatcher is to query a file of stolen vehicles, to determine if this is indeed a stolen vehicle, and, if so, to alert nearby patrol cars. The dispatcher is confronted with several problems. If the vehicle is stolen, its record will be on the file, but where? If it is not stolen, it will not be on the file, but how is he to know? In both cases the answer can be determined by checking sequentially through every record on the file. This defeats the major reason for using relative files which is the direct access of a record of interest or, alternatively, the direct determination of its absence. Thus the relative address must be known before *direct access* of a record can occur.

In applications programming, determining the relative record number of a given record can be more complex than simple recall. A relative record number is not usually fixed forever like a social security number. It is a function of the storage location of the record rather than its logical content. This address number will change if the record is relocated within the file or if the number of records between the beginning of the file and the record in question is altered during a recreation of the file. In addition, the record may not yet be a member of the file, and in this case there is no relative record number for it.

In this chapter, techniques will be developed to associate a relative record number with the primary key of each file record. We consider techniques that determine the relative key of a record in a file from the record primary key and determine whether or not a given record is a valid file member. The dynamic nature of a file largely determines the complexity of the method used to determine the relative key. Many methods only allow a limited amount of change and growth in a file; in some cases the file may be reorganized physically in a separate operation. Some techniques adapt better to periodic reorganization than others.

6.2 ADDRESS DETERMINATION

Although our immediate problem is to discover how to adapt Relative I-O to more general file organizational problems than those posed in Chapter 5, methods of determining the address of a record have wide and essential uses in file processing. Such techniques are fundamental to data base design, and our discussion is by no means limited to Relative I-O. The user of a file is only interested in the contents of the records and not in their physical locations. Knowledge of the physical location of a record is forced on the programmer, for instance, when he uses Relative I-O. Whenever possible, *a user should be relieved of the burden of knowing a record's physical location.*

The essential problem is to provide a mapping from the set of all possible keys, called the *key space*, to the set of all possible addresses, called the *address space*. Although the mappings from key space to address space can be viewed as mathematical functions (recall that a function is a set of ordered pairs), it should be noted that functions do not always have convenient representations such as those we see in algebra. This is further complicated by the fact that it is desirable for these address mappings to be dynamic, and, consequently, the definition of a *function may be violated*. Thus, while at a static point in time an address mapping is a function on its key space, we cannot ignore time when considering real files. For convenience we may consider a dynamic address mapping as a parametric set of functions on the key space.

From an abstract view, the addressing problem is one of functional representation. The difficulty is that the functions we desire do not always have convenient and concise representations.

An interesting result from computational theory proves that all sets of strings can be represented by the positive integers. Thus, for our discussion, we can assume that the address space always consists of relative addresses.

There are two basic types of methods for locating a record, given its primary key: search and calculation. There are many ways to search a file but we only consider some basic methods. The simplest method of locating a file record is to access each record of the file and examine its primary key for a match to the given key. Since this requires bringing each record into memory, it is crude and inefficient. It is more usual to keep a separate file of the primary keys and associated record addresses. This key file takes less storage space than the file and it can often be stored in memory or in large storage blocks which can be brought into memory as required. This separate file is usually arranged as a table and has various names, such as "directory," "index," or "dictionary," depending on its form.

There are many ways to calculate an address from a key. Calculation attempts to convert a primary key into an address by some sort of algorithm. When this can be done, it is faster than searching techniques. Unfortunately, direct conversion is not always possible and considerable complexity can then arise, as we shall see.

Each technique strongly affects the physical organization of data on the file, the speed of retrieval, and the problems of change associated with a dynamic file. The choice of technique is largely dependent on its characteristics and their resulting effect on the efficiency and performance of the file. In this chapter, we examine some of the better-known techniques and their relation to file organization. In particular, we examine in detail the important method of division hashing.

6.3 DIRECTORY TABLE

Conceptually, the most obvious solution to the problem of associating the primary key of each record with its relative record number is to keep a paired list of both. Such a list is shown in Fig. 6.1, where the social security number of a citizen is kept alongside the relative record number where his record is stored. The advantage of the list is that it is smaller than the file and can be more efficiently manipulated in memory than the file. As this list takes more than one page, we have shown only a small segment. No doubt the reader has recog-

KEY Social security number	ADDRESS Relative record number
⋮	⋮
400 70 0015	204
400 70 0016	16
400 70 0017	2016
400 70 0018	102462
400 70 0019	0
⋮	⋮

Figure 6.1 Directory table segment.

nized this functional representation as exhaustive enumeration. If a request is made for detailed information on the citizen whose social security number is 400 70 0016, his record can be fetched from the social security file by specifying relative record number 16. This list is called a *directory* and is usually stored on an auxiliary storage device because the number of entries matches the size of the file.

A directory may be created for an existing file by scanning the entire file and recording the primary key (the social security number in the above example) of each record fetched, along with the corresponding relative record number. This directory is often kept sorted by the primary key (as in Fig. 6.1) to enhance searching it, and we then call it a *dictionary* if the sort order is essential to its use.

In the event that a directory is very large, it may be partitioned into smaller segments, a segment being brought into memory only when that segment must be searched. One way of storing such a segment is to make it a record of a Relative I–O file. Such segments should be large in order to reduce file accesses. Once a directory has been created, it can be searched to locate the relative record number of a desired record.

6.4 SEARCHING

An important class of addressing techniques involves searching. Two search techniques are in common use: the *linear search*, which does not require the directory to be sorted on the search key and the *binary search*, which assumes that it is sorted on the search key.

In a search, the value being sought is called the *argument*. When the argument is located within the directory by a search routine, a *match* is said to have occurred. If a directory contains social security numbers and the relative keys of records identified by these social security numbers, one would hunt for a given social security number (the argument of the search) and once it was located (a match), determine from the directory the associated relative key.

6.4.1 Linear Search

In a linear search, the argument is compared against each successive entry of the directory until a match occurs or the directory is exhausted. For every comparison that fails, we must ask the question: "Are we at the end of the directory?" This test is extremely important when the argument value is not present in the table because then

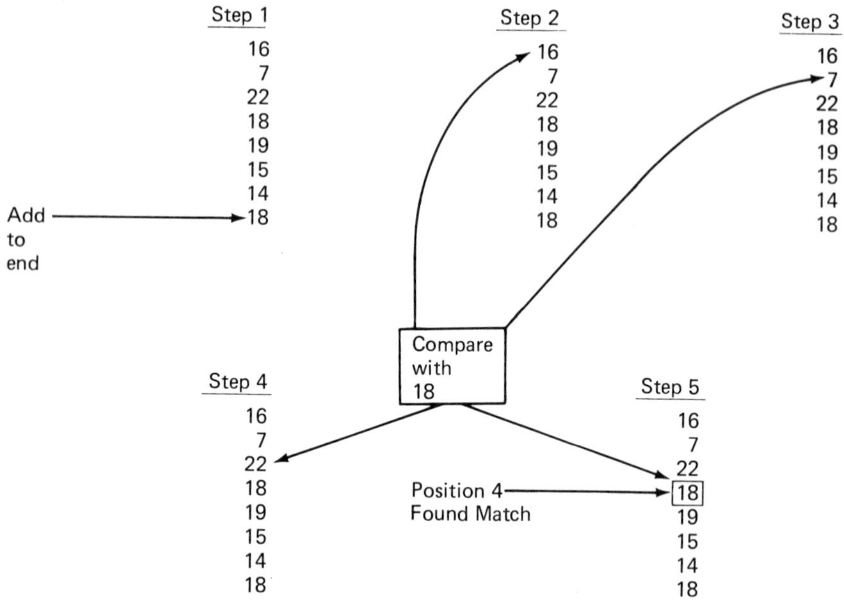

Figure 6.2 Linear search for segment 18.

the search would overrun the end of the directory. Thus two tests must normally be made at each step. "Do we have a match?" "Are we at the end of the directory?" If, however, we knew that a match for the argument would always occur, it would not be necessary to test for the end of the directory. This leads to a subtle improvement in the algorithm. If we place the argument at the end of the directory before beginning the search (as shown in Fig. 6.2), then there will definitely be a match. When a match occurs, it remains to determine if the match has taken place at the end of the table. If so, the argument was not present in the directory; otherwise it has been located.

Figure 6.2 shows five steps in a linear search. Each column shows one stage in searching for the number 18 in an unsorted list. In step 1 the number 18 is added to the bottom of the list. In steps 2–5 the numbers, beginning with the top number 16, are compared sequentially until 18 is located in step 5.

Exercise:

If we knew the list was sorted, how could we modify the linear search and the test in order to make the search more efficient when it fails?

6.4.2 Binary Search

In contrast to the linear search, the binary search requires that the directory be sorted, and we now refer to the directory as a "dictionary." The binary search proceeds in the following manner assuming the dictionary is sorted in ascending order. First, the argument is compared to the entry at the midpoint of the dictionary (if there are an even number of entries in the dictionary, pretend there is one more and take the midpoint). If the argument matches, then the search is finished. If the argument is less than the midpoint, then the entry at the midpoint and all larger entries are ignored and the search is repeated with the half of the table that remains. If the argument is greater than the midpoint, the midpoint and all smaller entries are ignored and the search is repeated on the half of the table that remains. At each successive search, one half of the remaining elements are eliminated. This procedure continues until the match is discovered or all the elements of the dictionary have been eliminated. Binary search is a recursive procedure. Each time a recursive procedure is repeated, something changes, in this case, the number of elements left to search at each step.

The entire routine can be programmed very easily with the use of three integer variables which we shall call FIRST, LAST, and MIDDLE. FIRST always points to the location containing the smallest element and LAST points to the location of the largest element (in that portion of the table left to be searched). At the start of the procedure, FIRST points to the first entry in the dictionary (and therefore the smallest) and LAST to the last entry in the dictionary (and hence the largest). The midpoint is calculated from

$$\frac{\text{FIRST} + \text{LAST}}{2}$$

If the argument being sought is less than the midpoint entry of the dictionary, then, since the dictionary is sorted, a match to this argument can only occur in the lower half of the dictionary. The midpoint of the lower half of the dictionary is now similarly examined. The new midpoint is obtained by setting LAST to the previous value of MIDPOINT and once more calculating

$$\frac{\text{FIRST} + \text{LAST}}{2}$$

If, on the other hand, the argument is greater than the midpoint, only the upper half of the dictionary need be considered. FIRST should be reset to the current value of the midpoint and a new midpoint calculated. The algorithm halts when a match is obtained or the dictionary is exhausted.

An example of a binary search is shown in Fig. 6.3, which indicates how 25 is located in a list of sorted numbers. The reader is urged to follow each step of the search. Note that the actual arithmetic is performed not on the elements of the array but on the index elements of the array. The reader should also spend a moment deciding how he would terminate the algorithm if 25 were missing from the array.

The binary search proceeds much more rapidly than the linear search because half of the list considered is removed at each step un-

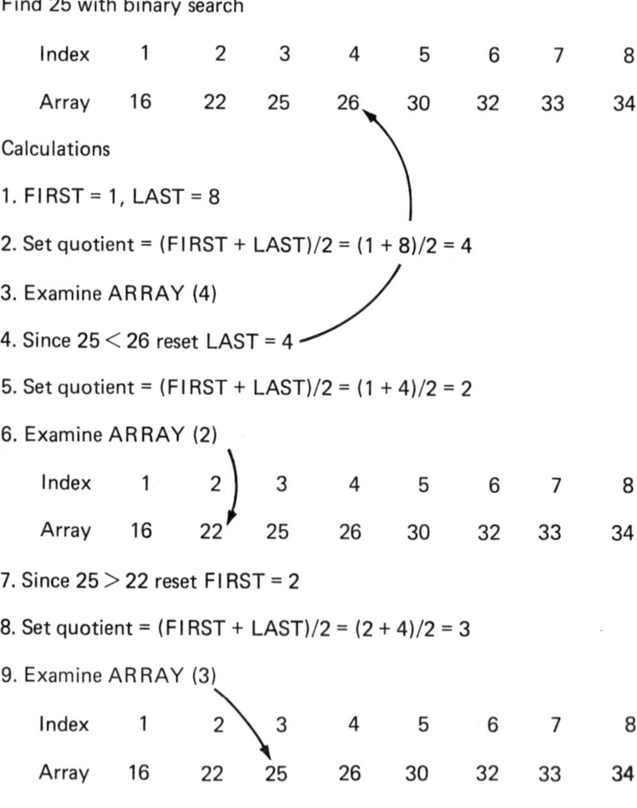

Find 25 with binary search
Index 1 2 3 4 5 6 7 8
Array 16 22 25 26 30 32 33 34
Calculations
1. FIRST = 1, LAST = 8
2. Set quotient = (FIRST + LAST)/2 = (1 + 8)/2 = 4
3. Examine ARRAY (4)
4. Since 25 < 26 reset LAST = 4
5. Set quotient = (FIRST + LAST)/2 = (1 + 4)/2 = 2
6. Examine ARRAY (2)
Index 1 2 3 4 5 6 7 8
Array 16 22 25 26 30 32 33 34
7. Since 25 > 22 reset FIRST = 2
8. Set quotient = (FIRST + LAST)/2 = (2 + 4)/2 = 3
9. Examine ARRAY (3)
Index 1 2 3 4 5 6 7 8
Array 16 22 25 26 30 32 33 34

Figure 6.3 Binary search.

til a match occurs. Since a binary search appears to be more efficient than a linear search and not difficult to program, why is it not always preferred to a linear search?

The main reason is the need to sort the dictionary on the search key and the difficulty involved in keeping it sorted in a dynamic environment. Dynamic file situations often exist in which records are continually being added, moved, or deleted; the cost of continually sorting can soon negate any savings realized by a more efficient search. Since the amount of dynamic change can be difficult to predict, it may be simpler to use a linear search.

6.5 ALTERING DICTIONARIES

6.5.1 Linear Insertion

In order to avoid the expense entailed in sorting when a new entry is added to an already sorted dictionary, the programmer may choose a less expensive procedure called *linear insertion*. With this technique, an entry is added at its correct sorted location by moving the following entries down one position, hence avoiding sorting altogether. Let us assume that an entry is to be added to a table sorted in ascending order. The argument is compared first with the *largest* and then successively smaller entries in the dictionary. For each comparison that is greater than the argument, the dictionary value is moved down one position in the array, thereby creating a free slot. When a dictionary entry is located whose value is less than or equal to the argument, the argument is inserted and we are done.

The process is illustrated in the code of Fig. 6.4 which compares the argument, data item A, with the elements of an array called DICTIONARY-TABLE whose current length is stored in the elementary item NUMBER-OF-ENTRIES. In this program segment, it has been assumed that the dictionary consists of both social security numbers and relative keys and that both of these items must be moved each time an unsuccessful comparison takes place. Upon termination of the routine, both a new social security number and a relative key are inserted into the dictionary.

6.5.2 Deleting Records

Whenever a record is deleted from the file, its corresponding entry must be removed from the dictionary. Physical removal means

```
WORKING-STORAGE-SECTION.
            .
            .
            .

01  DICTIONARY.
    02  NUMBER-OF-ENTRIES PIC 9(3).
    02  DICTIONARY-TABLE
            OCCURS   100 TIMES.
        03  SOCIAL-SECURITY-NUMBER
                PIC  9(9).
        03  RELATIVE-KEY
                PIC S9(8)COMP SYNC.
                            .
                            .
                            .

PROCEDURE DIVISION.
            .
            .
            .

        MOVE NUMBER-OF-ENTRIES TO I.
        PERFORM LOCATE-A UNTIL
            A IS GREATER THAN OR EQUAL TO
            SOCIAL-SECURITY-NUMBER (I)
            OR I IS EQUAL TO 0.
        MOVE A TO SOCIAL-SECURITY-NUMBER (I + 1)
        MOVE NEW-RELATIVE-KEY TO
            RELATIVE-KEY (I + 1)
                        .
                        .
                        .

        LOCATE-A.
            MOVE SOCIAL-SECURITY-NUMBER (I)
            TO SOCIAL-SECURITY-NUMBER (I + 1).
            MOVE RELATIVE-KEY (I)
            TO RELATIVE-KEY (I + 1).
            COMPUTE I = I - 1.
                        .
                        .
                        .
```

Figure 6.4 Example of a program for linear insertion.

leaving a gap, which must be compressed by moving all following entries up one table position. An alternative to this technique is simply to leave the dictionary entry present and set a flag that indicates that the record has been deleted. (The reader should determine how this affects the insertions of Fig. 6.4.)

This can be effected by setting the corresponding relative key to -1 or by some other manner that is convenient to the user. Using this technique, the programmer can find the entry to be deleted by using a binary search. When this technique is used, a check must be made to ascertain whether the argument of a search, once found, is actually a deleted record. As the dictionary will eventually become dense with deleted entries, the dictionary should be reorganized from time to time to physically remove these elements.

6.6 CALCULATION ADDRESSING

There are numerous methods of converting a key into a file address. Unfortunately, for some methods the resulting record address need not be unique. Surprisingly, the nonunique methods are more useful because the direct methods are either difficult to determine or have inefficient characteristics.

6.6.1 KEY-EQUALS-ADDRESS

In some applications the primary key is itself the record address. Suppose we assign consecutive account numbers to records beginning with 1. Then, by using Relative I-O, the account number can be used as the relative address. Thus the record key equals the record address. We have already used this method of direct addressing in Chapter 5.

Unfortunately, in most applications this direct and simple approach is not practical for two main reasons. First, it is not possible to identify each record by an integer in a natural way. Second, when the address space is larger than the file size, many of the physical addresses will not be used. For instance, social security numbers are not suitable as relative addresses of a personnel file. (Why?) If a number is not a natural part of a file, it should not be used. (Why?)

The major disadvantage of key-equals-address is that we must reserve a relative address for every potential record key and when these keys are not used, the space reserved is wasted. Because of low software overhead and the simplicity of implementation, it may be desirable to leave a large part of the physical file unused.

Exercise:

Discuss vector data structure access with respect to key-equals-addressing.

6.6.2 Key Conversion Algorithm

In the event that the key cannot be used as the record address, it is sometimes possible to transform or map the keys into the record addresses by means of an algorithm, which is often just an algebraic formula. As this is also a form of direct addressing (key-equals-address is really just a special case), it has essentially the same advantages and disadvantages as that of key-equals-address.

Exercise:

Discuss a vector data structure with symbolic indices and relate it to key conversion algorithm addressing.

6.6.3 Hashing

At first glance hashing resembles algorithmic conversion. The fundamental difference is that the result of hashing is not unique whereas the result of the algorithm method is. Hashing, in effect, operates like a pseudorandom number generator scattering consecutive keys in the address space and for this reason is often called *randomizing.*

Hashing is sometimes avoided on the grounds that it is too complex. When its advantages are considered, this is not so. Although record access is not as fast or as simple as direct methods, it can handle additions and insertions much more easily; and when properly designed, it generally has a much higher space utilization. With respect to search techniques and tables, it normally finds a record in one or two seeks. A major disadvantage is that sequential ordering of the key is lost.

There have been many techniques proposed for the hash transforms, and they have been studied and compared by many researchers, but a simple division method appears as good as any and better than most.[1] As it is beyond the scope of this text, we do not survey

[1] See, for instance, P.G. Sorenson, J.P. Tremblay, and R.F. Deutscher, "Key-to-Address Transformation Techniques," *INFOR*, 16, no. 1 (Feb. 1978), 1–33, and the references cited therein.

hashing techniques. Rather we concentrate on one specific technique, division hashing, and explore the problems associated with using a hashing transform along with some well-known solutions to them.

6.6.4 Division Hashing

A simple but effective method of hashing is based on the mathematical operation of division. In the following example we consider some of the aspects of division and in so doing develop division hashing.

Suppose we are given a group of 20 records with integer keys in the range of 150–200. Using a Relative I-O file, we could store each record at the relative address represented by the record key. However, at least 150 file locations will never be used and less than half of the remaining will store records. Let us further assume that at most 20 keys of the key space will ever be active.

To conserve space we would prefer to compress the address space of 50 values to 20 values. How can we convert records keys in the range 150–200 into relative addresses 1–20? We must attempt to discover an algorithm that maps a set of large numbers into a set of smaller numbers. One way large numbers are mapped to smaller numbers is through the operation of division. The decimal part of the result is meaningless as an address so we simply ignore it. The COBOL DIVIDE statement you will recall provides a quotient and a remainder. Ignoring the decimal result of division, we are left with the quotient.

The first difficulty is the choice of divisor. For a start, try the file size 20.

```
DIVIDE KEY BY 20
GIVING Q REMAINDER R.
```

Considering quotient Q(150/20) = 7, quotient Q(160/20) = 8, and quotient Q(200/20) = 10, we soon realize that only four quotients are possible. Why? Perhaps the divisor is too large. The smallest divisor that gives a quotient 20 as the maximum address is 10. Try it. Division does not appear to perform the compression of the key space we desire. Before giving up on division, let us tabulate (see Table 6.1) some results of divisor 20 on the key space to better understand what is happening.

As expected, the quotient is not of much use; however, the remainders run from 0 to 19, and by simply adding one we have the relative addresses from 1 to 20 as desired. There is only one problem; the remainders of 160, 180, and 200 are all zero. In fact, many other numbers have common remainders. But this is to be expected since we are mapping 50 numbers into 20 numbers. When two keys transform to the same address, we say a *hash collision* has occurred. The solution to this problem is known as a *hash resolution* technique. It reassigns the hash address when a collision occurs. We discuss several techniques in the following sections.

Table 6.1 An Example of Division Hashing

DIVIDE KEY BY 20	*GIVING Q*	*REMAINDER R.*
150	7	10
151	7	11
152	7	12
153	7	13
154	7	14
155	7	15
156	7	16
157	7	17
158	7	18
159	7	19
160	8	0
161	8	1
162	8	2
⋮	⋮	⋮
170	8	10
⋮	⋮	⋮
180	9	0
⋮	⋮	⋮
190	9	10
⋮	⋮	⋮
200	10	0

Our example illustrates the *division hashing* function, which, surprisingly, has survived considerable competition to emerge as the best all-around hashing function.

More formally, the division hashing function is expressed as

$$\mathrm{H\ (KEY) = KEY\ mod}\ d + 1$$

where H (KEY) is the relative address, KEY the primary key of the record, and d a divisor chosen to give the desired range of relative addresses. If d is not chosen carefully, many hashing collisions can occur and the method then gives poor results. (The reader is urged to experiment on the above example for different choices of d.)

6.6.5 Hashing Collisions

To minimize collisions we always attempt to choose a hash function with a uniform probability distribution of the function values. This is not always possible, so we must settle for a near-uniform function that works well on the most used set of keys. Research has indicated that, on average, division hashing is an excellent method where the divisor d is a prime or is relatively prime to the size of the address space and close to the number of file records. Also, the number of collisons that occur is smallest when there is no apparent ordering on the record keys.

The address space depends on the value of d. Given 20 records, should we actually choose an address space of this size? Choice of a prime d could be 19 or 23. As a general rule, to keep collisions under control, no more than 80% of the address space should be used. Since 20 is a little less than 80% of 29, a prime, an address space of 29 is a good choice.

Exercise:

Examine the results of using divisor 29 in the preceding division hashing example.

The following steps should be used to choose an appropriate address space size as a divisor:

1. Estimate the number of file records; call this N.
2. Find the prime nearest 125% of N.

The basic problem with hashing is that hash collisions can occur and must be somehow resolved. Many good techniques have been developed to handle collisions, and the result is that hashing has become a very useful addressing technique. A hashing algorithm consists of two major parts: a hash function such as we have seen and a collision resolution method. A general rule for controlling hash collisions is that not more than 80% of the address space should be used, therefore this must be larger than the file size. Thus a hashing method will always have a large amount of unused space. In spite of collisions, hashing is very fast and the average number of accesses is generally less than 2; a good method will have 1.2–1.8 accesses on average. Hashing is very flexible in a dynamic file.

6.6.6 Resolving Hash Collisions

The difficulty with hashing, as we have noted, is that collisions are usually inevitable. When a collision occurs, the colliding record, called an *overflow record*, must be stored elsewhere. Two questions naturally arise: where is it to be stored, and once stored how can we retrieve it since hashing the key now gives an incorrect address?

An obvious solution to the first question is to find some free space within the file and to store the overflow record there. Overflow records are then said to be stored in the *prime area*. The problem that arises is that we create *indirect* collisions in two ways. First, in searching for space we have a *secondary* collision each time an examined record location is full. Second, if we store an overflow record in free space, the first record hashed to that space will have a collision. Because of the second problem, a separate overflow area is often created and used only to resolve collisions. This gives a natural classification of solutions into *prime area* and *overflow area* techniques. We next give several important examples of each kind of technique. The reader should be warned that the nature of real files is such that the discussion is necessarily incomplete and provides guideposts rather than a detailed map.

6.6.7 Open Addressing

If a record key is hashed to a record location that is full, a simple resolution strategy is a linear search of the file records until a free location is found. The overflow record is then inserted at this point. To retrieve this record the process is repeated until a match occurs. Such a search as a primary addressing technique would be very inefficient; it can give satisfactory results only because the hashing function varies the initial point of the search. As the number of collisions at a given point increases, the method decreases in efficiency because the following unhashed locations have been used and the search may become very long. This is accentuated as the locations searched are filled by searches that began at other collision points, and we have many secondary collisions. Various search sequences can be used. Since there may be no free space following the collision, the search must, in effect, wrap around to the beginning of the file.

A problem occurs in retrieving records if we previously deleted a record. Then, in searching for a record, we would not know if it were absent from the file until an empty record were found. Therefore, if we delete records, we must be careful not to mark them as empty otherwise the search must be exhaustive.

The advantages of this method are that records are stored in the prime area and that usually only a short seek time is necessary. Simplicity is a major argument that should not be ignored. The major disadvantage is that the adjacent areas may be full and many addresses examined before space is found. Also, multiple collisions will fill adjacent space causing a domino effect when primary collisions occur at the stolen space.

Examples of open addressing are given by Programs 6.1 and 6.2.

Program 6.1 Narrative. The purpose of Program 6.1 is to build a hash table consisting of the relative record numbers of records in the VEHICLE-LICENSE-FILE. The index of a hash table entry is provided by applying the hashing algorithm to the associated VEHICLE-LICENSE-NUMBER. Hash collisions are resolved by open addressing; the first available slot following a collision is used to store the entry. In order to severely limit the number of hash collisions, the hash table has been set at size 200 although no more than 100 records are expected to be stored at any one time.

If k is the VEHICLE-LICENSE-NUMBER, then n, the value of the index of the hash table entry associated with key k, is defined as

$$n \equiv k \bmod 197 + 1$$

That is, n is the remainder +1 when the key k is divided by the prime number 197. We select 197 as a prime less than 200.

During initialization the entire hash table of 200 entries is set to −1. The program reads a record of the VEHICLE-LICENSE-FILE, hashes the VEHICLE-LICENSE-NUMBER, and stores the record's relative key in the hash table. The file is processed sequentially. Processing terminates on end-of-file.

Program 6.1

```
IDENTIFICATION DIVISION.
PROGRAM-ID. PROG6PT1.


ENVIRONMENT DIVISION.

CONFIGURATION SECTION.

SOURCE-COMPUTER. IBM-370-158.
OBJECT-COMPUTER. IBM-370-158.

INPUT-OUTPUT SECTION.

FILE-CONTROL.

    SELECT HASH-TABLE
        ASSIGN TO DISK-TABLE
        ORGANIZATION IS SEQUENTIAL
        ACCESS MODE IS SEQUENTIAL.

    SELECT VEHICLE-LICENSE-FILE
        ASSIGN TO DISK-LICENSE
        ORGANIZATION IS RELATIVE
        ACCESS MODE IS SEQUENTIAL
        RELATIVE KEY IS VEHICLE-LICENSE-KEY.


DATA DIVISION.

FILE SECTION.

FD  HASH-TABLE
    LABEL RECORDS ARE STANDARD
    RECORD CONTAINS 400 CHARACTERS
    DATA RECORD IS HASH-TABLE-RECORD.
01  HASH-TABLE-RECORD.
    02  TABLE-ENTRY                 PIC S9(4) COMP SYNC
            OCCURS 200 TIMES.

FD  VEHICLE-LICENSE-FILE
    RECORD CONTAINS 114 CHARACTERS
    LABEL RECORDS ARE STANDARD
    DATA RECORD IS VEHICLE-LICENSE-FILE-RECORD.
01  VEHICLE-LICENSE-FILE-RECORD .
    02  FILLER                      PIC X(88).
    02  VEHICLE-LICENSE-NUMBER      PIC X(6).
    02  FILLER                      PIC X(20).

WORKING-STORAGE SECTION.

77  EOF-FLAG                        PIC X(3).
    88  EOF                    VALUE IS 'ON'.
77  I                               PIC S9(8) COMP SYNC.
77  J                               PIC S9(8) COMP SYNC.
```

Program 6.1 (cont.)

```
       77  K                               PIC S9(8) COMP SYNC.
       77  NUMBER-OF-TABLE-ENTRIES         PIC S9(8) COMP SYNC.
       77  PRIME-NUMBER                    PIC S9(8) COMP SYNC.
       77  VEHICLE-LICENSE-KEY             PIC S9(8) COMP SYNC.


       PROCEDURE DIVISION.

           PERFORM INITIALIZATION.
           PERFORM HASHING-ROUTINE UNTIL EOF.
           PERFORM TERMINATION.
           STOP RUN.

       INITIALIZATION.
           OPEN  INPUT  VEHICLE-LICENSE-FILE
                 OUTPUT HASH-TABLE.
           MOVE 197 TO PRIME-NUMBER.
           MOVE 200 TO NUMBER-OF-TABLE-ENTRIES.
           MOVE 'OFF' TO EOF-FLAG.
           MOVE 1 TO VEHICLE-LICENSE-KEY.
           PERFORM INITIALIZE-TABLE-ENTRY
               VARYING I FROM 1 BY 1
               UNTIL I > NUMBER-OF-TABLE-ENTRIES.
           PERFORM READ-VEHICLE-LICENSE-FILE.

       INITIALIZE-TABLE-ENTRY.
           MOVE -1 TO TABLE-ENTRY (I).

       READ-VEHICLE-LICENSE-FILE.
           READ VEHICLE-LICENSE-FILE
               AT END MOVE 'ON' TO EOF-FLAG.

       HASHING-ROUTINE.
           TRANSFORM VEHICLE-LICENSE-NUMBER CHARACTERS
               FROM 'ABCDEFGHIJKLMNOPQRSTUVWXYZ'
               TO   '01234567890123456789012345'.
           MOVE VEHICLE-LICENSE-NUMBER TO K.
           DIVIDE K BY PRIME-NUMBER
               GIVING    I
               REMAINDER J.
           ADD 1 TO J.
           IF  TABLE-ENTRY (J) NOT = -1
               PERFORM INCREMENT-COUNTER
                   UNTIL TABLE-ENTRY (J) = -1.
           MOVE VEHICLE-LICENSE-KEY TO TABLE-ENTRY (J).
           ADD 1 TO VEHICLE-LICENSE-KEY.
           PERFORM READ-VEHICLE-LICENSE-FILE.

       INCREMENT-COUNTER.
           ADD 1 TO J.
           IF J > NUMBER-OF-TABLE-ENTRIES
               SUBTRACT NUMBER-OF-TABLE-ENTRIES FROM J.

       TERMINATION.
           WRITE HASH-TABLE-RECORD.
           CLOSE VEHICLE-LICENSE-FILE HASH-TABLE.
```

Program 6.2

```
IDENTIFICATION DIVISION.
PROGRAM-ID. PROG6PT2.


ENVIRONMENT DIVISION.

CONFIGURATION SECTION.

SOURCE-COMPUTER. IBM-370-158.
OBJECT-COMPUTER. IBM-370-158.

INPUT-OUTPUT SECTION.

FILE-CONTROL.

    SELECT HASH-TABLE
        ASSIGN TO DISK-TABLE
        ORGANIZATION IS SEQUENTIAL
        ACCESS MODE IS SEQUENTIAL.

    SELECT INPUT-FILE
        ASSIGN TO DISK-S-SYSIN
        ORGANIZATION IS SEQUENTIAL
        ACCESS MODE IS SEQUENTIAL.

    SELECT OUTPUT-FILE
        ASSIGN TO PRNT-S-SYSOUT
        ORGANIZATION IS SEQUENTIAL
        ACCESS MODE IS SEQUENTIAL.

    SELECT VEHICLE-LICENSE-FILE
        ASSIGN TO DISK-LICENSE
        ORGANIZATION IS RELATIVE
        ACCESS MODE IS RANDOM
        RELATIVE KEY IS VEHICLE-LICENSE-KEY.


DATA DIVISION.

FILE SECTION.

FD  HASH-TABLE
    LABEL RECORDS ARE STANDARD
    RECORD CONTAINS 400 CHARACTERS
    DATA RECORD IS HASH-TABLE-RECORD.
01  HASH-TABLE-RECORD.
    02  TABLE-ENTRY                PIC S9(4) COMP SYNC
            OCCURS 200 TIMES.

FD  INPUT-FILE
    LABEL RECORDS ARE OMITTED
    RECORD CONTAINS 80 CHARACTERS
    DATA RECORD IS INPUT-RECORD.
01  INPUT-RECORD.
    02  SEARCH-KEY                 PIC X(6).
    02  FILLER                     PIC X(74).

FD  OUTPUT-FILE
    LABEL RECORDS ARE OMITTED
    RECORD CONTAINS 133 CHARACTERS
    DATA RECORD IS OUTPUT-RECORD.
```

Program 6.2 (cont.)

```
       01  OUTPUT-RECORD.
           02  FILLER                      PIC X.
           02  OUTPUT-DATA                 PIC X(132).

       FD  VEHICLE-LICENSE-FILE
           RECORD CONTAINS 114 CHARACTERS
           LABEL RECORDS ARE STANDARD
           DATA RECORD IS VEHICLE-LICENSE-FILE-RECORD.
       01  VEHICLE-LICENSE-FILE-RECORD .
           02  FILLER                      PIC X(88).
           02  VEHICLE-LICENSE-NUMBER      PIC X(6).
           02  FILLER                      PIC X(20).

       WORKING-STORAGE SECTION.

       77  END-OF-SEARCH-FLAG              PIC X(3).
           88  EOS                    VALUE IS 'ON'.
       77  EOF-FLAG                        PIC X(3).
           88  EOF                    VALUE IS 'ON'.
       77  FOUND-FLAG                      PIC X(3).
           88  FOUND                  VALUE IS 'ON'.
       77  I                               PIC S9(8) COMP SYNC.
       77  J                               PIC S9(8) COMP SYNC.
       77  NUMBER-OF-TABLE-ENTRIES         PIC S9(8) COMP SYNC.
       77  PRIME-NUMBER                    PIC S9(8) COMP SYNC.
       77  VEHICLE-LICENSE-KEY             PIC S9(8) COMP SYNC.

       01  OUTPUT-LINE.
           02  FIRST-PART                  PIC X(38).
           02  TEMPORARY-KEY               PIC X(6).
           02  NUMERIC-KEY REDEFINES TEMPORARY-KEY
                                           PIC 9(6).



       PROCEDURE DIVISION.
           PERFORM INITIALIZATION.
           PERFORM SEARCH-ROUTINE UNTIL EOF.
           PERFORM TERMINATION.
           STOP RUN.

       INITIALIZATION.
           OPEN  INPUT   INPUT-FILE HASH-TABLE
                 OUTPUT  OUTPUT-FILE
                 I-O     VEHICLE-LICENSE-FILE.
           MOVE 'OFF' TO EOF-FLAG.
           MOVE 197 TO PRIME-NUMBER.
           MOVE 200 TO NUMBER-OF-TABLE-ENTRIES.
           MOVE 'THE GIVEN VEHICLE LICENSE NUMBER IS '
               TO FIRST-PART.
           READ HASH-TABLE.
           PERFORM READ-INPUT-FILE.

       READ-INPUT-FILE.
           READ INPUT-FILE
               AT END MOVE 'ON' TO EOF-FLAG.

       SEARCH-ROUTINE.
           MOVE 'OFF' TO END-OF-SEARCH-FLAG FOUND-FLAG.
           MOVE SEARCH-KEY TO TEMPORARY-KEY.
           MOVE OUTPUT-LINE TO OUTPUT-DATA.
```

Program 6.2 (cont.)

```
           WRITE OUTPUT-RECORD AFTER ADVANCING 2 LINES.
           TRANSFORM TEMPORARY-KEY CHARACTERS
               FROM 'ABCDEFGHIJKLMNOPQRSTUVWXYZ'
               TO   '01234567890123456789012345'.
           DIVIDE NUMERIC-KEY BY PRIME-NUMBER
               GIVING    I
               REMAINDER J.
           ADD 1 TO J.
           PERFORM RECORD-RETRIEVAL-ROUTINE.
           IF  NOT EOS
               IF  VEHICLE-LICENSE-NUMBER = SEARCH-KEY
                   MOVE 'ON' TO END-OF-SEARCH-FLAG FOUND-FLAG
                   ELSE
                   PERFORM CONTINUE-SEARCH UNTIL EOS.
           IF  FOUND
               MOVE VEHICLE-LICENSE-FILE-RECORD TO OUTPUT-DATA
               WRITE OUTPUT-RECORD AFTER ADVANCING 1 LINES
               ELSE
               MOVE '* NOTE * RECORD NOT IN FILE.'
                   TO OUTPUT-DATA
               WRITE OUTPUT-RECORD AFTER ADVANCING 1 LINES.
           PERFORM READ-INPUT-FILE.

       RECORD-RETRIEVAL-ROUTINE.
           MOVE TABLE-ENTRY (J) TO VEHICLE-LICENSE-KEY.
           READ VEHICLE-LICENSE-FILE
               INVALID KEY MOVE 'ON' TO END-OF-SEARCH-FLAG.

       CONTINUE-SEARCH.
           ADD 1 TO J.
           IF  J > NUMBER-OF-TABLE-ENTRIES
               SUBTRACT NUMBER-OF-TABLE-ENTRIES FROM J.
           PERFORM RECORD-RETRIEVAL-ROUTINE.
           IF  NOT EOS
               IF  VEHICLE-LICENSE-NUMBER = SEARCH-KEY
                   MOVE 'ON' TO END-OF-SEARCH-FLAG FOUND-FLAG.

       TERMINATION.
           CLOSE INPUT-FILE HASH-TABLE OUTPUT-FILE
               VEHICLE-LICENSE-FILE.
```

Because each license number consists of alphabetic characters and digits, the alphabetic characters are transformed into digits by means of the non-ANSI standard COBOL verb TRANSFORM available in IBM OS/VS COBOL. If this verb is not available, then a small program segment will need to be written.

Because this program is used for illustration only, error checking has not been provided. The reader should see the problems at the end of the chapter to follow the solution through.

Program 6.2 Narrative. The purpose of Program 6.2 is to read a deck of data cards containing vehicle license numbers and retrieve their corresponding records from the VEHICLE-LICENSE-FILE. If the record cannot be found, a message is printed. Processing is terminated when end-of-file is reached.

As each vehicle license number is read, it is hashed using the method described in Program 6.1. When a record is retrieved, its vehicle license number is compared with that given. If they are equal, we have found the record, and it is printed; otherwise, open addressing is used to fetch another record. The search of records halts when the record is found or a -1, denoting an empty entry, forces execution of the INVALID KEY clause or an attempt to read.

Note that the VEHICLE-LICENSE-FILE is now processed with ACCESS MODE IS RANDOM.

6.6.8 Chaining

There are numerous chaining techniques. Our discussion is limited to *separate chaining* which places the overflow records in a separate overflow area; this avoids the problem of indirect collisions that occur in open addressing when locations are stolen. Chaining consists of creating a linear list of overflow records for a hash collision. We may regard the hash function as pointing to a list rather than a record. Each record in the prime area represents the head of the list.

As discussed in Chapter 1, a list is connected by pointers and each record must have a pointer field. To indicate the end of the list, a null pointer is used, and the primary records must be created with the null pointer in the pointer field. When an overflow occurs, we follow the pointers to the record with the null pointer. A free record is obtained from the overflow area by a suitable algorithm and added to the end of the chain by replacing the null pointer with the address of this record. The pointer of the new record must be set to null. We may create the overflow records with null pointers or set the pointers when the records are used; it may be wise to do both.

It is easy to delete a record from the list (in Chapter 10 are detailed instructions, but you should be able to figure it out), and the record location should be made available for future use. To retrieve a record from a chained file, the following steps should be taken:

1. Hash the unique primary key to obtain a relative address.

2. Fetch the record at that relative address. If the search key equals the record key, then stop; the record is in the file. Otherwise continue.

3. If the pointer field is not null, do step 2 again using the

pointer to get next relative address. Otherwise stop; the record is not in the file.

Chaining is more complicated than open addressing. Since the overflow area will not be near the original collision, a second disk access is necessary. (Note that there are also chaining methods that embed the overflow areas nearby in the prime area to reduce disk accesses.) However, we should note that in open addressing, clustering can cause nearby records to fill and increase disk accesses. Since chains can be easily reordered, those records with a high probability of access can be moved to the front of the list. A simple strategy is to move a record up one list position toward the front of the list each time it is accessed.

6.7 ADDITIONAL ADDRESSING TECHNIQUES

6.7.1 The Bucket Concept

Until now we have considered mappings that obtain the desired address directly. In actual practice, methods are not as straightforward, and it is more usual to address a group of records, commonly referred to as a *bucket*. The group of records associated with a single address act as an adjacent overflow area. The obvious danger in reserving an overflow for each address is unused space when no collisions occur; however, by using consecutive spill addressing, a bucket can receive the overflow of other buckets. We leave the details to the reader. Alternatively, the hashing algorithm can be chosen to ensure ample collisions and pointers to overflow buckets used when the primary bucket is full. This combines spill addressing and chaining. There are indeed many techniques that attempt to handle hash collisions efficiently. Ultimately, the choice of technique depends on the file characteristics and the system design criteria. Analysis of what is best is always difficult.

6.7.2 Directory of Free Space

When many of the buckets are full, unnecessary searching is performed. One method of avoiding further searching is to use a directory of free space, which points to those buckets that have available space. When a bucket with space is found, a pointer to it is placed in the source bucket. The disadvantage of this method is the necessity of updating the directory when additions and deletions change the bucket full status. Also, space is required to store the pointers, and pointer overflow destroys the simplicity of record access. The advantage is that at most two bucket accesses are required for reading. Large bucket sizes are preferred. Why?

As a simple method, we suggest a full flag indicator for each bucket. This avoids a complete search of a full bucket; thus, we spill by bucket rather than record until a free bucket is reached. The flag updating is simple. Again, larger buckets improve the efficiency.

6.7.3 Optimization

Since it is apparent that overflow records take longer to access, frequently accessed records with primary and secondary collisions can seriously degrade file performance. One solution is to load the file in decreasing order of use. However, because of the nature of files, this is not usually possible because either usage is not known or the file grows. If a usage counter is placed in a record field, then usage statistics can be obtained and the file periodically reorganized. The cost of such statistics should first be related to the cost of using excess space to reduce collisions.

6.8 SUMMARY

The efficiency of the various hashing methods is highly dependent on the file characteristics. The difficulty in using hashing is in choosing good methods that best exploit the characteristics of the file in use. Indeed, analysis of a dynamic file is difficult and hazardous. In lieu of firm knowledge, we would suggest simple and known techniques. There is a definite danger in being too clever.

When it is clear that the simple techniques are not sufficient, the file can be analyzed empirically, based on usage and structure. We would suggest redesign in the context of the actual computing environment rather than complex analysis of what may well be fictional expectations. There are no hard and fast rules but we believe that it is better to lean to the side of simplicity rather than that of complexity.

PROBLEMS

1. We have noted that in studying addressing it can be assumed that the address space consists of integers from 1 to n. Why have we not done this for the key space?

2. (a) What is the disadvantage of a binary search?
   (b) Could you overcome this disadvantage by using a linked list as the data structure?

3. Your boss tells you to provide a procedure to assign storage in a vector where the address space is of size 1000. Unfortunately, budget restrictions only permit him to give you a vector of size 99.
   (a) How do you reply to this?
   (b) Your boss explains as follows, "But only about 50 elements are ever in the address space at any given time." What do you do?

4. Develop an algorithm to perform consecutive spill addressing in the primary area when buckets are used.

5. Develop an algorithm with chaining on buckets.

6. Suppose that the consecutive spill technique was used as the addressing scheme.
   (a) For N records in the file, what does the average time to access a record depend on, and what does the average time to store a new record depend on, assuming no deletions? Can you provide a formula?
   (b) Compare this method to sequential addressing.

7. Suppose you have an existing sequential file that you wish to change to a direct Relative I-O file with hash addressing. How would you go about it?

8. Devise algorithms for consecutive spill addressing with buckets.

9. Evaluate and compare two transforms on the address space of even numbers from 4000 to 6000, using

$$H(x) = x \bmod m + 1 \quad \text{for } m_1 = 2000 \text{ and } m_2 = 6001$$

10. In order to fetch a record using the open address hash algorithm of Program 6.1, a key must be hashed. Once the key is hashed, the hash value is used as an index into an array that contains record addresses. The record address in the form of a relative record number is used to fetch the record. Once the record is fetched, the key within it is checked against the original key to see whether or not the fetch was successful. An alternative is to keep the record key in the hash table along with the relative address. This way the record

need not be fetched unless the keys match, thereby saving I–O time.

(a) Modify Program 6.1 to include this feature.

(b) Modify Program 6.2 to fetch records in accordance with your modification for part (a).

11. Modify Programs 6.1 and 6.2 to permit a record on the file to be deleted. Be careful your modification does not interfere with the algorithm's ability to detect a missing record or locate one that is already there.

12. Change your solution to problem 10 to allow for record deletions.

13. Rewrite Programs 6.1 and 6.2 to use chaining of records instead of open addressing to resolve hash collisions.

7

IBM Direct File Organization

The file organization method discussed in this chapter is an IBM-designed file organization that does not conform to the specifications of ANSI COBOL but is available in the IBM OS/VS COBOL compiler. Other manufacturers have provided similar mechanisms for direct access. On the first reading this chapter may be skipped. You would not normally use this file organization because relative files can be used instead. However, the sophisticated file user should be acquainted with it, much as a high-level language user can benefit from an awareness of the machine assembler language.

7.1 INTRODUCTION

In comparison to relative file organization, direct file organization emphasizes the direct access storage device on which the records of a file are stored rather than the order of the records themselves. Any software that provides a file organization on disk must perform the kinds of elementary steps that we discuss here, although they need not be described in COBOL.

Of specific importance is the physical storage unit, called the *track*. A track is that storage section of a disk unit that passes under a READ/WRITE head when the disk undergoes one revolution. An integral number of tracks are required to store any given file.

On a disk, the tracks assigned to a file are numbered in increasing sequence beginning with zero and thus provide the track address. In order to store a record, a track number must be specified; this number is referred to as the *track identifier*. Most often the physical record size permits more than one record to be stored on a given track, and for this reason each record is also identified by a unique key, called the *record identifier*. A track identifier and a record identifier uniquely determine a physical record of the file on the storage device; consequently, the track identifier and the record identifier are combined to form a unique key designated as the ACTUAL KEY.

In order to use the direct file organization, it is necessary to determine for the file the track on which each record will be stored and to designate a unique identifier for each record. As this requires at the outset much more involvement with storage details than is required with Relative I–O, it is fair to ask why direct file organization is used at all. First, historically, it preceded relative addressing; that is, the implementation of Relative I–O was completed after direct file organization was already in use. Second, the move from direct to relative addressing was an early move toward the data base concept of isolation from the system hardware. Third, as a programmer you may often run into the problem of looking at someone else's code, in which case an acquaintance with direct addressing may well be necessary. In addition, the current version of the IBM direct file organization permits variable-length records while the IBM relative file organization does not.

An IBM direct file can be created either sequentially or randomly. That is, a file can be created by adding the records one at a time beginning with the first, then the second, and so on; or it can be produced by adding records at tracks chosen in some sequence predetermined by the programmer.

7.2 CREATING A DIRECT FILE SEQUENTIALLY

7.2.1 The SELECT Clause Entry

A typical SELECT clause for a direct file being created sequentially is:

```
SELECT file-name
ASSIGN TO DA-DISK-D-DD1
ACCESS MODE IS SEQUENTIAL
ACTUAL KEY IS data-name
TRACK-LIMIT IS integer.
```

The system name DA-DISK-D-DD1 indicates that this is a direct access (DA) file, stored on a disk (DISK) unit, with the direct file organization (D), and with the name DD1 as the system name of this file.

The ACCESS MODE IS SEQUENTIAL clause specifies that the file named will be accessed sequentially. The ACTUAL KEY clause names *data-name* as a data area within the WORKING-STORAGE SECTION that will provide the track and record identifier for each record. The TRACK-LIMIT clause is optional and informs the system that when the file is closed, enough dummy records are to be written to create a file using *integer* tracks. If the file already contains records written by the programmer utilizing more than this number of tracks, the clause is ignored.

The process of writing the initial data or dummy records onto a track is called *formatting* the track. If the user does not write records on to one or more tracks of the file or force the system to write dummy records for him (by using the TRACK-LIMIT clause), any tracks assigned to the file but not formatted are unusable. For example, suppose a user creates a file of 500 tracks, does not supply a TRACK-LIMIT clause, writes 100 tracks, and then closes the file. Then the 400 leftover tracks allocated to the file remain but (depending on how they were allocated) might not be used by the program. If a TRACK-LIMIT clause of the form

```
TRACK-LIMIT IS 500
```

is written, all the remaining 400 tracks can be used.

7.2.2 The ACTUAL KEY Entry

The track identifier and the record identifier constitute the ACTUAL KEY of each record. This key is a group item of the WORKING-STORAGE SECTION and might be defined as:

```
01  THE-ACTUAL-KEY

    02  TRACK-IDENTIFIER
            PIC  S9(8)
            COMPUTATIONAL
            SYNCHRONIZED.
    02  RECORD-IDENTIFIER
            PIC  X(10).
```

The data names shown here are user-defined COBOL words. The first part of the ACTUAL KEY must be reserved for the track identifier and must be described as a PIC S9(8) COMPUTATIONAL SYNCHRONIZED item. The record identifier portion can be defined in any manner by the programmer but must be at least 1 byte in length and not exceed 255.

When a record is to be written to the direct access file during sequential file creation, the track on which the record is to be written must be moved to the track identifier portion of the actual key and its unique distinguishing key placed in the record identifier portion. The record identifier need not also be stored within the logical record itself as the record identifier is placed alongside the record within the file automatically by the operating system. Placing it within the logical content of the record will cause two copies of the record identifier to be kept on the file. When a record is written to the file, its track identifier is returned in the ACTUAL KEY on the completion of a successful WRITE. On sequential output, the system automatically increments the track identifier whenever it is forced to advance to another track in order to store a record. The user need not advance it manually.

If a user wished to place some intervening dummy records between two records on the file, say records A and B, he should first write record A and then advance the ACTUAL KEY by the desired number of intervening tracks of dummy records and then write record B. For example, suppose record A is written as a record on track 10. If the user increments the track identifier to 20 and then writes record B, the system will first write dummy records to fill track 10, write dummy records onto tracks 11 through 19, and then write record B as the first record on track 20.

A dummy record, with fixed-length records, is a record of undefined information in which the first byte of the record identifier is set to HIGH-VALUES. The user may create his own dummy records by adhering to this method of construction.

When the user is writing variable-length records and requests the insertion of dummy records by the method indicated above, no actual record is written to the file by the system; however, some control information is placed on each track to indicate the capacity that remains on each track to store data. This "capacity record" is updated whenever the user writes data to a given track.

When the CLOSE is issued, the system will produce dummy or capacity records to fill the number of tracks specified in the TRACK-LIMIT clause. None are written when this clause is omitted during sequential creation of the file.

Program 7.1

```
       IDENTIFICATION DIVISION.
       PROGRAM-ID. PROG7PT1.


       ENVIRONMENT DIVISION.

       CONFIGURATION SECTION.

       SOURCE-COMPUTER. IBM-370.
       OBJECT-COMPUTER. IBM-370.

       INPUT-OUTPUT SECTION.

       FILE-CONTROL.

           SELECT INPUT-FILE
               ASSIGN TO CARD-SYSIN
               ACCESS MODE IS SEQUENTIAL
               ORGANIZATION IS SEQUENTIAL.

           SELECT OUTPUT-FILE
               ASSIGN TO DA-DISK-D-DD1
               ACCESS IS RANDOM
               TRACK-LIMIT IS 12
               ACTUAL KEY IS THE-ACTUAL-KEY.


       DATA DIVISION.
       FILE SECTION.

       FD  INPUT-FILE
               BLOCK CONTAINS 1 RECORDS
               LABEL RECORDS ARE OMITTED
               RECORD CONTAINS 80 CHARACTERS
               DATA RECORD IS INPUT-FILE-RECORD.
       01  INPUT-FILE-RECORD.
           02  FILLER                       PIC X(80).
```

Program 7.1 (cont.)

```
        FD  OUTPUT-FILE
            LABEL RECORDS ARE STANDARD
            RECORD CONTAINS 100 CHARACTERS
            DATA RECORD IS OUTPUT-FILE-RECORD.
        01  OUTPUT-FILE-RECORD.
            02  LICENSE-NUMBER           PICTURE 9(6).
            02  MAKE-OF-VEHICLE          PICTURE X(15).
            02  YEAR-OF-MODEL            PICTURE 9(2).
            02  COLOUR                   PICTURE X(9).
            02  TYPE-OF-CAR              PICTURE X(6).
            02  DATE-STOLEN              PICTURE 9(6).
            02  OWNER-ADDRESS            PICTURE X(18).
            02  CITY                     PICTURE X(10).
            02  STATE-OR-PROVINCE        PICTURE X(7).
            02  OWNER                    PICTURE X(16).
            02  FILLER                   PICTURE X(5).

        WORKING-STORAGE SECTION.
        77  HASH-QUOTIENT           PICTURE S9(8) COMP SYNC.
        77  HASH-REMAINDER          PICTURE S9(8) COMP SYNC.
        77  INPUT-FILE-EOF               PIC X(3).
                88  END-OF-FILE-IF VALUE IS 'ON'.
        77  OVERFLOW-RECORD-FULL-FLAG   PIC X(3).
            88 OVERFLOW-RECORD-FULL VALUE IS 'ON'.
        77  OVERFLOW-TRACK-NO       PICTURE S9(5) COMP SYNC
                VALUE IS +11.

        01  CARD-IN-FORMAT-1.
            02  MAKE-OF-VEHICLE            PIC X(15).
            02  YEAR-OF-MODEL              PIC 9(2).
            02  OWNER                      PIC X(16).
            02  LICENSE-NUMBER             PIC 9(6).
            02  DATE-REPORTED              PIC 9(6).
            02  OWNER-ADDRESS              PIC X(18).
            02  CITY                       PIC X(10).
            02  STATE-OR-PROVINCE          PIC X(7).
        01  CARD-IN-FORMAT-2.
            02  COLOUR                     PIC X(9).
            02  TYPE-OF-CAR                PIC X(6).
            02  FILLER                     PIC X(65).

        01  THE-ACTUAL-KEY.
            02  TRACK-IDENTIFIER    PICTURE S9(5) COMP SYNC.
            02  KEY-OF-RECORD       PICTURE X(6).


        PROCEDURE DIVISION.
            PERFORM INITIALIZATION.
            PERFORM READ-AND-STORE-RECORD
                UNTIL END-OF-FILE-IF OR
                    OVERFLOW-RECORD-FULL.
            PERFORM TERMINATION.
            STOP RUN.

        INITIALIZATION.
            MOVE 'OFF' TO OVERFLOW-RECORD-FULL-FLAG.
            MOVE 'OFF' TO INPUT-FILE-EOF.
            OPEN INPUT INPUT-FILE.
            OPEN OUTPUT OUTPUT-FILE.
            PERFORM READ-ROUTINE.
```

Program 7.1 (cont.)

```
       READ-ROUTINE.
           READ INPUT-FILE INTO CARD-IN-FORMAT-1
               AT END MOVE 'ON' TO INPUT-FILE-EOF.
           IF NOT END-OF-FILE-IF THEN
               READ INPUT-FILE INTO CARD-IN-FORMAT-2
               AT END MOVE 'ON' TO INPUT-FILE-EOF.

       READ-AND-STORE-RECORD.
           MOVE CORRESPONDING CARD-IN-FORMAT-1
                   TO OUTPUT-FILE-RECORD.
           MOVE CORRESPONDING CARD-IN-FORMAT-2
                   TO OUTPUT-FILE-RECORD.
           PERFORM HASH-ROUTINE.
       HASH-ROUTINE.
           DIVIDE 11 INTO LICENSE-NUMBER
               OF OUTPUT-FILE-RECORD
               GIVING HASH-QUOTIENT
               REMAINDER HASH-REMAINDER.
           MOVE HASH-REMAINDER TO TRACK-IDENTIFIER.
           MOVE LICENSE-NUMBER OF OUTPUT-FILE-RECORD
               TO KEY-OF-RECORD.
           WRITE OUTPUT-FILE-RECORD
               INVALID KEY PERFORM OVERFLOW-ROUTINE.
           PERFORM READ-ROUTINE.

       OVERFLOW-ROUTINE.
           MOVE OVERFLOW-TRACK-NO TO TRACK-IDENTIFIER.
           WRITE OUTPUT-FILE-RECORD
               INVALID KEY DISPLAY 'OVERFLOW RECORD FULL'
               MOVE 'ON' TO OVERFLOW-RECORD-FULL-FLAG.

       TERMINATION.
           CLOSE INPUT-FILE
                 OUTPUT-FILE.
```

Program 7.1 Narrative. The purpose of Program 7.1 is to read a deck of data cards and to transfer the information stored on them to a mass storage *direct access* file. Two data cards are needed to supply the information for one 100-byte record on the mass storage file. The mass storage file is called OUTPUT-FILE and it is created in the random access mode. The ACTUAL KEY is called THE-ACTUAL-KEY and contains a full word TRACK-IDENTIFIER declared as a computational synchronized item and a record identifier called KEY-OF-RECORD declared as a 6-byte display item.

TRACK-LIMIT IS 12 has been specified asking the operating system to format 12 tracks when the file is opened for output. These tracks are labeled 0 through 11. The last of these, it has been decided, will be used to store overflow records from a hashing algorithm.

Since each record of the file requires a track identifier from 0 to 10, the record key is divided by 11 and the remainder used as the track identifier. If a record cannot be stored on its designated track, an attempt is made to store it on track 11. Failing this, an "OVERFLOW RECORD FULL" message is printed and processing is terminated.

Note that this is a simplified version of the hashing algorithm used in the programs in Chapter 6. No hash table has been included. Here a bucket (track 11) has been used to store all overflow records. The operating system is responsible for finding the record, once its track address is known, by locating the corresponding record key. In Chapter 6, hashing collisions were resolved by storing their relative keys at open locations in the hash table.

7.2.3. The FD Entry: Defining the File

As an IBM direct access file can support both variable-length and fixed-length records but not blocking, the FD entries have either of two forms.

Fixed-Length Records

```
FD file-name
      LABEL RECORDS ARE STANDARD
      RECORD CONTAINS integer CHARACTERS
      DATA RECORD IS record-name.
01    record-name.
      02 etc.
```

Variable-Length Records

```
FD file-name
      LABEL RECORDS ARE STANDARD
      RECORD CONTAINS integer1 TO integer2 CHARACTERS
      DATA RECORDS ARE record-name1, record-name2, . . . .
01    record-name1.
      02 etc.
01    record-name2.
      02 etc.
01    . . .
```

It is assumed for variable-length records that at least two of the records described have different lengths or that an OCCURS DE-

PENDING ON clause is used within at least one of the record descriptions. (The reader is referred back to Chapter 3 where variable-length records are discussed in detail.)

7.2.4 Procedure Division Statements

The OPEN Statement

A typical OPEN statement for sequentially accessed files is:

```
OPEN INPUT file-name
```

used when reading the file and

```
OPEN OUTPUT file-name
```

used when writing to the file during file creation or subsequently.

The READ Statement

The general format of the READ statement to be used when the file is opened for input and the access mode is sequential is:

```
READ  file-name [INTO data-name]
      AT END imperative statement
```

Here *file-name* is the name of the file in question, and *data-name* names a data area within the WORKING-STORAGE SECTION to which the record read from the file is to be moved with a group MOVE if this optional INTO statement is employed.

The *imperative statement* following the AT END clause is invoked whenever an attempt is made to read beyond end-of-file.

The WRITE Statement

The standard form of the WRITE statement is:

```
WRITE record-name [FROM data-name]
      INVALID KEY imperative statement.
```

where *record-name* is the name of the level 01 entry within the FD describing the file, and *data-name* is the name of an area within the WORKING-STORAGE SECTION that is to undergo a group MOVE to the FD or buffer area of the file. The FROM clause is optional.

The *imperative statement* following the INVALID KEY clause is invoked if an attempt is made to write a record beyond the physical boundary of the file. Note very carefully that this clause is not invoked if an attempt is made to write a record to the file with the same record identifier as one already written on the current track or on any other. During random access processing the software is only capable of retrieving the first record on a track with a given record identifier thus making other records with the same record identifier on that track not retrievable. They can, however, be retrieved when the file is read sequentially.

The CLOSE Statement

The general form of the CLOSE statement is:

CLOSE *file-name*

This statement causes an end-of-file marker to be placed on the file after formatting any tracks as required by a TRACK-LIMIT clause.

7.3 RANDOM ACCESS OF A DIRECT FILE

A direct access file may be created in the random access mode and may be accessed in this mode once created (by either access mode).

Creating a direct file in the random access mode is quite different from creating one in the sequential mode. The major difference is that the tracks must be formatted first, this process being accomplished as part of the OPEN routine rather than during the CLOSE as is the case with sequential creation. For this reason the presence of the TRACK-LIMIT clause takes on greater importance. If the TRACK-LIMIT clause is present, the number of tracks specified is automatically formatted (that is, either dummy or capacity records are written onto the file). If the clause is not present, only the primary allocation is formatted. Unused tracks specified as secondary allocation are not formatted. Once the tracks are formatted, the user is free to write data records onto the track locations of his choice.

7.3.1 The SELECT Clause Entry

The general format of the SELECT clause entry is:

```
SELECT file-name
ASSIGN TO DA-DISK-D-DD1
ACCESS MODE IS RANDOM
ACTUAL KEY IS data-name.
```

where *file-name*, as before, names the COBOL file.

The system name DA-DISK-D-DD1 specifies that this is a direct access (DA) file, stored on a disk (DISK) unit, with direct file organization (D), and with the Job Control Language card of ddname DD1.

The file access mode is stated as random (ACCESS MODE IS RANDOM) and *data-name* specifies the name of a data area within the WORKING-STORAGE SECTION to be used as THE-ACTUAL-KEY.

When the file is opened for I–O, the system name may optionally be written as DA-DISK-W-DD1 with a "W" replacing the "D". The W allows the use of the REWRITE statement and shall be discussed presently.

7.3.2 The ACTUAL KEY Entry

A typical ACTUAL KEY entry is:

```
01  THE-ACTUAL-KEY.

    02  TRACK-IDENTIFIER
              PIC  S9(8)
              COMPUTATIONAL
              SYNCHRONIZED.
    02  RECORD-IDENTIFIER
              PIC  X(255).
```

set up exactly the same as with ACCESS MODE IS SEQUENTIAL.

In order to write a record in the random access mode, once the file has been opened, it is necessary to store the track identifier and the record identifier into the ACTUAL KEY before proceeding. The user is at liberty to specify the track identifier of his choice, and provided there is room on the named track, the record will be written. Once the record is written, the ACTUAL KEY will still contain the corresponding record and track identifiers. An example of the ACTUAL KEY entry in the random access mode is shown in Program 7.2.

Program 7.2

```
IDENTIFICATION DIVISION.
PROGRAM-ID. PROG7PT2.


ENVIRONMENT DIVISION.

CONFIGURATION SECTION.
SOURCE-COMPUTER. IBM-370.
OBJECT-COMPUTER. IBM-370.

INPUT-OUTPUT SECTION.

FILE-CONTROL.

    SELECT CARD-READER
        ASSIGN TO UT-CARD-S-SYSIN
        ORGANIZATION IS SEQUENTIAL
    ACCESS MODE IS SEQUENTIAL.

    SELECT INPUT-FILE
        ASSIGN TO DA-DISK-D-DD1
        ACCESS IS RANDOM
        ACTUAL KEY IS THE-ACTUAL-KEY.

    SELECT OUTPUT-FILE
    ASSIGN TO UT-PRNT-S-SYSPRINT
        ACCESS MODE IS SEQUENTIAL
        ORGANIZATION IS SEQUENTIAL.


DATA DIVISION.

FILE SECTION.

FD  CARD-READER
    LABEL RECORDS ARE OMITTED
    RECORD CONTAINS 80 CHARACTERS
    DATA RECORD IS CARD-READER-RECORD.
01  CARD-READER-RECORD.
    02  LICENSE-NUMBER              PICTURE 9(6).
    02  FILLER                      PICTURE X(74).

FD  INPUT-FILE
        LABEL RECORDS ARE STANDARD
        RECORD CONTAINS 100 CHARACTERS
        DATA RECORD IS INPUT-FILE-RECORD.
01  INPUT-FILE-RECORD.
    02  LICENSE-NUMBER              PICTURE X(6).
    02  MAKE-OF-VEHICLE             PICTURE X(15).
    02  YEAR-OF-MODEL               PICTURE 9(2).
    02  COLOUR                      PICTURE X(9).
    02  TYPE-OF-CAR                 PICTURE X(6).
    02  DATE-STOLEN                 PICTURE 9(6).
    02  OWNER-ADDRESS               PICTURE X(18).
    02  CITY                        PICTURE X(10).
    02  STATE-OR-PROVINCE           PICTURE X(7).
    02  OWNER                       PICTURE X(16).
    02  FILLER                      PICTURE X(5).

FD  OUTPUT-FILE
```

Program 7.2 (cont.)

```
            LABEL RECORDS ARE OMITTED
            RECORD CONTAINS 133 CHARACTERS
            DATA RECORD IS OUTPUT-FILE-RECORD.
       01   OUTPUT-FILE-RECORD.
            02   FILLER                     PICTURE X.
            02   FILLER                     PICTURE X(5).
            02   LICENSE-NUMBER             PICTURE X(6).
            02   FILLER                     PICTURE X(8).
            02   MAKE-OF-VEHICLE            PICTURE X(15).
            02   FILLER                     PICTURE X(5).
            02   COLOUR                     PICTURE X(9).
            02   FILLER                     PICTURE X(84).
       01   TITLE-LINE.
            02   FILLER                     PICTURE X.
            02   FILLER                     PICTURE X(5).
            02   LICENSE-NUMBER             PICTURE X(11).
            02   FILLER                     PICTURE X(3).
            02   MAKE                       PICTURE X(5).
            02   FILLER                     PICTURE X(15).
            02   VEHICLE-COLOUR             PICTURE X(6).
            02   FILLER                     PICTURE X(87).
       01   MESSAGE-LINE.
            02   FILLER                     PICTURE X.
            02   INVALID-LICENSE-NUMBER     PICTURE X(6).
            02   FILLER                     PICTURE X(3).
            02   MESSAGE-DESCRIPTOR         PICTURE X(18).
            02   FILLER                     PICTURE X(105).
       WORKING-STORAGE SECTION.
       77   CARD-READER-EOF                 PICTURE X(3).
                 88   END-OF-INPUT-CR
                      VALUE IS  'ON'.
       77   HASH-QUOTIENT                   PICTURE S9(8)
                                            COMPUTATIONAL
                                            SYNCHRONIZED.
       77   HASH-REMAINDER                  PICTURE S9(8)
                                            COMPUTATIONAL
                                            SYNCHRONIZED.
       77   OVERFLOW-TRACK-NO               PICTURE S9(5)
                                            COMPUTATIONAL
                                            SYNCHRONIZED
                 VALUE IS +11.
       01   THE-ACTUAL-KEY.
            02   TRACK-IDENTIFIER           PICTURE S9(5)
                                            COMPUTATIONAL
                                            SYNCHRONIZED.
            02   KEY-OF-RECORD              PICTURE X(6).
       01   RECORD-NOT-LOCATED.
            02   FILLER                     PICTURE X(3).
                 88   INVALID-READ VALUE IS 'ON'.
                 88   SEARCH-FAIL VALUE IS 'ON'.
                 88   SEARCH-POSITIVE VALUE IS 'OFF'.
       PROCEDURE DIVISION.
            PERFORM INITIALIZATION.
            PERFORM READ-KEY-FETCH-RECORD
```

Program 7.2 (cont.)

```
               UNTIL END-OF-INPUT-CR.
           PERFORM TERMINATION.
           STOP RUN.

       INITIALIZATION.
           MOVE 'OFF' TO CARD-READER-EOF.
           OPEN INPUT INPUT-FILE
                      CARD-READER.
           OPEN OUTPUT OUTPUT-FILE.
           PERFORM PRINT-TITLE.
           READ CARD-READER
           AT END MOVE 'ON' TO CARD-READER-EOF.

       TERMINATION.
           CLOSE CARD-READER
                 OUTPUT-FILE
                 INPUT-FILE.

       READ-KEY-FETCH-RECORD.
           PERFORM HASH-ROUTINE.
           PERFORM FETCH-RECORD.
           IF INVALID-READ THEN
               PERFORM OVERFLOW-SEARCH.
           IF SEARCH-POSITIVE THEN
               PERFORM PRINT-RECORD.
           IF SEARCH-FAIL THEN
               PERFORM PRINT-NO-RECORD-FOUND.
           READ CARD-READER
               AT END MOVE 'ON' TO CARD-READER-EOF.

       HASH-ROUTINE.
           DIVIDE 11 INTO LICENSE-NUMBER OF CARD-READER
               GIVING HASH-QUOTIENT
               REMAINDER HASH-REMAINDER.

       FETCH-RECORD.
           MOVE HASH-REMAINDER TO TRACK-IDENTIFIER.
           MOVE LICENSE-NUMBER OF CARD-READER
           TO KEY-OF-RECORD.
           MOVE 'OFF' TO RECORD-NOT-LOCATED.
           READ INPUT-FILE
           INVALID KEY MOVE 'ON' TO RECORD-NOT-LOCATED.

       OVERFLOW-SEARCH.
           MOVE OVERFLOW-TRACK-NO TO TRACK-IDENTIFIER.
           MOVE 'OFF' TO RECORD-NOT-LOCATED.
           READ INPUT-FILE
               INVALID KEY MOVE 'ON' TO RECORD-NOT-LOCATED.

       PRINT-RECORD.
           MOVE SPACES TO OUTPUT-FILE-RECORD.
           MOVE CORRESPONDING INPUT-FILE-RECORD
               TO OUTPUT-FILE-RECORD.
           WRITE OUTPUT-FILE-RECORD
               AFTER POSITIONING 1 LINES.

       PRINT-NO-RECORD-FOUND.
           MOVE SPACES TO MESSAGE-LINE.
           MOVE LICENSE-NUMBER OF CARD-READER
               TO INVALID-LICENSE-NUMBER.
```

Program 7.2 (cont.)

```
           MOVE 'RECORD NOT LOCATED' TO MESSAGE-DESCRIPTOR.
           WRITE OUTPUT-FILE-RECORD
               AFTER POSITIONING 1 LINES.

       PRINT-TITLE.
           MOVE SPACES TO TITLE-LINE.
           MOVE 'LICENSE-NO' TO LICENSE-NUMBER
               OF TITLE-LINE.
           MOVE 'MAKE' TO MAKE.
           MOVE 'COLOUR' TO VEHICLE-COLOUR.
           WRITE TITLE-LINE AFTER POSITIONING 0 LINES.
```

Program 7.2 Narrative. The purpose of Program 7.2 is to retrieve records whose record keys are given from the file created in Program 7.1. The record keys are read from the card reader and then divided by 11. The remainder on division is used as the track identifier to fetch the record. If the record cannot be located, an effort is made to locate the record on overflow track number 11. If the record is not located on track 11, it is considered to be missing from the file and an appropriate error message is printed. Processing halts when end-of-file is encountered.

7.3.3 The FD Entry: Describing the File

Fixed-Length Records

For fixed-length records, a typical entry is:

FD *file-name*

LABEL RECORDS ARE STANDARD
RECORD CONTAINS *integer* CHARACTERS
DATA RECORD IS *record-name.*

01 *record-name.*

02 etc.

where *file-name* is the name of the file, *integer* specifies the number of characters in each fixed length record, and *record-name* names the record in the following level 01 entry.

More than one level 01 entry may be present but each group item must have the same length. Multiple level 01 entries are treated as automatic redefinitions of the record. These additional record names may be named by the optional DATA RECORDS ARE clause as

```
DATA RECORDS ARE record-name1
                 record-name2 . . .
```

All clauses with the exception of the LABEL RECORDS clause may be omitted and entries may occur in any order.

Variable-Length Records

A typical variable-length entry is:

```
FD file-name
    LABEL RECORDS ARE STANDARD
    RECORD CONTAINS integer1 TO integer2 CHARACTERS
    RECORDING MODE IS V
    DATA RECORD IS record-name.
01  record-name.
    02  etc.
```

where *file-name* is the file being described.

The RECORD CONTAINS clause specifies the number of characters (*integer1*) in the minimum-sized, variable-length record and the number of characters (*integer2*) in the largest variable-length record. RECORDING MODE IS V indicates that this is a variable-length record file. The DATA RECORD clause indicates the name (names) of succeeding level 01 entry (entries).

Presumably (since this is a variable-length record file), there are present either multiple level 01 record descriptions of various sizes and/or one or more level 01 entries containing the OCCURS DEPENDING ON clause.

Before a record may be written to the file, the data portion of the record must be transmitted to the FD buffer area and its actual key specified.

As a reminder, we reiterate that the records of a direct file may *not* be blocked.

7.3.4 Procedure Division Statements

The OPEN Statement

Random access permits a direct access file to be opened in one of three modes: INPUT, OUTPUT, and I-O. The corresponding OPEN statements are:

```
OPEN INPUT file-name

OPEN OUTPUT file-name

OPEN I-O file-name
```

In the INPUT mode, file records can only be read; in the OUTPUT mode, file records can only be written. In the I–O mode, records can be both read and written.

The READ Statement

The general format of the READ statement in all three modes of the OPEN verb is:

```
READ file-name RECORD [INTO identifier]
        INVALID KEY imperative statement
```

where *file-name* is the name of the associated file. This statement causes one logical record to be made available in the buffer area or moved with a group MOVE to the data name *identifier* within the WORKING-STORAGE SECTION if the optional INTO clause is used. The *imperative statement* following the INVALID KEY is invoked if the record is not found or if the track address specified is not within the limits of the file.

Before a READ statement is issued, the ACTUAL KEY data item must be set to the track and record identifier of the desired record.

The WRITE Statement

The general format of the WRITE statement is

```
WRITE record-name [FROM identifier]
    INVALID KEY imperative-statement
```

where *record-name* is the name of the level 01 entry within the associated FD for the file. The record to be written to the file must be moved to this entry by the user or automatically from the data area named *identifier* by a group MOVE if the optional FROM clause is invoked.

The track and record identifiers of the record to be written must be placed in the ACTUAL KEY data item before the record is written.

If the ASSIGN clause contains a D in the system name entry,

as in DA-DISK-D-DD1, the WRITE statement will only write a record to the file to replace a file record already in existence if

(a) the record to be replaced has an ACTUAL KEY identical to the one in the record to be added and
(b) if the record to be replaced was read by the last READ statement executed.

The programmer should always READ a record before he replaces it to be sure it is eligible for replacement.

If a READ statement is not executed prior to writing, the record will not replace any record on the file but will be added as a new file record whether or not it duplicates the record key of another record on the file.

The INVALID KEY clause is invoked if an attempt is made to write a record with HIGH-VALUES in the first character position of the record identifier (you cannot create dummy records with ACCESS IS RANDOM) or if the ACTUAL KEY is outside the physical limits of the file.

The REWRITE Statement

Some users prefer to use the REWRITE verb when they wish to replace an already existing file record. This statement can only be used if a W is placed in the system name of the SELECT clause for the file as in DA-DISK-W-DD1. The general format of the REWRITE clause is:

REWRITE *record-name* [FROM *identifier*]
INVALID KEY *imperative-statement*

where *record-name* is the name of the level 01 entry within the FD of the file to which the record to be written must first be moved. The record can be moved there automatically by a group MOVE from the data area named *identifier* if the optional FROM clause is used.

In order to use the REWRITE statement, the following steps should be taken:

1. MOVE the record's track and record identifier to the ACTUAL KEY data item.
2. READ the record and check, now that you have read it, that it is eligible for replacement.

3. Issue the REWRITE statement before you issue another READ.

The INVALID KEY clause will be invoked if an attempt is made to replace a record that does not exist or if the record identifier is outside the limits of the file.

The REWRITE statement can only be used if the OPEN mode is I-O.

A WRITE statement used with a W in the system name of the SELECT clause will automatically add a new record to the file whether or not a duplicate exists. Files are closed by the normal use of a CLOSE statement.

7.4 CONCLUSION

The foremost difficulty with this direct access is record addressing. The address consisting of two parts is more complex than the simple relative address of Chapter 4 and all the difficulties of relative addressing as well as solutions apply. Unlike in relative addressing, knowledge of the storage device is essential to direct addressing. However, in any system direct physical addressing must be done somewhere. It need not be done in COBOL but the general problems remain the same.

The advantage of direct access is that it is fast, since there is no layer of software control between the program and the device. The disadvantage is that since there is no software control, all control, addressing, and data management must be performed by the programmer with device-dependent considerations. Direct access, as described in this chapter, should normally be avoided as a file access method. However, requirements of speed and flexibility could make it necessary, but the programmer should be prepared to demonstrate such necessity.

8

COBOL Indexed I-O Files

A COBOL Indexed I-O file is a mass storage file in which data records may be accessed by the *value* of a key. It is characterized by the fact that the physical relation of the records corresponds to the logical order of the file key values in so far as this can be maintained in a dynamic environment. Thus an Indexed I-O file allows records to be efficiently accessed in sequential as well as random order. For this reason a COBOL Indexed I-O file is an example of *indexed sequential* file organization and we sometimes refer to it by this general name. You will recall, however, that a Relative I-O file also allows such access. What then is the difference?

8.1 INTRODUCTION

A major feature of the Indexed I–O file organization is that each record address is *uniquely* named by the *value* of one or more keys that are part of the record. This is in contrast to a Relative I–O file which requires knowledge of the sequential ordering of records within the file (and thus their relative address) or the direct access file which requires both track addresses and record keys in order to locate a record. Recall that in a Relative I–O file the programmer was required to provide the relationship between the record key and the relative address at which the record was to be stored. Indexed I–O solves the addressing problem for the programmer.

Just as important, it is possible to add new records to an Indexed I–O file and place them between physically adjacent records when the record logically occurs between them, without recreating the file. Not only can additional records be added at will but they can also be deleted, making room for new records. Indexed I–O files provide system solutions to the problems the programmer encounters with relative files. As always, the system solution in relieving the programmer of tedious detail isolates the programmer from the mechanism of device access. Moreover, the solution to the problems encountered may not be suitable to the use the programmer intends. It is necessary then for the programmer to understand the particular method by which Indexed I–O files are implemented and its characteristics. Many IBM systems implement indexed files with ISAM or VSAM, and their general concepts are explained in Chapter 9. One can use indexed files without knowing how they are implemented but such use can be quite inefficient.

8.1.1 The Primary Key

When an Indexed I–O file is used, data records must be accessed by specifying the value of a key. The record layout or description of the file may contain one or more key data items. Each of these key data items is associated with a directory or index that links each key to the physical address of the record. Only one key, however, may be specified when records are to be added, deleted, or changed. This key must be the unique *primary key* of the record and may not be changed when the record is updated. This key is called the RECORD KEY of the file. Other data items used as keys are called ALTERNATE RECORD KEYs. These keys may provide alternate access paths for the retrieval of records and are not required to be unique.

8.1.2 Access Modes

Indexed I-O provides for both sequential and random access to records and permits the program to change freely from one form of access to the other, once the file has been opened. Records may be either fixed or variable length and both record formats may be blocked. When accessed sequentially, records are retrieved in ascending order of the RECORD KEY values. When accessed by ALTERNATE RECORD KEYs, records having duplicate keys are accessed in the order in which the records were written into the file.

When records are accessed in the random access mode, the order of retrieval is at the discretion of the programmer. Each record is accessed by specifying one of its record keys.

In this chapter, a COBOL program is discussed that will create an Indexed I-O file. Programs to add, delete, and change records should be written by the reader to process this file. The reader should compare the lengths of these programs to those used for the same purposes in Chapters 4 and 5 for Relative I-O files. It will be observed that considerably less code is required to achieve the same result.

The reader is cautioned that the use of Indexed I-O requires a fair amount of system overhead. There is a price to be paid for all the bookkeeping provided by the access method used. Whether the price is worthwhile depends on the value received as compared to the costs of programming, run time, maintenance, and delayed operation because the programmer chooses to write more code.

8.2 CASE STUDY: LEAKEY VALVE CREDIT UNION

The employees of the J.L. Leakey and Sons Valve Company have formed a small credit union. In essence, this is a small bank whose customers are company employees who lend their savings to the credit union in return for a higher rate of interest than is normally available at commercial banks. The credit union in turn invests this money by lending it back to members as mortgages and small interest loans. Each member is given a passbook; deposits and withdrawals are made in person. Check privileges are not possible. The accounts of the credit union members are kept on a mass storage device and accounts are updated when transactions are made. A monthly statement of account is also prepared.

8.2.1 Logical Analysis: Leakey Valve Credit Union

Each account is given a unique number that serves to identify it. This account number is written on the inside of the passbook and is thus available to the teller when the passbook is presented. It was decided to use an Indexed I–O file for this application because of the following facts:

1. Each account has a unique identifier.
2. Accounts are presented for updating at random by the credit union's customers.
3. Monthly accounts are rendered to each customer.
4. The number of transactions per customer is variable.

Monthly accounts can be produced by listing the month's transactions for each customer. This can be done by sequentially processing the records of the file.

Random accessing is necessary so that bank tellers can enter transactions immediately at a terminal. This terminal data entry need not concern us. Modern sophisticated operating systems allow the programmer to write his application program as though the data were to be entered on punched cards. Once the program is written and debugged, the operating system is instructed to treat a given terminal as though it were a card reader. No change in the COBOL program is required.

For each customer the account will contain the following fields:

(a) credit account number
(b) customer name
(c) customer address
(d) credit rating
(e) current amount borrowed from credit union
(f) loan account number if applicable
(g) current credit balance in savings account plus any number of transactions of the form

- date
- amount
- transaction code

The possibilities for transaction code are D for deposit, W for withdrawal, S for service charge, L for loan payment, and B for amount loaned.

In view of the fact that the monthly transactions must be kept on the file and because the number of these entries is variable, the Indexed I–O file is created with variable-length records.

8.2.2 Indexed File Processing: Leakey Valve Credit Union

Records may be added to an indexed file in either of the access modes: sequential or random. If records are added to the file in the sequential access mode, they must be sorted in ascending order on their primary keys. Records need not be sorted if they are added to the file in the random access mode.

Program 8.1 adds the initial records to the Indexed I–O file called the CREDIT-UNION-FILE. The reader should familiarize himself with this program as he studies this chapter.

Program 8.1

```
IDENTIFICATION DIVISION.
PROGRAM-ID.  PROG8PT1.
DATE-WRITTEN.  MAY 31,1979.
DATE-COMPILED. MAR 19,1980.
AUTHOR. R H COOPER.
SECURITY. UNCLASSIFIED.
ENVIRONMENT DIVISION.
CONFIGURATION SECTION.
SOURCE-COMPUTER. IBM-3032.
OBJECT-COMPUTER. IBM-3032.
INPUT-OUTPUT SECTION.
FILE-CONTROL.
    SELECT INPUT-FILE
        ASSIGN TO CARD-SYSIN.
    SELECT OUTPUT-FILE
        ASSIGN TO DISK-DD1
        ORGANIZATION IS INDEXED
        ACCESS MODE IS SEQUENTIAL
        RECORD KEY IS CREDIT-ACCOUNT-NUMBER
        OF OUTPUT-FILE
        FILE STATUS IS STATUS-VARIABLE.
DATA DIVISION.
```

Program 8.1 (cont.)

```
       FILE SECTION.

       FD  INPUT-FILE
               LABEL RECORDS ARE OMITTED
               RECORD CONTAINS 80 CHARACTERS
               DATA RECORD IS INPUT-FILE-RECORD.
       01  INPUT-FILE-RECORD.
           02  CREDIT-ACCOUNT-NUMBER   PIC 9(4).
           02  CUSTOMER-NAME   PIC X(20).
           02  CUSTOMER-ADDRESS        PIC X(20).
           02  CREDIT-RATING           PIC 9.
           02  AMOUNT-BORROWED         PIC 9(7).
           02  LOAN-ACCOUNT-NUMBER     PIC 9(4).
           02  CURRENT-BALANCE         PIC 9(7).
           02  FILLER                  PIC X(13).

       FD  OUTPUT-FILE
               BLOCK CONTAINS 1 RECORDS
               LABEL RECORDS ARE STANDARD
               RECORD CONTAINS 70 TO 1159 CHARACTERS
               DATA RECORD IS OUTPUT-FILE-RECORD.
       01  OUTPUT-FILE-RECORD.
           02  CREDIT-ACCOUNT-NUMBER   PIC 9(4).
           02  CUSTOMER-NAME           PIC X(20).
           02  CUSTOMER-ADDRESS        PIC X(20).
           02  CREDIT-RATING           PIC 9.
           02  AMOUNT-BORROWED         PIC 9(8)
               USAGE IS COMP.
           02  LOAN-ACCOUNT-NUMBER     PIC 9(4).
           02  CURRENT-BALANCE         PIC 9(8)
               USAGE IS COMP.
           02  NUMBER-OF-TRANSACTIONS  PIC 9(4)
               USAGE IS COMP.
           02  TRANSACTIONS
               OCCURS 1 TO 100 TIMES
               DEPENDING ON NUMBER-OF-TRANSACTIONS.
               03  TRANSACTION-DATE    PIC 9(6).
               03  TRANSACTION-AMOUNT  PIC 9(8)
                   USAGE IS COMP.
               03  TRANSACTION-CODE    PIC X.

       WORKING-STORAGE SECTION.

       77  INPUT-FILE-EOF              PIC X(3).
           88  NO-MORE-DATA-CARDS
               VALUE IS 'ON'.
       77  OUTPUT-FILE-EOF             PIC X(3).
           88  END-OF-FILE-OF VALUE IS 'ON'.
       77  STATUS-VARIABLE             PIC 99.


       PROCEDURE DIVISION.

           PERFORM INITIALIZATION.
           PERFORM BUILD-FILE
               UNTIL NO-MORE-DATA-CARDS.
           PERFORM TERMINATION.
           STOP RUN.

       INITIALIZATION.
           MOVE 'OFF' TO INPUT-FILE-EOF.
```

Program 8.1 (cont.)

```
           OPEN INPUT INPUT-FILE.
           OPEN OUTPUT OUTPUT-FILE.
           READ INPUT-FILE
               AT END MOVE 'ON' TO INPUT-FILE-EOF.

       BUILD-FILE.
           MOVE CORRESPONDING INPUT-FILE-RECORD
               TO OUTPUT-FILE-RECORD.
           MOVE 1 TO NUMBER-OF-TRANSACTIONS.
           WRITE OUTPUT-FILE-RECORD.
           IF STATUS-VARIABLE NOT EQUAL ZERO
               PERFORM ERROR-ROUTINE.
           READ INPUT-FILE
               AT END MOVE 'ON' TO INPUT-FILE-EOF.

      * **** SUPPLY ERROR ROUTINE FOR PRODUCTION RUNS ****
       ERROR-ROUTINE.
           DISPLAY 'FATAL ERROR'.
           DISPLAY STATUS-VARIABLE.
           DISPLAY OUTPUT-FILE-RECORD.

       TERMINATION.
           CLOSE INPUT-FILE
                 OUTPUT-FILE.
           PERFORM VERIFY.
       VERIFY.
           OPEN INPUT OUTPUT-FILE.
           READ OUTPUT-FILE
               AT END MOVE 'ON' TO OUTPUT-FILE-EOF.
           PERFORM READ-AND-DISPLAY
               UNTIL END-OF-FILE-OF.
           CLOSE OUTPUT-FILE.
       READ-AND-DISPLAY.
           DISPLAY OUTPUT-FILE-RECORD.
           READ OUTPUT-FILE
           AT END MOVE 'ON' TO OUTPUT-FILE-EOF.
```

Program 8.1 Narrative. The purpose of this program is to create the credit union file and add new customer records to it.

The file is called OUTPUT-FILE, and the record key for this file is called CREDIT-ACCOUNT-NUMBER. Note that the file consists of variable length records; the variable part is described under the level 02 entry TRANSACTIONS within OUTPUT-FILE-RECORD.

The OCCURS clause for this file states

```
02 TRANSACTIONS
   OCCURS 1 TO 100 TIMES
   DEPENDING ON NUMBER-OF-TRANSACTIONS.
```

The data item NUMBER-OF-TRANSACTIONS is stored above the data item TRANSACTIONS in the fixed part of the record as required.

Since the OCCURS clause ranges from 1 to 100 times the data

item NUMBER-OF-TRANSACTIONS is given the value 1 in the paragraph BUILD-FILE even though there is no data as yet for this part of the record.

8.3 INDEXED I-O MODULE

8.3.1 The RECORD KEY

When the random access mode is employed, the primary key of the record to be added must be placed in a data item designated as the RECORD KEY. This RECORD KEY in the Indexed I–O module of COBOL is the unique primary key of each record. In ANSI COBOL, the RECORD KEY is a data item whose value is the unique primary key of the record that is to be added, deleted, or updated. In IBM OS/VS COBOL, the RECORD KEY may be any fixed-length item within the record. It must be less than 256 bytes in length.

If more than one description of a record is provided within the FD of the file (with either fixed- or variable-length records), the data item designated as the RECORD KEY must have the same description and must appear at the same location within each record relative to the start of the record. It is not, however, required that the same data name be used in each instance.

It is suggested in IBM OS/VS COBOL that this data item be defined to exclude the first byte of each record, in view of the fact that it is used to mark deletions. In particular, it *must exclude* the first byte in the following cases:

1. The file contains records that *may be deleted.*
2. The file contains *unblocked* records.
3. The file contains one or more records whose primary key has HIGH-VALUES in the first byte position.

With these exceptions, the primary key may occur anywhere within the record.

8.3.2 Environment Division: Defining the Indexed I-O File

The Indexed I–O file is defined by a SELECT clause within the INPUT-OUTPUT section of the environment division. The following is a standard ANSI COBOL entry:

```
SELECT file-name
ASSIGN TO implementor-name
ORGANIZATION IS INDEXED
                 { SEQUENTIAL }
ACCESS MODE IS   { RANDOM     }
                 { DYNAMIC    }
RECORD KEY IS data-name-1
ALTERNATE RECORD KEY IS data-name-2
FILE STATUS IS data-name-3.
```

These clauses are permitted to occur in any order after the SELECT *file-name* entry. The clause ORGANIZATION IS INDEXED specifies that this is an Indexed I–O file.

ANSI COBOL permits one of three access modes for Indexed I–O files. ACCESS MODE IS SEQUENTIAL indicates that access is sequential. This is assumed if the ACCESS clause is omitted. For sequential access, the records in the file are retrieved or stored in sequential order by ascending order of the RECORD KEY. *If records are to be stored in the sequential access mode, the records must be sorted in ascending order by primary key before they are written to the storage device.*

When ACCESS MODE IS RANDOM is specified, records may be stored or retrieved in any order. The order is determined by the programmer, and any record to be stored or retrieved is designated by its RECORD or ALTERNATE RECORD KEY. To retrieve records from the file, this key should be placed in a data item named as part of the READ statement. To store records, the user must ensure that the primary key of the record is stored within the record.

ANSI COBOL permits switching from the sequential access mode to the random access mode or vice versa any number of times during one OPEN of the file provided ACCESS MODE IS DYNAMIC is specified.

The RECORD KEY clause specifies the name of the data item, i.e., *data-name-1*, that locates the primary key of the file within the record description of the file FD.

The ALTERNATE RECORD KEY clause names one or more data items that may be used as alternate keys instead of the RECORD KEY to locate a record within the file. These ALTERNATE KEYs need not be unique, as is the case with the RECORD KEY of the file, and they can only be used to retrieve records. When two or more records have the same alternate key values, the first record encountered containing this key will be fetched. The following format should be used to specify that duplicates on the file may exist:

```
ALTERNATE RECORD KEY IS data-name-2 WITH DUPLICATES
```

Any number of alternate keys may be specified. As previously mentioned, ALTERNATE RECORD KEYs are not used to add, change, or delete records. They can only be used for record retrieval.

The FILE STATUS clause names a data item, *data-name-3*, that is updated by the operating system after every operation that references the file to indicate the execution result of the statement. Programmers wishing to check the success status of an operation should consult the manual for the appropriate return codes.

8.3.3 Data Division: The FD Entry for an Indexed I-O File

The FD entry supplies information relating to the identification, record names, and physical structure of a file. A standard ANSI COBOL entry is as follows:

```
FD file-name
BLOCK CONTAINS integer-1 TO integer-2 CHARACTERS
RECORD CONTAINS integer-3 TO integer-4 CHARACTERS
                       { STANDARD }
LABEL RECORDS ARE      { OMITTED  }
DATA RECORDS ARE record-name-1
                 record-name-2
                       .
                       .
                       .
```

The order of the clauses following the FD *file-name* clause is immaterial. It is assumed that this FD description entry is followed by descriptions of the records within the file with record names of *record-name-1*, *record-name-2*, . . . , the number of which must be at least 1. The description of each record must, of course, contain the primary key and secondary keys named in the RECORD KEY and ALTERNATE RECORD KEY clauses of the file.

The BLOCK CONTAINS clause denotes the size of a physical record as stored on the mass storage device. This clause is not required if one logical record is to constitute the block or if the hardware device has only one physical record size. Respectively, *integer-1* and *integer-2* specify the minimum and maximum physical record sizes. If only *integer-2* is given, the physical record is a fixed-length record; otherwise, it is a variable-length record.

The RECORD CONTAINS clause is optional and specifies the length of a logical record. Respectively, *integer-3* and *integer-4* designate the minimum and maximum record lengths of the records within the file. If only *integer-4* is specified as in

RECORD CONTAINS *integer-4* CHARACTERS

the logical records are considered to be fixed-length records. When the RECORD CONTAINS clause is omitted, the logical record size(s) is determined from the level 01 record descriptions which follow the FD. Variable-length records are assumed if these record descriptions have different lengths or if they contain one or more OCCURS clauses with the DEPENDING ON option.

The LABEL RECORDS clause is required. The option STANDARD indicates that labels exist for the file that have been generated according to the format of the installation's routine for creating file labels. The option OMITTED indicates that the file possesses no labels.

The DATA RECORDS clause is optional and serves to document the names of the level 01 record description entries that follow the FD.

8.3.4 Procedure Division: Statements in an Indexed I-O File

The full power of the Indexed I-O module of COBOL is reflected in the range of COBOL statements available for use within the PROCEDURE DIVISION. The user may update records, delete records from the file, and add records to the file. These operations may be done in sequential mode, random mode, or in a combination of both. A record is identified during random processing by its primary key. A secondary key can be used instead of the primary key when retrieving records. During sequential processing, records are stored and fetched in ascending order by primary key. When adding records sequentially, the burden of sorting by primary key is a user's responsibility.

In this subsection, we shall discuss the relevant COBOL statements for adding, deleting, and updating records. For each statement, a discussion of sequential processing will be followed by a discussion on random processing.

Adding Records

The addition of records may take place at any time during the execution of a COBOL program once the file has been opened. In this respect, the initial creation of a file can be considered as the addition of records to an empty or null file.

Sequential access. When ACCESS MODE IS SEQUENTIAL is specified, records to be added to the file must be presented to the file in sorted order on ascending primary key.

The file can be opened either for OUTPUT or for I–O by using, respectively:

```
OPEN OUTPUT file-name
OPEN I-O file-name
```

If the file is being opened for the very first time (that is, it is being created), only the form

```
OPEN OUTPUT file-name
```

should be used. If the file is already in existence, either form may be used, but the programmer is cautioned that *opening the file for* OUTPUT *will destroy the current content of the file.*

Only one form of the WRITE statement may be used in either case. If the file is being opened for OUTPUT, the user must code:

```
WRITE record-name [FROM identifier]
      INVALID KEY imperative statement
```

in order to logically transfer a record to the file. (Physical transfer may be delayed until sufficient records are available in the buffer to constitute a block.) The *record-name* is the name of the level 01 record description data name within the FD associated with the file. The optional FROM statement names a data area within the WORKING-STORAGE SECTION that is to be first moved to the buffer area before writing. The *imperative statement* following the INVALID KEY clause is executed whenever

(a) the primary key of a record is out of order with respect to those that have preceded it or

(b) the record contains a secondary record key that is not permitted to have duplicates but for which another record in the file possesses the same secondary record key or

(c) an attempt is made to write a record beyond the physical limitations of the file.

In the event that the INVALID KEY clause is invoked, the record stored within the FD area is not affected or written, and the reason the clause is invoked is reflected in the current value of the data item named in the FILE STATUS clause of the SELECT entry for the file.

If the file is opened for I-O, the assumption is made that the record being added is logically replacing a record currently existing within the file. While this is perfectly valid, we prefer to consider this as a change or update to the file in which the entire record with the exception of keys is being made. Discussion of this is deferred until later.

Random access. Records may be added to a file in the random access mode. Each record to be added is specified by its primary key or RECORD KEY within the record itself. Records may be added to the file in any order. Additions can take place until the physical limitations of the file are exhausted. It is not required (as with relative files) that records having the same primary keys exist within the file; indeed we consider such cases as changes not additions.

Records to be added to the file should first be moved to the program area by the execution of one or more MOVE statements or the FROM option of the WRITE statement should be used.

The programmer has two options for the OPEN statement:

```
OPEN OUTPUT file-name

OPEN I-O file-name
```

The former should be used if the programmer wishes during one particular OPEN of the file to only add records to an existing file. If some records are to be changed or deleted as well, he should code the second of these options.

To add a brand new record to the file, the programmer should code the following form of the WRITE statement:

```
WRITE record-name [FROM identifier]
      INVALID KEY imperative statement
```

The *record-name* is the name of the level 01 record description data name within the FD associated with the file and record. The optional FROM statement names a data area within the WORKING-STORAGE SECTION that is to be first moved to the buffer area before writing. The *imperative statement* following the INVALID KEY clause is executed in any of the following eventualities:

(a) if a record with the same primary key already exists within the file

(b) if there exists within the file a record that has a secondary key in common with this record and this secondary key is not permitted to have duplicates

(c) if there is not enough physical room left in the file to store the record.

If the INVALID KEY clause is invoked, the data item designated in the FILE STATUS clause of the associated SELECT statement is updated to indicate the cause of the problem. The record transferred to the buffer area of the file is not affected.

Changing Records

The programmer should always approach the idea of changing a record on a mass storage device with a certain amount of trepidation. A change can consist of an addition of new information to a record, or the deletion of items within a record, or a combination of both. The user should view a change to any of the primary or secondary keys as a deletion followed by an addition not as a change or update. If you are looking for instructions in order to change the keys of records, read the following and then reconsider the previous "Adding Records."

The first thing that is required when changing a record is to read the current record as it now exists. Verify that the record just read is indeed the one you want to change (once it's gone, it's gone), change the record, and then rewrite it. During this process, the total length in characters of the record being changed must not be modified. If the logical record size of the record is to change, it must first be deleted and then added.

Sequential access. When changing records, the file may only be opened in the I-O mode. This is accomplished by specifying

```
OPEN I-O file-name
```

Records to be changed must be processed in sequential order in ascending sequence by RECORD KEY. Records to be changed must first be read and then rewritten. Intervening file records in the sequence of records to be changed must be read unless a START statement intervenes. Such records need not be rewritten.

Records should be read with the following format of the READ statement:

READ *file-name* RECORD [INTO *identifier*]
AT END *imperative statement*

This statement causes one record to be read from the file named and stored in the program buffer area. If the INTO option is specified, the record is moved to the *identifier* data item in the WORKING-STORAGE SECTION by a group MOVE.

The AT END condition occurs when there is no logical record left in the file to read. Control then passes to the *imperative statement* following the AT END clause.

Each READ causes the FILE STATUS data item associated with the file to be updated.

Once a record has been read, it may be changed and then rewritten back to the file. The format for the REWRITE statement is as follows:

REWRITE *record-name* [FROM *identifier*]
INVALID KEY *imperative statement*

The *record-name* is the data name of the logical record in the FD associated with the file. The record must be moved to the buffer area previous to the REWRITE if the optional FROM feature is not specified. In the event the FROM option is specified, the record is moved from the data area named as *identifier* within the WORKING-STORAGE SECTION by a group MOVE.

The INVALID KEY clause is invoked if the primary key of the record to be rewritten does not match that of the last record read successfully from the file. The INVALID KEY clause will also be invoked if the record whose primary key is given has been deleted from the file since the time it was last read.

The value of a secondary key may be changed at the discretion of the user provided it does not equal the secondary key of another record stored on the file for a secondary key that may not have duplicates. As previously mentioned, changing the value of a secondary key is a very serious operation that is perhaps best considered as a deletion of a record followed by an addition of a new record. The decision to change a secondary key may affect other programs used to retrieve records.

Very often during sequential processing of a file, it is desirable to start somewhere in the file other than at the beginning (where you are always left by the action of an OPEN statement) or to skip over records during the processing of the file. The START statement is provided for this purpose. The general format of the START statement is:

```
START file-name
        ⎧ IS EQUAL TO         ⎫
        ⎪ IS =                ⎪
    KEY ⎨ IS GREATER THAN     ⎬ data-name
        ⎪ IS >                ⎪
        ⎪ IS NOT LESS THAN    ⎪
        ⎩ IS NOT <            ⎭
INVALID KEY imperative statement
```

The START statement is used to position the current record pointer to any record. The OPEN statement automatically positions this pointer at the start of the file. Sequential reading of records will begin from whichever record is pointed to by the START statement.

Each record is located within the file by its primary key. The *data-name* is the name of a data item that contains a primary key. The START statement will locate this primary key within the file or the first one greater than this value depending on whether the programmer specifies IS EQUAL TO or IS GREATER THAN, respectively. If the programmer specifies IS NOT LESS THAN, he is indicating that he wants the current record pointer set at the value of *data-name* or, if a record with that primary key is missing, at the first record with a primary key greater than *data-name.*

The INVALID KEY clause is invoked if a record that satisfies the KEY IS condition cannot be found. Thus, there are three conditions that will trigger an INVALID KEY condition:

1. KEY IS EQUAL TO is specified and no key with this exact value found.
2. KEY IS GREATER THAN is specified and no key with a value greater than the given key can be found.
3. KEY IS NOT LESS THAN is specified and no key can be found either equal to the primary key specified or larger than it.

If the INVALID KEY clause is invoked, the current record pointer is not changed.

In summary, records can be changed or updated sequentially by using a combination of READ and REWRITE statements interspersed with one or more START statements. As the condition value that a START statement relies on is stored in *data-name*, the START statement can be inserted between a REWRITE statement and the following READ. It can then be executed conditionally whenever the difference between the primary key of the record to be added and the value of the current record pointer is large, thereby skipping over many records. For example, if the current record pointer points to primary key 600, the record to be added is 900, and there is a high probability that there are many records in between, then it would make sense to use a START statement prior to the next READ to skip records.

Random access. When records are to be changed with ACCESS IS RANDOM specified, the record to be changed should first be read and verified and then updated and rewritten. It is not permitted during this process to change the actual length in characters of the logical record. The primary key of the record should not be modified and extreme care should be observed if secondary keys are to be modified. Changing secondary keys might logically be considered as a deletion followed by the addition of a new record.

The file whose records are to be changed should be opened in the I-O mode with the statement:

```
OPEN I-O file-name
```

The only two statements needed are READ and REWRITE. The record should be retrieved by specifying one of its keys (either a primary or a secondary key) in a READ statement. Once the record has been verified as eligible for change, the update should be made and a REWRITE issued to restore the record in its updated form. The general format of the READ statement is:

```
READ file-name RECORD [INTO identifier]
     KEY IS data-name
     INVALID KEY imperative statement
```

This statement causes one logical record to be made available in the buffer area or in the area named as *identifier* if the optional INTO clause is specified. If this INTO clause is specified, the record is moved to the *identifier* by means of a group MOVE.

The *data-name* specifies the name of a data item that has been named as RECORD KEY or ALTERNATE RECORD KEY of the file. If the KEY IS clause is omitted, the primary or RECORD KEY is assumed. The INVALID KEY CLAUSE is invoked if no record can be found on the file that matches the key specified.

The general format of the REWRITE statement is:

```
REWRITE record-name [FROM identifier]
    INVALID KEY imperative statement
```

where *record-name* is the name of the logical record described in the FD associated with the file. The contents of the record must be moved to the buffer area by the programmer or by the optional use of the FROM clause, which causes the record stored at *identifier* to be moved to the buffer by means of a group MOVE. The number of character positions in the logical record length cannot be changed.

The execution of this statement causes the record stored in the buffer area to replace the record on the file with the same primary key value. If any secondary keys are changed, they must not be duplicates of any other secondary keys stored in other records of the file unless ALTERNATE RECORD KEYS has been specified as allowing duplicates.

Strictly speaking, it is not required in random accessing to READ the record before rewriting it. This technique is, however, strongly recommended.

The INVALID KEY clause will be invoked if an attempt is made to REWRITE a record that contains a primary key whose value is not the same as the primary key of any record on the file or in the event that a secondary key contains a duplicate of a secondary key of another record on the file when duplicates are not allowed. The execution of the REWRITE statement causes the data item associated with the FILE STATUS clause to be updated. The reader should be aware that *the result of an attempt to change the logical record length is undefined.*

Deleting Records

The Indexed I–O module of COBOL provides a single statement, the DELETE statement, that is used to remove a record from an indexed file. Care should always be exercised when using this statement because a record that is deleted cannot be READ again. A suggested procedure is to READ the record first, apply a verification test to it, and after valid verification DELETE the record. A deleted record should, in most instances, be moved to a save area before it is deleted.

Sequential access. The DELETE statement may be used with ACCESS IS SEQUENTIAL but must only be used in the I-O mode of the OPEN verb with the statement:

OPEN I-O *file-name*

Each DELETE command that is executed must be preceded by a successful READ of the record to be deleted. This READ should be the last I/O operation executed for the file in question before the DELETE is performed, and it must be a successful READ. However, it is permitted to have I/O operations on other files between the executions of the READ and DELETE statements (indeed it is wise to save a copy of the record prior to its deletion). The general format of the READ statement to be used is:

READ *file-name* RECORD [INTO *identifier*]
AT END *imperative statement*

This statement causes the next record in sequence on the file to be read into the buffer area (or made available if blocking is employed). The record is moved to the data name designated *identifier* by means of a group MOVE if the optional INTO statement is included. The AT END clause is invoked if an attempt is made to read beyond the physical bounds of the file. The START statement discussed previously may also be used in this case to position the file at the desired record.

The general format of the DELETE statement is:

DELETE *file-name* RECORD

This statement causes the record previously read by the last READ statement on the file in question to be logically removed from the file. The data item named in the FILE STATUS clause is also updated at this time.

The reader should be aware that *the* DELETE *statement used with* ACCESS IS SEQUENTIAL *has no* INVALID KEY *clause to escape to if something goes wrong.* The last record successfully READ is simply removed; hopefully it is the record the programmer would like to have removed but the responsibility is the programmer's. *The result of a* DELETE *statement if no successful* READ *precedes its execution is not defined.*

Random access. The DELETE statement may also be used if ACCESS IS RANDOM is specified, provided the file is opened for I-O with the statement:

```
OPEN I-O file-name
```

Although it is not required that a successful READ precede the execution of this statement, it is suggested that a record be read before an order to delete it is given for purposes of verification. The general format for the READ statement is:

```
READ file-name RECORD [INTO identifier]
     KEY IS data-name
     INVALID KEY imperative statement
```

where *data-name* is the name of a data item that has been designated as a primary or secondary key for this file. The record on the file to be read matches the key that is the current value of *data-name.* Once read, the record is made available in the buffer area for the file or transferred to the data item *identifier* by a group MOVE if the optional INTO clause is used.

The INVALID KEY clause is invoked if a record cannot be located on the file that matches the value of the key in *data-name.* If the KEY IS clause is omitted, it is assumed that the key meant is the RECORD KEY of the file.

Once the record is read and verified as eligible for deletion it may be deleted. Again we suggest that first the record should be copied to a save area. The general format of the DELETE statement is:

```
DELETE file-name RECORD
     INVALID KEY imperative statement
```

This statement causes the record whose key is the current contents of the primary key data item (the RECORD KEY) to be logically removed from the file. The data item associated with the FILE STATUS clause is updated to reflect the results of execution.

The INVALID KEY clause is invoked if a record cannot be found that has the primary key specified. The contents of the buffer area associated with the file are not affected by the execution of this statement.

8.3.5 Summary of Statements

Within the procedure division we have examined five language verbs in their various formats; namely, the READ, WRITE, REWRITE, DELETE, and START verbs. Each of these verbs performs a specific task and is subject to various rules depending on the access mode and the format of the OPEN verb employed. For quick review and reference, the rules for the use of these verbs are summarized in the Tables 8.1 and 8.2. Table 8.1 summarizes the various statement formats for each verb and Table 8.2 keys the use of these formats to the access mode and the OPEN format.

Table 8.1 Verb Formats for Indexed I-O

Verb	*Format*	*Statements*
READ	1	READ *file-name* RECORD [INTO *identifier*] AT END *imperative statement*
	2	READ *file-name* RECORD [INTO *identifier*] KEY IS *data-name* INVALID KEY *imperative statement*
WRITE		WRITE *record-name* [FROM *identifier*] INVALID KEY *imperative statement*
REWRITE		REWRITE *record-name* [FROM *identifier*] INVALID KEY *imperative statement*
DELETE	1	DELETE *file-name* RECORD
	2	DELETE *file-name* RECORD INVALID KEY *imperative statement*
START		START *file-name* KEY { IS EQUAL TO | IS = | IS GREATER THAN | IS > | IS NOT LESS THAN | IS NOT < } *data-name* INVALID KEY *imperative statement*

Dynamic access. The Indexed I–O module of COBOL allows one further feature, namely, ACCESS MODE IS DYNAMIC. In this mode, the user may switch from using random access instructions to sequential access instructions at will and in any order without closing and reopening files. There are no changes in the formats of any instructions with the exception of the READ statement which must now take the following form when sequential access is employed:

```
READ file-name NEXT RECORD INTO identifier
     AT END imperative statement
```

(The change here is the addition of the word NEXT.)

The use of statements is still governed by the mode in which the file is opened. All statements can be used if the mode is I–O; only the WRITE verb can be used if the mode is OUTPUT; and only the READ and START verbs can be used if the mode is INPUT.

Table 8.2 Summary of Formats from Table 8.1 and Access Modes

Access	*Input*	*Output*	*I-O*
Sequential	READ format 1 START	WRITE	READ format 1 REWRITE DELETE format 1 START
Random	READ format 1	WRITE	READ format 2 WRITE REWRITE DELETE format 2

PROBLEMS

1. Use Program 8.1 to create a credit union file. Do not forget that you will have to run an Access Method Services Procedure to allocate the file.

2. Prepare some transactions for the credit union file and write a program to update it.

3. Delete and add some records to the credit union file.

4. Set up an index file of the students in your class or of the people with whom you work. Employ at least two secondary keys and fetch records using these secondary keys.

5. Upon admission to the emergency room of the local hospital, a patient is required to give the information described in COBOL below.

```
01  ADMITTING-RECORD.
    02  MEDICAID-NUMBER       PIC X(10).
    02  NAME-LAST             PIC X(15).
```

```
02 NAME-FIRST              PIC X(15).
02 ADDRESS-OF-PATIENT
   03 STREET               PIC X(16).
   03 CITY                 PIC X(10).
02 MILITARY-IDENT-NUMBER
                           PIC X(10).
```

Other information is also taken but will be ignored for this example.

Write a COBOL program that creates an index sequential file on primary key MEDICAID-NUMBER for these admitting records. Keypunch and store at least ten such records.

6. Write a COBOL program that reads in a deck of data cards each containing a ten digit MEDICAID-NUMBER. Access the file you created in question 5 and print out the records corresponding to the MEDICAID-NUMBER read in. Print an appropriate warning message if no admitting record corresponds to a particular MEDICAID-NUMBER read in.

7. Below is a partial description in COBOL of a military record keyed on the MILITARY-IDENT-NUMBER. Create an index sequential file of these records as you did in question 5. In addition modify the program from question 5 so that MILITARY-IDENT-NUMBER can be a secondary key for the admitting records file (no duplicates allowed). If your system does not allow for secondary keys, create a directory of MILITARY-IDENT-NUMBERs and corresponding MEDICAID-NUMBERs. It will now be possible to read a record from the military file, then to read the corresponding record from the admitting file. Try this in a COBOL program.

When files are linked together this way, we call the admitting record file an index coordinated file. This technique is very useful in data base technology because it allows information needed in one file application to be stored in a separate file, perhaps in a file updated by another party.

Do you see any connection between index coordinated files and variable length records? Index coordinated files can be used to store information that would normally be stored in the variable length portion of a record in situations where the use of fixed length records is preferable.

```
01 MILITARY-RECORD.
   02 MILITARY-IDENT-NUMBER PIC X(10).
   02 SERVICE-UNIT          PIC X(10).
   02 RANK                  PIC X(10).
   02 YRS-IN-SERVICE        PIC X(2).
```

9

Physical Organization of Indexed I-O Files

This chapter provides insight into two file access methods used by IBM to implement the Indexed I–O module discussed in the previous chapter. As such, this chapter is not strictly necessary, and the reader may skip to Chapter 10. However, the Indexed I–O module is easier to understand if one has a grasp of the kind of physical organization that underlies it.

9.1 INTRODUCTION

A well-known implementation of a file structure for the Indexed I–O module (serving other languages as well) is the IBM indexed sequential access method (ISAM) system. Unfortunately, a generic name was used for a system implementation and much more than *access* is intended. Because this method does not give total support of the Indexed I-O module of COBOL, certain features, such as the DELETE statement, ACCESS MODE IS DYNAMIC, and ALTERNATE KEY, are not available. While ISAM is gradually being phased out by IBM, it remains in wide use and is an interesting example of an implementation of Indexed I-O. Although ISAM is a file access method available to a host of different languages on IBM machines, other manufacturers have provided similar forms of file structures for their computers. IBM supports full ANSI Indexed I-O files under another file access system, which is discussed later in this chapter.

When COBOL is the language to be used, we often speak of the Indexed Sequential method of file organization in preference to Indexed I-O. The COBOL compiler contains routines that link the Indexed Sequential language features into the ISAM system. It is *not* our purpose to give a detailed description of ISAM but rather to examine the physical organization of the records on a DASD and to see how the sequential nature of the file is maintained. The purpose is to give the programmer insight into the advantages and limitations of the Indexed I-O module and to see how its use is system dependent.

9.2 A BASIS FOR AN INDEXED SEQUENTIAL ORGANIZATION

Suppose we are faced with the problem that we want the records of a file to be organized sequentially by ascending key order and yet at the same time want to be able to fetch records directly. One solution is to sort the records before creating a Relative I-O file. (Remember that a Relative I-O file is created sequentially.) Let us complicate the issue a little further by imagining that the file is to contain in excess of a million records. Most medium-sized credit card companies have file systems much larger than this. As we are using Relative I-O, we must create either a directory or invent a good hashing algorithm. We can, if we wish, create a directory containing a million entries. This will be a nontrivial task as it is most unlikely, at least at the present time, that there will be enough cheap memory available. The directory will therefore need to be stored on disk or on some other auxiliary storage device. Parts of the directory can be read into memory in small segments and table lookup performed there. If the binary search is being used for table lookup, keeping the dictionary sorted will be a nightmare, because as records are added to the file, their keys and relative addresses need to be placed in the directory at the correct locations to maintain sorted key order. These same space restrictions in memory will also keep a hash table small if we choose the hashing method. This could mean large linked chains in the file and a consequent increase in the I/O time for record retrieval as these long chains of hash colliding records are searched. None of our options are very attractive.

There is, however, an alternate solution. Suppose we logically block the records into groups and maintain a pointer to the first record in each group. We could arbitrarily let each group consist of 100 records with a dictionary entry for the first record in each of these groups. As there are 10,000 of these groups ($10{,}000 \times 100 = 1{,}000{,}000$), the directory will have 10,000 entries and can remain in memory. To search for any given record, we first determine which group it is in. Then we sequentially fetch (by adding one each time to the relative key) each record in the group until we find the required record. To illustrate the ideas involved, we shall fix our attention on a smaller file. The reader should keep in mind whenever we do this that it is only for purposes of illustration. With small files practically any method will do.

Consider the file of Fig. 9.1, which consists of four groups of three records each and a directory which is used to provide the pointers to the groups. Each record contains a unique key. Only the

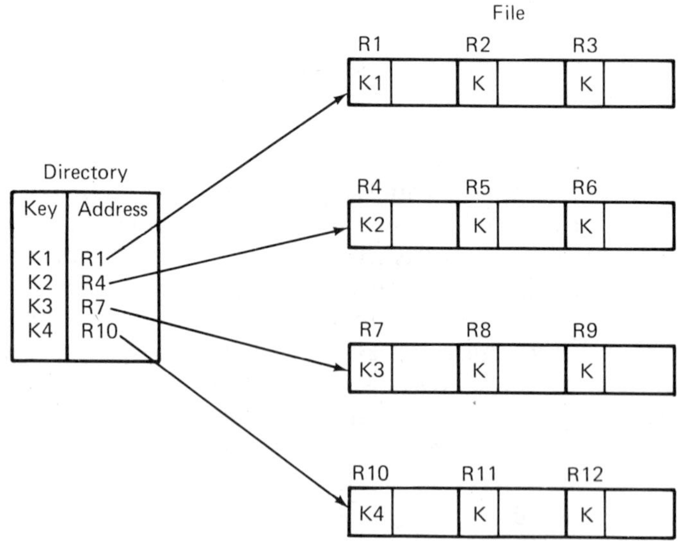

Figure 9.1 Indexing block records.

key of the *first* record in each group is placed in the directory along with a pointer to its record. The records are stored sequentially in order of the key. Note how this keeps the directory much smaller than the size of the file.

To locate a record we first find (from the directory) the group to which it belongs. This is done by locating the two adjacent directory key entries that bracket the desired key. We then go to the group pointed to by the lower-valued key and search this group sequentially for the desired key.

For example, in Fig. 9.2, to find record K38, we check the directory and find that keys K31 and K78 bracket this value. The record must be in the group whose leading record is K31. Since this has address 7 in the directory, we start sequentially searching this group for the record we want. We examine records 7, 8, and 9 in turn. Record 9 is the one we want.

It is an idea like this for data organization that forms the basis

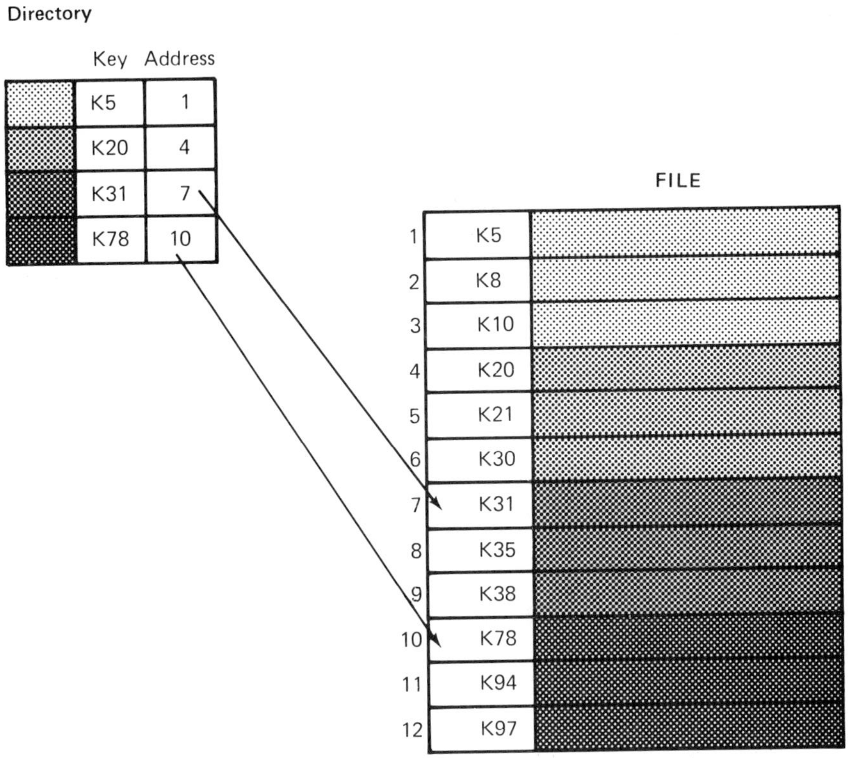

Figure 9.2 Directory for blocks of records.

of the ISAM method. ISAM is a little bit more clever even than this, however, because its designers decided to utilize some of the characteristics of the physical storage devices themselves.

Recall that a disk is cylindrical in shape and consists of a series of *platters* which visually resemble phonograph records. Each surface of a platter can be selectively magnetized to store information. The areas of magnetization are called *tracks* and can be thought of visually as concentric rings. The platters are vertically stacked and joined on a central spindle with a gap between each platter to allow space for a READ/WRITE mechanism to travel along the surface of a platter thereby allowing access to each surface. In addition, the disk revolves at constant speed to bring, eventually, all the recording area under the READ/WRITE mechanism fixed in place at the side of the disk.

Disks have two main designs: the fixed disk, where the disk unit is permanently mounted on the drive; and the removable disk pack, where the disk on the drive can be removed and interchanged. With a fixed disk each track usually has its own READ/WRITE head. A fixed disk is less flexible, but as rotational time is the only significant contributor to access time when each track has its own READ/WRITE head, it is usually faster.

The disk pack unit, as shown in Fig. 9.3, has a movable arm, resembling a comb, with READ/WRITE heads mounted on it for each platter surface. This arm moves laterally in and out of the space between the platters seeking a track. To reach any point on the surface of any platter, the following three steps take place. First,

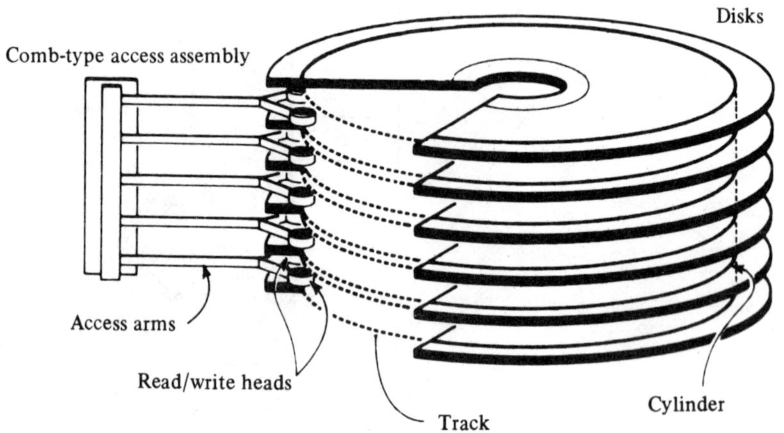

Figure 9.3 Disk pack unit.

the unit moves inward toward the central spindle (or away from it depending on its position relative to the track sought). Then one of the READ heads is selected by the hardware. Finally, a waiting period takes place until the rotation of the drive mechanism brings the desired location on the track under the head, at which time it is then read.

There are as many tracks on a platter as there are fixed stops for the READ arm in its movement from rim to spindle. When the arm is in position at one of these stops, it can select either of the surfaces on any platter. The set of those tracks that can be read when the arm is stopped is called a *cylinder.* If the movement of the arm is much slower than the rotation of the disk, sequential processing should proceed by cylinder rather than by platter. This was true at the time ISAM was designed and it is this feature that ISAM is designed to exploit.

9.3 PHYSICAL DATA ORGANIZATION UNDER ISAM

When a record is stored by ISAM, its unique key must be one of the fields in the record. In ISAM this key is referred to as the *record key.* The records themselves are first sorted by record key into *ascending order* before they are stored on one or more disk drives. ISAM will always maintain the records in this sorted order. Each record is stored on one of the tracks of a disk. Those records that follow it in sorted sequence are placed directly after it on the same track or, if room does not permit, are spilled over onto the next track in the same cylinder. In other words, they are dropped down to the next platter surface. The arm does not move. Looking downward, the next READ head is selected. Since the tracks on a cylinder are labeled 0, 1, 2, . . . , the records that follow those on track 1 are placed on track 2. Track 0 is reserved. Records that follow those on the last track of a cylinder are moved over to the next cylinder. The cylinders are also labeled 0, 1, 2, ...

Figure 9.4 shows two cylinders of records with just their keys being shown. Note that the keys are in ascending sequence throughout their storage on both cylinders. We have not shown record 0 on either cylinder as this is kept for the track index. Of course the number of tracks on each cylinder is a function of the size of the disk pack.

When ISAM retrieves a record, it needs to know the record key, its appropriate cylinder, and track address. Thus these are the com-

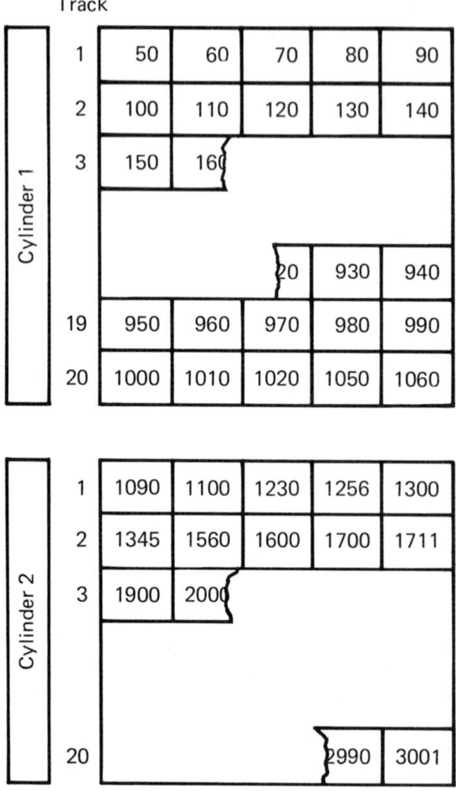

Figure 9.4 Record storage.

ponents that must make up the directory entries for the ISAM file. In ISAM a directory is called an *index*. For example, if a directory entry for record 1500 gave cylinder 9 and track 3, then ISAM would direct the READ/WRITE mechanism to move in toward cylinder 9. The READ head associated with track 3 would then be activated. Since the bottom side of the top platter is usually track 0 (because the top being exposed is subject to damage), the READ head selected would be that for the top side of the third platter, as shown in Fig. 9.5. Of course, the required record might be one of many records stored on track 3. Rotation of the drive would eventually bring the required record under the READ head. ISAM can check to see which record is the correct one by comparing the record keys on each record with the one it is looking for.

As the records in an ISAM file are kept in sorted order by

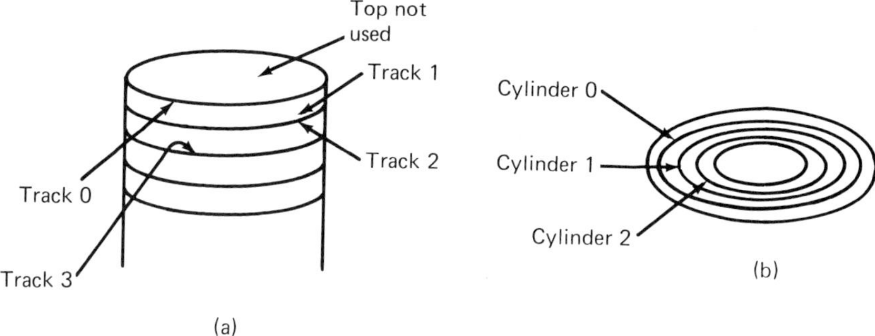

Figure 9.5 Disk organization: (a) disk; (b) top view of platter.

record key, it is not necessary to have a directory entry for every single entry. *It is sufficient to know the largest key on every track of the file.* For example, suppose the largest key on track 3 is 100 and the largest on track 4 is 200. A record with key 175, if it exists in the file at all, must be on track 4. It cannot be on track 3 as the largest key on that track is 100.

The most obvious place to keep the directory for each cylinder on the file is, of course, on the cylinder itself, and it is on track 0 of each cylinder that ISAM keeps its directory. This directory is known as a *track index;* it contains the largest key on every track and the hardware address of that track. Figure 9.6 shows a typical track index for one cylinder of a file. In this cylinder, for example, 400 is shown to be the largest key on track 3 and 700 the largest key on the cylinder. Later we will see that this directory is slightly more complicated than the version presently shown. This will be clarified when we discuss how ISAM keeps track of records that are added to the file after its original creation. For the moment, this simplified version of the directory is more than sufficient.

How does ISAM use this directory to find a record on the file? First it positions the READ/WRITE mechanism arm over the appropriate cylinder and selects track 0. Let us suppose that the index on track 0 has the entries shown below in Fig. 9.6 and the system seeks

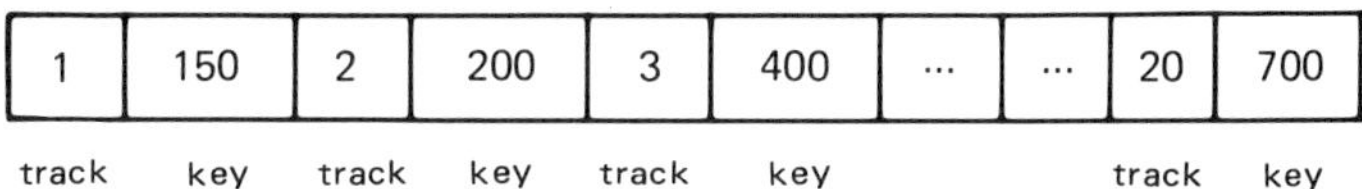

Figure 9.6 Track index.

the key 350. The entry

indicates that the record, if it is to be found, will be on track 3. The READ/WRITE unit need not move. The READ head for track 3 is selected and the rotation of the drive will eventually bring the record with key 350, if it exists, under this READ head. The fact that the index for this cylinder is on the cylinder itself means that no additional movement of the READ/WRITE mechanism is necessary. Selecting between READ heads is a far less time-consuming operation than mechanically moving the entire arm unit. It is for this very reason that ISAM organizes its index on the same cylinder as the data indexed. The reader may now be beginning to understand why we mentioned at the start of this chapter that ISAM takes into account the physical characteristics of the device on which it stores its data. It is an attempt to minimize the delay in fetching a record.

When an ISAM file is spread over several cylinders, there is, of course, more than one track index. One track index is placed on track 0 of each cylinder used. There remains then in this case a further problem. When a record is being sought, which track index should be examined? Not surprisingly, ISAM keeps a cylinder index with an entry for each of its track indexes. Each entry in this index specifies the address of every track index and the largest entry in each track index. In other words, the cylinder index has an entry for each cylinder of the file and the largest entry on that cylinder. The following is a typical cylinder index:

13	1650	14	1750	15	2000	16	3000	. . .
cyl	key	cyl	key	cyl	key	cyl	key	

This cylinder index shows that on cylinder 15 the largest key that will be found is 2000. If ISAM is seeking record 1886, an examination of this cylinder index reveals that the record, if it exists, can be found on cylinder 15. The READ/WRITE mechanism moves inward to cylinder 15, selects track 0, and consults the track index. If that track index is:

1	1800	2	1890	3	1900	. . .
track	key	track	key	track	key	

then track 2 is selected and eventually the revolution of the drive will bring the record, once again stressing if it exists at all, under the READ head.

The cylinder index is not associated with any particular cylinder of the file and is stored on a separate area of the disk pack or on another disk pack altogether. This area is referred to as the *cylinder area.* The file itself along with the track indexes is called the *prime area.*

Sometimes a file may be very large, even extending across several disk drives. In this case hundreds of cylinders may be involved causing the cylinder index itself to be several tracks or cylinders in size. In this eventuality, ISAM may even create an index of the cylinder index. Such an index is called a *master index.* Each entry of the master index then points to a track of the cylinder index and specifies the largest key given on this track of the cylinder index. Even another master index might be made of this index. Perhaps now the reader can appreciate why the name "Indexed" is the first word in ISAM.

Figure 9.7 shows segments of each of the three types of indexes. The reader should see if he can follow the search algorithm, beginning at the master index, for the location of record 45. Only two tracks of both the master index and cylinder index are shown. The first entry in the master index says that the largest key mentioned in track 1 of the cylinder index is 211. The first entry on track 1 of the cylinder index shows that 95 is the largest key on the track index on cylinder 6. Checking the track index of cylinder 6 shows that record 45 is located on track 2. Record 45 also happens to be the largest record key on track 2.

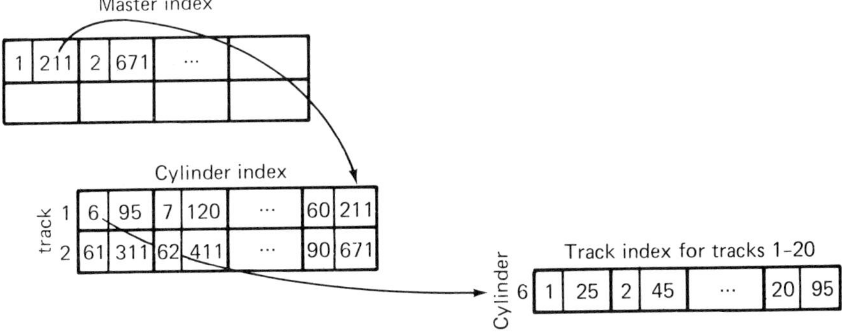

Figure 9.7 Search algorithm through three indexes.

9.4 OVERFLOW RECORDS IN ISAM

Unlike Relative I-O, which does not permit the addition of a new record to a file unless an empty slot is available, ISAM allows any number of new records to be added to an already existing file. The number is, however, obviously limited by the availability of sufficient storage space. As mentioned earlier ISAM also maintains the original ordering of the sorted file. Any record to be added is inserted into the file at an appropriate place. To accomplish this insertion, it is required that room be made available for the record on its track by shifting each record *that logically follows the one to be added* forward on the track and dropping the last record on the track off the end. For example, if the records at the end of a track are:

...	26	28	30	31	33	35	37

and record 34 is to be added, then the track will be changed to:

...	26	28	30	31	33	34	35

and record 37 will be dropped off the end. The track's highest key is now 35 and the track index is changed accordingly. The question, of course, is what to do with record 37 that was dropped. If it is added to the next track, it will cause the record at the end of that track to be dropped off the end and a domino effect will cascade through all the records on the file. In each case, the track index will need to be changed as will the cylinder index when the last record on the cylinder is forced off. To avoid this problem, the record dropped off the original track is removed from the file altogether and placed in an overflow area. This overflow area may be on another disk unit, elsewhere on the same disk unit, or even perhaps on the same cylinder if several tracks on each cylinder are set aside and designated for overflow use. The exact placement of the overflow area is determined when space for the file is requested from the operating system. When a record is added to this overflow area, a pointer to it is created in the track index.

Earlier, it was noted that a simplified version of the track index had been presented. This version can now be upgraded as, in actual fact, there are two entries for each track on a given cylinder. We shall designate them as "N" and "O" entries, where "N" denotes a normal entry and "O" an overflow entry. Originally, that is, before overflow records are added to the file, both entries are the same. For example, the track index for cylinder 6 of a file might appear as:

N		O		N		O		N		
1	120	1	120	2	200	2	200	3	250	. . .

In this case, both the N and O entries for track 2 designate that 200 is the largest key on this track. Suppose, in fact, that track 2 contains the following records (only the keys shown):

130	145	150	. . .	180	190	200

As indicated by the track index, the largest key to be found on track 2 is 200. Now suppose record 185 is to be added to this track forcing record 200 off the end into the overflow area. Track 2 now becomes:

130	145	150	. . .	180	185	190

As the largest key on track 2 is now 190, the N entry for this track in the index must be changed to 190 as follows:

N		O		N		O		N		
1	120	1	120	2	190	2	200	3	250	. . .

Suppose further that record 200 is placed in an overflow area on track 10 and is the first record on this overflow track. If this is designated as 10:1, the overflow area should be changed as follows:

N		O		N		O		N		
1	120	1	120	2	190	10:1	200	3	250	. . .

In effect, then, record 200 has become the first of many possible records in the overflow area.

If record 186 is added to track 2, forcing 190 off the end into the overflow area leaving track 2 as:

130	145	150	. . .	180	185	186

then record 190 will be added as the second record in the overflow area, namely 10:2, and the overflow entry on the track index will be replaced by 10:2 so that the track index becomes:

N		O		N		O		N		
1	120	1	120	2	186	10:2	200	3	250	. . .

Note that in the O entry the 200 is not changed as it still represents the largest record key in the overflow area. In fact the previous entry 10:1 is added to the latest record to be added to the overflow area, record 190, so that it is not lost. The overflow area now looks like:

#	200	10:1	190	. . .

with record 190 pointing to record 200. The symbol "#" indicates that record 200 does not point to another record. The overflow entry always contains two values: one represents the largest primary key value in the overflow area that has been moved there from an individual track (200 in the above example) and the other contains a pointer to the smallest primary key in the overflow area (190 in the above example). If record 194 is now spilled to the overflow area, the O entry will not be changed as 190 is still the smallest record key value in the overflow area. As the record with primary key 194 comes after 190, record 190 is adjusted to point to record 194 and 194 to 200. The sorted order is maintained in the overflow area, which now appears as:

#	200	10:3	190	10:1	194	. . .

It is not necessary that the records stored on a track in the overflow area be associated with only one track of the prime area. This is only the case here because we have assumed that all the overflow records on track 10 come from track 2. This is not always so. It is quite possible to have overflow records from many other tracks so that we could well imagine an overflow area as follows:

#	200	10:4	190	#	216	10:1	194	10:3	214	···

where records 214 and 216 have arrived from track 4. Record 214 is the second overflow record from track 4 and points to the first from track 4, namely 216, at location 10:3.

The algorithm to be employed in adding a record to the overflow area can now be stated:

ALGORITHM: OVERFLOW ADDITIONS

1: Find the first available position in the overflow area.

2: Move the record to this position.

3: If this record is the record of lowest primary key in the overflow area, place the pointer to this record in the overflow entry of the track index and move the old value in the track index to the pointer field of the newly added record. If this is not the case, move the address of the new record to the pointer field of the record in the overflow area that precedes it in sorted sequence and place the old value of the pointer into the pointer field of the new record.

9.4.1 Overflow Considerations

If a record is in the prime area of a file, its retrieval is straightforward. The master, cylinder, and track indexes are examined; the appropriate track selected; and finally, after rotational delay of the drive, the record is retrieved. This is not true if the record has been moved off to an overflow area.

Depending on when the record being sought was added to the overflow area, its retrieval can take a long time. Suppose, for example, that record 16,000 is the first record moved to an overflow area followed later by 60 more such records. As these 60 later records are all chained together in key sequence order by pointers, all 60 records will have to be read before record 16,000 can be located. As each READ is a time-consuming process, this can take a very long time. The efficiency of ISAM is defeated by allowing large numbers of records to overflow from a single track.

There are two possible approaches to be used in relieving this problem. The first is to write a "clean up" program which reads all the records on the file, including those in the overflow areas and recreates a bigger file. This can be done whenever the time taken to retrieve records is becoming prohibitive. *The time taken for retrieval is the dominant criterion here as it is acceptable to have a large overflow area if the records in it are seldom retrieved.*

The other possibility is, as with Relative I–O, to create dummy records. In ISAM a dummy record is a record that contains HIGH-VALUES in the first character position but must, as with all records in ISAM, also contain a unique key. During file creation these records are sorted along with all the other file records and scattered wherever desired within the file.

Dummy records prevent growth in the overflow area in two ways. First, if a record to be added to an ISAM file has the same key as a dummy record, it merely replaces the dummy record. This is the ideal situation as no records are shifted along a given track and none of the indexes are changed. The second service rendered by dummy records is that they are not moved to the overflow area if they are forced off the end of the track by the insertion of a new record. They are simply ignored. The N entry in the track index is, however, changed to reflect the fact that a different record now holds the last position on the track. If both the O and N keys are the same before the addition takes place, they are both changed. Suppose, for example, that the N and O entries for track 7 of a certain cylinder are given as:

N		O	
7	100	7	100

and that track 7 has the following keys:

50	60	70	...	90	100

with record 100 being a dummy record. The addition of record 55 would change track 7 as follows:

50	55	60	70	...	90

and since record 100 is a dummy record (and therefore not transferred to the overflow area), the N and O entries become

N		O	
7	90	7	90

9.5 CREATING AN ISAM FILE

Since an ISAM file must be created in sorted order, the records to begin the file must first be sorted in ascending order by record key and the file created sequentially. ISAM will detect an attempt to create the file with a record not in its proper place in sorted order. Any dummy records to be added to the file should be placed in the input data stream in sequence. These records are best added in sections of the file where addition most commonly will take place. For instance, a credit card company may well expect in the near future to add records whose keys range between 416 250 000 and 416 275 000 as a new district of credit card holders is opened up. In this case, dummy records with these keys can be created and added to the file during file creation. Another possibility is simply to scatter a certain percentage of dummy records throughout the file if possible. This is not nearly as effective nor always possible (there may be no free keys throughout the file). Recall that a dummy record is only ignored if it is at the end of a track. It will stay on a track until it is replaced by a valid record with the same key or pushed off the end by a new insertion.

Once the file is in use, any record whose deletion is desired can be made a dummy record by writing HIGH-VALUES in its first character position. This is a useful feature, especially in a credit card situation or phone number list where inactive customers can be replaced. Of course, this would be done by reading the record with a READ verb in COBOL, checking the validity of the record, and then replacing the record with a REWRITE statement.

9.6 VSAM

ISAM is gradually being replaced by a new access method on IBM machines called the Virtual Storage Access Method (VSAM), which organizes physical files in an entirely different manner than ISAM, and IBM has been able to implement the full ANSI COBOL Indexed

I–O module with it. VSAM is a very complex access method and can also be used to implement the Relative and Sequential I–O modules.

In VSAM, logical records are stored in packets called *control intervals.* A control interval may contain one or more logical records. On the mass storage device the control interval is a continuous area of storage that has the format depicted in Fig. 9.8. From the figure it can be seen that the control interval contains three entities: records, free space, and an area of control information. The records are the logical records as viewed by the COBOL program. The size of a control interval is determined by the user (or the system by default) and is a function of the logical record size, the buffer size, the storage device characteristics, and the amount of free space requested by the user. The control interval in a sense is the VSAM physical record; it is the unit of continuous storage that it transmits from I/O device to buffer and from buffer to I/O device. Once the control interval is in the buffer, logical records are released to the user program to satisfy READ requests.

To the user a file is a collection of logical records. To VSAM the file is a collection of control intervals. There is, in fact, an intermediate collection of control intervals called a *control area.* Thus when a file is created it contains one control area consisting of several control intervals. The number of control intervals that make up a control area is determined by VSAM.

It is very important to note that a control interval requires contiguous area on a storage device. A control interval would thus reside on one track of a mass storage device or (failing enough room) on one or more contiguous tracks. This is not so in a control area. Control intervals within a control area need not be physically contiguous.

9.6.1 Record Organization

There are three possible organizations for the logical records in control intervals: entry sequenced, relative record, and key se-

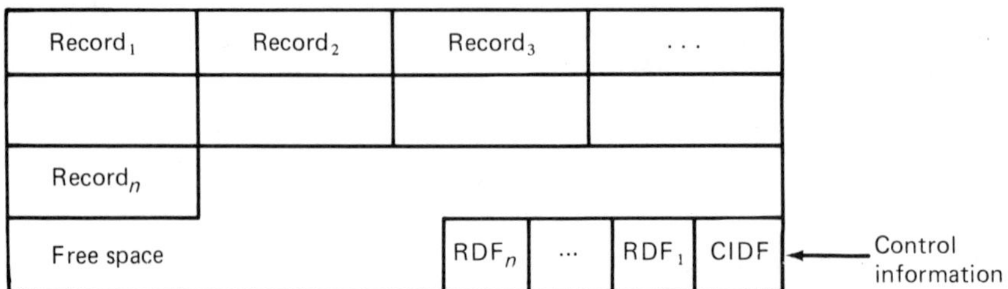

Figure 9.8 Control interval.

quenced. Normally, we refer to a physical file of control intervals as a *data set.* We thus speak of entry-sequenced data sets (or ESDS), relative record data sets (or RRDS), and key-sequenced data sets (KSDS). These three types of data sets are used to implement the file organizations of COBOL. We shall study each one separately.

Entry-Sequenced Data Set

An entry-sequenced data set (ESDS) consists of one or more control intervals in which the logical records are loaded in their entry sequence, that is, in the order in which they are received for storage. No attention is paid to any field or fields within each logical record. It can be used to implement the Sequential I-O module of COBOL.

Relative Record Data Set

A relative record data set (RRDS) consists of one or more control intervals in which the number of logical records is fixed. Each logical record is identified by a relative record number, the lowest such number being 1. Records may be stored sequentially, with each logical record receiving the relative record number in sequence, or loaded directly (randomly), with each record receiving the relative record number specified. Each control interval contains the same number of logical records. If n records are stored in the first control interval, the second control interval (if loaded sequentially) has relative record numbers $n+1$ through $2n$. It is permitted to delete logical records, replace existing logical records, and add new records to vacant relative record number positions. It is used to implement the Relative I-O module of COBOL.

Key-Sequenced Data Set

The logical records within control intervals of a key-sequenced data set (KSDS) are stored in ascending order by a given primary key. A KSDS permits insertion, deletion, and retrieval of a logical record. In addition, the logical records are permitted to change in length. A KSDS can only be created in sequential mode. It is used to implement the Indexed I-O module.

9.6.2 A Closer Look at Control Intervals

A control interval, as previously mentioned, is a physical record that requires a contiguous area of an auxiliary mass storage device. Each control interval is given an address by which it is made known to VSAM. This address is called a *relative byte address* (RBA). The first control interval in a VSAM data set has an RBA of zero. The RBA of the second control interval is the length in bytes of the entire first control interval, the RBA of the third is the sum of the lengths of the first two, and so on. The relative byte addresses are independent of the physical location of the control intervals and are a function only of the length of other control intervals.

KSDS Control Intervals

Because the KSDS permits the most in storage flexibility it is worth studying it in more detail. You will recall from Chapter 8 that an indexed file is created sequentially but that later records may be added to the file with random access by specifying a primary key. During the sequential creation it is understood that records will be written in key sequence order. These logical records, accessed by the COBOL program through READ and WRITE statements, are processed by VSAM and are stored on the auxiliary mass storage device within the control intervals of a KSDS. The first record that is stored takes up logical record position number 1 in the first control interval, whose relative byte address or RBA is zero. The length of this record is stored in the record definition field (RDF) at the right-hand end of the control interval, as shown in Fig. 9.8. The second record follows the first and its RDF is placed to the left of the first RDF. Logical records are thus added to the control interval from left to right but the RDFs are added from the right to the left. Thus the records and RDFs grow from opposite sides inward toward the center of the control interval. The user can request VSAM to leave a certain percentage of the control interval as free space during initial file creation. This request is made outside of the COBOL program before the first run and is discussed later in the section "Creating a VSAM Data Set." In Fig. 9.8, the area labeled "free space" lies in the middle between the end of the logical records and the beginning of the RDF control area.

Once the first control interval has been filled to capacity, with due regard being given to keeping the free space free, the next group of records is entered into another control interval. This process is repeated until all the records have been added to the file by the COBOL program during initial file creation.

The reader may well be asking at this point what all this has to do with the keys. Are these records, stored in a KSDS, in any way indexed? They are, to be sure, stored in key-sequenced order but how does VSAM respond to a request to fetch a record, given its primary key, when a READ statement is executed in a COBOL program?

To understand how this is accomplished, it is important to remember that the primary key of each logical record consists of one or more adjacent fields within the record itself. Since the records are added in key-sequenced order, each control interval has a maximum key value.[1] Determining in which control interval a given logical record can be found is a matter of finding that control interval whose maximum key is greater than or equal to the hunted key and is the smallest maximum key with this property. Table 9.1 shows these maximum key values and the relative byte addresses of corresponding control intervals. For example, key 20 will be found in the control interval whose RBA is 400 as shown in the table. Once the RBA of the appropriate control interval is established, the control interval can be transferred to the buffer area and the desired logical record released to satisfy the READ request.

The VSAM operation corresponding to Table 9.1 is the creation of one or more special control intervals, called an *index control*

Table 9.1 Maximum Key Values and Corresponding Control Inverval RBAs

RBA	*Maximum Key*
0	5
100	10
200	16
300	18
400	25
500	56

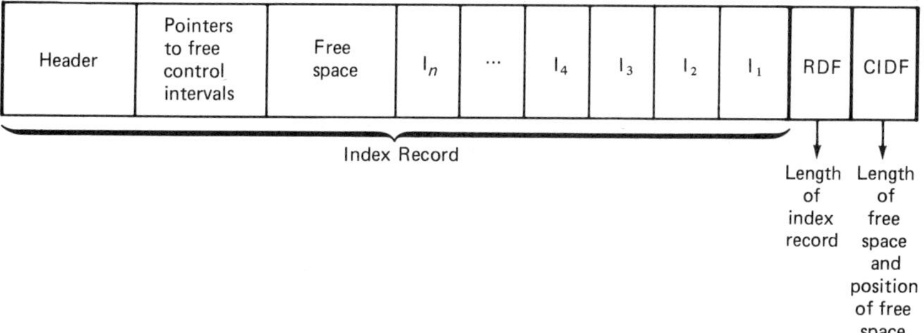

Figure 9.9 Index control interval.

[1] If the keys are not numeric, then they are ordered by the collating sequence of the machine and their ordinal position in this partial ordering can be taken as the key for purposes of this discussion.

interval (ICI). This type of control interval consists of one record, called an *index record*, followed by its own RDF and a control interval data field (CIDF) containing overall control information, as shown in Fig. 9.9. The index record itself is broken down into four areas as illustrated in the figure. Of special concern is the area of index entries.

The Index Entry

Each index entry consists of two parts, as shown in Fig. 9.10: the RBA of a control interval and the value of the maximum key stored within the control interval. As there may be many control intervals and an equivalent number of index entries, the index entries are grouped into sections, as in Fig. 9.11. At the head of each section the maximum key of the entire section is stored. This setup is used to enhance the index entry search. The search procedure is in two steps. First, the section headers are examined to determine which section of index entries should be searched. Then, the index entries are examined to determine which control interval is the required one.

It remains for us to determine what happens when a new logical record is added to a control interval. First, it should be understood that a record is added to the control interval whose maximum key is nearest the key being added but still exceeding it. If enough free space is available, records whose keys are greater than the key of the given record are shuffled aside and into the free space in order to make room for the new record. The new record is inserted and an RDF pointer is added to the control interval.

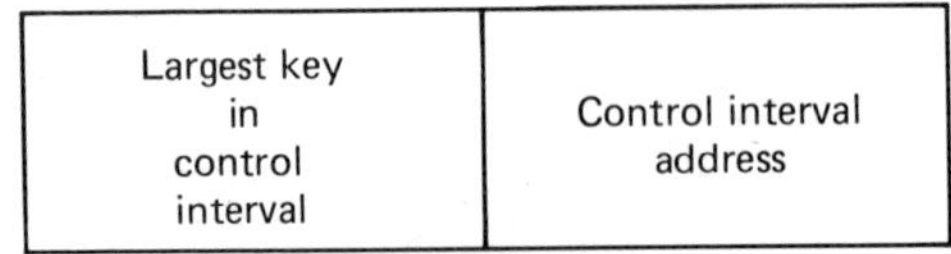

Figure 9.10 An index entry.

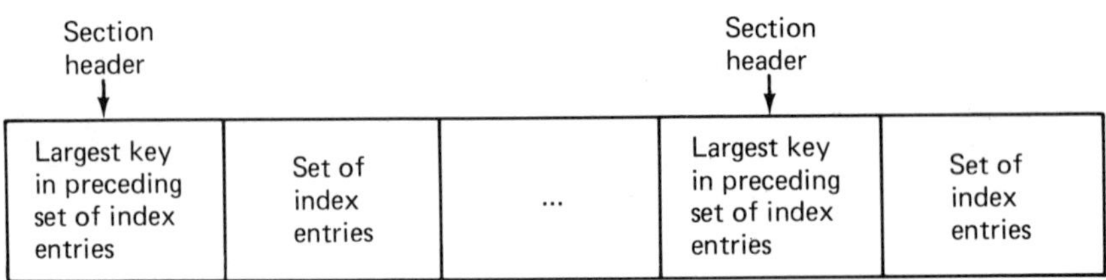

Figure 9.11 Grouping index entries by sections.

It may be that there is not enough space available in a control interval. In this event a *control interval split* takes place. This means that an empty control interval is found. Half of the records and their associated RDF fields are moved to this new control interval, the index control interval is updated to reflect the existence of this new control interval, and then the new logical record is added in whichever of the now two control intervals it should be. The addresses of empty control intervals are stored in the index record associated with the file (Fig. 9.9).

In the case where there is no free control interval available, a *control area split* takes place. The following steps are performed: more auxiliary storage is requested from the operating system; half of the control intervals are moved into the new control area; a new index control interval is created to provide entry addresses into the new control area; and, finally, a control interval shuffle takes place to make room for the new record in the appropriate control interval.

As there are now two index control intervals where there used to be one and later there may be many others, VSAM keeps track of these index control intervals in a higher-level index control interval. There is thus a hierarchy of control intervals, control areas containing control intervals, index control intervals pointing to control intervals, and index control intervals pointing to index control intervals.

9.6.3 Creating a VSAM Data Set

The non-IBM user is invited to skip this section. It is included only for completeness.

A VSAM data set is created by using a special utility program package, called *Access Method Services* (AMS). The utilities available through this package can also be used to delete, print, and locate data sets. In addition, in VSAM, each data set name and related information is stored in a catalog. Access Method Services is used for the purpose of creating these catalogs. We shall not attempt to cover AMS in any depth, but we shall show a typical file definition to give the flavor of what can be done.

A VSAM data set is called a *cluster* and is defined with the DEFINE CLUSTER statement. A typical example of such a file definition is:

```
DEFINE CLUSTER
(NAME (VEHICLE.FILE)
```

```
FILE (DD1)
RECORDS (250 100)
RECORDSIZE (50 100)
FREESPACE (20 30)
KEYRANGES (000000 999999)
MASTERPW (COOPER)
INDEXED
KEYS (6 0) )
CATALOG (USER.CATALOG)
```

These statements are selected from among many options available to the user. They ask VSAM to create a data set according to the following:

```
NAME (VEHICLE.FILE)
```

The cluster is to be called VEHICLE. FILE.

In FILE (DD1), DD1 is the ddname of a job control language card that indicates on what volume and unit type the file is to be stored. A typical example might be

```
//DD1 DD UNIT = DISK, VOL = SER = 111111
```

According to RECORDS (250 100), room is to be set aside to store a file of 250 records. Should more space be required, the system will supply up to 15 more areas (called *extents*), each capable of storing 100 more records as needed. RECORDSIZE (50 100) indicates that the file records average 50 bytes in length, and none are larger than 100 bytes in length.

The FREESPACE (20 30) clause specifies that 20% of the space in each control interval is set aside as freespace and 30% of the space in each control area is set aside for free control intervals. KEYRANGES (000000 999999) means that the smallest key permitted in the data is 000000, and the largest is 999999.

The MASTERPW (COOPER) clause indicates that the data set is password protected. Access is not possible without specification of the word COOPER. INDEXED means that this is a KSDS-type data set. The KEYS (6 0) clause requires that the key in each record be 6 bytes long and begin at position 0 (the first byte of each record).

Finally, CATALOG (USER.CATALOG) indicates that cataloging information for this file is stored in the data set, with name USER.CATALOG. These cards are keypunched and submitted as data to Access Method Services. The file is now ready to receive records from a COBOL program.

From this example it should be clear that there are many other options available, giving the user more say over the actions undertaken by VSAM.

9.7 SUMMARY

In this chapter we have superficially explored ISAM and VSAM—two access methods that have enabled one manufacturer, IBM, to implement the Indexed I-O module of COBOL. Other manufacturers will link this module to their hardware in other ways. These other approaches must be explored by our readers as necessary; it is our firm belief that this effort will be worth their while. This sort of knowledge helps in providing an educated guess to such questions as, "Can it be done?" and "How much can easily be done?" The latter question is one of the many ways people have of asking the real question, "How much will it cost?"

PROBLEMS

1. What access method does your installation use for handling index sequential files? If yours is a non-IBM installation prepare a short description of the access method used.

2. IBM provides a utility to convert an ISAM file to a VSAM key sequenced data set. Learn how to use this utility if it is available.

3. Ask a systems programmer or consult your job control language manual to find out the job control language for creating an IBM ISAM file or to find out the index access method at your installation. Learn the meanings of the keywords involved and relate these meanings to the physical implementation of an indexed file.

10

Data Structures

So far we have mainly considered how to store and access records in COBOL. The COBOL file structures we have examined have been in many respects quite limited and far from ideal. Nevertheless, a programmer can use these file structures to devise a wide variety of logical structures, a much more complicated procedure. Indeed, an examination of the limitations posed by COBOL illustrates the problems that occur in the external physical storage of data.

There are two major difficulties that arise when the programmer superimposes another structure on a file structure: he must devise an often-complex set of programs to create and manipulate the new structure via the physical file structure, and the performance of his creation may be extremely poor because the organization of the underlying COBOL file may be unsuitable to his purpose and, therefore, inefficient in terms of the operations required. Even so, the programmer is never limited to the forms of data organization provided by a programming language. The trick is to determine when it is worthwhile to program a more complicated organization for data.

As a rule of thumb, data should be organized to reflect the manner in which we perceive it. To do this, we must often go beyond the simple file structures of COBOL. In fact, we should actually think of COBOL files as host organizations that store the logical organizations we impose on our data.

It is desirable, then, to study the relationships that occur among data, independently of COBOL or any programming language for that matter. The theory of the structural relationships of data and of the manipulation of these relationships is called *data structures.* When we consider the abstract relationships of physical records and their contents, we see that certain fundamental types of structure are recognizable and reoccur so frequently that they are worthy of close study, independently of any programming language. This can be done because the study of data structures ignores the physical realities of storage and discusses only logical properties and relationships. Such a simplification of the detail necessary to a physical organization of data can be important in determining the kind of data base organization desired, since it is useful first to consider the best way to organize data independently of how it will be organized in an implementation. It may well be that, in order to implement a data base, the ultimate form of data organization chosen will be compromised by the available file structures and the characteristics of the system used. Nevertheless, only by considering an ideal structure can we determine the degree of compromise in effect and thus determine the degree of efficiency gained by such compromise.

Data structures are the subject of intense mathematical analysis; however, this need not concern us greatly here. Our intent is a *practical* consideration of data structures as the underlying logical theory for file organization. As such, we provide some abstract tools for the programmer that will release him from the confines of a particular computer language.

In Chapter 1 we briefly considered several data structures: stack, queue, linear list, and tree. This was necessary because reference to the data structure concept was required in the intervening chapters. Vectors, arrays, and tables are also data structures with which the reader is no doubt more familiar. Now we are concerned with four important aspects of a data structure: how it is described or represented, how it is organized, how it is accessed, and how the organization is changed. Since the last does not always apply, we may classify data structures as static or dynamic.

10.1 STATIC DATA STRUCTURES

If we think of a data structure as consisting of a number of storage cells that can contain data, then a static data structure is one with a fixed number of cells whose relationship to each other does not change, where the relationship refers to the cell organization not the cell content. Vectors and their generalization, arrays, are static. Usually, as in vector algebra for example, they are of fixed size, but some programming languages allow dynamic size definition. In an array, all elements are homogeneous (i.e., of the same type and size). When the elements of an array are not homogeneous, then we have a table.

The data structures available in most languages are static. This is because static data structures having efficient addressing schemes are easy to implement. A serious drawback is the difficulty involved in logical reorganization; because of the static structure, we must move the contents of cells rather than change the relationships of the cells, which are fixed. Ideally, the structure of the data we perceive should directly correspond to the structure of the cells. We can, of course, devise complicated mappings to obtain the desired correspondence, but it is more fruitful to attempt to obtain a cell structure that directly corresponds to the structure of the data.

10.2 DYNAMIC DATA STRUCTURES

Our intent here is to introduce several fundamental data structures and to highlight some of their important aspects. In the space allotted, we can do no more. The reader is referred to a rich and growing theory of data structures: (See the References section at the end of the book.) However, for practical programming, much of the theory is not relevant. We defer the actual form of operations on these data structures to the section on linked lists as this form is very dependent on the representation chosen.

10.2.1 Strings

Generalizing from the idea that the letters in a word constitute a string of symbols, we could state the following primitive definition: a string is a linearly ordered collection of homogeneous elements. If we consider a sentence as a string of words, then clearly the elements need not be homogeneous. This definition is too restrictive.

We will consider the concept of a string as follows: *A string is a finite sequential collection of elements.* These elements are representations of some entity; they may, in fact, be strings. If the elements are not homogeneous or single symbols, (a list could be a list or a sentence, for example) then they must be separated by delimiters that can be recognized, and no decomposition is allowed within the delimiters. A string does not have a fixed length. We do not consider it to be indexed as is a vector, although in many representations (such as a vector) this is possible. The definition of a string poses some difficulty, in part, because it is often represented as a vector and appears to have the characteristics of a linear list. On the other hand, the operations we perform on a string appear to differentiate it from a list.

A fundamental requirement is that string operations are not restricted to elements but operate on substrings of strings. A *substring* of a string is any contiguous collection of elements of that string. Figure 10.1 gives an example of string S and substring S′. We should point out that the prime symbol (′) is a commonly used delimiter for strings. There are many interesting operations on substrings, but since they are not pertinent to this book, we refer the reader to the string language SNOBOL[1] for an interesting example of an implementation of the string concept.

10.2.2 Lists

A *linear list* is a sequential set of elements that are accessed from *logically* adjacent elements. Any element may be added or deleted. Elements are stored in cells; therefore we will often use the term *cell* rather than *element.* The physical list consists of its storage cells. The representation of a linear list takes many forms, but the linked list form, as indicated in Chapter 1, is most commonly used in computing. The concept of a list is not new to the reader.

String S	′abcde′
Substring S′	′bc′
Concatenation of S and S′	S•S′ = ′abcdebc′

Figure 10.1 String examples.

[1] R.E. Griswold, J.F. Poage, and I.P. Polonsky, *The SNOBOL 4 Programming Language* (Englewood Cliffs, N.J.: Prentice-Hall, 1971).

For instance, if you write the first five names of people that occur to you one after the other, you have a linear list. When written on a single page, this is a static list and not easy to modify. This single-page list can be considered as a model of a sequential file. However the elements need be neither physically adjacent nor homogeneous. Vectors and tables are also examples of lists.

The simplest way to represent a list is to order it by physical location, as we do when we write a list on a sheet of paper. Then, as shown in Figure 10.2, to insert C following B we must first move the contents of cells 3 and 4 into cells 4 and 5. In a dynamic list this form of representation causes a great deal of work. Later we introduce a more flexible representation, known as a "linked list."

Henceforth, we shall refer to linear lists simply as *lists.* Lists have a beginning, called the *head,* and an end, called the *tail.* The tail cell must be somehow marked, and normally it contains an indicator, such as the symbol ∅, that no cells follow in the list. In a *one-way list,* a cell is only accessed from the preceding cell. In a *two-way list,* a cell is accessed from either the preceding or following cell. A two-way list is not logically more powerful than a single list. For instance, while it is easy to find the preceding cell in a two-way list, this can still be done in a one-way list by beginning at the head and locating the current cell by always remembering the preceding cell location. Pictorially, list structures are usually represented as in Fig. 10.3.

Stack

A *stack* is a list in which additions and deletions are restricted to the head of the list. As an example of a stack, consider empty railroad cars placed on a dead-end siding. As shown in Fig. 10.4, car G is the tail and A is the head. We can only move a car onto or off of one end of the stack, namely the head. Therefore, the first car

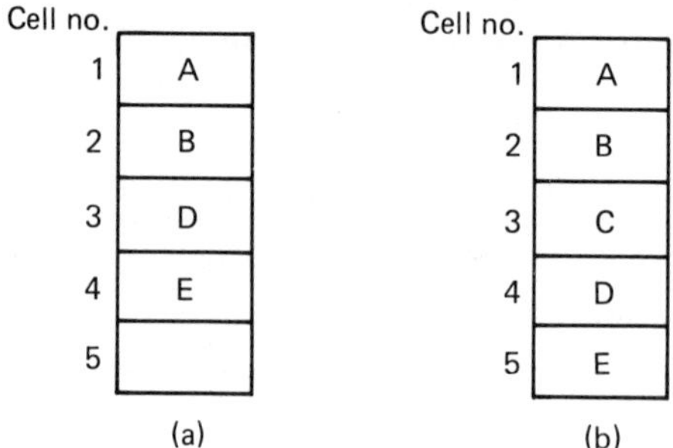

Figure 10.2 Insertion of "C" in list: (a) before; (b) after.

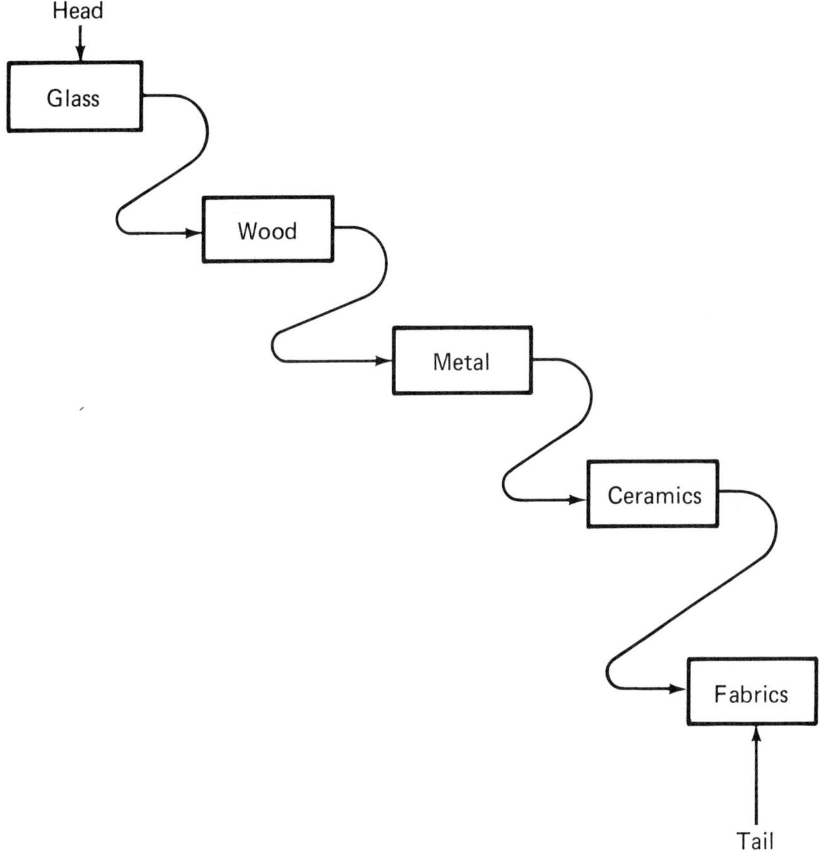

Figure 10.3 Linear linked list of materials sold by Profit, Inc.

removed must always be removed from position 1. After car A is removed, then car B can be removed, and so on. Similarly, new cars can only be added at one end of the track.

Queue

A *queue* is a list in which additions are restricted to the tail and deletions are restricted to the head. As an example of a queue, or a "first-come-first-served" linked list not in physical order, consider the example of customers waiting to be served at a bakery, as shown in Fig. 10.5. In order to serve customers in their order of arrival, suppose a set of consecutive numbers are available on tags. On arrival customers take the top tag from a stack of available tags arranged in

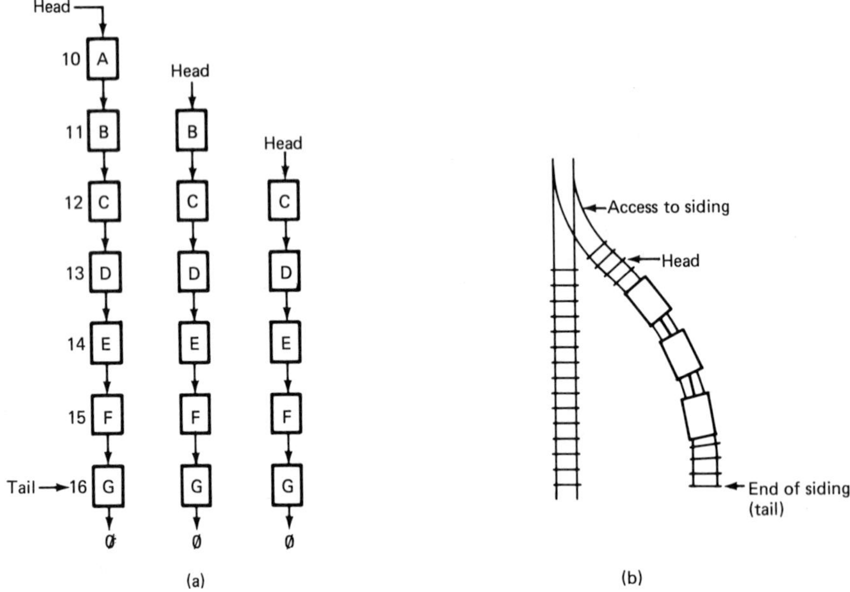

Figure 10.4 Dead end siding as an example of a stack.

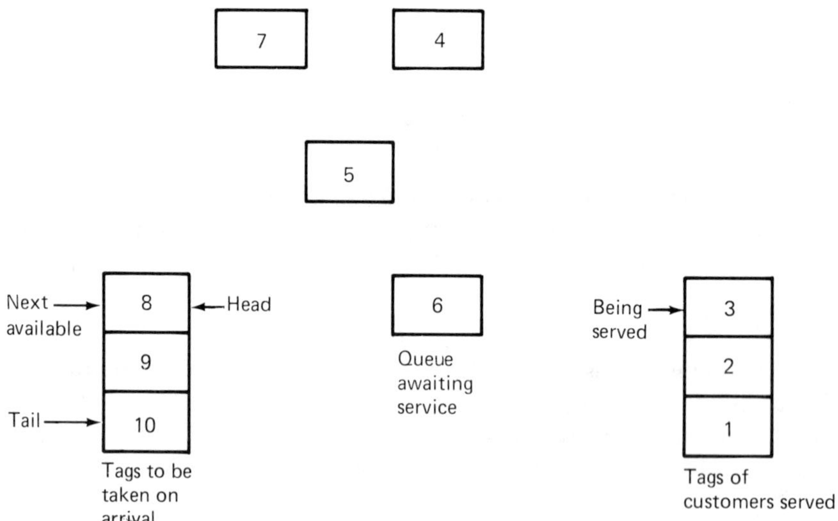

Figure 10.5 Serving queue.

ascending order. There may be several tags out awaiting service. When a person's number is called, that person is served and his or her tag is placed on another stack of tags belonging to previously served customers. Then the next tag to be served is determined as the lowest number among the unserved tags.

Deque

A *deque* is a list in which additions and deletions are restricted to the head or the tail. As an example of a deque, suppose that we wish to store empty boxcars at a given position along a north–south railroad line. For this purpose the stack cited in Fig. 10.4 is not a good organization. In the stack example only a train bound in a single direction (either north or south) can properly access a dead-end siding because a boxcar must couple behind the engine of a regular train. If we use a shunt siding, as shown in Fig. 10.6, then a north-bound train can access the siding when coming from the north junction, while a south-bound train can access the siding from the south junction. Boxcars are bidirectional, so they can be accessed from either junction. This shunt siding is equivalent to a deque.

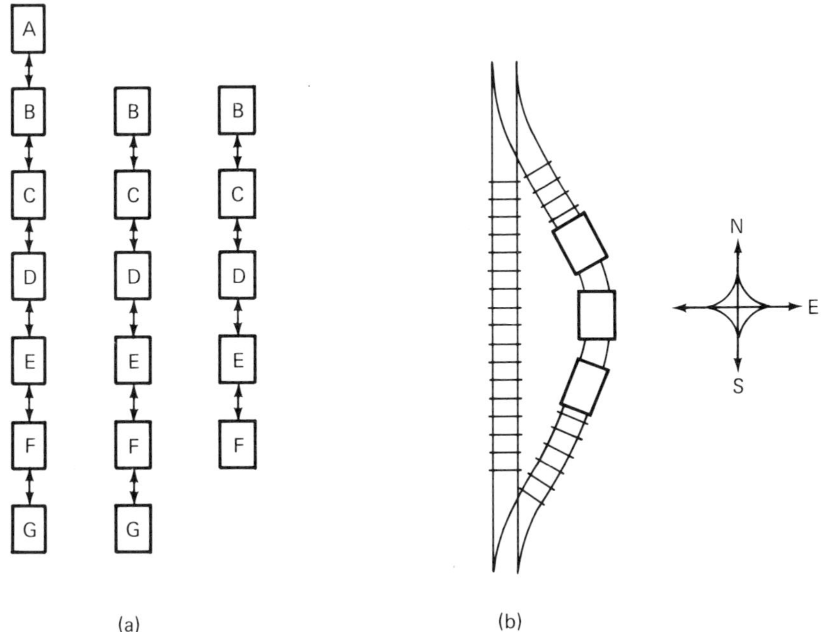

Figure 10.6 Shunt siding as an example of a deque.

The reader should be aware that although the preceding restrictions are placed on additions and deletions, we have not restricted the operation of access, as some authors do. We feel that for programming purposes this is unnecesarily restrictive.

10.2.3 Trees

Most people have an intuitive concept of a hierarchical structure: the familiar family tree is a convenient illustration. The command structure of the military or the administrative organization chart of a business is also a hierarchical structure. An important property of the definition of a hierarchical structure is that there are no circles or cycles in the structure; that is, once leaving an element in the structure there is no return to that element following the structure.

A *tree* is simply an abstract model for a structure that has a hierarchical form. It is difficult to overstate the importance of trees; they occur everywhere; and in computing they are indispensable. Because trees occur in so many guises, they have been independently discovered many times by theorists.

Trees are a special class of discrete structures known as *graphs* for which there is now a vast and interesting mathematical theory. While in our view graph theory is fundamental for the foundations of computer science and should be familiar to any serious programmer, we shall treat trees in a simple descriptive manner, which is sufficient for our purposes.

A *tree* is a set of related *nodes*, or hierarchical elements such that no node is indirectly related to itself. That is, no circle of related nodes can exist. Pictorially we indicate the direct relationship of two nodes (represented by points) by a line, called an *edge*, joining each node as shown in Fig. 10.7.

In a hierarchical structure, the relationship of two entities is not symmetric. In a business, commands flow down the organization chart and information up the chart. Thus a tree is not a complete model for all aspects of the organization of people in an enterprise. When the relation between nodes is asymmetric, a tree is directed or called a *ditree.* This is indicated, as shown in Fig. 10.8, by an arrow, called an *arc*, that is added to the lines between nodes to show the asymmetry of the relations.

The trees discussed most often in computer science are special cases of the ditree just defined and are actually called "ditrees" in graph theory. The relationships depicted by these trees are not symmetric but directed, and the nodes are thus ordered. Pictorially,

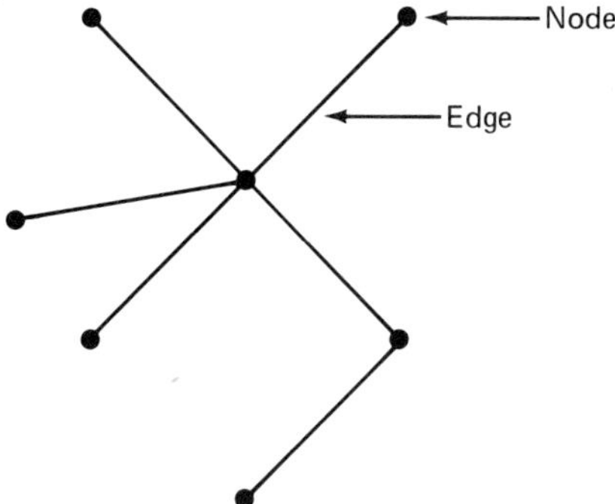

Figure 10.7 A tree.

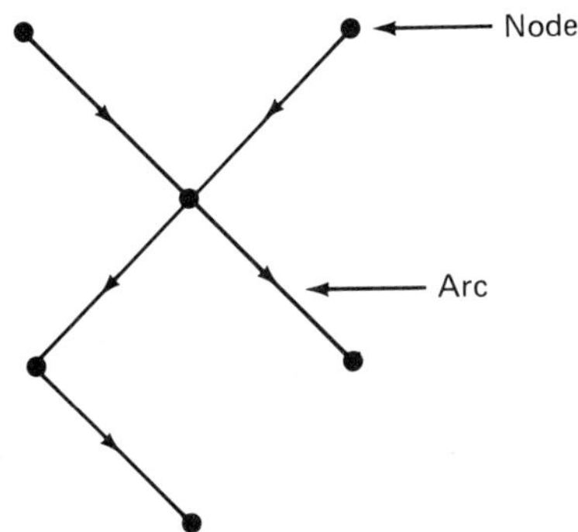

Figure 10.8 A ditree.

the direction implied is down, and two joined or *adjacent* nodes are always pictured at different vertical positions. In addition, the nodes are ordered. That is, a node to the left of a node at the same level cannot be moved to the right of that node. Such directed and ordered trees are called *oriented trees* and are represented by Fig. 10.9.

In an oriented tree, there is a unique node that cannot be reached from any other node; pictorially, it is the highest node and is called the *root*. Given two related nodes, the higher of the two is the *father* and the lower is the *son*. A root then is fatherless. By definition each node with the exception of the root has exactly one father. Nodes with no sons are often called *leaves* or, as we prefer, *terminals*.

A tree is an important example of a nonlinear data structure. The reader should observe that a list may be considered as a special

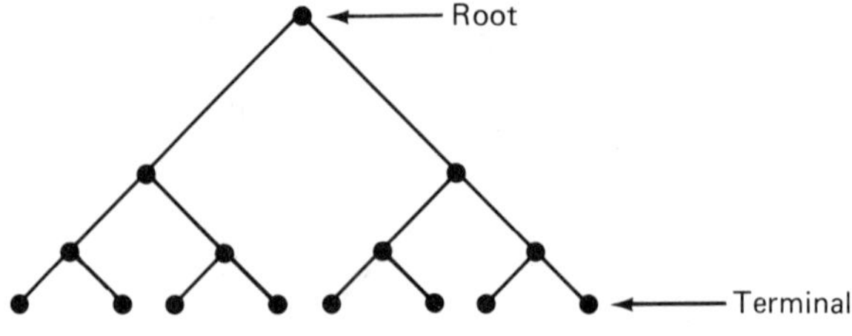

Figure 10.9 An oriented tree.

oriented tree where each father has at most one son and the head is the root and the tail the only terminal.

10.2.4 Plexes

Often data relationships are too complex to be represented as trees. Certainly, circular relationships are common: the highway network is an obvious example if we think of the nodes as cities. By removing the "no-cycle" restriction from trees, we obtain a network structure, and this generalization of a tree is then a *graph*. In computer science, the graphs have node labels (or are cells), and these structures are called *plexes.*

A plex is a general nonlinear data structure. Two representations of plexes are shown in Fig. 10.10. There are, however, other structures which have more than one relationship between two nodes, so a plex is not the most general form of structure.

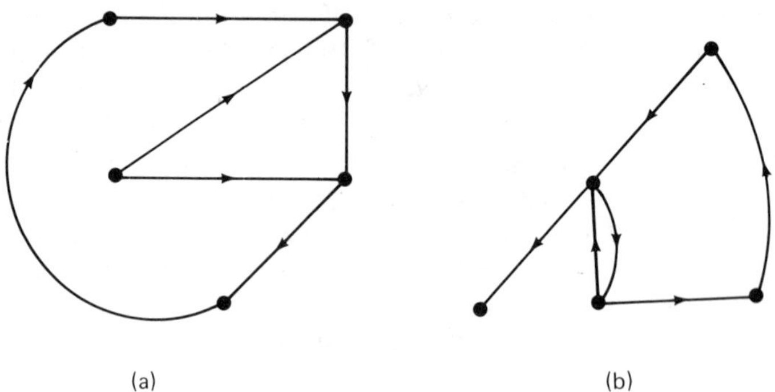

Figure 10.10 Plex structures.

10.3 LINKED LISTS

Our discussion so far has made no reference as to how these data structures are to be stored or represented within a computer. In the representations chosen for the data structures we have discussed, the logical and physical relationships of data have agreed. Certainly, this is visually convenient, and indeed we always attempt to find a physical structure that directly represents the logical structure of the data. Visually, this allows us to view directly the logical structure; storagewise, this correspondence can also be invaluable. Unfortunately, a subtle difficulty arises when we realize that this direct correspondence is not always possible nor is it even desirable when using storage. The problem is how conveniently to divorce the logical structure from that of the physical representation when it is appropriate to do so.

Fortunately, this can be done. We have a powerful and flexible tool for structural representation using a concept based on the idea of storing structural information within the elements of the structure itself. This concept, the *linked list*, is simply a set of data elements where each element contains its directed relationship to the other elements; the receiving element need not explicitly store its relationship with the sender. Previously, we found it convenient to view a directed relationship as a pointing arrow between related cells. Obviously, within the computer we cannot draw pointed arrows; however, we certainly can represent pointers. To do so the following steps should be taken:

1. Assume a single list.
2. Assign to each data cell an address and add to a data cell a cell address field which we call a *link*.
3. Then in the address link of a cell store the address of the cell that is related.

This address then effectively points to the related cell, and we call the address a *pointer*.

It is important to note that we consider the linked list concept as a powerful representational tool for data structures not, as some authors do, as just another data structure. We feel that the latter is not only misleading but confuses a data structure model with a particular representation. To do so unnecessarily restricts the process of generalization and inhibits insight into the study of structure.

Let us now use linked lists to reexamine the data structures of the last sections and to consider reorganization operations on them.

10.3.1 Linked List Stack

The stack of Fig. 10.4 is implemented in Fig. 10.11. As can be seen, the pointers are replaced by adding a link field to each list data cell and making the cells addressable. Pictorially there is no great advantage, and in fact it is harder to follow.

It is still not obvious how to describe a linked list in a computer. Let us suppose that the cells are rows of a table; the data fields of the cells are the first element and the link fields the second element. We may now define the cells of a linked list in COBOL as follows:

```
WORKING-STORAGE SECTION.
        .
        .
        .
01  LINKED-LIST.
    02  CELL OCCURS 100 TIMES.
        03 DATA PIC X(30).
        03 LINK PIC 99.
```

To determine the head of the stack, we must know the index that points to the head. We will use the data name HEAD as the location in which this head index value is stored. The tail indicator is chosen as zero: thus, initially LINK(HEAD) = 0.

To add a new cell to the stack that has address NEW and that contains data, we add to the head of the list as:

```
MOVE HEAD TO LINK (NEW).
MOVE NEW TO HEAD.
```

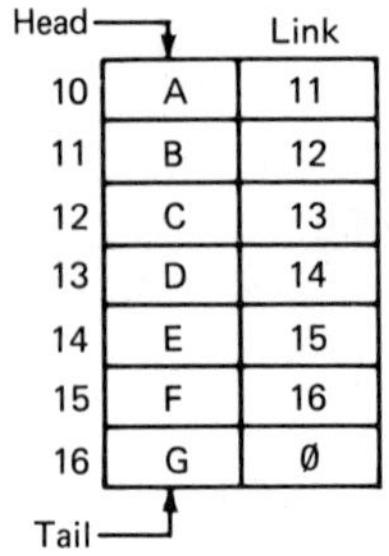

Head ↓

		Link
10	A	11
11	B	12
12	C	13
13	D	14
14	E	15
15	F	16
16	G	Ø

Tail ↑

Figure 10.11 Linked list stack.

Of course we must now update NEW:

```
MOVE free cell name TO NEW.
```

To delete a cell from the stack is simpler:

```
MOVE LINK (HEAD) TO HEAD.
```

The former head cell is then lost. If we want the data, we must refer to DATA (HEAD) before HEAD is changed. The add and delete operations for queues and deques are similar, and we leave them to the reader.

10.3.2 Algorithms

Let us examine several operations on a linked list. We shall consider them as general algorithms rather than as COBOL programs and leave it as an exercise for the reader to make the necessary translations.

Operation NEXT

First suppose we are at cell x as indicated by POINTER and wish to obtain the next cell.

ALGORITHM: NEXT(POINTER)

1: POINTER ← LINK(POINTER)

2: RETURN

This is the basic operation by which we move to the next cell.

Operation ACCESS

More generally, suppose we wish to move to the cell that contains the value KEY.

ALGORITHM:ACCESS(KEY,HEAD,POINTER)

1: POINTER ← HEAD

2: WHILE (POINTER ≠ 0) DO
IF KEY = VALUE (POINTER)THEN RETURN
ELSE POINTER ← LINK(POINTER)

3: RETURN

Note that the variable HEAD and step 1 can be moved outside the algorithm but this is not a good idea if we always start at the head of the list. Why? On the other hand, if we do not always need to start at the head of the list, is there a disadvantage to the above algorithm?

Operation DELETE

To delete cell *x* we must know the address of the preceding cell. Suppose the preceding cell is pointed to by POINTER.

```
ALGORITHM: DELETE(POINTER)
1: LINK(POINTER) ← LINK(LINK(POINTER))
2: RETURN
```

Operation ADD

To add a cell pointed to by NEW we must know the address of the cell that precedes the new cell.

```
ALGORITHM: ADD(POINTER,NEW)
1: LINK(NEW) ← LINK(POINTER)
2: LINK(POINTER) ← NEW
3: RETURN
```

To determine the appropriate cell that precedes an addition or deletion, we can use the algorithm ACCESS. These algorithms have only dealt with the organization of a single linked list, and the operations on the data contained have been purposely omitted. From these algorithms we can see that there is an increased flexibility of cell organization but this is at the cost of increased access time and storage.

A two-way list requires that two pointers must be reset for addition and deletion. Multilinked lists require increasing storage as the number of pointers per cell grows.

The advantage of a two-way list is that it is as easy to find the predecessor as it is the successor cell. Two-way lists also provide some protection against the possible loss of a single cell when external storage is used. If a tail pointer is kept as well as a head pointer the list on either side of the lost cell can be found.

Because of the possibility of losing a cell in writing to external storage, the sequence of writing is chosen to allow recovery. The pointer to a new cell is written first and if successful then the data to that cell. If we wish to insert an existing record X in between records A and B, first point X to B and then point A to X. Then by saving the location of X or X itself, we can recover if A fails to point to X and B will not be lost.

Two advantages of linked lists over physical lists are that insertion and deletion are easy and that by adding more pointers to a cell we are no longer restricted to linear lists but can represent any complex relationship we wish. Two disadvantages are the extra storage required for the pointers and the cost of traversing pointers to locate a cell. Pointer traversal is essentially a linear search and thus random retrieval can be slow.

Binary trees, which are trees that have at most two sons, are usually implemented as linked lists and have been widely studied. Since only two pointers per cell are required, they are easy to implement.

We have glossed over the fact that to add an element to a list a free cell must be available. Where does it come from? There are various techniques for obtaining a free cell. One method is to keep them in a stack. Then to acquire a free cell, you obtain the stack head and to delete a cell, you return it to the stack head. Initially all cells are placed in the free cell stack. In the linked list concept, the pointer is considered part of the cell. When a linked list is stored on external memory, a long search through embedded pointers can require many record fetches. Another technique is to remove the pointers and place them in separate directories that can be searched more efficiently.

10.4 INVERTED LISTS

If the record keys are organized in lists by attributes, with one list for each attribute to be ordered on that attribute, then structure is stored outside the file and it is called an *inverted file.* We can now access a record by attribute rather than by primary key if we examine the appropriate inverted list (the attribute list). Addition and deletion of a record can become quite complicated, as each attribute list is affected. This type of organization can take many forms and is particularly useful for information retrieval; we examine inverted files in more detail in the next chapter.

10.5 FILE STRUCTURES

Data structures are generally considered as memory-based structures. This is because consideration of the pure structure is simplified by ignoring the physical details required of an implementation in a physical media. Implementation in memory is fairly straightforward, and efficient access to all memory cells allows us to ignore address determination as a problem.

A file structure of a programming language is a data structure on the set of physical records of a file defined by that file structure. Moreover, the logical organization of a logical record is a data structure. Ideally, the logical and physical organization of a file should coincide. Since the appropriate file structure may not exist in the language used, this is not always possible.

It should now be apparent to the reader that data structures provide important concepts that can be used in the creation of useful file techniques and in the understanding of these techniques. Also, data structures provide a formal way of looking at a data base organization independent of the contents of the data base.

The prime problem in the physical and logical organization of records on external storage is that record access is much more complicated than in memory. The prime consideration is not the representation of structure but rather the manner in which a structure can be appropriately manipulated. It must be possible to efficiently traverse both the physical and logical records of a file structure and to keep the physical size of the file related to the logical size.

PROBLEMS

1. Devise an algorithm to insert a cell in a physical list stored in consecutive addresses within memory.

2. Devise an algorithm to delete a cell from the list in Problem 1. Use the simplest method possible. What is the disadvantage of your simple method?

3. Give a COBOL definition of a storage structure capable of representing a binary tree of up to 200 cells where each cell has elements key, data, and appropriate pointers.

4. Investigate the storing of file record keys and record addresses in a binary tree form rather than as a table. To locate a key some form of searching the binary tree must be devised. Some methods are exhaustive, but if the tree is properly constructed only one path from the root to a terminal need be examined to see if a key is present.

5. Implement your solution to Problem 4 in COBOL.

11

File Query

In the previous chapter, we studied data structures that could be used to organize the fields and records of a file into networks of interlocking relationships. The structures studied were internal as opposed to external; that is, the paths that linked data items together were located within the file itself, either through the use of stored pointers or indirectly by means of language data structures used to store fields or records. In this chapter, we shall study techniques that impose structure on a file by organizing a logical adjacency of records and storing information concerning this organization external to the file.

11.1 CASE STUDY: ICTL CAR LEASING AGENCY

The ICTL (It's Cheaper to Lease) Car Leasing Agency offers automobiles for rental on a daily, weekly, monthly, or annual basis. Their cars are available at major airports in the midwestern United States. Each office of ICTL has an on-line terminal to a data file that describes the automobiles available at that location. This file can be examined by an agent in order to choose a car that best suits the needs and price range of a prospective client.

11.1.1 Logical Analysis: ICTL Car Leasing Agency

The basic component of ICTL's computer information system is a file of information about each automobile owned by the company. Random accessing is required because many rental customers request an automobile on the spot. In addition, ICTL wishes to show a customer a list describing only those cars he might be interested in leasing. A good choice of primary key for such a file is state vehicle license number, in view of the fact that it is unique. For simplicity, the file can be created as an index sequential file. Thus our attention need only focus on how to obtain the license numbers of those cars the client might wish to lease. Once this is done, these license numbers can be used to fetch each automobile's record from the index sequential file and the client can base his decision on the descriptions that these records provide.

The problem of obtaining these vehicle license numbers is clearly a complex issue because it depends on the individual whim of the customer. The list cannot be predetermined until the client has made his wishes known. In order to design a system that can produce the list of vehicle license numbers required, some restrictions must be imposed on the nature of the description the customer is allowed to give. We could not do much with a description such as: "I want a car my wife would like but I don't want one of those chrome-plated lemons like my mother-in-law has." Rather, the description must be restricted to a list of attributes possessed by the company's automobiles and about which the file contains information. It might be possible, for example, to locate a car that is "blue," "four-door," "air conditioned," "with a V-8 engine." Even if a customer desired such a car, the description provided could only prove useful if the records on the file contained information about engine sizes, air-conditioning, number of doors, and colors.

One way of viewing such a request is to see it as describing a subset of the group of records that contain blue cars. Among these blue cars there is a, possibly smaller, set that have V-8 engines, and among these a set that have four doors. The request is ultimately the intersection of the set of blue cars, with the sets of air-conditioned cars, four-door cars, and cars with V-8 engines. The first technique that we describe in this chapter, inverted lists, is based on this observation.

We refer to a request to locate a group of records having certain characteristics in a file as a *file query*. If a query is regarded as a request to locate a set of records that is derived from the intersection of sets of records that share one attribute in common, such as blueness or air-conditioned, then the license numbers (primary keys) pertaining to these common attribute sets must be readily available. A list of the primary keys of records that share one attribute in common is called an *inverted list*. In order to process the aforementioned query, it is necessary to have inverted lists of blue cars, cars with V-8 engines, air-conditioned cars, and four-door cars. The cars that the customer is interested in are those cars whose primary record keys appear on each of these inverted lists.

The inverted lists are not part of the data file but are data structures that are stored outside of the data file, either in main memory or in auxiliary storage. Normally, inverted lists are stored in ascending order by primary key. If AAA 111, EMG 425, COB 162, TRE 645, and XMC 219 are the only license numbers on the file of blue cars, the inverted list of blue cars is simply:

AAA 111

COB 162

EMG 425

TRE 645

XMC 219

An inverted list for a particular attribute such as color may be created by opening a file for sequential reading, extracting and examining each record, and adding primary keys to an inverted list only when the records match the inverted list attribute. Afterwards, the inverted list is sorted. When an index sequential file is used, the inverted list created will already be sorted. Why? Remember that records in an index sequential file are stored in order of primary key.

In some files, the inverted lists for particular attributes may be very large (as, for example, the inverted list that points to verses in the Bible that contain the word Jesus). Such lists can be stored in segments as records in a file that are chained together using the linear linked data structure described in the previous chapter. As new records are added to a file and old records are deleted, the inverted lists must be updated to reflect current status. The problems faced here are very similar to those encountered in maintaining dictionaries.

Given that the inverted lists have been created, it remains to process a query. Let us suppose that the customer presents a request for a blue air-conditioned car. We may denote this request as

Q (BLUE ∧ AIR-CONDITIONED)

using the symbol ∧ for the Boolean operator AND. The codes BLUE and AIR-CONDITIONED are the names of two inverted lists. These lists are brought into memory for examination. Because these lists are sorted in ascending order, they resemble two sequentially ordered files. We seek those primary keys that occur in both lists. If we regard the lists as sequential files, this is very much like a request to update a master file from a transaction file. (In sequential file processing we update only those records whose keys appear on both the transaction and master files; here we want only those keys on both inverted lists.) The balance line algorithm discussed in Chapter 3 can be modified to do the task. Instead of issuing a READ instruction to advance along a file as we would when processing records with the balance line algorithm, we merely advance a *pointer* along the list in question. When the pointers for each list match an active key, the record pointed to is fetched. Processing is continued until one of the inverted lists is exhausted. Why? Clearly the ∧ operation requires the primary key to be on both lists.

Sometimes the queries can be much longer, such as:

Q(BLUE ∧ AIR-CONDITIONED ∧ V-8 ∧ FOUR-DOOR)

but the basic algorithm does not change. Each attribute entry in the query is called an *operand* of the query and the inverted list for each operand is fetched. The active key of the balance line algorithm is initially set to the smallest vehicle license number that appears at the front of the lists. The pointers on each list are advanced and compared with the active key which, of course, is always updated to point to the smallest primary key of those at the head of the lists. If at any point in the process all five keys pointed to match the active key, that record is fetched, as it satisfies the query. Processing is halted whenever one inverted list is exhausted. The basic algorithm can now be stated.

ALGORITHM: ANDQUERY

1: Fetch each inverted list that appears as an operand in the body of the query.

2: Set a pointer to the head of each list. If any list is empty, stop.

3: Set the active key to the smallest value pointed to by the inverted list pointers.

4: Compare the key pointed to on each inverted list with the active key. If every key matches the active key, fetch the record whose key is the active key.

5: Advance each list pointer whose current value matches the active key one position. If any list is exhausted, stop. Otherwise return to step 3.

It is often very useful to allow the Boolean OR operator ∨ to be used in a query. A client may wish either a blue or red car that has air-conditioning. Such a query could be represented as:

Q[(BLUE ∨ RED) ∧ AIR-CONDITIONED]

Parentheses have been added to indicate the priority of operations. The car must be either blue or red and in addition it must be air-conditioned. If the parentheses were omitted, the query could mistakenly be read as a request for either a blue car or an air-conditioned red car.

The balance line algorithm can easily be modified to handle the OR operator. This is simply a request for a key that is on at least one of several lists. Let us consider a query such as:

Q(RED ∨ YELLOW ∨ BLUE ∨ GREEN)

Such a query is very easy to process. *A record is fetched for every value the active key assumes during the execution of the balance line algorithm.* The balance line algorithm for a series of OR operators can now be stated.

ALGORITHM: ORQUERY

1: Fetch each inverted list that appears as an operand in the body of the query.

2: Set a pointer to the head of each list. If all lists are empty, stop.

3: Set the active key to the smallest value pointed to by the inverted list pointers.

4: Fetch the record whose primary key is the value of the active key.

5: Advance each list pointer that matched the active key by one position. If all lists are exhausted, stop. Otherwise return to step 3.

The reader would be wise to compare this algorithm with the one for the Boolean operator $\wedge$.

The real difficulty, of course, comes in processing a query that contains both types of operator, $\wedge$, and $\vee$.

11.2 THE HSIAO-HARARY ALGORITHM

Suppose we have a *compound* query, which is a query consisting of both the OR and AND operators, such as:

$$Q[(L_1 \wedge L_2 \wedge L_3) \vee (L_4 \wedge L_5)]$$

where each L_i represents the name of an inverted list. From the preceding discussion we could perform the modified balance line on $L_1 \wedge L_2 \wedge L_3$ and instead of fetching each record when the primary keys on L_1, L_2, and L_3 match, we could instead store the matching keys in a new inverted list, say L_6. We could then perform a similar process on $L_4 \wedge L_5$, creating another new inverted list L_7, which would be a list of keys on both lists L_4 and L_5. Then we could perform the OR version of the modified balance line algorithm on lists L_6 and L_7. The records whose keys are on either of L_6 or L_7 should be fetched.

ALGORITHM: COMPOUNDQUERY

1: Fetch each inverted list that appears as an operand in the body of the query.

2: For each set of operands bracketed together and joined by $\wedge$ operators, create a new inverted list by using the ANDQUERY routine suitably modified to output an inverted list rather than a series of file records.

3: Employ the ORQUERY routine on all the inverted lists that remain after the completion of step 2.

The Hsiao-Harary algorithm is a modification of this idea. Consider once again the query

$$Q[(L_1 \wedge L_2 \wedge L_3) \vee (L_4 \wedge L_5)]$$

It is clear that any record that is on all three lists, L_1, L_2, and L_3, is certainly on the smallest of these three lists. Suppose this list is L_3. Similarly, records whose primary keys are on both L_4 and L_5 are on the shortest of these, say L_5. Clearly, the records desired by this query are a subset of the records on L_3 and L_5. Using the ORQUERY version of the balance line algorithm, fetch all the records of L_3 and L_5. As each record is fetched, it is examined to see whether or not it satisfies the original query. Those that do can be processed for whatever reason they are needed. As an example, returning to the ICTL Leasing Agency, suppose that the customer asks for details on the following group of records:

Q[(CONVERTIBLE ∧ BUCKET SEATS ∧ AUTOMATIC TRANSMISSION)
 ∨ (LUXURY CAR ∧ AIR-CONDITIONING) ∨ (FOREIGN ∧ SPORTS CAR)]

Then suppose that Table 11.1 gives the number of primary keys on each inverted list. From the part of the query (CONVERTIBLE ∧ BUCKET SEATS ∧ AUTOMATIC TRANSMISSION), we select the smallest list, the one for bucket seats. Similarly, we select the lists of luxury car and foreign car as the smallest lists from their respective parts of the query.

Using the ORQUERY algorithm, we fetch all the records whose keys are on these three lists. As each record is fetched, it is examined

Table 11.1 Primary Keys

Name of List	*Size of List*
Convertible	60
Bucket seats	10
Automatic transmission	100
Luxury car	4
Air-conditioning	75
Foreign car	20
Sports car	40

to see whether or not it satisfies the given query. Remember, in the example, that while a car occurs on the short list of cars with bucket seats, the query demanded it also be a convertible with automatic transmission. Those that do, can be shown to the customer. Of course, any car that appears on more than one of those three lists is only fetched once. Thus, in all, the maximum number of records fetched is 10 (bucket seats) + 4(luxury cars) + 20(foreign) or 34 cars. The figure will be less if any car shares two or more of these characteristics. Many of the foreign cars, for instance, may have bucket seats.

As an alternative to fetching the records to determine whether or not they satisfy the given query, the balance line algorithm can be further modified. Normally in the balance line algorithm, the active key is set to the value of the smallest primary key at the head of all the inverted lists; alternatively, it can be set as follows: Suppose the query to be given is:

$$Q[(L_1 \wedge L_2 \wedge L_3) \vee (L_4 \wedge L_5)]$$

where each of L_1, L_2, L_3, L_4, and L_5 are the names of inverted lists. Let L_3 be the shortest list of L_1, L_2, and L_3, and let L_5 be shortest of L_4 and L_5 as before. The balance line algorithm then becomes the Hsiao–Harary algorithm.

ALGORITHM: HSIAO–HARARY

1: Set the active key to the smallest primary key selected from L_3 and L_5. If both lists are empty, stop.

2: Advance the pointers on all lists until they point to primary keys larger than or equal to the active key. If the keys pointed to on L_1, L_2, and L_3 are the same as the active key or if those on L_4 and L_5 are the same as the active key, fetch the record.

3: Move all pointers ahead one position on their respective lists if they have just matched the active key. If lists L_3 and L_5 are exhausted, stop. Otherwise reset the active key to the smallest of the keys now pointed to on lists L_3 and L_5 and return to step 2.

The advantage gained, of course, is in using the smaller inverted lists. The algorithm can easily be modified to handle any given query.

11.3 THE TRACE ALGORITHM

An alternative to the Hsiao-Harary algorithm is the trace algorithm of Welch and Graham. This algorithm requires the recursive calculation of a value called the "trace" which helps to maximize the movement of the pointers along the inverted lists in satisfying a query.

Let P(L) be the pointer associated with a given list L. The *trace* T(L) of a list L is defined as the value of P(L). The trace of a query on two lists, L_1 and L_2, ANDed together as $L_1 \wedge L_2$ is defined as

$$T(L_1 \wedge L_2) = \max[T(L_1), T(L_2)]$$

The trace of a query on two lists, L_1 and L_2, ORed together is defined as

$$T(L_1 \vee L_2) = \min[T(L_1), T(L_2)]$$

The trace function is defined recursively so that

$$T((L_1 \wedge L_2) \vee (L_1 \wedge L_3 \wedge L_5)) = \min\{T(L_1 \wedge L_2), T(L_1 \wedge L_3 \wedge L_5)\}$$

but

$$\begin{aligned} T(L_1 \wedge L_2) &= \max\{T(L_1), T(L_2)\} \\ &= \max\{P(L_1), P(L_2)\} \end{aligned}$$

and

$$\begin{aligned} T(L_1 \wedge L_3 \wedge L_5) &= \max\{T(L_1 \wedge L_3), T(L_5)\} \\ &= \max\{\max\{T(L_1), T(L_3)\}, T(L_5)\} \\ &= \max\{P(L_1), P(L_3), P(L_5)\} \end{aligned}$$

So the original expression gives

$$\begin{aligned} &T((L_1 \wedge L_2) \vee (L_1 \wedge L_3 \wedge L_5)) \\ &\quad = \min\{\max\{P(L_1), P(L_2)\}, \max\{P(L_1), P(L_3), P(L_5)\}\} \end{aligned}$$

Thus the trace algorithm can be used to modify the balance line algorithm:

ALGORITHM: TRACE

1: Let $P(L_i)$ be the pointer to inverted list L_i for all inverted lists, $L_1, L_2, L_3, \ldots, L_i, \ldots, L_k$, given in the query for $i = 1, 2, 3, \ldots, k$. If list L_j is an empty set, $P(L_j) = \infty$ (HIGH-VALUES in COBOL).

2: Set the active key to the trace of the query Q. Stop if $T(Q) = \infty$

3: Advance all inverted list pointers until the value of each pointer is greater than or equal to the current value of the trace function. If the record whose primary key is the value of the active key satisfies the query (that is, its primary key is a member of the appropriate combination of lists), fetch the record.

4: Advance the pointers of all inverted lists whose pointer values match the current value of the active key. Set the value of any pointer that now points to an empty list to ∞ or HIGH-VALUES. Return to step 2.

As an example, suppose we are given the query $Q((L_1 \wedge L_2) \vee L_3)$ on three lists, L_1, L_2, and L_3. The value of the trace function by definition is

$$\begin{aligned} T((L_1 \wedge L_2) \vee (L_3) &= \min\{T(L_1 \wedge L_2), P(L_3)\} \\ &= \min\{\max\{P(L_1), P(L_2)\}, P(L_3)\} \end{aligned}$$

Suppose the following inverted lists were given:

L_1	L_2	L_3
11	6	9
9	5	4
7	4	
2	3	

The first value of the trace function is

$$\min\{\max\{2, 3\}, 4\} = 3$$

Record 3 does not satisfy the query; it is not fetched. The inverted lists become

L_1	L_2	L_3
11	6	9
9	5	4
7	4	

The trace function is now

$$\min\{\max\{7, 4\}, 4\} = 4$$

Record 4 satisfies the query (since it is on L_3); it is fetched. The inverted lists become

L_1	L_2	L_3
11	6	9
9	5	
7		

The trace function is now

$$\min\{\max\{7, 5\}, 9\} = 7$$

Record 7 does not satisfy the query; therefore it is not fetched. The lists become

L_1	L_2	L_3
11		9
9		

The trace function is now

$$\min\{\max\{9, \infty\}, 9\} = 9$$

Record 9 satisfies the query; it is fetched. The inverted lists become

L_1	L_2	L_3
11		

The trace function becomes

$$\min\{\max\{11, \infty, \}\, \infty\} = \infty$$

The algorithm terminates.

11.4 RECORD ORGANIZATION TECHNIQUES

Rather than use inverted lists of record keys that satisfy a particular record attribute in common and then use techniques such as those just described to scan these various lists, it is sometimes decided to store the records into groups that share the various attributes demanded by queries. For example, we might agree to put all blue, air-conditioned, V-8 cars into one bin or bucket. This makes the process of finding records satisfying a given query extremely fast. Unfortunately, it leads to a lot of storage redundancy because many of the blue, air-conditioned, V-8 cars may also be stored in the bucket pertaining to luxury four-door cars with automatic transmissions. A file that has a separate bucket for every possible query is called a *query-inverted* file. It has minimum look-up time and maximum redundancy. The former methods we studied in the beginning of this chapter have minimum redundancy but high look-up times or *search times* (the times needed to search the inverted lists).

Between these two extreme approaches is a halfway ground called *balanced* filing techniques. The idea of a balanced filing technique is to store records into groups called subbuckets. These subbuckets are then grouped together into buckets, the understanding being that each bucket will contain the *same* number of subbuckets. In addition, the method provides an algebraic formula that maps a given query directly to the bucket that contains it. Redundancy is limited by the further restriction that records will not be duplicated within a given bucket but will be stored in only one of the subbuckets. If a record belongs in any other subbucket of the same bucket, a pointer to it will be stored rather than another copy.

Very often the buckets may be separate disk packs or complete cylinders. Subbuckets could then be cylinders or tracks, respectively.

There is a great deal of mathematics used in these types of systems. For example, a bucket in one algorithm is considered as a line in a finite geometry; the subbuckets of the bucket are considered as the points which lie on the line. Finding a subbucket of records involves considering the query as composed of points. These points are used to generate the equation of the line, which in turn yields the bucket address.

11.5 BINARY TABLES

The algorithms just presented require a scanning algorithm to dissect the query into its basic components, to locate imbedded brackets, and to inform the overall program which operands (lists) are associated with which operators. If the number of operators is small, there is a very simple technique that can be used which avoids using brackets and allows the user to give priority to either $\wedge$ or $\vee$ as he chooses. It is best illustrated by example. Suppose the following query is given:

BLUE $\wedge$ TWO-DOOR $\vee$ GREEN

Since the symbols $\wedge$ and $\vee$ are not available on a keypunch, it is more likely we would have been presented with

BLUE AND TWO-DOOR OR GREEN

using the character strings AND and OR as the operators $\wedge$ and $\vee$. Let us examine this query. BLUE, TWO-DOOR, and GREEN are the names of inverted lists. In actuality they are not really that important. One inverted list is like any other; all it contains is a list of primary keys. Presumably the program has a directory of inverted lists. If each inverted list is stored as one or more linearly linked records in a Relative I-O file, the directory might look something like the following:

BLUE	2
BROWN	6
GREY	3
GREEN	14
.	
.	
.	

This is merely a list of the names of inverted lists and their relative record numbers. Each list involved in the query could be fetched from disk and brought into core.

What is important are the operators present and their order of priority. Does AND take precedence over OR or vice versa? Suppose, as in the above query, we are restricted to exactly two operators. Clearly, for any query there are then four possibilities for the pair of operators:

OR	OR
OR	AND
AND	OR
AND	AND

If there are two operators, then there are three operands or inverted lists involved, say L_1, L_2, and L_3. The question of concern is: Given the two operators involved in the query, on what lists must a primary key be in order for it to be the key of a record that satisfies the query?

For example, if we are given the query

$$L_1 \text{ AND } L_2 \text{ OR } L_3$$

and AND is given preference over OR, any primary key that is on

(a) both L_1 and L_2
(b) only on L_3
(c) on L_1, L_2, and L_3

is a primary key that satisfies the query. There are two possibilities for each list: a primary key is either on it or it is not. Since there are three lists, there are 2^3 or eight possibilities in all for any given primary key.

Let us label these eight possibilities with the binary numbers 0 through 7:

000
001
010
011
100
101
110
111

and make the following correspondence. A 0 in the first column means a given primary key is not on list L_1; a 1 means it is. A 0 in the second column means a given primary key is not on list L_2; a 1 means it is. A 0 in the third column means a given primary key is not on list L_3, a 1 means it is. Thus 011 means a given primary key is not on list L_1 but is on both L_2 and L_3. For each of these eight possibilities it is for the user to decide whether or not a primary key satisfies the query. With the query

$$L_1 \text{ AND } L_2 \text{ OR } L_3,$$

we have the results shown in Table 11.2, which gives us all the information we need to know. If a primary key is found only on list L_2 (thus the case 010), the table tells us that it does not satisfy the query.

Usually column three of Table 11.2 is shown as a row in a *binary table* of eight columns as in

AND OR	0	1	0	1	0	1	1	1

The complete binary table as the reader should verify is

OR OR	0	1	1	1	1	1	1	1
OR AND	0	0	0	1	1	1	1	1
AND OR	0	1	0	1	0	1	1	1
AND AND	0	0	0	0	0	0	0	1

As an example, suppose we are given the query

$$Q(L_1 \text{ OR } L_2 \text{ AND } L_3).$$

Table 11.2 Summary of AND OR Results

Base 10	*Base 2*	*Query Satisfied (1 is Yes, 0 is No)*
0	000	0
1	001	1
2	010	0
3	011	1
4	100	0
5	101	1
6	110	1
7	111	1

The operators involved are OR AND. Thus we consult row 2 of the table. Suppose the keys at the head of each list at some point during processing are

L_1	L_2	L_3
5	4	4

The active key will, of course, be set to 4 (always set to the smallest). Does record 4 satisfy the query? Since 4 is not on L_1, on L_2, and on L_3, the binary number generated is 011. This is 3 in base 10, so we consult column 4 of row 2 (the first column is labelled 0). Since it contains a 1, record 4 does indeed satisfy the query. Binary tables can be created for all orders. If three operators are involved, there will be 2^3 or 8 rows and since there are now four operands there will be 2^4 or 16 columns.

It should be remembered that since the user sets the binary table, he can decide what each operator means and the order of precedence of the operators.

The following algorithm can be employed to process queries using a binary table.

ALGORITHM: BINARY TABLE QUERY

1: Fetch each inverted list that appears as an operand in the body of the query.

2: Set a pointer to the head of each list. If any list is empty, set the pointer to ∞ (HIGH-VALUES in COBOL).

3: Set the active key to the smallest value pointed to by the inverted list pointers.

4: Generate a binary number by assigning a 0 digit (working from left to right in the order in which lists are given in the query) if the active key does not match a given pointer and a 1 digit otherwise. Use the binary number thus formed as the column index into the binary table whose row is given by the operators present in the query. Fetch the record whose key is the same as the active key if a 1 is found in the table; otherwise ignore the active key.

5: Advance each list pointer whose current value matches the active key one position. If all lists are exhausted, stop. Otherwise return to step 3.

11.6 SUMMARY

The reader now may sense that a lot has been left unsaid. Designing techniques and algorithms that permit a file to be queried bring us to an area of ongoing research in computer science. Storing data is one problem but retrieving the information from it is quite another. The brief overview presented in this chapter should suggest, however, the following requirements for file query:

1. Analysis of the nature of file queries should come early in design.
2. Techniques for file queries depend very heavily on the type of query.
3. Efficient general browsing of a file would be very difficult to implement.
4. *Efficient* retrieval algorithms will be very difficult to design.

The greatest information retrieval system that has ever been developed is the human brain. Some information there is certainly very well indexed. Think of the names of four Presidents of the United States. Any four. How did you accomplish the retrieval of information? You were not prepared for the query. Does your brain contain a partial inverted list of Presidents? Was it an exhaustive search or did the brain use an algorithm for retrieval beyond the scope of our current knowledge? Students often use the word "cram" when they talk of studying as though the purpose was only to store material, stuff it in so to speak. How often the student learns that getting it in is easy; it's getting it out that is the hard part.

PROBLEMS

1. Baseball fans love to collect statistics of baseball players. They keep track of the following information:

(a) name of player

(b) names of teams played on

(c) number of times at bat

(d) number of hits

(e) number of hits to 1st base

(f) number of hits to 2nd base

(g) number of hits to 3rd base

(h) number of home runs

(i) number of strike-outs

(j) number of times walked

(k) batting average (number of hits per number of times at bat)

(l) positions played by player when team is not at bat.

You have just been hired by the New York Yankees to design an information retrieval system for them about baseball players. Discuss how you would do this with emphasis on record layout, file organization, the inverted list(s) employed, and query processing.

2. Go to the library and obtain a copy of *Gone With the Wind.* Suppose the entire text of the novel were entered into the computer. Suppose further that you had to write a COBOL program that reads in a keyword such as RHETT and returns the passages printed in your novel. How would you use the techniques of this chapter to carry out such a task? Give some consideration in your reply to the record layout you would use and the nature of any key(s) you would establish.

12 Security and Integrity

In this chapter we shall be concerned with two problems: What reasonable precautions can be taken to ensure that the data stored in files is accurate and what measures can be employed to protect against the unauthorized disclosure or loss of stored information? Data *integrity* refers to the accuracy of stored data, whereas data *security* refers to the privacy of stored data. As data integrity is of fundamental importance (there is after all no point in trying to keep data secure if it is garbage to begin with) we shall consider it first.

12.1 DATA INTEGRITY

Occasionally we read in the newspapers that a computer somewhere has issued a check to someone for an exorbitant amount of money.

On other occasions, not nearly as enjoyable to the recipient, someone is sent a bill for a ridiculous amount.

In the early days of computing, such events provided comic relief and quickly faded as the favorite story at cocktail hour. Today they are viewed by most people as symbols of gross incompetence, and their occurrence can often be enough to terminate an otherwise brilliant career.

The real problem, aside from any embarrassment that occurs, is the fact that such errors tend to cast serious doubts on the reliability of the system and the files involved. It is, after all, a truism that usually only the large mistakes are discovered. The question then becomes "Just what other things are going wrong?"

Somewhere in the internal workings of the system inconsistent information lies at the heart of the difficulty. Like a malignant tumor, it may creep into otherwise healthy computations, get added into record fields, grow across record boundaries, and spread into other files. All too often warning signs are diagnosed during the funeral. A credit card customer discovers to his delight that his monthly bills do not reflect his purchases. He continues to spend long after his credit limit is reached and when the mistake is finally discovered, he cannot pay his debts. Such accounts are often never reconciled. Litigation is expensive and civil court action, viewed by many as brush fires in the war against the individual in society, loses more customers than the effort is worth.

There may even be a deliberate attempt to destroy the integrity of a system. A bank manager opens an account for a fictitious individual and loans him some money. Later, when a payment comes due, another individual is invented, a new loan is made, the original payment is met, and any extra money is spent. As the payments become heavier and heavier, more and more loans are made. The data, however, is never in error. Accounts balance nicely, loan payments are made on time, and there is genuine cash flow. For a limited time the individual may even be praised for his aggressive and dynamic business sense. When the bubble collapses, it is far too late for correction. Confidence in the institution is destroyed, and widespread public knowledge can cause a significant loss of business.

Clearly, no system can afford to ignore the integrity of its data. Prevention and early detection of errors are as important in this respect as they are with human diseases. There are no clearcut solutions to the problem of ensuring data integrity but some techniques have been learned, often through bitter experience.

12.1.1 External Validation

Every effort should be made to correct bad data before it is entered into a system. Errors in data input are caused in one of two ways: either the source documents that describe the data are in error or an error is made in transcribing data from source documents into machine-readable form.

Verification is a test of the correct transcription of data. When keypunch cards are used as the vehicle for data input, a keypunch verifier should be used. This device is very similar to a keypunch except that cards that have already been keypunched are placed into the card hopper. The cards are then repunched (preferably by another keypunch clerk). The machine detects any discrepancy between what is punched the second time and what is originally keypunched on the card. The machine halts and the offending card can be retyped.

The weakness in keypunch verification is that some transcription errors are easy to repeat and may not be caught. In the case of numbers, control totals provided on the source document can be compared against machine computed totals to test for correct transcription. When using batch entry, batch totals will test for missing records and correct transcription.

A far more serious error, of course, is that introduced by a source document. Only quality control on the part of the users and good system design that expects human error can prevent this. Our consulting work has indicated that employees who introduce errors into source documents have often been brainwashed into believing they need not be careful as "the computer will catch their mistakes." They are consequently less careful. A frequent contributor to carelessness is the individual who works in a large department where it has been made impossible to single out who actually produced a given source document. People are more cautious when the mistakes they make can be traced back to them. Our own experience suggests that effective liaison should be created between the computer personnel and the department in charge of source documents. Most people are not anxious to create a lot of work for others, particularly, when they have met the possible victims. A little psychology, a dash of education, and the personal touch are the only ways to really make progress in solving this type of problem.

When documents are entered by terminals instead of by keypunch machines, editing of errors is much easier but workers unfortunately tend to rely on this fact and sometimes are less concerned about making errors. There is a mistaken tendency on the part of managers to prefer terminal input to keypunches because they can do without verifier operators and save money. A much safer approach is to design the terminal system to require the reentry of data by a verifier operator to warn of any discrepancy. The terminal only makes it easier to correct errors not to eliminate them. Computer programmers can take a lesson from accounting. Double entry accounting is an error detection system that can be applied. For instance, enter hand totals to be checked against machine totals.

12.1.2 Internal Validation

Once the data has been placed on a card or transaction file, every effort should be made to ascertain its accuracy before it is applied as an update to a master file. The process of verifying records is called *edit checking* and, as suggestions, fields of records can be checked with the following tests in mind:

1. If the field is alphabetic, a test can be made to ascertain if it contains only alphabetic characters. Always describe purely alphabetic fields in COBOL with the "A" designation as in

   ```
   77 ITEM PICTURE A(20)
   ```

   rather than as

   ```
   77 ITEM PICTURE X(20)
   ```

   The COBOL language provides an alphabetic test to be used with the IF statement:

   ```
   IF ITEM NOT ALPHABETIC
       THEN imperative statement
   ```

2. If the field is numeric, it should contain only integers. Always describe purely numeric fields with the "9" designation as in

   ```
   77 PART-NO PIC 9 (6)
   ```

   rather than as

```
77 PART-NO PIC X(6)
```

The COBOL language also provides a test for numbers:

```
IF PART-NO NOT NUMERIC
    THEN imperative statement
```

3. If the field is numeric, question whether or not it contains a reasonable value. Verification should be required for excessively small or large amounts. If a bank teller, for instance, enters a $100,000 deposit, he should be asked to verify that he indeed intends to do that.
4. Reasonable value checks can also be made by checking against previous entries in the file to which an update is to apply. For instance, a monthly gas meter reading can be checked against last month's reading. A large discrepancy can be noted.
5. If the field is limited to specific values, such as an airline flight number, a check can be made against a table of valid entries. Invalid entries can be flagged.
6. Occasionally a field cannot take on one or more specific values, such as a purchase order for $0.00 of merchandise or a request for 30.5 cars, and appropriate arithmetic checking can be made.
7. An entry in one field of a record may invalidate another field of the same record. This should be checked. For example, an American citizen is not permitted to vote for both the Republican and Democratic candidate for president.
8. Some numeric fields, such as a bank account number to which a transaction is to be applied, contain critical values. If a single digit is incorrectly entered, the results may be catastrophic; and yet a one-digit slip may leave a value that passes all the validation tests. If a 2 is typed instead of a 3 in a credit card account number, for example, the account number may remain a valid account number but it will be someone else's. In these instances a check digit should be added to the number. This is simply a digit that is produced by applying a mathematical operation on the number in question and that will change if any digit within the number is changed. One such method for forming a check digit is as follows:

- Working from right to left, write the successive digits 2,3,4, 5,6,7,8,9,2,3,4, . . . one at a time under each digit of the given number.
- Multiply each digit in the given number by the number just written below it.
- Add together all the products developed in step 2.
- Divide the sum by 11 and subtract the remainder on division from 11. This last number, referred to as P, is the check digit. An example is given in Fig. 12.1.

Given:	
An Account Number	416 247 819
Step 1:	
Write the digits 2,3,4, . .	416 247 819
under the Account Number	234 567 892
Step 2:	
MULTIPLY	4 1 6 2
	× 2 × 3 × 4 × 5 . . .
	8 3 24 10
Step 3:	
ADD	8 + 3 + 24 + 10 + 24 + 49 + 64 + 9 + 18
	= 209
Step 4:	
DIVIDE by 11	209 = 19 × 11 + 0
AND TAKE REMAINDER	
Step 5:	
SUBTRACT REMAINDER	11 - 0 = 11
FROM 11	
This is	
CHECK DIGIT	11
Step 6:	
REWRITE NUMBER GIVEN AS	416 247 819 11

Figure 12.1 Check digit.

Validation is a test of the completeness of a set of data. Information generated from an entire batch of records may prove useful in validation checking. Random samples of records can be printed for hand verification. Subtotals from various fields of all the records can be very useful as estimates of the range of their values can often be made. For example, the sum of requests for new credit cards may be unusually high for a given run or the amount of cash flow may appear unusually high. A large batch of customer transactions that include only payments but never purchases may be highly improbable. A large batch of transactions that have invalid fields probably signals a catastrophic situation as would information that a batch of transactions was about to delete an enormous number of master records. Once sorted, transaction records should be checked for duplication. A source document may be processed more than once or an error left in the system even if it was corrected.

In data processing a large portion of most programs is concerned with testing and maintaining integrity. We have discussed entering correct data. A second major problem is maintaining integrity. There are three major hazards: hardware failures, software failures, and operational errors. It is important then that the integrity of data be tested beyond its point of original entry. Many of the ideas we discussed for testing at entry can be used.

Designing for the maintenance of integrity is very much an art. It requires considerable foresight as to what could go wrong. A very useful idea is to have an audit of a program performed by another programmer to test for integrity weaknesses.

The ideas that can be considered to eliminate errors are endless. We have found that getting a representative from each area of the enterprise that uses a data base system into one room is a rich growth medium for ideas to track down the elusive and destructive error. Design audits will catch many software weaknesses and expose potential operational errors. Any idea that has a reasonable likelihood of detecting an error should be considered. The determining factor in which ideas are chosen, apart from the obvious ones, is the cost of error detection weighed against the cost of that error.

The costs of achieving integrity will be high and difficult decisions are necessary to determine the degree of integrity checking to be done as the costs of integrity failure may be difficult to calculate.

12.2 DATA SECURITY

As the true cost and value of data have become widely recognized, the protection of data against unauthorized access has become a major problem and, indeed, a major design criteria that, along with integrity, can make or break a system. The problem extends beyond the enterprise. We do not treat here the ethical and social implications of an invasion of privacy nor the political aspects of multinational firms. Although we limit our discussion to some basic technical aspects of security and their relations to file design, this should not in any way be considered as a measure of the relative importance of data security in system design.

Data security involves the protection of data against unauthorized disclosure, modification, or destruction. Security also provides protection against accidental modification or destruction and thus cannot be separated from the problem of data integrity. Security can be divided into two aspects: *internal*, having to do with file access and machine form, and *external*, having to do with the operational procedures and ordinary text.

12.2.1 Internal Security

An important basis for the protection of machine-stored data is text encryption. This involves a *cipher*, which is a mapping that transforms data (the plaintext) into an unreadable or unintelligible form (the ciphertext).[1] The transform must have an inverse if we wish to decipher the ciphertext; that is, it must be possible to change the ciphertext back to the plaintext.

There are three distinct approaches used to encrypt data.

Transposition

One approach to text encryption, called *transposition*, involves permuting the letters of the original plaintext message. Since this method involves no change to the frequency of occurrence of letters, only their rearrangement, cryptanalytic attack methods rely on discovering the algorithm for permutation.

Substitution

A second approach, called *substitution*, involves the actual replacement of symbols in the plaintext with those of one or more other alphabets. The letter A, for example, may be coded by the letter X at one point and by the letter T at another.

[1] The study of ciphers, known as cryptography, is an ancient art. Computers now assist in cryptanalysis, or the breaking of ciphers, by reducing the human work factor and by the application of statistical methods.

Polygraphics

The third, and probably the most fruitful approach, is to map large groups of letters onto other groups. Such methods, called *polygraphic* ciphers, are a derivative of substitution ciphers. In such methods the letter combination FINANCE, for example, may be mapped to the letter combination XTMZNFI. Any other grouping of seven letters is mapped to an entirely different set of seven letters. These methods have been discussed in recent literature.[2] These methods are not easily broken by statistical techniques but involve complex mathematical sophistication for their employment.

Passwords

There are a number of cases where high school students have used a computer to breach the security of timesharing companies, much to their embarassment. It is now common practice to assume that any ciphering method used will not be kept secret since it is part of the data base. For this reason, ciphers that require a key or *password* to be provided in order to perform the correct transformation are used to provide security.

Since the password is critical to security, the following procedures are recommended for the creation and use of passwords:

1. Do not use short passwords such as your initials.
2. Avoid single English words; use a sentence instead.
3. Commit passwords to memory; do not leave them written in unsecure areas.
4. Change passwords frequently.
5. Destroy hard copy containing passwords (i.e. back space and overstrike).
6. Allow the user to invent the passwords.

Access

While it is not always necessary to encrypt data, file access should be controlled and limited to authorized users. Data access should consist of identification and authentication of authorized users. For instance, the employee number followed by a password could be used. This process may be repeated, consisting of a dialog between computer and user:

[2] See, for example, Cooper (1980) and Diffie and Hillman (1976).

```
ENTER ACCOUNT NUMBER
     2001
WHAT IS YOUR ID
     LFJ-007
YEAR OF EMPLOYMENT
     1971
PASSWORD
     SUPER AUTHOR
PROCEED
```

It is a good idea to log invalid authentication. However, since many valid users require more than one attempt, we might wish only to log, say, five or more invalid attempts. Exception reporting could be used to detect a serious attempt to penetrate security. Logging users is a good way to discourage browsers who may penetrate security. If a user knows that security breach detection methods are watching, he is less likely to browse. Also, the less he knows about how the system is watching, the better. The use of terminals can make it difficult to detect illegal use. Call back for hardware terminal identification can increase the difficulty of illegal access and discourage the casual offender.

Although a measure of security is cheaply obtained by using a cipher only to control access to the file (in this case an inverse need not exist but do not lose the password), the data should also be encrypted if important. If not, an easy way to bypass access control where data is not encrypted is to steal a tape copy of the data.

The design of a good cipher is a difficult problem. Because of the computing cost of encrypting data, cipher systems have been implemented in hardware. Such systems are based on the password concept, since the cipher can hardly be secret. The United States government has approved a standard for computer encryption, called the Data Encryption Standard. Recently, however, the method has been under criticism by cryptographers who claim that the government knows a secret method of decryption.

Although many proponents of cipher systems claim that their system is virtually unbreakable, new mathematical discoveries can quickly invalidate such claims.

A breach of machine security can occur in many ways. For instance, in a terminal system, wire tapping can directly bypass an otherwise sophisticated system. The solution, of course, is encryption at the terminal, but that is expensive. Cheap hardware cipher devices at the terminal are necessary to control cost.

One of the major problems in a data base is that different levels of security must be present that correspond to the degree of authorization a user has to access and alter data. Such flexible security must be incorporated into the data base design and adds to system overhead. Security is an installation and enterprise problem and should not be left to the individual programmer.

12.2.2. External Security

Although a great deal of security concern has involved the protection of data within the computer, perhaps the greater danger and weakness lie outside the file access mechanisms. There are a number of external points that can lead to a security breach: improper handling, defective procedures, and uncontrolled dissemination of data.

Improper handling is treated by rigid internal procedures that are well supervised. The accounting profession has developed many good techniques to deal with the improper handling of money, and these can be applied. Procedures for physical security are also well known. It is pointless to design a highly sophisticated security system if sensitive computer printouts are left lying on a desk for unauthorized eyes. *Defective procedures* are more a matter of hindsight, but design review and audit by consultants can decrease the risk of the unforeseen. Unfortunately, even when data is properly controlled, collation of that data may lead to *unauthorized disclosure*. Public data, for instance, can be used to crack encrypted files.

Security does not necessarily require great expense or total encryption of data. Physical isolation can give a fair degree of security. For instance, controlled access to machine rooms and external memory devices is cheap. The tape library should also have controlled access. Librarians and operators should clearly understand that they are guardians of data and a breach of trust will cost them their job.

Any system that is designed to protect data is vulnerable to a determined attack. Nevertheless, such an attack is not without cost for the perpetrator. A good security system should increase the cost for penetration sufficiently to discourage penetration. As the cost for penetration approaches the value of the data, penetration is discouraged. Although many techniques for data security can be attacked by other computers or by your own, the cost of the attack may not be worth the value of the information.

Similarly, the cost of losing data determines how much we should pay to protect it. The value of the data being protected should be clearly understood. It is not enough to realize that the loss of data is bad but rather how bad. There is no point going to great expense to secure data that is superficially confidential. It may be enough for management to take reasonable precautions and to be seen as having done so.

Data should only be protected in the system if it is not otherwise available. Although this may seem obvious, such assumptions are dangerous. As an example, consider the data processing manager who informed us that the payroll file had been scrambled to prevent disclosure of salaries. To circumvent the security, we phoned the payroll office, impersonated the manager, and indignantly claimed an overpayment of salary had been made. A breathless clerk, on obtaining the manager's file, verified the error giving the correct amount. When we told the manager what his salary was and how we had obtained the information, the payroll office procedure was subsequently changed. Information on salaries is now only given in person after suitable identification. It is most important to realize that as data must flow throughout an organization, often beyond control of the data base, so too must security precautions.

A breach of security concerns people not machines, and it is wise to locate potential sources of a breach rather than attempt to detect that a breach has occurred. Potential sources generally fall into three classes: foolish employees, dishonest employees, and disgruntled employees. If you fire a programmer, prudence dictates that you take precautions to prevent him from destroying data or taking it with him when he leaves. Above all, the seriousness of such offences must be made clear to employees.

12.3 SUMMARY

The degree of security achieved is directly related to the cost of providing it. The cost can be difficult to determine and arise, for example, from increases in design time, implementation, complications, access time, user frustration, and system overhead. It must be stressed that no system can be made secure; all that can be done is to increase the cost of penetration so that unauthorized access is effectively discouraged.

If we think of system security as a chain of entry points, a system is only as strong as its weakest link. Thus in designing security for a data system, optimization requires a balanced approach to the possible entry points. The problems of integrity and security as well as the solutions are intermingled. If we can give warning for integrity failure, we can also give warning of security breaches. A major drawback to the data base concept is that multiple and concurrent users of data vastly increase the magnitude of the problems of integrity and security.

PROBLEMS

1. The Canadian postal code consists of six alphanumeric symbols ldl dld, where l is a letter and d a digit. Compare it to the American integer zip code with respect to integrity.

2. Examine and report on the security of your computer installation.

3. If you are a student, examine the integrity of your grades. Are they really a correct assessment of your performance? If not, where does the problem(s) lie?

4. In this chapter we discussed error detection. Correcting an error is called *recovery*. What would happen if you dropped a deck of 500 cards on the floor? How would you recover? Should error recovery be designed into a system as well as error detection?

13

File Design

Now that we have dealt in some detail with basic techniques for data base design, a consideration of when to use or not to use various access methods and, in particular, which file organization to use is now appropriate. File design is difficult, and often many compromises are necessary. It is the choice and degree of compromise, necessitated by conflicting requirements, that make good file design both frustrating and challenging. Our approach is top down as in the programming methods that we have used. So, first, we consider just what constitutes good design, keeping in mind that our ultimate interest is file design in a data base context. Then, we review the main attributes of various general file organizations. With this preparation, we attack the problems of how to *design* and *implement* files and consider their place in a data base.

13.1 AN APPROACH TO DESIGN

So far we have assembled some basic tools for file design that have been specifically related to COBOL but are also generally applicable to any programming language. It should be noted that the file capability of COBOL has increased over the years with successive standards.

Suffice it to say that the problems of definition and access encountered in COBOL resemble those of other high-level languages such as PL/1. There is considerable advantage to be gained from a comparison of file organizations of different languages; unfortunately, this must be left to another book.

When it comes to technical work, the facts are all important. Details are the nuts and bolts that hold the structure firmly together. These nuts and bolts stare us rudely in the eye and cannot be avoided; the concepts, on the other hand, are hidden and elusive. It would be remiss of us, indeed, if we did not stop to consider in the design process what it is we are building, why we are building it, and, moreover, why we choose to build it in a particular way. Good design begins with a conceptual view of how to satisfy the user's needs.

It cannot be overemphasized that the nuts and bolts of a system are but the means to an end—*not* the purpose of the system. There are many types of nuts and bolts, all of which are useful to a degree in their many properties. It is usually the case that no one type is the best. We may agonize over the choice of nut and bolt to use in a particular case; however, once the choice is made, it must be used.

Within a system be *consistent;* should your choice be less than perfect, change it in the next *system* that you design; otherwise, you will never complete a design, never meet schedules, never be recognized as a good designer. Remember, design is an iterative process but *do* restrict the number of iterations so that the end result is achievable within the constraints of the given problem.

It does happen that some design decisions can only be made after the user has received initial output from the system. Although this is to be expected, it is not always easy to predict what will be affected. For example, in a system we had designed for job accounting, an upper limit on the number of jobs was required. The client was asked to analyze the number of jobs he had active and to give an upper limit on future growth. It is a good approach to let the user design his system and we were earnestly trying to employ this technique. The end result was that the client provided us with an average figure based on past accounting records. It was agreed to double this figure for future growth. In addition, we thought we would be clever and added 50% more to be safe. After testing, the system was turned over to the client. Surprisingly, only two bugs occurred: an update function did not work properly and—you guessed it—the client had more jobs that we had allowed for, and redesign was required. What happened? The client had three kinds of jobs: those that were on his mind, small jobs that were not important and consequently had not been counted, and jobs that were not very active but not dead either. This problem might have been avoided if we had more vigorously analyzed the number of jobs, but at the time we were trying to build a relationship of trust and cooperation. Surely the client should know his business and how many jobs he had.

A second factor that was not predicted was that the client decided to view other activities as jobs by adding them to the system. Also, the convenience of the computer system led him to break jobs into subjobs for more detailed information. Not only was the job estimate incorrect, but a clever programmer took advantage of the low value for the number of jobs and simplified the design. Thus, the correction of the problem, although not too serious, was nontrivial.

To be successful in making continuous progress, major and measurable milestones of a design should last no longer than three months. Why three months? The human factor dictates that a person's enthusiasm and progress deteriorates into discouragement and vacillation without frequent and regular success. We feel that three months is long enough to wait for a major success and yet sufficient time in which to achieve one. Others may find different time spans more attuned to their nature. The main point is that progress is based on success and both must be seen to happen to keep a project on target. Planning, measurement, and success are essential to continuous forward progress.

In the analyst's approach to file design, two essential and overriding points must be kept firmly in mind: people and communications. But what about the details—protests the keen analyst who wishes to proceed to the real problems of design? The details are *not* the real problems of design; the designer knows all too well the need for details, and since after all, it is design not basic research that is required, the details are available without great difficulty.

People have needs and desires that give purpose to their life. If a project is not seen to be consistent with these needs and desires, not only may you lose their cooperation but you may well be faced with an active, resourceful, and powerful enemy. That the enemy is at work may not become clear until after your system has failed or been degraded. The politics of the design may well be more important to success than the actual technical choices.

The user may well feel that he is losing control of a part of his operations and sabotage may be seen as protection of his interests. Members of a design team may be more interested in promotion at the expense of others and the project. Communication failure while not malicious may be as destructive. It is difficult, if not impossible, to achieve good results on misinterpreted information. When the left hand does not know what the right hand is up to there is bound to be confusion and conflict. Minor changes in specifications can cause major changes in the design and, consequently, massive and costly modifications. It is surprising how a minor change can ripple through a design building into a wave of modifications. Ideally, designs should be easy to modify, but this is difficult to achieve overall since we must anticipate the unexpected. Good communication will hopefully decrease the unexpected from occurring.

File design, or any design for that matter, has two important aspects we choose to call the *metatechnical*, which is the main subject of this chapter, and the *technical*, which is the main subject of the next chapter. The metatechnical aspect is the *why* of file design. By this we mean the reasons for the existence of the file, its record structure, and its content. Why does it contain this particular information, what use is it put to, and what use will it be put to for a given period, say, five years? The answers lie in a thorough analysis of the problem that is to be solved. There must be sufficient understanding of an application before a solution is proposed in order that the solution be suitable. The metatechnical aspects of design are difficult and frustrating, make no mistake about this. It is for these very reasons that they are scandalously neglected. In contrast, the technical aspects are the *how* of file design and are more immediately satisfying. This will be discussed later.

The fundamental questions of design is: What does the user need? The fundamental problem of design is that most often these needs are not explicitly known. Unfortunately, they may only be discovered after the system is up. The human aspect of the design question is: What does the user want? The cardinal sin of design is to give the user what *you* think is *best* for him. Now it may well be that the user does not know what he requires. Then, it is the analyst's or designer's job to *uncover* the user's requirement and to demonstrate this requirement to the user. Note that we did not say *convince*; it is not the analyst's job to score debating points or sell his personal beliefs. Rational arguments are sometimes set aside in favor of intimidation. A statement such as "this is the *logical* way to do it" implies that the listener does not understand the *correct* solution; "the truly professional way would be this" implies that the listener does not know anything about the solution and should leave the judgement to the speaker, who is of course the expert.

The designer considers a system that does what he intended and provides what he desires to be a good system, if not an excellent one; however, the user considers a system that does not fulfill his needs (not his desires but his needs) to be a bad system. Thus, depending on the individual's viewpoint, a system can be considered both good and bad, both workable and unworkable. The *mature* designer will realize that, given such a contradiction, the user's view must prevail. Unfortunately, all too often the designer's *ego* takes charge and the user's wishes are ignored. Examples of bad design abound; to the uninitiated, the extremes of good and bad design are often confused. Good design requires clearly stated and achievable objectives; objectives that the design judiciously attains. Overdesign is bad design; avoid it.

Although good design has been discussed, the details for achieving it have not been explicitly expressed. That is beyond the scope of any one book. We can however, list the following criteria for good design:

- simplicity
- meeting specifications
- user acceptability
- cost effectiveness
- adaptability to change
- maintainability.

The design process is best approached in an orderly manner through several stages. In Table 13.1 we give a suitable sequence of stages applicable to any system design along with typical activities at the end stage. A similar table should be used to describe any proposed system; this table should result from the design proposal and describes the key system activities up to actual operation.

Systems are not eternal. Table 13.2 describes a basic life cycle common to all systems that reach the operational stage. The rate of flow through the various stages is unpredictable and will vary from system to system, but estimates are useful as design parameters.

We hope the reader will appreciate the importance of the approach to design, for it is all too often the weak link in the design

Table 13.1 Activities in System Development

Stage	*Activity*
Planning	Problem analysis Problem definitions Interviews Plan attack Feasibility study, general system requirements, solution proposal
Development	System requirements General system design Sign off, design freeze, system manual
Solution	Design Program specifications Programming System testing, software manual
Implementation	Installation plan User training, user's manual System installation, maintenance manual Review and complete all documentation
Follow-up	Audit evaluation and report Maintenance

Table 13.2 System Life Cycle

Processes

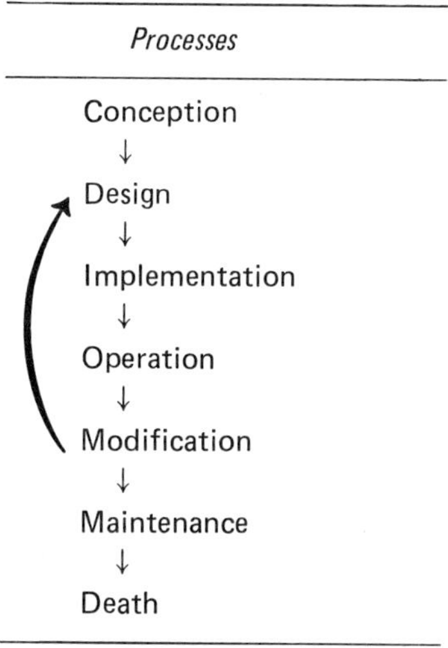

chain. The methodology of design has been considered by many authors whose works the reader is advised to study (see the References section at the end of this book). A good source to the literature is Brooks (1975). Above all, think of good design as a problem to be solved. *Work at it* steadily until it is solved; there is always room for improvement.

13.1.1 Design Quality

Overdesign is the design of features that are not required by the application. One of its main causes is the designer's need for artistic reward from his work; the need to feel that he is good at his job. It is designing a cable to withstand a tension of 1000 pounds when the required use cannot possibly exceed 50 pounds. It stems from neglecting the consideration of cost, if not function, as a design criterion.

Primarily, overdesign results from a lack of appreciation of cost as a major factor to be considered in any design and a lack of management control. In many people's minds, economy is confused with cheapness, which in turn implies inferiority. No designer would want to be considered a purveyor of inferior designs. Thus the tendency to overdesign is a natural one, but this insidious people problem of design can often be solved by the communication of upper bounds on specifications that must not be exceeded as well as the usual lower bounds that must be exceeded. Often the absence of management control results from a lack of technical knowledge. The first level of management should contain sufficient technical expertise to maintain control of products. One solution to control at the design process is the *design review*. A design is subjected to critical evaluation *before* it is executed, and, when necessary, appropriate changes are made.

That overdesign is serious is evident from the fact that a branch of engineering, known as *value engineering*, has arisen in an attempt to deal with the problem. It is not our purpose, nor is it possible, to treat this question here. However, we can give a framework that will ensure that the problem is not neglected by default.

Let us choose the degree of *luxury* as a measure of the quality of a design so that we can discuss the positive limits that a design should not exceed. Remember it is essential to use neutral terms since people respond in undesirable ways to the emotional content of words. It is convenient and instructive to divide the level of design luxury into three groups: Volkswagens, station wagons, and Cadillacs.

After people problems the subordinate problem of communication ranks next in elusive difficulty. Misunderstanding the required luxury of a design is common and generally due to lack of *effective* communication. This results from the use of vague generalities when measurable specifics are required, or more often simply the failure of the designer to listen to requests. The failure to specify the luxury level required of a design results in the designer doing his best design, his Cadillac. But Cadillacs cost money, and if the user wants to buy only a Volkswagen, he does not want to pay for a Cadillac. Money may not even be the prime consideration. For instance, if the user wants a unique and expensive sports car, he will find a Cadillac equally unsuitable.

Mixed with the problem of overdesign is the coproblem of underdesign. Here the problem is a failure to analyze and solve the metatechnical problems we have mentioned. This largely results from a confusion of the interests of the designer with the requirements of the design solution. Programmers are notorious for their interest in programming detail and neat tricks that lead to bad design. The result is all too often a cheap imitation of a Cadillac that is outperformed by a Volkswagen. A number of programming disciplines, such as structured programming, have been created to force the programmer to behave in the prescribed manner. Unfortunately, good tools do not necessarily make a craftsman.

The luxury level of a design must be clearly discussed, agreed to, and written down in specific terms that can be measured. This will protect both the designer and the user. Another term for "luxury" might be level of "sophistication." *Never*, under any circumstances, mistake unnecessarily complicated design for sophistication or quality. Always remember, when in doubt, make it simple, simple, simple.

13.1.2 Documentation

An essential part of any design and its quality is the documentation of the design process and the operational procedures for the completed system. Any design should start with a *feasibility study* or proposal, which will contain the reasons why the system should be built and the general specifications of the system and its objectives. From this, the *system description* is generated through the design process. The system description can take many forms. It should be such that new people can take over the project when others unexpectedly leave, as they invariably do. Although never up-to-date, it must be sufficiently current to achieve this. When a system is completed, the original designers are not apt to be available for solving bugs that arise, changing requirements, and generally maintaining the system; thus the description must be complete enough that the system can be modified without undue effort.

Although it may seem a management function, the designers must be aware of the *schedules* and *budget* if they are to create a system within the time and cost constraints of the system objectives. Too often analysts and programmers are kept in the dark concerning time and cost. Consequently, they can hardly be blamed if the system is late and costly. *Time* and *cost* are parameters of a design as much or more so than the technical objectives. Time is mainly a function of the availability of manpower and skills to design, implement, and operate the system. Cost is mainly a function of the failure to have the required manpower and the lost opportunity to the enterprise as a system is debugged. We like to believe that if you give designers and programmers the proper objectives to optimize, they will do so. Bringing a system in on time under budget can be as gratifying as developing an obscure programming trick. But it must be realized that people optimize on their own reward structure. It is the job of management to see that the individual's reward structures correspond with the enterprise's reward structure and its objectives. Moreover, this correspondence *must* be perceived by the designer or the programmer for it to be effective.

It seems that program documentation must be more difficult than programming, since most programmers are unable to document effectively. Documentation of a program is, without doubt, a learned skill, and to do it well requires a lot of thought and hard work, as does programming itself. Many programmers (coders) do not find documentation rewarding, so they ignore it or produce at best a feeble attempt. It is difficult to understand why, if the programmer is truly proud of his work, he does not wish to publicize it through good documentation. One might conclude that the programmer knows what a rotten job he did and does not want anyone else to know; thus, his documentation is obscure at best.

In terms of technique, it is best to document a program within that program as it is easier to keep the documentation current and to spot errors. External program documentation may be necessary, but since it is difficult to keep current, it should be designed as an overview and functional specification leaving detail to the program. For simplicity, installation standards should be adhered to. Documenting files separately from programs can be advantageous, particularly when they are used in more than one program.

Documentation per se is not the subject of this book and we can do no more than emphasize its importance in successful file design. The reader will note that we have not taken great care to document our programs or our files; this is because our examples would become unwieldy and would obscure the points we wish to make. Our programs are for illustration; they are not production programs.

Obvious as it may seem, it is important to date every document and to date every revision. Every page should indicate its revision status. Obsolete documents can cause significant problems. Any project of more than two people requires assigned responsibility for documentation control.

13.2 FILE ORGANIZATIONS

File structures are data structure systems on which the physical world poses additional design constraints of time and space because files are incorporated in a programming language and resident on external storage. When a data structure is discussed abstractly or stored in memory, neither addressing nor access are a particular problem, since memory cells are indexed by their address. For instance, memory is organized as a vector. Programming languages provide structured access for traversing their data structures. While we tend to classify data structures by form, file structures are more often classified by address technique. (This is not strictly true; for instance, compare a stack to a list.)

We refer to a file class as a *file organization.* After we have encountered several types of file organizations, the reader will recognize the COBOL file structures we have so far studied as examples of these general types. There are some terminology difficulties in doing this since the terms used to describe programming language files and file structures overlap with and are inconsistent with those describing file organizations. For instance, an Indexed I-O file is not an example of an indexed file but rather an indexed sequential file. The differences will, we are sure, be appreciated when the reader examines the file structures of more than one programming language.

Some major types of file organizations are: pile, sequential, direct, indexed, indexed sequential, inverted, and pointer lists. We briefly examine their defining features and design attributes.

13.2.1 Pile

Perhaps the most primitive file structure is the pile. A *pile* is a group of records with no restrictions on individual records except that the record consists of related items. For instance, in preparing this book, the data on the top of our desks most often was organized as a pile. In a pile the records may be quite unrelated other than the fact that they belong to the same pile. However, as a file structure, we need a few restrictions.

The pile records are arranged sequentially in order of arrival. Since the records differ, each record contains identification of the meaning of its elements. Since there may not be an item common to all records, it is not always possible to order a pile on its contents. In COBOL, some sequential files can be constructed as piles by declaring alternate record formats. Thus we could consider a pile as a sequential file. Nevertheless, the distinction appears worthwhile.

13.2.2 Sequential File

As we have noted, records in a sequential file can only be addressed by moving from one logically adjacent record to the next. The records are most often identical in format and length. In COBOL, provision is made for alternate record formats and variable-length records.

Use

The most common use for sequential files is when cost is the prime consideration and large volumes of data are accessed sequentially. Their use is restricted to batch processing operations, such as data back-up, archival purposes, and the physical transmission of data.

Advantages

Sequential files can provide the best utilization of space and are fast when the records are accessed sequentially. In addition, with sequential files the record address is implicit in the file and is invulnerable (i.e., it is not lost) to system failure. Also, the system overhead is low and operation is inexpensive when tape drives are used with large files.

Disadvantages

Single record access time is poor, bordering on disastrous, and random access is impractical.

13.2.3 Direct File

When the location of a file record is known, either because a record key value is the location or can be used to calculate the location, we have a *direct* file. Relative I-O files (and the files of Chapter 6) are direct files when key-equals-address or hashing is used to determine the relative address.

Use

The primary use of direct files is when fast access is important and sequential ordering is not important. It is best used where the file is relatively stable, such as for tables, or where the need to reorganize the data between capture and use is not significant.

Advantages

The direct file has the fastest access: one access for key-equals-address and algorithm addressing and, on the average, less than two accesses for a well-designed hashing algorithm. Also, by using direct files, the knowledge of a record location is invulnerable to system failure.

Disadvantages

The direct file is difficult to reorganize or expand because of the fixed binding of addresses to locations. A second disadvantage is the poor utilization of space because unused addresses can reserve space. Also, records are sequentially organized by a key attribute whose order may be of little use. Therefore, records cannot be ordered within the file except on the access key, and they may require separate sorting.

13.2.4 Indexed File

We say a file is *indexed* when record keys and record addresses are stored in a table, called an *index table* or a *directory*. To retrieve a record, search the index table until the desired key is found and then use the key address to locate the record. To insert a record, simply enter the key and an available record address in the table. To delete a record, erase the desired entries.

We can create an index table for each record key. The key need not be unique if we allow more than one address for a key entry. COBOL Relative I-O files or direct files (as in Chapter 7) can be used to create indexed files.

Use

While indexed files may or may not be fast depending on the level of indexes, they are very popular in software and application programs because they provide the most suitable solution to the demands of dynamic files and multiple key files.

Advantages

Indexed files provide fast access for single-level tables, assuming that they are not too large. Excellent space utilization is another advantage, although some space is required for the index tables. In addition, indexed files are easy to reorganize and allow multiple key access since we can order the tables on the keys. In short, indexed files are the most flexible organization and can coexist with any one of the direct addressing techniques.

Disadvantages

An important disadvantage is that indexed files are vulnerable to system failure when a table is lost in main memory. To remedy this either a back-up table can be kept (except for the problem with updates) or, preferably, each record should contain a self-identifying item that can be used to reconstruct the index table. Another disadvantage is the time required to maintain the index tables in a dynamic file, particularly if several keys are used.

13.2.5 Indexed Sequential File

An indexed sequential file orders the records sequentially on a principal primary key and provides an index for direct access. (Normally a bucket is located and then searched sequentially.) Thus an indexed sequential file is a compromise combination of sequential and index organizations. Sometimes secondary index keys are provided. COBOL Indexed I–O is an example of indexed sequential organization.

Use

Indexed sequential files are best used where random access is required and where significant sequential processing of the file will occur. Also, when primary key addressing is handled by the file structure, indexed sequential files are efficient to program. They may be used where processing inefficiency is acceptable.

Advantages

Indexed sequential processing is efficient as compared to non-sequential files. Other advantages are that addressing can be done by primary key and records can be added in sequence without reorganizing the entire file.

Disadvantages

Because of its compromise nature, the processing of indexed sequential files is not as efficient as compared to sequential, direct, or indexed files, and more information must be read to locate a record (see Chapter 9). Another disadvantage is that when records are added, they are placed in overflow areas and a very active file can soon become very inefficient to process. However, this can be corrected by periodic reorganization.

13.2.6 Inverted File

If we think of a file stored as rows of records in a table, we may consider an inverted file as those same records accessed by columns of the table. Each column represents some attribute of the record. To access, an index of attribute values for a particular attribute is kept and each attribute value is associated with all the records that contain it. If the attribute values are ordered, then the index can efficiently be searched.

Use

This organization should be used when fast access on multiple keys is required, where a general query on record attributes is required, for on-line systems where file search would be too slow, and for text retrieval systems. Because inverted files have poor characteristics for general processing, they are restricted to specialized uses.

Advantages

Inverted files allow random access on multiple keys, are suitable for queries on file attributes, and provide fast location of records.

Disadvantages

The principle disadvantage is the cost of storing and maintaining inverted indexes (a fully inverted file requires more space for indexes than the file data). In addition, inverted files are difficult to update, and it is necessary to update an index to accommodate a change in record attribute value of that index.

13.2.7 Pointer File

A pointer file interconnects records by means of pointers embedded in the records. Thus, addressing is contained in the records. This organization is based on the concept of the linked list. Chains, rings, trees, and plexes can all be implemented as pointer files. While in many structures one-way pointers will logically suffice, it is often advisable to use two-way pointers.

Use

Pointer files are used primarily where other file organizations cannot as conveniently provide the flexibility of structure provided by embedded pointers.

Advantages

This extreme flexibility of structure, which results in freedom of organization such as variable-length records obtained by using overflow pointers, is the primary advantage of pointer files.

Disadvantages

When linked records span many blocks, many READs will be required to traverse a path through the records; consequently, search time is slow. In addition, traversing a path of records treats records as logically sequential, so the drawbacks of sequential organization apply. Also, a pointer file is vulnerable to the loss of a record, since it may contain the addresses of other records. More storage for pointers is required in each record. There is a considerable increase in processing overhead because of the pointers.

13.2.8 File Classification by Content and Use

There are other ways to classify files, such as by content and by use. In particular, systems files will be classified by the actual file structures provided. The content classification of files will consist of the following types of files:

- master
- transaction

- dictionary
- table
- work.

The use classification of files will consist of the following types of files:

- current
- backup
- archival.

Ultimately, a major criteria of any file organization is its cost. The costs arise from many factors of the file such as creation, processing, maintenance, media, and, in particular, installation limitations of equipment as well as available expertise. It may be desirable to increase costs in order to enhance user requirements such as immediate, on-line, low-volume transactions rather than delayed, high-volume, batch transactions. It may even be that because of the firm's overhead costs, on-line is actually cheaper than batch. Remember, there are rules of thumb that usually hold but blind application in the exceptional situation can be disastrous.

13.2.8 Selection of File Media

Ideally, the use of memory for file storage would simplify file processing. Although it is possible to store files for use in memory, the cost of doing so makes it impractical. There are times, however, when performance can be greatly enhanced by using memory when it is available; thus, while we associate files with external storage, memory should be considered as a possible medium.

Figure 13.1 indicates some of the possible media for storage. On large systems the choice is usually between magnetic tape reels and magnetic disk. In Chapter 2 we discussed their properties. In many cases, the choice is dictated by the hardware configuration or installation standards. Of course, the choice should only be made by the analyst when he thoroughly understands the advantages and disadvantages of the various media and the local constraints of hardware and cost. These depend in turn on the file size, file organization, and type of processing required.

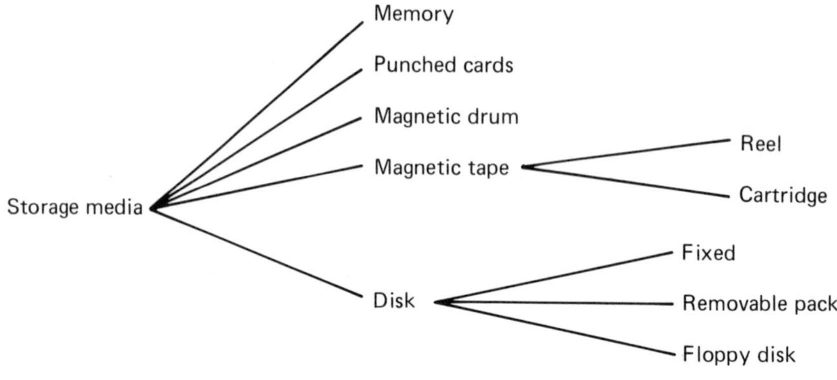

Figure 13.1 Storage media.

13.3 PRACTICAL CONSIDERATIONS

The effective use of any software system involves a number of practical considerations and these are often ignored or neglected by the programmer and designer swamped with the problem of finding a solution and creating it in code. This bias is aptly illustrated by the programmer who declares his system to work because it happens to run error-free on his test data. Certainly, this is necessary, but to the user a system works because it runs on real data over a significant period of time.

We must first assume that there will always be errors. Since specific errors are unexpected, a general error recovery must be planned and built into a file system. Errors occur from three sources: people, bugs, and installation generation. (*Bugs* is a euphemism for programmer errors that are not fatal.) Second, we must assume that the system will require change and that files are dynamic.

Security, integrity, backup, recovery, maintenance, and future uses and requirements are important factors in a practical system. Security and integrity as discussed in Chapter 12 are essential considerations in the original design. The other practical factors are a function of the operational environment. What factors are most important and how they are to be provided for requires careful consideration based on experience and foresight.

13.3.1 Backup

Although it is widely recognized that copies of programs and data should always be kept, it is not as widely recognized that current master copies should be kept in a fireproof vault with controlled access, with "current" being defined by the cost of recovery. There are several stages of backup ranging from transaction logging on an on-line system to vault storage.

At the first level, errors undetected by edit will occur. They arise from program errors or deficiency, hardware failure, and operational errors. Such errors may cause loss of a file or serious modification of a file. Since loss of file data cannot be permitted, it must be possible to recover such data and restart processing properly.

A transaction file can be recreated by reprocessing the input transaction. This can be difficult on an on-line system and so transactions should have a backup log. Backup of master files can be by an old master or by making periodic copies. In order to recover, all transactions processed against the master file since backup must be rerun.

The frequency of backup is determined by balancing the cost of backup against the cost of backup recovery. Some estimate of the frequency of recovery is required. It may be best to use a safe frequency of backup and decrease it as experience with the system is acquired.

As we continue to make backup copies, we must decide what to do with previous backup files. File retention depends on the backup cycle and the successful creation of new master files. If a batch processing cycle occurs every week, then the backup for the previous week could be destroyed on successful completion, but it would be wise to wait one more accounting cycle. What normally happens is that a safe number of backup copies for several periods are maintained and the oldest file is overwritten by creation of the current backup file.

Some files must be retained after they cease to be updated. This may be to provide historical data or because of legal requirements for retention. Any information that determines taxes must usually be retained for a fixed period.

13.3.2 File Reorganization

The process of adding and deleting records causes a file to lose the original structure it had when initialized. At some point a file may overflow or be largely empty, and reorganization is required. Overflow will become apparent when the file fails to store a new record. In a complicated file organization, the processing of a file may slowly become very inefficient. The designer must take this into account and provide some means of determining disorganization in a file. This can be done by accumulating statistics on the file processing time or by regularly scheduled reorganizations. For instance, a COBOL Indexed I–O file can lose physical sequentiality of the logical sequence of the records. Some compilers will indicate this condition.

13.3.3 Audit Trails

When we think of errors in a system, we tend to think of programming errors and neglect data errors. In large systems it may not be feasible to scratch data and start again. Therefore, it is important to understand and control the flow of data generated by an initial input transaction. The logical path of data in the system is called an *audit trail*, and it is important to be able to examine and verify that proper actions are taking place. Certainly, in a computer accounting system, auditors want to verify that correct accounting procedures are taking place. The concept of audit should be extended to other computer systems. In particular, it should be possible to independently audit the computer data of an enterprise.

13.3.4 Data Compaction

Files consume a great deal of space, but many methods of compacting files are available. Even the simple method of suppressing blanks may give considerable savings on some files. The less frequently a record is used, the more suitable it is for compaction because the cost of space saved must be balanced against the additional processing cost. The possibility of file compaction should be considered during the design stage.

13.3.5 Portability

The portability of software refers to its degree of machine independence. If software is portable, we can expect it to run correctly at a new installation with only minor bookkeeping changes. COBOL is intended to be portable and the bookkeeping changes should be confined to the environment division and the external job control language.

Portability is enhanced by late binding of addresses to physical storage. The system designed can achieve portability by interfacing with standard software rather than the machine. While at some point software must be machine dependent, interfaces can and should be machine independent. Where the designer must interface with the physical machine, for instance in a mini, where full software support is not available, careful isolation of the machine dependencies into modules will buffer their effects from the main software of the designer's system.

While it is useful to be able to transfer software from installation to installation, the most important need for portability is within an installation. The continual upgrading of hardware will play havoc with machine-dependent programs and create a nightmare of program maintenance that will devour program development time and machine resources.

13.4 FILE DESIGN CRITERIA

In order to choose a file organization, a file structure for program implementation, and a storage medium, knowledge concerning the use and nature of the file must be acquired. Those factors that are the most important to consider are:

- file capacity
- file activity
- file access
- file processing speed
- cost of a file design.

File capacity is the maximum size of the physical storage required and is the record size times the number of records plus the filler space required by the system. While both tape and disk can store files of any size, nonsequential files require that the whole file be mounted, and the hardware configuration may not have the capacity to do this. Thus large files may require sequential organization since only a single disk or tape need be mounted. In such an event, batch processing is required. *File activity* is defined as the number of transactions processed against a file for a specified period of processing time. The period of time must be chosen to reflect the average activity expected of the file. For files with high activity, sequential organization is very efficient. Other organization should be considered for low activity files.

It is desirable to quantize the operational parameters where possible. When choice of a single number is not practical, range bounds should be chosen. Values may be obtained by various calculations based on a thorough analysis of the expected file operations or, as often happens, simply based on the best guesses and experience of an analyst. Calculations are based on three methods:

- empirical formulas based on experience and common sense
- simulation
- mathematical models.

The performance of a file (or any system for that matter) must be measured in terms of criteria determined by the design goals. The following are suggested file organization performance measures:

- READ time
  arbitrary record/next record
- WRITE time
  arbitrary record/next record
- update time
  insert record/delete record
- file processing time
- file reorganization time
- storage required by a record
- storage utilization of space reserved.

13.5 STEPS IN FILE DESIGN

A common error in designing files is to quickly determine what the input will be and then to decide on the file layouts to contain this input. The importance of the creation and processing costs as well as the difficulty in changing files demand that considerable thought be given to the purpose of the file and what the enterprise can obtain from it before layout. Ultimately a file exists for one purpose only, *output*. The contents, layout, and file organization are determined by the nature of the information to be obtained from a file. The user must participate in the design of the output, and the final approval is a management function.

There are three aspects to adding a file to a data base that determines its ultimate value to an enterprise, and the design of every file must be tested against these. First, what is the cost to the enterprise of this file? The file cost consists of data capture, processing, and maintenance. These costs should be balanced against the cost of lack of information from the file. Second, what new information will be made available to the enterprise? Third, will it be timely, that is, will the information be available when required?

In short, we must first determine the value of the proposed file to the enterprise. This can be a difficult question, and for this reason it is often ignored in the rush to get on with the job. We propose a checklist of five general steps to use in file design.

1. Determine the objectives of the enterprise.
2. Determine the objectives of the proposed system.
3. Determine what output we want to provide, based on the file.
4. Decide what the logical aspects of the enterprise operation to be modeled are and what data is necessary to obtain the output of step 3.
5. Design the file repeating the preceding steps as necessary.

Like all checklists this can and should be modified to suit the application. Steps 1 and 2 are crucial in deciding step 3 and in deciding if a file should be created at all.

As part of step 2, the following four file objectives must be considered:

- to minimize file accesses
- to minimize file space
- to minimize data migration
- to maximize file system integrity.

When we have decided on the output required and the transformation process that will be used to obtain this output, then we can decide what data the file should contain. Programming does not enter at this stage, only a good knowledge of the file organizations available and the application. It is important that files be defined and structured by a *senior* person. The user should have considerable input and be asked to approve the file design.

Step 5 in the checklist requires a good technical understanding of file techniques and should be done by an analyst. It is not necessary that he do the programming of the file description, but he should do the system file description. Also, the analyst should be familiar with the other files of the organization. *Never* consider a file in isolation, but strive for integration of all data files.

To effectively define a file, the analyst goes, roughly, through the following processes, revising his answers as new information is provided:

1. How much do we wish to spend?
2. What are the data base goals?
3. What kinds of application programs are required?
4. What is the dynamic nature of the file?
5. How should the data be processed?
6. What file organization should be used?
7. What is the difficulty of implementation?
8. What is the system overhead?
9. How much will these choices cost?
10. How much should we spend?
11. What are the data base goals realized and what alternatives are there?
12. Reiterate until answers are satisfactory.
13. Generate system description of file.

A word of caution is in order about the design of a file processing system. Among programmers there is often a great concern for efficiency. Unfortunately they tend to concentrate on local efficiency and thereby neglect and even degrade global efficiency. Any attempt to obtain efficiency must be balanced against the cost of doing so which involves the *total costs* of a system. In our view it is better to take the approach that a system be tunable. It is often not clear where the bottlenecks in processing or execution time will occur until the system is in operation. For instance, sorts can be tuned later when they become a problem and more knowledge of the structure of the files to be sorted is available. If sorts consume insignificant resources, why optimize them? Where possible and when the solution is not well understood by the designer, we would advise incremental design of the system—build usable parts of the system and get the user involved with computer-assisted manual procedures. It can be too much to expect a complex system to function smoothly without some trial-and-error development.

PROBLEM

You have been asked to head a research group to investigate drug use among high school students. You are to prepare a plan for carrying out a study of this problem and submit it to a committee of the state legislature.

As a start you decide to prepare a questionnaire.

Write up this plan, paying attention to the appropriate steps in the design process. Remember that you are not required to implement the study, but you are responsible for detailing exactly how it is to be carried out. Your plan must convince members of the legislature review board that you have thought through the design steps carefully. You will not be called in person and you will not be given a second chance.

Ask your professor or a colleague to read your plan and offer constructive criticism.

14

File Implementation

The ultimate requirement of data processing is, of course, to implement design—to translate blueprint into production. The previous chapters, through discussion of file organizations, data structures, query techniques, and design considerations have filled the workshop with programming tools. Implementation involves choice; choosing the tools that will do the job effectively subject to the contraints of time, money, personnel, availability of storage, CPU cycles, security requirements, data integrity, and end use. In this chapter we shall highlight by way of an example the process of choosing tools.

14.1 CASE STUDY: THE STOLEN VEHICLE FILE

The data bases used to keep track of crimes and criminals are extensive, complex in design, international in scope, and extremely expensive. If we restrict our interest, however, solely to the one crime of auto theft, we can build with what we have learned in this book a small version of such a data base. The design is straightforward and the reader may even be able to use the design to create a little system of his own for another purpose; some of our students already have.

14.1.1 Logical Analysis: The Stolen Vehicle File

Let us suppose that we are to create a data base of stolen vehicles for use in a midwestern state. Each stolen car listed in the data base is to be kept active for five years after which it is to be assumed unrecoverable and the associated records removed to the document storage section. We shall assume the data base has at any time information about at most 20,000 cars.

Information on these cars is to be kept in a format that makes the information readable and understandable. This information is often to be radioed to law enforcement officers in the field and there is little room for the error that might result in transmission of incorrectly understood data. Information requests are to be of three types:

1. Each state patrol car team is to be given, at the start of their six-hour duty period, a list of those vehicles reported stolen in the past two weeks; this is the so-called "hot" list.
2. If a car is reported stolen during one officer's shift, he is to be notified immediately by radio.
3. Should an officer request information by radio regarding a particular vehicle, the stolen car data base is to be queried in case the car described is one of those reported stolen.

In addition to these three kinds of information requests a "broad-banded" request facility is to be added. Specifically a *broad-banded* request is a request for those vehicles in the stolen vehicle data base that share common characteristics. A list of all stolen vehicles that are red station wagons or foreign sports cars are two examples of broad-banded requests. Very often criminals switch license plates on cars so that stolen cars are not as easily detectable. It is very common to use out-of-state plates for such purposes, making it difficult to determine whether or not a car is stolen simply by checking its license registry.

From the data base point of view the broad-band requirements would suggest a file organization that has the following capabilities:

(a) storing pertinent information on each car that is stolen

(b) providing access to the records by
- date (all records added to the file in the past two weeks are to appear on the hot list)
- specific descriptive data (such as color, make, and year)
- exact data (such as the uniquely occurring license number)

(c) adding and deleting records (as cars are reported stolen or located)

(d) instant retrieval.

Which file techniques, sequential, relative, or index sequential, provide this kind of capability?

None of the file techniques discussed have this kind of capability, and yet we must choose one of these methods because in COBOL we have no other file organization techniques with which to work.

Clearly, sequential organization is not the way to go. There is no obvious sequential ordering of the stolen vehicle records (unless we take the last one reported stolen as the last one on the file, which is meaningless in this context). Furthermore, there is a need for fairly instantaneous (or at least quick) retrieval of the records given that a police officer requests information suddenly, and surely, randomly on a given car he has under surveillance. This leaves us with relative file organization or index sequential organization to choose from. The latter requires that we choose a unique key for each file record and this could clearly be the license number. If there is a possibility that license number is not a unique identifier because the same license number is used in other states, the unique identifier can be a concatenation of license number and state. It is clear that there will be a need to retrieve records on license numbers so there is some justification for preferring index sequential to Relative I–O. On the other hand using Relative I–O gives the programmer control over the mapping between identifier and storage location (see Chapter 6). If small file sizes are involved, Relative I-O may be preferred over index sequential because implementations of index sequential usually require a minimum commitment to auxiliary storage. (Index I-O is almost always employed if the file requires more than one disk pack.) In addition, experience indicates that the binding of track addresses with keys is a little more inflexible with index files than with relative files in some implementations, and given a free choice, some computer centers might prefer relative to index. We shall choose Relative I-O for illustrative purposes and because, as we shall see, the file is not very large.

The first step in any implementation is to focus attention on the input and output of a system, and in view of the fact that the system required has clear guidelines as to what is expected in terms of the reports to be generated, we can now focus our attention on what the nature of the input is.

Clearly, at least the following information is needed for each stolen vehicle:

(a) license number
(b) make of vehicle
(c) year of model
(d) color
(e) number of doors
(f) date reported stolen
(g) address of owner
(h) city where car was stolen
(i) state of registration
(j) name of owner
(k) type of vehicle

Making the record layout is an easy process, and for simplicity we might choose the following COBOL format:

```
01  STOLEN-VEHICLE-RECORD.
    02  LICENSE-NOS         PIC 9(6).
    02  MAKE-OF-VEHICLE     PIC X(15).
    02  YEAR-OF-MODEL       PIC 9(2).
    02  COLOR               PIC X(9).
    02  NOS-DOORS           PIC 9(2).
```

```
02  DATE-REPORTED     PIC 9(6).
02  OWNER-ADDRESS     PIC X(18).
02  CITY              PIC X(10).
02  STATE             PIC X(7).
02  OWNER             PIC X(16).
02  TYPE-OF-VEHICLE   PIC X(13).
```

The last entry TYPE-OF-VEHICLE has the following possibilities:

```
LUXURY
NORMAL
COMPACT
FOREIGN
SPORTS CAR
TRUCK
STATION WAGON
4 WHEEL DRIVE
```

Whenever a field of a record in a data base has a fixed number of possibilities, the programmer can consider the idea of coding each possibility by a number. In this case we can choose to enter the vehicle type as a one-digit number from 1 to 8 as in Fig. 14.1.

Of course, whenever any record is to be printed, the coded value must be looked up in the translation table before proceeding. It is especially important to remember that the table must be changed if the number of or designation of coded values is changed.

In this example we might also choose to code color and car make. Street address could not be coded, and it would be a blunder to code cities.

The reader will remember from Chapter 5 that it is necessary to create a relative file sequentially but that once created it may be accessed randomly. It would be a good idea at this point to review

COMPACT	1
FOREIGN	2
LUXURY	3
NORMAL	4
SPORTS CAR	5
STATION WAGON	6
TRUCK	7
4 WHEEL DRIVE	8

Figure 14.1 Translation table.

Chapter 5 before reading further and to skim the section in Chapter 6 on hashing.

Since each record is 92 bytes long and *fixed* in length, a total of 92 × 20,000 or roughly two million bytes of auxiliary storage will be needed. The most common IBM disk packs presently in use store either 100 million or 200 million bytes so that the data base will not spill over onto more than one disk pack. The word "fixed" is emphasized above: Remember that Relative I-O cannot be used for variable-length records in IBM OS/VS COBOL.

It is clear that one entry to the file must be by means of the unique key license number. For this reason a hash table must be created linking each license number with the relative address of the record in the file with which it is associated. The file contains (at maximum) 20,000 entries. Since the hash table should be at least 125% of the required size to lessen the number of hash collisions, the hash table should be a minimum size of

$$20{,}000 \times \frac{125}{100} = 25{,}000$$

entries. Relative addresses can be kept in binary as COMPUTATIONAL SYNCHRONIZED items.

In IBM OS/VS COBOL, binary halfwords can be used to store the relative addresses. At 2 bytes/address this requires 2 × 25,000 or 50,000 bytes of core. This is far too much of the WORKING-STORAGE SECTION that is made available at run time so the hash table will have to be subdivided, stored on disk, and brought into core as needed. Suppose we agree to use 10,000 bytes of core for the hash table as in:

```
01   HASH-TABLE.
     02   RELATIVE-ADDRESS
          OCCURS 5000 TIMES
          PIC S9 (4)   COMP  SYNC.
```

There are thus 5 segments of 10,000 bytes each, each of which could be stored in one 10,000-byte, fixed-length record of a separate Relative I-O file and retrieved as needed.

What hashing algorithm should be used? As suggested in Chapter 6, division hashing is preferred. Since the hash table can contain no more than 25,000 entries, we need as divisor the largest prime smaller than 25,000. From number tables this is found to be 24,989. Hence the index into the hash table will be X, where

```
X ≡ KEY MOD 24989 + 1
```

In order to determine the segment of the hash table containing the appropriate relative address of the record, the value X should be *integer* divided by 5,000 and 1 added as in

```
COMPUTE Y = X/5000 + 1
```

Take, as an example, license number 500,000. This hashes to (500,000 MOD 24,989) + 1 = 221. This entry is in the hash table in the (221/ 5,000) + 1 = 1st segment. Any of the techniques suggested in Chapter 6 can be used for resolving hash collisions. Let us adopt the following version for the stolen vehicle file:

1. The addresses in the hash table point to the head of a chain of records.
2. The links between each record in the chain are kept within records themselves.
3. A "-1" indicates the tail of a chain.

The file is thus organized as shown in Fig. 14.2.

At this point two programs have been made necessary. A program is needed to transfer information from keypunch cards onto the Relative I-O file. These cards represent information coded from historical documents about stolen vehicles. From now on programs will be available to add new stolen cars to the already existing file. A second program is needed to create the hash table and link the file records together.

After the hash table is designed, a third program is needed to read a license number in and fetch the appropriate record by hashing. In addition, a fourth program is needed to add, change, and delete any record on the file given its unique key.

Implementation proceeds by stages. For each specifically different function there is an individual program. Each program uses techniques already known to perform a specific task. Each program runs independently of the others and therefore can be tested separately. Of course, some programs cannot be properly tested until others have been tested and proved reliable. We cannot, for instance, test the program that reads a license number and fetches the associated record until we have created and tested the hash table. In larger projects, it is sometimes useful to assume that another program already works (as an example, we could keypunch part of the hash

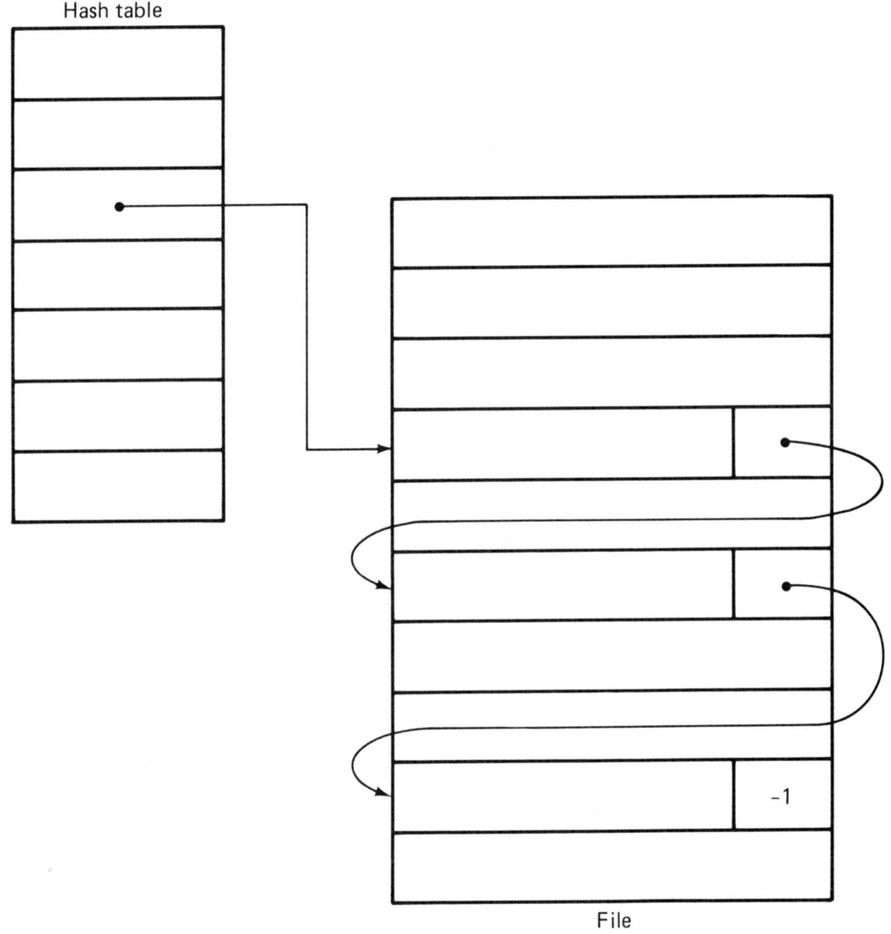

Figure 14.2 Relating the hash table to the stolen vehicle file.

table and insert it into a program for testing before the real hash table was ready).

It is obvious that the hash table should be kept along with the data file as it may need to be updated as records are added to or deleted from the file. It can be stored as a separate file or as a special record within the file itself. We have decided in this example to keep the hash table as a separate file.

To this point we have not accomplished anything very dramatic. Even the hash table would not have been necessary had we decided to use Indexed I-O. There has been no attempt to go beyond the simple file organization described in Chapters 5 and 6. The demands of the case study, however, require a more advanced view of the data. Other routes than the license number are required to link the physical storage of the records to the end use of the system.

The program that produces the "hot sheet" listing does not require access to the entire file. Only those records that pertain to cars stolen over the preceding two weeks are needed. One solution is to provide another file of stolen vehicle records that migrate on and off the file over a two-week period. This is probably a very satisfactory solution in this case as the file needed is relatively small. It would not be appropriate if both the files were extremely large as might be the case if we were considering all North American stolen vehicles as a subset of a world-wide system. The problem, of course, is redundancy; many of the records appear on both files.

Another approach, and the one we shall take, is to restrict the view of one program, the "hot sheet" program, to those records on the data file that have appeared on the file within the past two weeks. This is done by providing an inverted list of those cars on the data file active over the past two weeks. This list could be a list of relative addresses or a list of license numbers. The former lends itself to faster access to the records but has the drawback that any movement of records within the data file requires an updating of this list. This is a design decision. We shall choose to store license numbers as it is logically simpler.

The inverted list of vehicles stolen over a two-week period is a logical data structure. It is left to the designer of the system to implement the data structure and to decide how to save it for future reference. One method of implementation is to store the linked list of license numbers in an array, as illustrated in Figure 14.3. This array is two-dimensional (it has rows and columns). There are three columns, each with a specific purpose. The entries in the first column are the license numbers of those cars recorded on the data file that were stolen in the most recent two-week period. The second column contains the Julian date that the car was stolen. This second column contains redundant information as DATE-STOLEN is also kept on the file itself. The system designer should have a good reason when he stores redundant information. The reason here is to indicate when the license number should be removed from the linked list. Had these dates not been included, it would have been necessary to periodically fetch all the records pointed to by this list and determine whether or not to remove them. Remember that the records themselves are not being removed from the file. Records

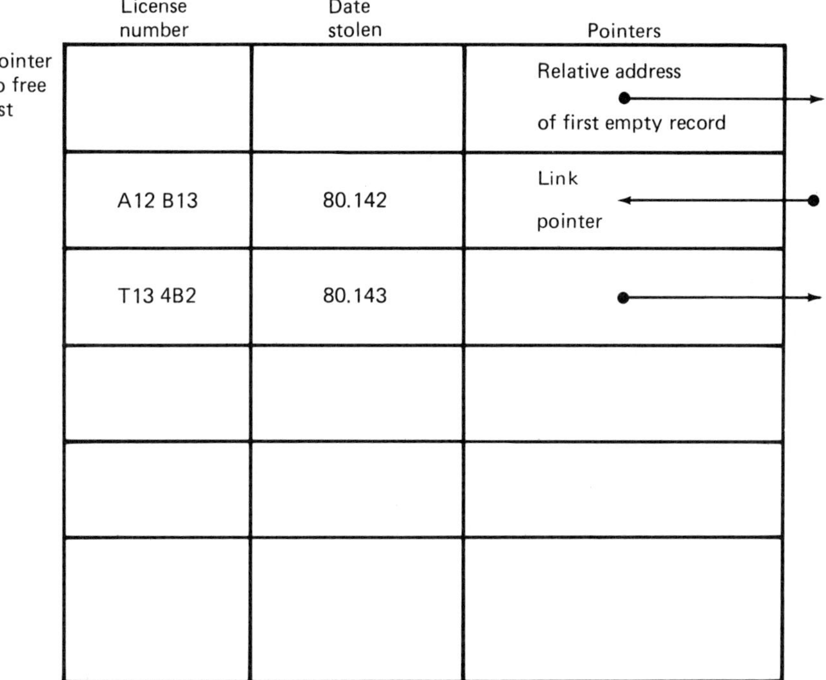

Figure 14.3 Inverted list of license numbers on the "hot sheet."

on the file are kept for five years before being removed. The third column contains the list pointers. They point to another element of the list or contain a -1 to indicate the end of the list.

Row 1 of the array is a special entry. It contains a pointer to the free list, the linked list of all those elements of the array that are available to contain the license number of a car that has yet to be stolen.

In order to maintain a consistent addition (of records) algorithm, it is sensible to set the linked list up at file creation as shown in Fig. 14.4. In this original setup, each row of the array is linked to the one following it. All rows are members of the free list and the head of the free list at row 1 points to the first free cell in row 2.

Now that this data structure has been decided on, three programs are necessary and perhaps even more will be used if the designer should decide to split these programs up into smaller programs. The programs are as follows:

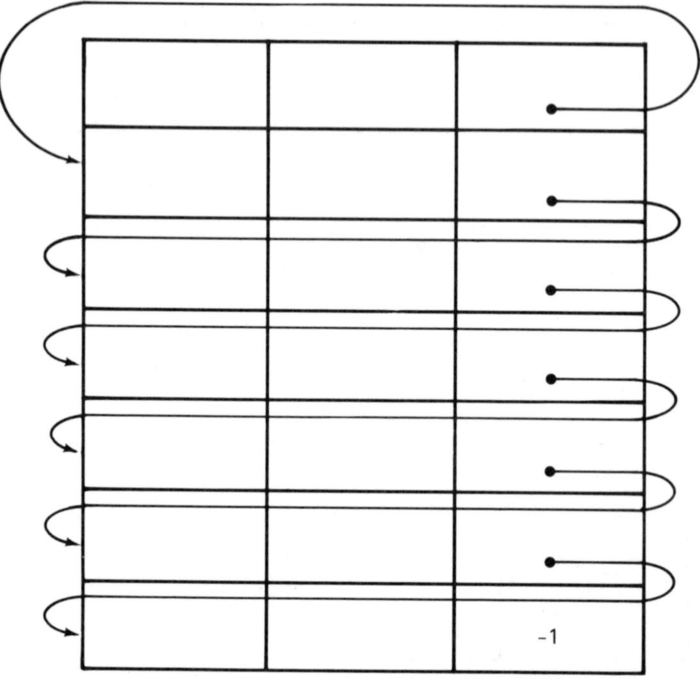

Figure 14.4 Linked list setup.

(a) a program to set up the original array or linked list and initialize the free list

(b) a program that adds and deletes license numbers on this list as cars are reported found or stolen or two weeks pass

(c) a program to prepare the hot list for police officers, given that the inverted list has been prepared.

Another implementation problem is how this linked list that has been physically realized as an array is to be stored when the program is not in use. One solution is to store the array as a large single record in a physical sequential file (the equivalent of storing the level 01 entry associated with the array). If the array is very large, it can be stored in sections; one section per record.

Some programmers prefer to keep inverted lists in the same file as the original data. We do not subscribe to this view, preferring to keep the files as homogeneous as possible.

We are in the process here of creating a small system of programs. Each program has its own specific function and together they carry out the function of making the data on the file accessible in many different forms. So far, in this system two views of the same data file have been created. One set of programs, those that use the hash table, permit a program to "see" only one record at a time, given a license number. The record whose license number is given can be read, changed, added, or deleted. The hash table has access to any record on the original data file; indeed a record cannot be added to the data file unless it is linked through the hash table. The programs, such as the "hot list" printer, that use the inverted list of stolen cars by date do not have access to all the records on the original data file. These programs have access to or "see" only those records associated with stolen cars reported in the past two weeks. The data structure thus narrows the vision through an imaginary window. Any program that has access to the data file through this window can only interact with a limited subsection of the file. It is as though there really was a *two-week* stolen vehicle file. Physically, there is only one file, but by the use of the linked inverted list, there logically appears to be another. This rather different way of looking at what is happening when a data structure is used as a window on a data file is of fundamental importance to the idea of data bases. Data structures can be used not only to restrict access to a select subset of records but can also be used to restrict access to subsets of the set of fields of a record. We can have not only a logical view of the data file itself but also a logical view of each physical record. What is being gained is a saving in the proliferation of redundant information. One file is needed instead of two; one record is needed instead of two.

In this example an inverted list was created; a list of records associated with recent car thefts. In order to implement the inverted list into a language data structure, an array was chosen with three columns. We have already mentioned that we could have done without one of the columns. We could even have done without the entire array. As an alternative we could have kept another link field within each record of the file. These fields could be used to point to records stolen within the two-week period. The head of the chain and the free list pointer could be kept in a special record of the file such as record 1. When a record is added to the data file, it is added to the head of the chain and, later, when recovered or its two-week waiting period is over, it is removed. This does not destroy the concept of an inverted list but merely transfers its implementation from an array into the file itself. This has the advantage that there is no more array, and it has the disadvantage that in order to print the license numbers of the most recently stolen cars, the records must be read. The implementation is left to the designer.

By similar procedures we can produce inverted lists of cars by color, one list for the red cars, another for the green, and so on. Inverted lists can be kept of car makes, car types, two-door cars, four-door cars, engine sizes (if kept on the file), recovery dates, etc. Each list provides a different window into the file; another logical file. Sometimes it will be useful to merge these logical files as would be the case when we want a list of all red and blue cars. These logical files can be treated in the same way as real physical files, provided we proceed through the appropriate data structures. A list of all two-door red cars stolen in the past two weeks requires selecting those cars found on three inverted lists. Algorithms that deal with logical files are discussed in Chapter 11.

Now that all the basic design criteria and implementation techniques have been decided, there remains the tedious translation of these decisions into the COBOL language. This will result in a number of fairly substantial programs and those readers tempted with time and access to computing facilities may want to code this or a similar system. Our students have accomplished very pretty realizations of this system in an average of 1,000 to 2,000 COBOL statements.

Next we shall examine this last phase of the actual programming. It is not, as many managers have learned to their chagrin, the simple part of system implementation.

14.2 THE ROLE OF THE PROGRAMMER

If you look at the organization chart of a business that uses computers and is of any reasonable size, you will generally find the programmer's box drawn somewhere very close to the bottom of the chart, buried perhaps off to one side or even left off altogether. He is very far removed from the center of power in the corporation. Ahead of the programmer lies a long, winding, and tortuous climb up the ladder of success away from his origins. Advancement in the organization is very often blocked. A high barricade that can rarely be leaped is raised between those who program the computer and the senior executive positions of management. Senior management positions are reached only from areas of the company such as sales, marketing, advertising, research, finance, accounting, and production. This is a grim picture and to many an affront to the spirit of capitalism. Fortunately it is only a mental picture held by beginning programmers and bears no relationship to the real world. In fact, good programmers in most of the large companies and particularly in some of the smaller ones are extremely well paid, earn in most cases more than their contemporaries in other areas of the business, have unlimited futures, and can and do rise rapidly to areas of major corporate responsibility. But we should go back and underline the word "good." The dim picture just painted is certainly reality for the *poor* programmer. Why is it true that so many programmers—intelligent individuals, with college-level courses behind them, fired with ambition and opportunity—take off in their careers with great expectations and confidence only to fall flat on their faces to be buried alive forever inside the organization?

The answer is extremely simple. *The programmer, by the very nature of his job, already has a share in corporate responsibility that he cannot afford to ignore.* If he cannot rise to the challenge of that responsibility, he can never be promoted into a position that would force him to assume a greater responsibility. It is just that simple.

What makes this seemingly universal requirement particularly applicable to a programmer is that there is no time to train him to accept responsibility as there is in so many other corporate positions. Once code starts to flow off the programmer's desk toward integration into production systems, he has implicitly assumed responsibility for the integrity of these systems. If his code fails, the systems fail. The more complex the system is of which his code is a part and the more heavily the organization comes to depend on it, the greater are the consequences of his failure. Neither the experienced nor the inexperienced programmer has the luxury of performing poorly on off days without the risk of exposure. *Poor coding is almost certain to be discovered.*

But the programmer is human and he is going to make mistakes. How then does one succeed as a programmer? What differentiates the good programmer from the poor one?

A good programmer strives to reduce the frequency of his failures, to minimize the consequences of his failures, and, most importantly, to make it as easy as possible to recover from his failures. This is true of all professions. A doctor cannot save every patient; a dentist cannot restore every tooth; a police detective cannot solve every crime; and a teacher cannot instruct every student. Professionals are measured by the percentage of successes they have in relation to their failures. This is a challenge that faces every good programmer and it requires all the creative energy of which he is capable.

Since failure is something to be overcome, it would do us well to study what is viewed as failure from the point of view of a corporation. For some reason one of the most frequently occurring problems among both novice and expert programmers is the failure to meet deadlines. What is even more shocking is the frequency with which such failures are discovered at the final hour. The bad news descends at the eleventh hour, often in spite of numerous promises and protestations to the contrary whenever the subject of the deadline is discussed. Often a deadline must be changed for perfectly good reasons but it is usually true that the consequences of changing a deadline vary in degree of severity as the deadline approaches; the closer the deadline the more severe the consequences of not making it. The shock waves of a missed deadline may reverberate throughout an organization, reaching sometimes to the senior executive level where a decision to dismiss those involved may be made (an event not nearly as rare as programmers believe). Programmers can avoid this most important of failures or at least minimize its consequences by communicating an accurate and truthful report of the status of a project as work progresses and by asking for changes in deadlines as early in the life of a project as possible with reasonable justification and with the expectancy that a deadline will not be reached. Following these procedures will allow management to *minimize* the consequences of possible failure. A deadline that is missed because it was changed before it was reached is not as drastic a failure as one that is simply not met.

The second most important failure that a programmer must learn to avoid is the failure to accomplish that which was required. Such a failure *cannot* be blamed on management. It is the programmer's responsibility to ensure that he understands what is expected of him. When in doubt, ask. The programmer who works hard, programs efficiently, and makes his deadlines is a failure if he has not done the job according to the specifications. Beginning programmers are particularly prone to this problem. The question, "Are there any questions?", often asked at the end of a meeting, should not be taken as a signal to prepare to leave the room. No question is considered stupid if it is asked at that point. Managers want to be sure you know how to proceed.

We should also caution the reader that both managers and programmers have the same memory problems as other people. Write project requirements down and send copies to all participants. Refer to such documentation from time to time.

The third failure that occurs widely among poor programmers is the failure to adequately document work. Documentation serves two purposes: First, it serves as a record of accomplishment. Managers rarely study code (although they would be well advised to do so) and documentation may be all that there is to indicate achievement; second, it enables individuals, including the programmer, to use, modify, and repair the code efficiently.

Documentation must be considered as part of the coding effort and must be developed in parallel with the code. Documentation should never be left to the end. Exactly what constitutes documentation is hard to define without a specific project in mind and without clear knowledge of the intended user. Those who use the documentation should be considered as the judges of what constitutes proper documentation.

A fourth failure that will ultimately lead to greater failure is the inadequate use of the resources available. In particular, avoid spending unreasonable amounts of time studying things or thinking through problems when there are people around who know the answers or have previously found solutions to the problems being faced. Ignorance should not be encouraged, and time is more important than pride. A programmer should never be afraid to ask.

Finally, the programmer should always provide adequate protection for routines that are thoroughly debugged and tested. Programs ready for production should be frozen and copies of them used for future modifications. All too often modifications cause formerly working versions to fail.

14.3 THE ART OF PROGRAMMING

Programming, like almost all other forms of creative work, is an art and there are programmers that invent algorithms and write programs that are as expressive of this art as Michaelangelo's ceiling of the Sistine Chapel is of painting. These people are geniuses but they are as rare among programmers as the great painters are in the world of painting. Fortunately, programming is a science as well as an art and the very act of programming has been studied in that light. In the past twenty years there have been some revolutionary ideas in the science of programming; these realizations and generalizations can be applied to programming to actually help the programmer write a better program. One of these is the concept of structured programming. The ideas of structured programming have been followed in the programs in this text. Specifically the ideas behind structured programs in COBOL are that they:

(a) contain only one STOP RUN statement
(b) use few if any GO TO statements
(c) use only forward GO TO statements; that is, GO TO statements that cause control to jump to an *imperative statement* which follows that GO TO itself. There are, in other words, no backward jumps in the program.

In COBOL structured programs use the PERFORM statement to transfer to another statement outside the range of sequential statement execution. This implies a return to the statement following the PERFORM and a return to the normal sequence of flow in the program. The result is a gentle forcing of the programmer to contemplate carefully why he wishes to leave the normal sequence of statement execution, and this very fact is an aid to program creation. There are many program designers who believe that the GO TO is a very powerful and often misused statement in programming languages and that we should avoid it unless we are convinced we have a good reason to use it. Some managers have increased the productivity of their employees by forcing them to record every use of the GO TO statement and to state clearly why they felt obliged to use it. Those programmers who have studied their own and other people's programs that are full of GO TOs, trying hopelessly to discover what is going on within them, would welcome such an idea.

Another good idea is that of writing programs in small sections, called *modules*, and later joining all the modules together. A module should have a carefully defined purpose and clearly defined input and output. It should have only one entry and one exit point. A module should be a subroutine in COBOL or a paragraph that is to be executed under the control of a PERFORM statement. Programs in this book are always divided into little paragraphs that have specific functions clearly defined by their paragraph names, for example, a READ-PARAGRAPH or a TRANSACTION-ROUTINE. A group of paragraphs can be considered a module, and when this is the case they should be designated as a SECTION in the program.

How large should a module be? That decision is up to the discretion of the programmer, but we would suggest no more than could be printed on an 8½ × 11 inch sheet of paper.

The third major idea is the suggestion that a program should be designed in a top-down manner. In other words, the details should be added later rather than in the beginning. Our programs in this text are designed in this manner. Each program begins with the four statements or something very similar:

```
PERFORM INITIALIZATION.
PERFORM PROCESS-ROUTINE.
PERFORM TERMINATION.
STOP RUN.
```

Except for a few details, this is a complete program. Of course, we have to describe the PROCESS-ROUTINE which might consist of:

```
PERFORM READ-A-CARD.
PERFORM ADD-1-TO-AMOUNT.
PERFORM WRITE-CARD.
```

and these routines in turn have to be further described. Eventually, every added paragraph has no further PERFORM statements and the process terminates. There is some advantage in considering the name of a paragraph as a kind of super COBOL verb. It would be nice to have a verb in COBOL called INITIALIZATION that would run away and get all those switches set, files opened, and initial reads done but, alas, the language is not as yet that rich. One day it may be. For the moment invent the verb by sticking the word PERFORM out in front and describe what it is supposed to do in a paragraph called INITIALIZATION. A program can then be thought of as defining a few commands in terms of others. Eventually, in the process of defining a new verb one uses a verb such as READ or ADD that already exists and the job is done.

The fourth consideration does not really have a name but we might think of it as "Do yourself a favor; you might have to read your own program one day." Under this heading we would suggest that you:

(a) use COBOL variable names, file names, and paragraph names that are meaningful to you and that would make sense to someone else

(b) document your program in-line whenever you do something that is not obvious

(c) avoid using tricky programming techniques but thoroughly document them when you do. There is an old adage in computing that says, "The first person to forget what a trick is supposed to do is the inventor."

14.4 TESTING AND PROGRAM VALIDATION

Enough can never be said about testing and validation. It is probably the least organized part of a job and in many cases the one area of programming responsibility that always seems to be ignored in the design process. And yet it is at least as important as system design. It is so important that we would like to suggest that it be removed as a separate part of a given job and be considered as an integral part of the design process itself. As an algorithm is designed, provision should be made to test it. Testing should proceed in parallel with program creation. Code should not be considered as written until it has been tested.

Fortunately, this is not as difficult to do when a program is being written in modules. Since each module has only one entry point and one exit point and no backward GO TOs, it is possible to test it independently of other code. The programmer should make up dummy input of various types for his module to test. Every statement of the module should be tried and every branch of an IF statement executed in a proper test. Program testing is made easier if nested IFs are prohibited and compound conditions within IF statements and PERFORMS avoided. A great help to testing is to document code as the writing proceeds. Take the time to describe what a statement or group of statements are expected to do and what data is expected to reach them. If you suspect that bad data or a bad environment at statement execution time may occur, provide a test for it. It is far better for your program to signal an error condition than to have the operating system do it for you. If you suspect, for example, that a zero value may be passed on as a divisor to an arithmetic calculation, provide a test for it and signal an error condition. This is especially important when you can determine beforehand that there is a condition that will upset a section of code. There is only one way to be really sure that it will not and that is to let the section be conditionally executed. The ELSE part of the appropriate IF statement can generate an appropriate error message.

Be very careful in making value judgements about data that someone else is providing. It is very unlikely that payroll has anyone on its staff making more than $100,000 a year but that does not mean they will not make a mistake and indicate a salary of that amount.

14.5 SOME FINAL PROGRAMMING AND DESIGN DETAILS

In many of the language modules the statement

```
BLOCK CONTAINS { RECORDS    }
               { CHARACTERS }
```

is used. How is this number of records or characters decided on?

First, it is important to recognize that the size of a block is a programming decision. It affects the amount of core a program uses and the execution time but it does not affect system design. As review, recall that no matter how large a block is, one logical record is made available each time a READ is executed and one logical record is written each time a WRITE statement is executed. This reading and writing of logical records should not be confused with what electronic operations are actually taking place. At the hardware level there may be no data transfer taking place at all.

When data transfer is initiated, a block of logical records is transferred. Before data transfer these records are located as one group on an I/O device or together in an area of core, called a "buffer." Thus, in determining the size of a buffer, the user must decide the amount of core he can set aside for logical record storage in addition to the core he must set aside for utilizing the code compiled by COBOL from the source documents and the area reserved for elements in the WORKING-STORAGE SECTION. When the block of logical records, on the other hand, is transferred to a physical storage device, another consideration applies. Because of the gaps left between adjacent blocks, space is wasted. The larger a block, the less the number of gaps and the less space lost. The electronics involved also add restrictions as it is not recommended with disk devices that blocks span more than one track. Most manufacturers provide a table that tells the programmer for each given device the best size for a block given the logical record lengths involved. Consult the programmer's guide of your installation's COBOL compiler.

14.5.1 JCL Considerations

No matter which operating system or computer is eventually used, it will be necessary to supply some JCL with your COBOL program. If you are using IBM OS/VS COBOL, you will have two choices: You can use the VSAM facility for all three I–O modules (Sequential, Relative, and Indexed) if it is available on your machine or you may elect to use non-VSAM file organizations. The former is preferable; the latter may be necessitated. When VSAM is used, files must be created using the utility called Access Method Services (AMS). An example of a program in AMS is given at the end of Chapter 9. AMS has a command language that is described in the IBM publication, *ACCESS METHOD SERVICES*. If you wish to create a physical sequential file for use with the Sequential I–O module, you will need to create an ENTRY SEQUENCED DATA SET; a Relative I–O file requires a RELATIVE RECORD DATA

SET; an Indexed I–O file is implemented with a KEY SEQUENCED DATA SET. Very little JCL is required when using VSAM-type data sets.

Non-VSAM data sets must be created on the system with the job control language. Space does not permit us to give details here. To help get you started here is the JCL statement needed to create the Sequential I–O file described in the COBOL clause SELECT FILEA ASSIGN TO UT-DISK-S-DD1 at our installation.

```
//DD1  DD  DSN = MYFILE,
VOL = SER = 111111, UNIT = DISK,
SPACE = (TRK, (2, 1)),
DISP = (NEW, KEEP),
DCB = (DSORG = PS, RECFM = FB)
```

This is a DD or data definition statement. It is labeled DD1. This label connects it with the system name in the ASSIGN TO clause of the SELECT statement. DSN stands for data set name. MYFILE is the name of the physical sequential data set in this example. VOL = SER = is a key word which specifies the name of the volume on which the physical data set is to reside. In this example it is labeled 111111. UNIT is used to describe the type of device used. Here a DISK is implied.

```
SPACE = (TRK,(2,1)),
```

is a request that two tracks be set aside for the data set on disk. Should more space be needed, it is to be made available one track at a time. The system will permit this a maximum of fifteen times.

```
DISP = (NEW, KEEP),
```

informs the operating system that this is a new data set and that it should be kept at the end of the job (otherwise it would be automatically deleted).

```
DCB = (DSORG = PS, RECFM = FB)
```

is the DCB or data control block parameter. Specifically, this informs the system that a physical sequential (PS) file is to be created consisting of fixed-length blocked records (FB).

14.6 SUMMARY

In this chapter and in the preceding one we have looked at design and implementation from a people perspective. In essence these two chapters serve to advise the reader. The authors' advice contains what we have learned both from our own and others' mistakes and from inquiries when things went right. We cannot guarantee that this advice will make everything our reader does turn out well, but we hope that it may save him a baptism by fire.

PROBLEM

You have been hired by a hotel to write a small data base system to keep track of rooms and their occupancy. The hotel has 1200 rooms of various kinds, and naturally you will not have to keep the room assignments up-to-date yourself. You will, however have to write the following COBOL programs.

1. A program that creates and Indexed I–O file of room assignments. This file is to contain such information as room number, size of room (single, double, presidential suite, etc.), name of registered guest, number in party, his or her address, form of payment for room (i.e. check, cash, or credit card), cost of room, and one or more room charges and for what purpose (an example might be $2.40 PHONE, $8.00 BREAKFAST).
2. Set up a few inverted lists such as OCCUPIED-ROOMS, SINGLE-BEDS, NUMBER-IN-PARTY, COST-OF-ROOM.
3. Write a query program to handle such queries as

   UNOCCUPIED *and* SINGLE-BEDS

   and the more difficult

   OCCUPIED *and* COST-OF-ROOM < $50.00.

Basically we want you to design a nice little system that a hotel manager might like to have. If you want to get serious, visit a local hotel and discuss the project with a real manager. One of our students did and a hotel chain gave him a job when he showed them the program.

15

Data Base Systems

So far we have considered a number of file organization techniques and examined the file structures available in COBOL. Advantages and disadvantages were discussed in the light of technical problems. As experience with large files has grown, a number of serious problems have been recognized as increasingly important. These we consider as metatechnical problems, in that they go beyond the kind of technical details we have so far discussed.

15.1 METATECHNICAL CONSIDERATIONS

The data base concept is an attempt to provide technical solutions to these metatechnical problems. A new file technology is developing that views data as independent of the programs that process it and as independent of physical storage. We first discuss the metatechnical problems that have caused this shift and then we give an overview of a general data base system that arises as a reaction to these problems and, consequently, examine some of the major requirements for a data base system.

When we reconsider our study of file techniques in the previous chapters, we realize that we were concerned with only three essential functions:

- creation
- retrieval
- maintenance

The metatechnical problems we pose concern these three functions. How, for instance, do we minimize the creation of files? It is extremely expensive to create files, and it is foolish to add files that are largely redundant. Nevertheless, this is exactly what has happened time and time again. How can we efficiently access and use other people's files or indeed even our own when the file structure is no longer convenient? How do we maintain files that have multiple users? It is difficult to change files and programs, and it is difficult to query files when the query has not been anticipated. This can be nontrivial when the file definition is lost and the god-like creator has vanished. How can an enterprise best control the creation, dissemination, and protection of data consistent with its importance?

These problems are not necessarily new but were overshadowed by the difficulties of programming and of hardware technology or its lack. In the broadest sense, the problem is this: data stored in a computer is of no value if it is not accessible when required and at an acceptable cost. Conceptually, the data base solution is to integrate the data into a single rational system that can be defined and manipulated in a general way and easily accessed from an applications program. Although we are a long way from the pure concept of a data base, many working systems have been built.

15.1.1 The Data Definition Language

In the past, it has not been easy to share files. The problem has been recognized as essentially due to ownership of a file by its processing program or indirectly by the application programmer. The solution proposed is to make data independent of the processing programs and to centralize it. Obviously, some means of defining data external to such programs is necessary. This has resulted in the design and implementation of data definition languages. These languages allow us to model the data relationships that concern us. Such a descriptive representation of data is called a *schema.* Since an applications programmer may not be interested in the total schema, nor in the model of data provided, provision should be made to extract a submodel of the data pertinent to his use, and such a representation is termed a *subschema.* We consider these concepts in more detail, subsequently.

15.1.2 The Data Manipulation Language

As we have seen, hardware independence has been developed to avoid program change when a file is physically moved. A further step of data base independence is logical. Since the program no longer owns the data, we wish to protect the program from changes in the structure of data as stored in the data base.

Data independence implies that the user no longer talks directly to the data base files but rather to logical files of the data base system defined in the user's subschema. For this, a *data manipulation language* (DML) may be necessary, and it is embedded in an application language which we regard as the *host language.* This is similar in nature to and could be the file control statements of the host language but then the user is forced to go through the data base for all file requirements. In our view the DML should be distinct from the file control statements of the application language. There are good reasons for allowing a file capability independent of the data base. These will become clear as we discover the complexity of the data base system overhead. The DML connects the program subschema to the physical data base via a schema.

15.1.3 The Data Base Administrator

Since the programmer no longer controls the data, he can no longer name it. The many uses of the same data require a data dictionary to provide the names, the relevant attributes of data, and its use and meaning within the enterprise. Who is to control data in the enterprise?

The responsibility for defining schemas, subschemas, actual file structures, and overall control is centralized in the *data base administrator* (DBA). Although often referred to as a person, this is a human function and in a large organization would be a department.

To execute his functions, the DBA has a system of software programs that control and manipulate the data of the data base. We will think of this software collectively as the *data base control* (DBC). Ideally, the DBA speaks to these programs via a data control language (DCL). The DCL would contain the DDL and contain or have access to a file control language such as JCL.

15.1.4 A Data Base Management System Architecture

The solution just proposed for the metatechnical problems can be represented in the data base architecture of Fig. 15.1. Solid lines indicate the flow of data or its definition; dashed lines indicate the flow of control. It must be emphasized that this is a general scheme and a particular data base architecture may differ. Since we show that the DBMS has access to the data base (DB), we will refer to all computer-stored data for an enterprise as a *data bank*, although "data base" is often used in this sense.

15.2 REQUIREMENTS AND OBJECTIVES OF A DATA BASE SYSTEM

With hindsight we can see that the prime objective of a data base system is the centralized control of data consistent with its now recognized importance. Secondary objectives and advantages are:

- sharing of data files
- protection of processing programs and logical files against changes in physical files
- enforcement of standards
- ease of querying
- simplicity
- interface with future needs.

The advantages of file sharing decrease data redundancy and inconsistency. By allowing new applications to use existing files, large savings can be made. We effectively share the cost of files over many applications, present and future. It is much easier to write processing programs than it is to create large files. There is, as usual, a major disadvantage, and this results from the problems of concur-

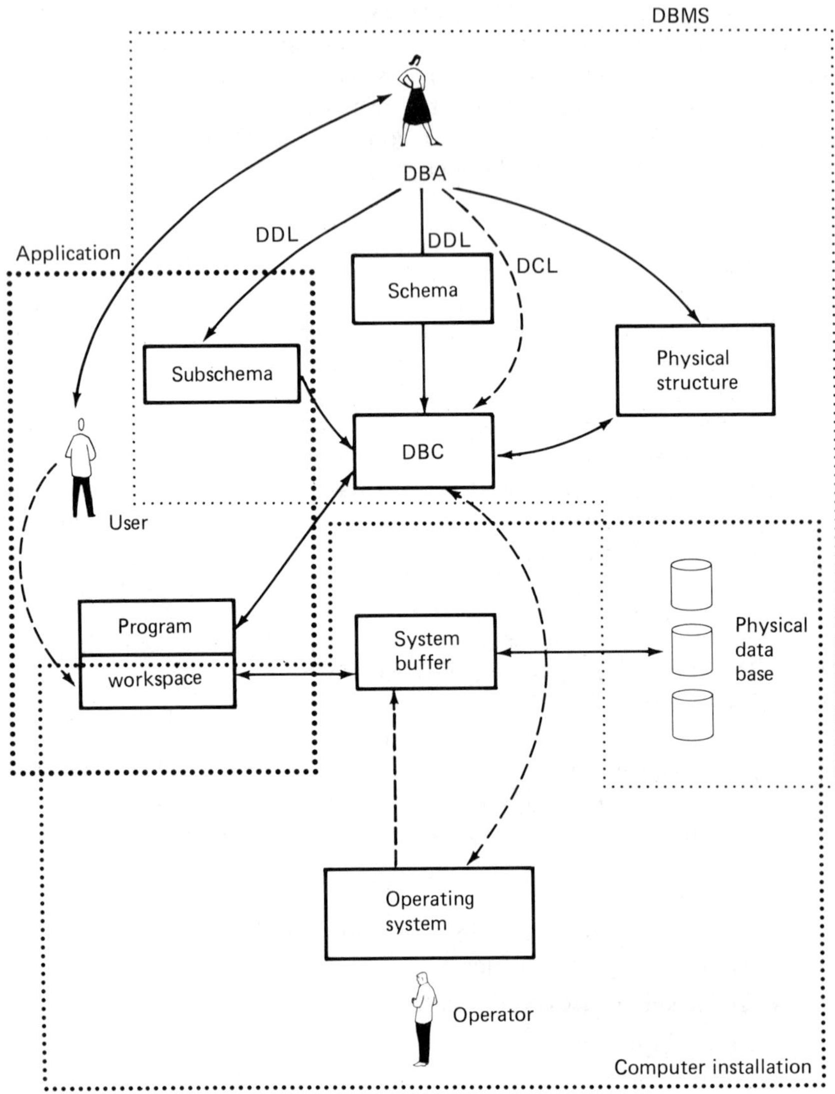

Figure 15.1 Data base architecture.

rent access of files by multiple users along with the status of updates. On-line systems have similar problems. Since files are shared and controlled external to an application, the data base can be structured to serve the enterprise rather than the individual. By balancing conflicting requirements, optimization occurs at the enterprise level rather than at the individual level.

The file techniques of previous chapters are data dependent. The physical file structure is built into the applications program. Any change in the physical file structure necessitates change in the program file access structure. Data independence separates the logical file of the program from the physical file structure, which is not the same as physical location of the file.

The enforcement of standards because of centralization of control provides increased security and integrity; conversely, these problems are of increased magnitude because of centralization. Integrity, security, and privacy of data require special attention in a data base. In the long run, installation and industry standards are economical, simplifying maintenance and data interchange. The DBA plays an essential role here. There is a vast difference between having standards and applying them. Responsibility is assigned to the DBA.

With the completion of this overview we have two remaining objectives: a consideration of data models and an examination of the CODASYL proposals for a DBMS standard linked to a COBOL environment. This work is of major importance—even if accomplished by committee—and will eventually result in an industry standard for data base design. It is for this reason we have chosen it as the basis for discussion. We cannot treat these objectives in depth; however, we do hope to give a flavor of some requirements for the design of a general DBMS. We again point out that the large general DBMS is not necessarily the best solution for an enterprise.

To emphasize the potential advantages of a DBMS, we list the following important qualities:

- access to data in a natural manner
- definition of relationships between files
- all data transactions logged
- standardization of data
- amortization of the cost of data over many applications
- versatile representation of data relationships that can be redefined independently of processing programs
- better availability of enterprise data
- reduced application program maintenance

It is equally important to list the following potential disadvantages of a DBMS:

- operational inefficiency due to software overhead

- higher storage cost of data and increased hardware requirements
- software cost
- organizational cost due to system complexity
- serious program failure if data incorrectly modified
- complicated security and integrity requirements
- vulnerability of all systems of an enterprise to a single DBMS failure

15.3 DATA MODELS

Given the real world, an observer does not see everything but only representative parts. How indeed are we to know that the images that impinge upon the brain are the real thing? Consider the person with defective eyesight. Certainly, without glasses he only sees a representation of what the normal viewer sees. A model is a representation that is necessarily incomplete. Language is a model for thinking. For instance, the word "house" is an abstract model for all the homes that exist.

More technically, a *model* is a representation of some reality that we can manipulate and expect the results to correspond to like changes in that reality. We deal daily with models; data files are models of the information we collect.

From an abstract point of view, a data base is a representation of the facts that pertain to an enterprise. Those facts that we collect and store in the data base we call *data*. Since it is not possible to collect all such facts, the data we have represents or models the collection of facts that is the enterprise. A model has structure but by its nature a model's structure need not be unique.

No doubt the reader has perceived by now the different aspects of logical and physical realms and even more the difficulty of doing so. We have, for instance, an object, a name for that object, and a place where that object or a suitable representation of that object is located. That is, an entity is some item that we place in a field. Similarly, the problem of multiple aspects extends to facts or information. In discussing information, we can consider three viewpoints which we call *realms* (Mealy, 1968). As with the logical and physical viewpoints, we tend to carelessly jump back and forth between these viewpoints and this often results in considerable confusion.

The first realm is the real world; the second is our perception of that world; and third is the data model we construct to represent that world. In the first we have entities and their properties; in the second we have attributes and attribute values; in the third we have data items and their values. Data models concern the relationships of the third aspect.

There are many ways that we can impose structure on a collection of data; what is important is that the structures we impose or the models we create bear a useful relation to the structure of facts concerning the enterprise that are perceived to be important by the enterprise now and in the future. Many models have been proposed for data files ranging from the simple, early, flat file to set-theoretic models of extreme mathematical complexity.

At present, data models are divided into three general classes, each supported by large groups of proponents: hierarchical, network, and relational. We will concern ourselves mostly with hierarchical and network models since they have been the most used in commercial systems. This is not an implied criticism of relational models but rather a decision forced upon us by the objectives of this book and the choice of the CODASYL work as an example.

15.3.1 Hierarchical Models

A hierarchical model is one in which the data relationships are restricted to a tree structure. A hierarchical model, viewed abstractly, is a forest of trees. Although this may sound imposing, it is just the kind of abstract structure we can describe in the data division of COBOL. Many DBMS handle only hierarchical models, and this is perfectly satisfactory for many applications.

The data division of COBOL, we now realize, provides a data definition language, and the data division section of a program is a data model of the program data.

15.3.2 Network Models

A *network* is a generalization of a tree. Recall that in a tree the path from the root to any member is unique. Relaxing this restriction gives a network. Thus an element of a network may have more than one parent and interestingly can be fathered by its offspring. If that sounds circular, then you have got the point. Networks allow cycles or circular relationships. The most important attempt at DBMS standardization was the CODASYL DBTG report (1971) which is based on the network data model.

15.3.3 Relational Models

The hierarchical and network models arise naturally from the way files were handled prior to the inception of DBMS. The relational model attacks the relationship of entities directly. Consider a binary relation B, this is a set of ordered pairs $<x, y>$ or *tuples*, where the first member x is selected from a set called domain A and the second member y from domain B, say. Then the relation is some set of $<x, y>$ tuples where $x \in A$ and $y \in B$ and this set defines the relation.

More generally, given sets $D_1, D_2, \ldots, D_n$, a relation R is a set of n-tuples, which are members of sets D_i. The ith element of the tuple is selected from D_i. Simply stated, a relational model represents the relationships of the data as a set of appropriate relations. Of course, there is more to it than this. An important result is that there is a well-understood mathematical theory of relations. The interested reader should refer to the papers of E.F. Codd, the major pioneer in the study of relational models. An attractive advantage of relational models is that they are conceived independently of physical structure.

With respect to DBMS, relations are usually represented as tables where a row is a tuple or member of the relation. The principal idea is that any structure can be reduced to two-dimensional tables by a process called *normalization*. Thus we may consider the relational model as consisting of a set of two-dimensional tables.

15.3.4 Perspective

Before we have a look at the CODASYL data base model, let us pause briefly to get our bearings. We are attempting to get a feel for data base technology at this point, not detailed knowledge, so we will try to get a perspective.

Our view of data has been conditioned by the writing of COBOL programs. Records are groups of data items strung together in a contiguous line and made available to us by opening files and issuing READ statements. They may be fixed-length or variable-length. We may retrieve them sequentially, which is easy, or randomly, which is more difficult. When we want to obtain them randomly, we have to be able to specify which record we want. We do this in one of three ways: by specifying track addresses (IBM DIRECT ACCESS), by specifying relative addresses, or by specifying primary or secondary keys. There are no other methods available to us in COBOL automatically. But there are far greater drawbacks than this. Let us examine some of them.

Suppose we want to drop or add a field to a record. What a lot of work has to be done. The file has to be recreated. The record description in the DATA DIVISION has to be changed and the program recompiled. But not just one program; every program that uses the file has to be changed. The data is not independent of the application programs. In addition, every user who accesses a file has to have the same description of the records in his program as everyone else. But every user may not need the same fields for processing. And even the order of the fields in a record cannot be changed. This problem is often solved by having more than one copy of the file. The data is made redundant to satisfy each user. This regretfully leads to difficulty when data is updated. Forget to update one of the many copies and the several reports generated by all these user programs may be inconsistent. Inconsistency can be extremely dangerous in data processing. When users confront inconsistencies in their reports they may lose confidence both in the reports and in those responsible for preparing the reports.

An even greater drawback to COBOL data definition is that the language provides no facility for one type of record to have a relationship to another type or for a field to point to another record. For example, suppose we have a record detailing a part number, quantity on hand, price, and the names of one or more suppliers:

PART NO.	QTY	PRICE	SUPPLIER	SUPPLIER

Each supplier has a record specifying his address and a list of the part numbers of parts he manufactures. In COBOL, both of these record types have to be stored in separate files, and getting from a part number to the supplier records associated with it requires programming effort. Yet the association is, or ought to be, intrinsic. We would prefer to be able to say:

```
FETCH RECORD FOR PART #5
OBTAIN ASSOCIATED SUPPLIER RECORDS
```

Logically, we see the record types as associated or having a relationship with each other. Physically, unfortunately, they are on separate files, maybe on separate devices, and programming is involved to get all the records together. Data base technology is designed to overcome this problem.

The logical relationships of record types to each other are

specified with a data definition language and access to records is made (by means of statements very much like the FETCH above) with data manipulation languages. The DDL which describes the logical view of the data is said to provide a schema. In Fig. 15.2, we illustrate the overall process. The user sees his data logically through the model or subschema. The data base management system passes information back and forth from its physical reality via a schema to the user's program where the view is governed by the subschema instead of by its physical or actual schema structure.

Since the user is freed from knowing anything about the way data is really stored, his world can be involved with only the data important to his program. If he wants a record to have three fields, the data base management system can provide him with such a record although it may pull these three fields off three different files. Thus, in the future, the data division of COBOL will describe the user's view of data not the system's.

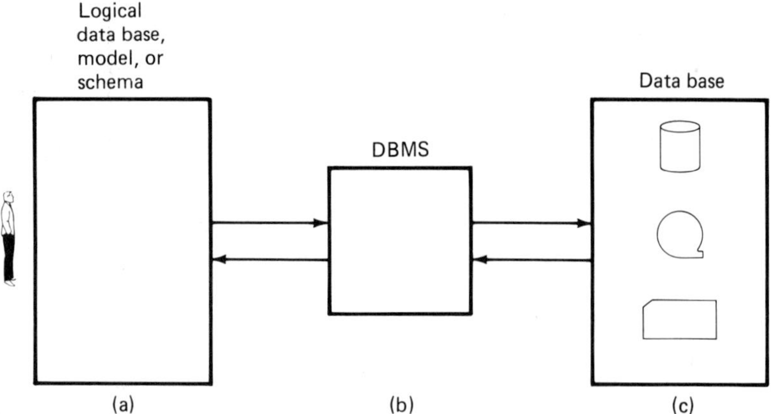

Figure 15.2 The DBMS interface: (a) User view of data (b) System view of data (c) Physical data.

15.4 CODASYL DATA BASE MODEL

There are many implementations of DBMS. The first attempt at standardization has been made by the CODASYL (Conference on Data Systems Languages) DBTG (Data Base Task Group) Proposal published in 1971. This work has evolved and is an important landmark in the development of DBMS. Furthermore, it will remain important in the future as a data base facility is incorporated in COBOL. Such a facility was proposed in the 1976 *CODASYL Journal of Develop-*

ment and is under constant review. For these reasons we will approach the concept of a DBMS in more detail strictly in terms of the CODASYL approach. As this work evolves, current CODASYL documents should be referred to for precise reference. However, their approach is now relatively firm and future standards should not differ significantly from the overview we present here.

It should be noted that the CODASYL approach is intended as a large general DBMS to be implemented by various vendors and consequently is quite complex.

An important design criteria of the CODASYL work is that it is to find practical application. In practice it is not easy to change existing procedural languages because of the large investment involved so that the data base application should be expected to be written in a host programming language. Although we may view a DBMS as a generalized file processing system, in practice a file is usually processed by well-defined applications and transactions run at high frequency; therefore, it is important that the DBMS application can be tuned for efficiency.

The DDL of CODASYL is a separate language and naturally enough is similar to COBOL in syntax. We examine some important features of DDL in the next section. In order to achieve efficiency and machine independence for the schema, a separate data storage description language (DSDL) has been conceived. DSDL defines the representation of a data base in storage. It defines how the data described in a schema may be organized in terms of an operating system and storage devices. The resulting description is known as a *storage schema*, and it is created by the data administrator (DA). Although the DSDL is important because its purpose, ideally, is to separate the logical description of a schema from its physical description and permits tuning for efficiency without alteration to other parts of the DBMS, we shall not consider it further.

The DML devised by CODASYL is embedded in COBOL and intended to interface with the CODASYL DDL. We consider some of DML's important features in Section 15.6.

15.5 CODASYL DATA DESCRIPTION LANGUAGE

The CODASYL data description language (DDL) is complex, and we make no pretense to examine it in detail. We do, however, propose to deal with several of its salient features that relate to its ability and limitations in dealing with modeling a data base. Any concern with syntax should be considered only as illustration. The objective of

DDL is to describe the data contained in a data base and their interrelationships or structure. Such a description is called a "schema" by CODASYL which refers to DDL as a "schema language."

A program that references a data base requires its own interpretation of the data; this interpretation is referred to as a subschema. In the CODASYL view, it is not necessary that the subschema language be the schema language. This has advantages in implementation when the syntax of a programming language does not resemble that of the DDL or the DBMS.

In Chapter 1 we discussed the need for and the definitions of various subgroupings of data and gave some general names for useful groups of data. In DDL there are seven ways in which we consider data: data item, data aggregate, record, set, area, schema, and data base. These are defined in Table 15.1.

Table 15.1 CODASYL Data Groupings

Term	*Definition*
Data item	Smallest accessible unit of named data
Data aggregate	Named collection of data items within a record; they may be vectors or repeating groups
Record	Named collection of data items or data aggregates
Set	Occurrence of a named collection of records where one of the record types is said to be the owner record and the other record types are said to be members
Area	Named collection of unique records which need not preserve owner/member relationships
Schema	Complete description of a data base
Data base	All records, sets, and areas controlled by a particular schema; the contents of different data bases is assumed to be disjoint

15.5.1 Record Type

The nature of a data base requires a more precise view of the different levels of abstraction. Recall that for a file we can distinguish three levels of the concept of a record: the record structure, a particular record associated with an entity or an occurrence of the record structure, and an instance of the record with values assigned to each of the record attributes. CODASYL refers to the record structure as a *record type*, the record associated with a particular entity as a *record*, and the set of values assumed by a record as an *instance of the record*. The COBOL definition of a *record type* is a collection of records described by a RECORD DESCRIPTION entry.

Thus we may have a record type AUTHOR and the occurrence of records for JOHNSON and for COOPER. An instance of a JOHNSON record would contain fixed values for its attributes which would be expected to change with time.

15.5.2 The Set Concept

The nature of a data base requires a flexible way to relate records that is independent of physical or internal pointers in records. CODASYL introduced a simple one-to-many construct that forms the basis of DDL. This construct is called a *set* (an unfortunate choice; owner set might be a better choice) but is not a set in the set theory sense of the word. A set contains two kinds of records: an owner record of which there is exactly one and any number of member records. If there are no member records, the set is said to be *empty*.

The different levels of abstraction regarding a record also pertain to sets. The general form of a set is a set type and this consists of exactly one owner record type and a number of member record types. CODASYL defines a *set type* as a named relationship between record types. There may be many sets for a set type just as there may be many records for a record type. Again we distinguish between a set type and an occurrence of a set of that type: *set* will denote a set occurrence. There is a set whenever there is an owner record. A set is said to *empty* when there are no member records. Figure 15.3 shows an example of this relationship.

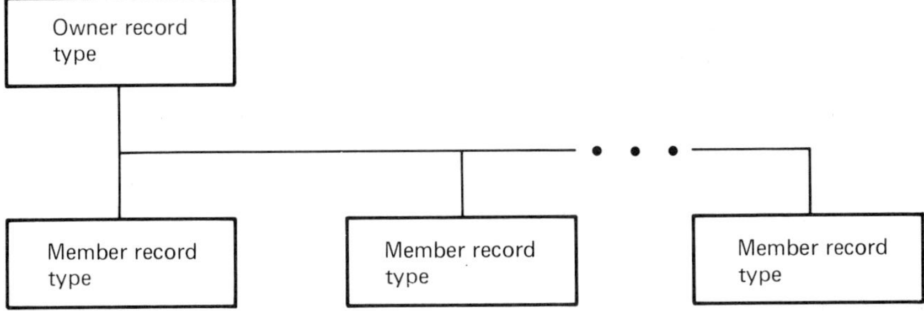

Figure 15.3 Relationship of record types.

15.6 CODASYL COBOL DATA BASE FACILITY

CODASYL has defined a data base facility within COBOL. A DBMS environment for COBOL consists of a data base, a data base control system that provides an interface between the physical data base and the schema, a schema to describe the data base, a subschema to describe the data base as seen by the user, and a COBOL program containing instructions to manipulate the data of the subschema. Our purpose here is to examine some of the features of a data base facility within COBOL in order to gain insight into the requirements of a DBMS and, in particular, DML.

As in the previous chapter, we have chosen to follow the development in the *CODASYL Journal of Development* (1978) in order to facilitate more particular reference by the reader. As such, our purpose is a general overview of the important concepts of a DBMS as seen by an applications programmer. Our objective is twofold: insight into the requirements of a DBMS and a survey of necessary features as seen by CODASYL.

15.6.1 Data Base Records and Related Terminology

Although a data base record is conceptually like a record in a file, it is *not* necessarily a physically contiguous collection of data items. In fact some of the items may not physically exist but be derived in the act of access. A data base record type is described by a RECORD DESCRIPTION entry in the subschema.

Data Base Keys

Each data base record is uniquely identified by a *data base key* which is not part of the record. The data base key is a conceptual entity and, while the value pertaining to a record can be accessed by a COBOL program, this value is invariant for the life of the record.

Currency

The concept of currency is important to indicate the state of interaction of the program with the data base. Currency indicators are conceptual entities that act as pointers into the data base to keep track of record retrieval and storage. There is one currency indicator for each run unit.

15.6.2 Record Selection

In DB processing as well as file processing, the basic unit of data that we manipulate is the record and the basic problem is to select a record. To select a record we require some means of identifying the record we have chosen so that we can find it. In files, we can identify a record directly by its primary key and indirectly by logical position as, for instance, the next record of a sequential file.

The COBOL data base facility allows selection of records based on data base key value, logical position, or currency indicator. The rule for selection is based on a record selection expression of which there are seven formats. The selection expression can only occur in a FIND statement.

Simple Format of FIND

FIND *record-selection-expression*

Some Simple Record Selection Expressions

record-name DB-KEY IS *identifier*

NEXT *record-name* WITHIN *set-name*

CURRENT *record-name* WITHIN *set-name*

15.6.3 DML Verbs

Given a subschema, the user requires a data manipulation language to access the data he views through the subschema. As the user wishes to access the data base via his application language, the DML should be contained in the application language which is, thus, a host for DML. The commands of the CODASYL DML are COBOL verbs, fifteen in number, which provide for data base access in the PROCEDURE DIVISION:

ACCEPT
CONNECT
DISCONNECT
ERASE
FIND
FINISH
FREE
GET
KEEP

```
MODIFY
ORDER
READY
REMONITOR
STORE
USE
```

We briefly indicate the function of each DML verb and a sample format to indicate the possible manipulation of the data base by a user. For convenience of reference we have chosen alphabetic order.

1. ACCEPT accesses the contents of a specified currency indicator.

   ACCEPT *identifier* FROM CURRENCY

2. CONNECT places a record occurrence into a set or sets. Note that the record type must have been defined as a member of such a set.

   CONNECT *record-name* TO *set-name*

3. DISCONNECT logically removes or deletes a record occurrence from one or more sets.

   DISCONNECT *record-name* FROM *set-name*

4. ERASE logically removes one or more records from the data base.

   ERASE *record-name* PERMANENT MEMBERS

5. FIND establishes a specific record occurrence as the current record of the run unit. This prepares it for further manipulations.

   FIND *record-selection-expression*

6. FINISH terminates the availability of one or more realms to the program. It acts like CLOSE for a file. An affected realm must first be in READY mode. (Recall that you cannot close a file that is not open.)

```
FINISH set-name
```

7. FREE removes records from extended monitored mode.

```
FREE record-name
```

8. GET places part or all of a current record in its user work area. To retrieve a record, execute a FIND followed by a GET.

```
GET
```

9. KEEP establishes an extended monitored mode for the current record of the run unit which must already be in monitored mode.

```
KEEP
```

10. MODIFY changes the contents of the current record of the run unit in the data base according to the contents of that record in the user work area.

```
MODIFY record-name
```

11. ORDER allows the logical reordering of the members of a set.

```
ORDER set-name ON DESCENDING
    KEY DB-KEY
```

12. READY prepares one or more realms for processing.

```
READY set-name
```

13. REMONITOR terminates a monitored mode or extended monitored mode followed immediately by the establishment of a new monitored or extended monitored mode for the same records.

```
REMONITOR record-name
```

14. STORE inserts a new record in the data base if its record type is defined.

STORE *record-name*

15. USE specifies procedures to be executed when the execution of a statement results in a data base exception condition. It must immediately follow a section header in the declarative portion of the PROCEDURE DIVISION and be followed by a separator period. The remainder of the section defines the procedure to be used.

USE FOR DB-EXCEPTION

We have done no more than highlight some major aspects of the CODASYL data base facility of COBOL in order to contrast the DBMS requirements with those of the file structures we have examined. It should now be clear that the potential increased flexibility of a DBMS is at the cost of increased complexity of programming record access and increased analysis of the data requirements of an enterprise.

15.7 CONCLUSION

When we consider a DBMS such as the CODASYL concept, we have in mind a rather large and complicated system. The potential advantages of such a large system involve many potential disadvantages. Such a large system is not always necessary.

At the very lowest level of a data base, we can begin by viewing data files as belonging to the enterprise and neither to the program nor, more dangerously, to the programmer. By considering files as a unified group and placing management control on their design and maintenance, the enterprise can begin to move toward a data base/data bank concept.

Many of the advantages claimed for DBMS are the result of defacto standardization instituted by the use of a single system. Manual standards and management control can also claim many of these advantages. Data base management as a philosophy has many manifestations. We would emphasize that if simple control can achieve the objectives of the enterprise, then more sophisticated control is not required. Indeed, we view simplicity as the golden rule of design.

PROBLEMS

1. The intent of a DBMS is to isolate the application programmer from the storage structure of the data. Discuss the advantages that might be obtained. Are there any disadvantages?

2. Is a DBMS a better approach than a file management system?

3. What requirements must a DDL satisfy? Should it be a separate language?

4. What purpose is satisfied by inserting a DML in a host language? Give some reasons for making it a stand-alone language. Sketch how it might then be used.

5. Design high-level functional specifications for a *simple* DBMS.

6. What DBMS or file processing systems are available at your installation? What data models do they use?

Postscript

In our view many programming systems fail or are very unsatisfactory not because of insufficient technical knowledge but because of lack of discipline and understanding of the relative importance of the many facets of a project to the objectives of the enterprise. Computing as a relatively new discipline attracts those who enjoy the freedom to innovate attendant on a new area that does not have a well-defined rigorous body of knowledge that must be painfully acquired by a long arduous apprenticeship. Until programming changes from art to craft, the artist programmer will abound. If we are aware of the incredible amount of bad art, we will appreciate that the creations of the artistic programmer seldom are what they pretend to be. Few enterprises can afford to be patrons of artistic programming.

We realize that this attitude destroys much of the fun of programming. We do not expect the building of a bridge to be fun, and although we can appreciate the creativeness of a new bridge design, we do not want it to fall down or to exceed the cost estimates. Because of this, the building of bridges is a carefully controlled activity, indeed, a craft. The design of programming systems is developing as a craft to be practiced with discipline and understanding.

References

BOOKS

Alexander, M.J., *Information Systems Analysis: Theory and Applications.* Chicago: SRA, 1974.

Brooks, F.P., *The Mythical Man-month.* Reading, Mass.: Addison-Wesley, 1975. Essays on the design process based on the author's experience as project manager for the development of the IBM System/360. Supplements Chapters 13 and 14.

Cooper, R.H., D.D. Cowan, P.H. Dirksen, and **J.W. Graham,** *File Processing with COBOL/WATBOL.* Waterloo, Ont., Canada: WATFAC, 1973.

Freeman, D.E., and **O.R. Perry,** *I/O Design: Data Management in Operating Systems.* Rochelle Park, N.J.: Hayden Book Company, Inc., 1977. Detailed reference for Chapter 2 and the physical aspects of data storage.

Ghosh, S., *Data Base Organization for Data Management.* New York: Academic Press, 1977.

Griswold, R.E., J.F. Poage, and **I.P. Polonsky,** *The SNOBOL 4 Pro-*

gramming Language (2nd ed.). Englewood Cliffs, N.J.: Prentice-Hall, 1971.

Knuth, D.E., *The Art of Computer Programming, Volume I: Fundamental Algorithms* (2nd ed.). Reading, Mass.: Addison-Wesley, 1973.

Knuth, D.E., *The Art of Computer Programming, Volume III: Sorting and Searching.* Reading, Mass.: Addison-Wesley, 1973.

Kroenke, D., *Database Processing.* Chicago: SRA, 1977. Considerable information on data base models and extant data base systems.

Lefkovitz, D., *File Structures for On-Line Systems.* New York: Spartan Books, 1969. An early book on techniques for direct access.

Lucas, H.C., *The Analysis, Design, and Implementation of Information Systems.* New York: McGraw-Hill, 1976. Readable management-level discussion related to Chapters 1, 13, and 14.

Lyon, S.K., *The Database Administrator.* New York: Wiley, 1976.

Martin, James, *Computer Data-Base Organization* (2nd ed.). Englewood Cliffs, N.J.: Prentice-Hall, 1977. Good general reference for many of our topics. It is language independent and very readable.

——, *Principles of Data-Base Management.* Englewood Cliffs, N.J.: Prentice-Hall, 1976.

——, *Security, Accuracy, and Privacy in Computer Systems.* Englewood Cliffs, N.J.: Prentice-Hall, 1973.

Meadow, C.T., *Applied Data Management.* New York: John Wiley & Sons, 1976. A general reference that is language independent.

Sprowls, R.C., *Management Data Bases.* New York: Wiley, 1976.

Tremblay, S.P., and P.G. Sorenson, *An Introduction to Data Structures with Applications.* New York: McGraw-Hill, 1976.

Tsichritzis, D.C., and F.H. Lochovsky, *Data Base Management Systems.* New York: Academic Press, 1977.

Walsh, M.E., *Information Management Systems/Virtual Storage.* Reston, Va.:, Reston 1979. This book describes the practical application of the IMS/VS data base system.

Watson, R.W., *Timesharing System Design Concepts.* New York: McGraw-Hill, 1970.

Wiederhold, G., *Database Design.* New York: McGraw-Hill, 1977. Highly technical treatment of files and data base concepts.

PAPERS

Codd, E.F., "Recent Investigations in Relational Data Base Systems," *Information Processing '74.* Amsterdam: North-Holland, 1974.

Comer, D., "The Ubiquitous B-Tree," *ACM Computing Surveys,* 11, no. 2 (June 1979).

Cooper, R.H., "Linear Transformations in Galois Fields and their Application to Cryptography," *Cryptologia,* 4, no. 3 (July 1980), pp. 184–88).

Denning, D.E., and **P.J. Denning**, "Data Security," *ACM Computing Surveys,* 11, no. 3 (Sept. 1979).

Diffie, W. and **M.E. Hellman**, "A Critique of the Proposed Data Encryption Standard," *Communications of the ACM,* 19, no. 3 (March 1976), 164–65.

Dobosiewicz, Wlodzimiera, "Sorting by Distributive Partitioning," *Information Processing Letters,* 7, no. 1 (1978).

Hoare, C.A.R., Quicksort," *Computer Journal,* 5, no. 1 (April 1962), 10–15.

Lempel, A., "Cryptology in Transition," *ACM Computing Surveys,* 11, no. 4 (December 1979).

Maryanski, F.J., "Backend Database Systems," *ACM Computing Surveys,* 12, no. 1 (March 1980).

Maurer, W.D., and **T.G. Lewis**, "Hash Table Methods," *ACM Computing Surveys,* 7, no. 1 (March 1975).

Mealy, A.H., "Another Look at Data," *Proceedings of the AFIPS 1967 Fall Joint Computer Conference,* vol. 31. Montvale, N.J.: AFIPS Press, 1968.

"Special Issue on Database," *ACM Computing Surveys,* 8, no. 1 (March 1976).

Sorenson, P.G., **S.P. Trembley**, and **R.F. Deutscher**, "Key-to-address Transformation Techniques," *INFOR,* 16, no. 1 (February 1978).

Williams, J.W.J., "Algorithm 232 Heapsort," *Communications of the ACM,* 7, no. 6 (June 1964), 347–48.

COBOL SOURCE DOCUMENTS

American National Standard Programming Language COBOL, ANSI X3.23-1974. New York: American National Standards Institute, Inc., 1974.

"CODASYL COBOL 1976," *CODASYL Programming Language Committee Journal of Development.* Hull, Que., Canada: Supply and Services Canada, 1976.

"CODASYL COBOL 1978," *CODASYL Data Description Language Committee Journal of Development.* Hull, Que., Canada: Secretariat of the Canadian Government EDP Standards Committee, 1978. This is a working document of the Committee in preparation for the next version of the COBOL standard. It contains a definition of a COBOL data base facility within COBOL.

"Data Description Language 1978," *CODASYL Data Description Language Committee Journal of Development.* Hull, Que., Canada: Secretariat of the Canadian Government EDP Standards Committee, 1978.

Data Base Task Group (DBTG) of CODASYL Programming Languages Committee Report. New York: ACM (Association of Computing Machinery), April, 1971.

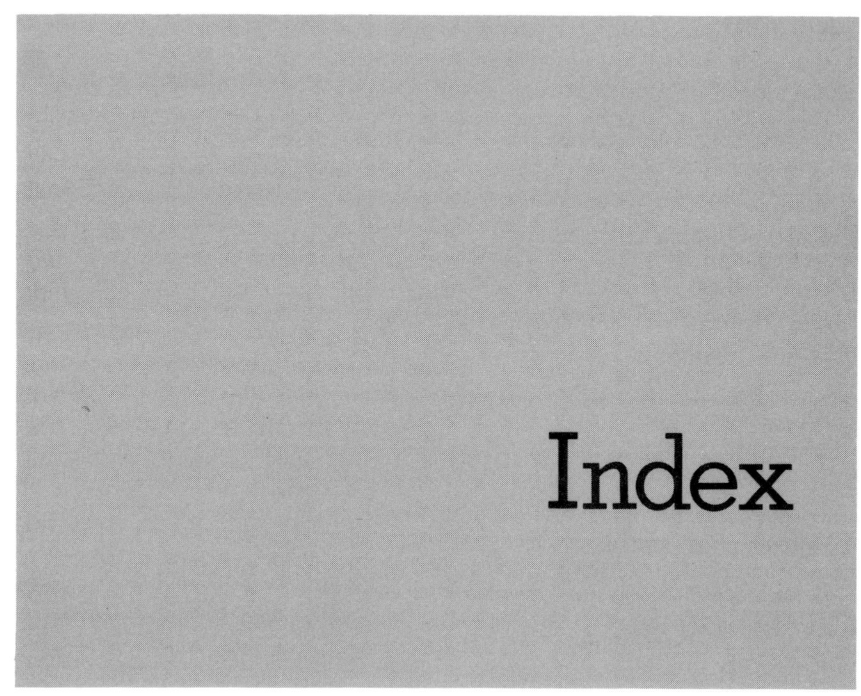

Index

H

I

J

K

L

M

N

O

P

Q

R

S

T

U

V

W